I0222780

At Home on the Waves

Studies in Environmental Anthropology and Ethnobiology

General Editor: **Roy Ellen**, FBA
Professor of Anthropology, University of Kent at Canterbury
Interest in environmental anthropology and ethnobiological knowledge has grown steadily in recent years, reflecting national and international concern about the environment and developing research priorities. Studies in Environmental Anthropology and Ethnobiology is an international series based at the University of Kent at Canterbury. It is a vehicle for publishing up-to-date monographs and edited works on particular issues, themes, places or peoples which focus on the interrelationship between society, culture, and the environment.

For a full volume listing, please see the series page on our website:
http://berghahnbooks.com/series/environmental-anthropology-and-ethnobiology

At Home on the Waves

Human Habitation of the Sea
from the Mesolithic to Today

Edited by Tanya J. King and Gary Robinson

berghahn
NEW YORK · OXFORD
www.berghahnbooks.com

First published in 2019 by

Berghahn Books

www.berghahnbooks.com

© 2019, 2022 Tanya J. King and Gary Robinson
First paperback edition published in 2022

All rights reserved. Except for the quotation of short passages
for the purposes of criticism and review, no part of this book
may be reproduced in any form or by any means, electronic or
mechanical, including photocopying, recording, or any information
storage and retrieval system now known or to be invented,
without written permission of the publisher.

Library of Congress Cataloging-in-Publication Data

A C.I.P. cataloging record is available from the Library of Congress
Library of Congress Cataloging in Publication Control Number: 2018055830

British Library Cataloguing in Publication Data

A catalogue record for this book is available from the British Library

ISBN 978-1-78920-142-0 hardback
ISBN 978-1-80073-448-7 paperback
ISBN 978-1-78920-143-7 ebook

https://doi.org/10.3167/9781800734487

To Elliotte and Olivia: my home
—Tanya J. King

To Geneviève and Maxime
—Gary Robinson

Contents

Figures

Tables

Foreword

Bonnie McCay

People who do not work at sea often think of the sea as a frontier, not yet peopled and civilized—as a watery playground for surfing and sailing; as a handy wasteland capable of lapping up and dispersing all that is discarded; or as a fragile source of biodiversity to be protected from human action. Marine scientists rely on fisheries' harvest data for clues to fish populations but until recently did not see why one should collect data on the people who catch those fish. Social scientists, in their studies of fishing communities or coastal communities, are intrigued by the livelihoods and cultures of people who live by and on the sea, but tend to focus on the implications of "going to sea" from family and community life on shore rather than acknowledging the extent to which people actually live with and within the realm of the ocean.

This volume, strongly influenced by the thinking of environmental anthropologist Tim Ingold (2011), explores the mutually constituting interactions between people and fishing places. The notion of mutually constituted relationships is a way that social scientists problematize all sorts of received oppositions, including "nature and culture," "land and sea." We sometimes use the term "seascape" as distinct from "landscape," but even these terms can distract from appreciation of the complexities (in Ingold's term, the "meshwork") of a world that is, as the editors write, "simultaneously earthy and watery." In the book, this is shown vividly in chapters that concern people who dwell and work in estuarine areas, the ever-dynamic littoral. Throughout, the authors explore the shifting dynamics and permeable boundaries that constitute the ecosystems, fishing grounds, and marine zones of the seas as places that are lived in and created by people.

Human actions affect the abundance and balance of marine species, the quality of marine waters and habitats, and even now, we learn, the acidity of the ocean; in another vein, we can talk about the social production of marine ecosystems (Olson 2011), as evocatively shown in this book's chapter on the creation of named fishing grounds in Scottish waters. In turn, people are dependent on and shaped by the oceans in so many ways, not least of which is their role in maintaining the climate that has made life possible. Oceans provide food and ways of traveling from one place to another, and for those who have most directly worked with and on the seas—the main actors in this volume—oceans and their inhabitants are simply part of life, part of one's identity and dreams, a focus of one's social and private worlds.

The world's seas have become the marine components of the Anthropocene, an Earth transformed by human action, and human activities must be constrained and regulated to protect valued and essential parts and processes. But forgotten in that perspective is the notion that the very sources of overharvesting, pollution, and carbon dioxide emission are also thinking, responding actors. It can be more productive to think of people as active parts of marine ecosystems rather than solely as external, intruding forces (McCay 2012).

Scientists for example, watch, record, monitor, and try to explain what is happening in the seas. Environmental and social activists cry out against perceived wrongs and losses, and politicians and officials may have the mandate and authority to regulate and judge. In this book, the important actors are those who have immediate and embodied engagements with the places and things of estuaries and seas. Their livelihoods are of the sea; these are people who come to know and understand marine worlds through dwelling, working, moving through, and interacting with them. By and large, they bear the immediate costs of interventions such as the establishment of marine protected areas and fishing closures, even though subsequent benefits flow on to broader publics and other special interests. They do, then, deserve the special attention given them in *At Home on the Waves*.

The editors and authors of *At Home on the Waves* are influenced by relatively new theoretical and epistemological realms, employing concepts such as "taskscape" (Ingold 1993) and "affordances" (Gibson 1979) to signify and represent different ways of handling the complicated matter of mutual constitution. "Taskscape" refers to the notion that human understandings of landscapes or seascapes are produced through "tasks," through work and movement, nicely shown in chapters on sea peoples in Scotland and India. The notion of "affordance" respects the power of material attributes of places and things in the process of mutual constitution of the marine world. Home-making at sea is addressed, within this overall framework, in a fascinating chapter on Philippine seafarers. The emphasis on practice, which is embedded in this theoretical orientation, appears throughout, as in the chapter on subsistence and recreational fishing in a coastal area of the southern United States.

Archaeological findings underscore the depth of human–ocean interdependence and cocreation—through investigations of the vast coastal mounds found in Brazil and the rich evidence of the interpenetration of land and sea in ancient Britain. Archaeology is also an entry into the problem of defining land and sea, given the dynamics of sea level in both the British Isles and Australia. The fluidity of boundaries arises in theory as well as with rising sea levels, and the liminal in its many dimensions might be considered a condition of land–sea interfaces (McCay 2009). For sea people, this can also be a condition affecting social identity in tightly gendered occupations such as fishing, shown here in an Icelandic case that addresses the remarkable presence of women in the fisheries, as well as the equally remarkable cultural silence on the matter.

Communication is a rich topic that arises in several chapters of the book. It is discerned in unexpected ways in the "active silences" of Greenlanders finding their way, and the choreographed gestures of underwater archaeologists trying to explain the location of a submerged Pleistocene site in Chile. A chapter on traditional fish traps and one on the geomorphology of long-abandoned islands in Australia incorporate elements of community engagement and revitalization, so very important to the welfare of marginalized coastal and sea peoples.

One strength of social science has been measuring the effects of major developments and regulations on the social and economic wellbeing of affected populations. Applied to studies of hazards and disasters, this has become the important realm of risk and vulnerability analysis. However, like the notion that humans are relevant to marine systems solely as external forces of change, this perspective can have unintended consequences, too, in eliding the agency of people, leaving them solely in the role of victims. A chapter on western Greenlander Inuit addresses how "crisis narration" leaves out crucial aspects of interaction with the natural environment and diminishes the role of human agency, intentionality, and flexibility in shaping responses to environmental threats and opportunities. Appreciating the latter requires research that studies indigenous knowledge in its social and environmental contexts.

The ethnographic and archaeological case studies in *At Home on the Waves* are wonderfully various in space and time and topic, while being knit together with shared commitment to this business of mutual constitution of people and the sea, of challenging conceptual boundaries and drawing attention to how social practices and the physical features of the natural world come together in creating new boundaries. The significance of this work has a compelling immediacy, as many public discourses and actors seek to stop fishing and limit other human interactions with the oceans. How that is done, by whom, and with what tools and cognitive understandings will have profound effects on the seascapes of the future.

Bonnie McCay has worked with fishing communities in the Northwest Atlantic region as well as Mexico's Pacific coast. An ecological anthropologist by training, her practice has been interdisciplinary, spanning cultural studies, fisheries biology and marine ecology, economics, and political economy. The challenge of "the commons" is her main theoretical interest, leading to studies of community-based and participatory management of common pool resources as well as the unfolding social and ecological dynamics and consequences of privatizing marine fishery resources. She has also been engaged in science policy through institutions such as the US Ocean Studies Board and the Mid-Atlantic Fisheries Management Council. She held a faculty appointment in the Department of Human Ecology, Rutgers University, New Jersey, from 1974 to 2015 and is now Distinguished Professor Emerita.

References

Gibson, J. J. 1979. *The Ecological Approach to Visual Perception*. New York: Houghton Mifflin.

Ingold, T. 1993. "The Temporality of the Landscape." *World Archaeology* 25, no. 2: 152–74.

———. 2011. *Being Alive: Essays on Movement, Knowledge and Description*. New York: Taylor & Francis.

McCay, B. J. 2009. "The Littoral and the Liminal: Or Why it is Hard and Critical to Answer the Question 'Who Owns the Coast?'" *MAST* (Maritime Anthropology Studies, University of Amsterdam) 17: 7–30.

———. 2012. "Peopling the Marine Ecosystem." In *Advancing an Ecosystem Approach in the Gulf of Maine*. Edited by R. L. Stephenson, J. Annala, J. A. Runge, and M. L. Hall-Arber. Vol. 79. Bethesda, Maryland: American Fisheries Society, Symposium.

Olson, J. 2011. "Producing Nature and Enacting Difference in Ecosystem-based Fisheries Management: An Example from the Northeastern US." *Marine Policy* 35, no. 4: 528–35.

Acknowledgments

It's been nearly a decade since the 2009 meeting of the European Association of Social Anthropologists (EASA), where archaeologists and anthropologists came together under the banner, *Anthropological and Archaeological Imaginations: past, present and future*. It was in the convivial setting of a Bristol spring that ideas were exchanged, imaginations stretched, commonalities explored, and—after some scholarly binge-drinking—it was agreed that an edited collection was warranted.

Since then, research projects have moved on, over (and under), some people have found or changed academic or research positions, and others have found their jobs increasingly difficult and time-consuming to retain. Babies have been born.

Despite the multitude of changes that have come about, both personally in the lives of authors and editors, as well as professionally within anthropology and archaeology, the volume has finally come to fruition in a tome that aspires to be worth the wait. Through chapters richly detailing communities in five continents, we anticipate this volume will offer ethnographic insights that will remain relevant to scholars, as well as those with an interest in maritime cultures, for many decades to come.

It is with this aspirational prediction that we begin by thanking the patient contributors to this book. Your insightful research, and your commitment to presenting the reality of those with whom you engage with humanity and beauty, is what has inspired this collection.

To those whose lives are on show in this book: thank you for tolerating the nosey questions of researchers with such grace and generosity. We sincerely hope we present your experiences with credibility, and we wish for others to see and appreciate your wonderful worlds as we do.

To Katia Ariel, our brilliant and professional editor. If anyone reading this needs a dynamite set of eyes across their work—someone who will engage generously with the material and work with their strengths and limitations—Katia is the person to contact.

To a long list of past Berghahn Book editors, culminating in the fabulously attentive Harry Eagles, we offer our thanks—gratitude for your patience and willingness to see our vision realized.

To the two anonymous reviewers who provided helpful advice and encouragement on the manuscript, we're sorry the book is so long and that you probably received no formal professional recognition for the onerous and important task of reviewing. Please be assured that we are grateful; once the book is in print, please identify yourselves so we can thank you properly!

Donna Squire, you fabulous, image-enhancing wizard! Thanks for taking the time to teach us the mad skills necessary to make the book look spectacular. Any glitches in cropping, vignetting, or tone are ours.

To Bonnie McCay, who helped at various stages of this book with encouragement, general advice, and a steady faith in the value of the collection, and who remains an all-round inspirational human.

To Tim Ingold, who inspired so many of the authors in this volume to see, to know, and to write about the world in a way that so aptly captures the reality of the human experience in "scapes."

To Caroline Wickham-Jones, who contributed the glossary, and the sparkling gift of some last-minute editorial undertakings.

This manuscript was completed (in various stages), while generously supported by Deakin University (Australia), Bangor University (UK), on sabbatical at Rutgers University (USA), and on exchange at the Alfred Deakin Research Institute (Australia).

* * *

Tanya J. King would also like to thank her friends and family; Monica Minnegal, Peter Dwyer, and Simone Blair for endless conversations about fishermen and the world; Bronwyn Hicks, for saving us from living in complete squalor and delivering me a weekly dose of mental serenity; the many generous fishermen of Bass Strait, and their families, especially Brian "Daffy" Daff, Michael "Mick" Hobson, and Andrew "Fat" Hicken.

At Sea in the Twenty-First Century

Tanya J. King and Gary Robinson

Contrary to the idiom, people "at sea" have always been "at home." Since the Mesolithic and before, human communities have lived closely with the ocean, not simply as a domain to visit temporarily in order to extract resources, food, specimens, experiences, or literary analogies. Figurative depictions of seascapes as vast, unpeopled, and temporally constrained are at odds with the evidence depicted in this volume. Rather, oceans persistently constitute the principal organizing spaces through which many communities dwell in the world.

In this volume, we present rich ethnographic data, both archaeological and anthropological, demonstrating the centrality of marine environments to the lives of peoples around the globe. While the majority of people experience the ocean as an alternative to a largely terrestrial existence, the voices we present in this volume tell a story with a very different emphasis. For these people, the sea "grounds" them in a way both figurative and literal.

The book is decidedly Ingoldian. This is unsurprising, given that the volume sprung from a conference panel organized by a number of Ingold's students and where Ingold acted as the panel discussant. In particular, Ingold's notion of "meshwork" emerges as a binding feature of most chapters, albeit implicitly. The concept itself draws on the phenomenological characteristics of much of Ingold's anthropology, harnessing the metaphor of the "network" as a point of contrast with which to depict the fluid and perpetual coming-into-being of creatures and materials:

> I return to the importance of distinguishing the network as a set of interconnected points from the meshwork as an interweaving of lines. Every such line describes a flow of material substance in a space that is topologically fluid. I conclude that the organism (animal or human) should be understood not as a bounded entity surrounded by an environment but as an unbounded entanglement of lines in fluid space. (Ingold 2011, 64)

It is Ingold's refusal to imprison materials and organisms in the categories fabricated by humans—animate and inanimate, static and dynamic, animal and material, terrestrial and marine—that enables him to conceive of a world that is mutually constituting. For Ingold, ontological genesis is a continuous state, brought about by the movement of people and things and ideas as they go about their daily business. "In this animic ontology, beings do not propel themselves across a ready-made world but rather issue forth through a world-in-formation, along the lines of their relationships" (Ingold 2011, 63).

This volume compiles a number of ethnographic stories in which humans "issue forth through a world-in-formation," encompassing both terrestrial and marine locations. Indeed, the chapters encourage us to look at the world in a way that problematizes the distinction between land and sea, and to recognize the continuity with which people live and enliven their surroundings.

Human Engagement with the Sea: A Shifting Discourse

For some forty years of Western thought, the nature of the relationship between people and the ocean has been under increasing scrutiny. Key reasons for this scrutiny include the intense industrialization of commercial fisheries since the 1970s, the expansion of oil and gas exploration, the development of the *United Nations Convention on the Law of the Sea* (1982) (which seeks to protect the marine resources of sovereign nations from outsiders), and the "awakening" of those in the West to "environmental" concerns. Under discussion has been the rightful place of humans in the marine environment: How should people engage with the sea? What, if anything, should be extracted? What limits and allowances should be imposed in order to ensure people engage with the ocean properly? The answers have been varied and often contentious, reflecting the myriad ways in which people engage with, and attribute meaning to, the ocean. As such, nation-state restrictions and affordances have been applied to individuals, corporations, firms, categories of people, and even to the personification of "the environment" itself, each group seeking to establish that its way of valuing the ocean is best. As Castree (2010, 1731) explains, "Struggles over nature are always already struggles over meanings."

Examples of such "struggles" include those between commercial and recreational fishers (Kearney 2002; Cooke and Cowx 2006), where competition for a shared resource, as well as the perception of incongruous ideological motivations, can prompt antagonisms on the water as well as in the political realm (Voyer et al. 2017). Likewise, there are heterogeneous views on how the resource should be used and by whom within the angling sector itself (e.g., Arlinghaus et al. 2007), as well as among those focused on commercial fishing communities (Smith, Sainsbury, and Stevens 1999; Beddington, Agnew, and Clark 2007; Hilborn 2007). The dynamics between commercial fishers and indigenous resource users (whether commercial or subsistence) can also be characterized by disagreements over who has the right to engage the environment in a particular way (Barber 2010; McCormack 2012; Breslow 2014). Neither commercial, recreational, or traditional fishers have been particularly successful in asserting their rights to the ocean over those claimed by powerful multinational corporations such as BP (formerly British Petroleum), who supply the world with oil and gas (Cicin-Sain and Tiddens 1989; McCrea-Strub et al. 2011; Pinkerton and Davis 2015; Pomeroy, Hall-Arber, and Conway 2015). Of course, those who advocate for "the environment" may argue that extractive resource use of any kind—by fishers, oil and gas companies, wind and tidal energy developers, bioprospectors, or beachcombers—is incommensurate with the preservation ethic of nonextraction (Drengson and Devall 2010; King 2005, 356).

Underlying these attempts to control human engagement with the sea has been an assumption that it is possible for humans to remove themselves from the ocean, a perspective reinforced by the almost exclusively terrestrial or coastal experiences of humans. As King explains (2005, 353): "Most people experience the ocean in absentia. Unchallenged by conflicting experiences, the public is potentially able to imagine an ocean ecosystem without humans." This "imagined" environment informs the expectations that people and their governments have of the human–marine relationship; conflicts can arise when incongruous meanings converge to challenge the lived experiences of diverse user-groups (King 2005).

It is in the context of such struggles, and public discourses that seek to limit—or even halt—human interactions with the ocean, that we present this volume. In these pages, we challenge the notion that the sea is not the proper domain of people. Acheson has stated: "The sea is a dangerous and alien environment, and one in which man is poorly equipped to survive. It is a realm that man enters only with the support of artificial devices . . . and then only when weather and sea conditions allow" (Acheson 1981, 276). However, people *do* live at sea, and with far more domesticity and less drama than Acheson's oft-quoted passage suggests. The case studies we present range from industrialized commercial fisheries in Iceland, Australia, and the US to combined commercial and subsistence focused ocean-goers in Greenland to car-carrier employees from the Philippines. Evidence of past, intimate associations with the ocean is provided by archaeological accounts from the UK, South America, and Australia. Proposing a marine environment without human interaction ignores the evidence that humans have a long-spanning and rich relationship with the ocean.

Uniting Landscape and Maritime Archaeology

The significance of the sea to sites on the land has a long but sporadic history within archaeological research. Davies argued that the location of megaliths along the shores of the Irish Sea could be linked to navigation markers within the Irish Sea (1946). Bowen (1972) considered the geographical distribution of megaliths in the light of later sea traffic, the voyaging of Celtic saints, and pilgrims using skin boats. He concluded that as far back as the Mesolithic and Early Neolithic, an established pattern of movement and trading, from peninsula to peninsula and coast to coast, had been established and that the origin of this movement was the pursuit of migratory fish. In response to Bowen, Clark (1977) suggested that the apparent cultural continuity seen in the occurrence of passage graves along the Atlantic fringes of northwest Europe could be best explained as being the result of sea-born fisher-peoples. The distribution of megaliths throughout this region was thus accounted for though the movements of people following the migratory movements of fish along the Atlantic seaboard. These views were developed when modified diffusion was deemed the social mechanism behind the appearance of similar monuments in various sea-separated places (Renfrew 1973, 20–47). From the 1970s onward, reaction against the idea of diffusion within British prehistory, in conjunction with the failure of finding a common origin for megaliths, has served to exclude movement as a variable in the lives of prehistoric people.

In the past twenty years, landscape archaeology in Britain has developed in many directions, providing increasingly sophisticated understandings of past peoples' sense of place. In part, this change of perspective has come about through a growing awareness of indigenous peoples' perceptions of landscape and the realization that landscapes are deeply ingrained with meaning for the people who inhabit them (Basso 1984; Hirsch and O'Hanlon 1995; Ucko and Layton 1999). A central theme within studies of prehistoric landscapes has been a focus on the settings of sites and monuments and how they emphasize and signify certain aspects of the lived landscape (Thomas 1993; Tilley 1994; Richards 1996; Cummings and Whittle 2003). While this work has certainly energized debate and research within archaeology, it has equally received criticism for both its interpretation of the archaeological record and its lack of a coherent fieldwork strategy (Fleming 1999, 2005; Brück 2005; Barrett and Ko 2009).

In contrast to the growing body of work that considers the social construction of landscape, little attention has been given to the sea. Some archaeologists have noted the significance of the sea to the settings of monuments, where the sea is interpreted as a symbolic or metaphorical backdrop to life, and death, on the land (Scarre 2002; Cummings and Whittle 2003). But prehistoric coastal and island communities did not simply gaze across the sea—they physically engaged with it through the daily practices of seafaring and fishing. In this respect, the sea was not a neutral backdrop for human action but an active medium through which prehistoric communities lived, experienced, and ordered their world. A consideration of social practices associated with the sea is thus central to any interpretation of the archaeological record of island and coastal communities.

The research agenda of maritime archaeology has traditionally focused on technical aspects of boat construction and seaworthiness, the identification of landing places, and the role of both activities in exploring movement and trade (Muckelroy 1980; Wright 1986; McGrail 1987, 1988, 1989; Johnstone 1988; Robinson, Shimwel, and Cribbin 1999). While there is clear overlap in research between landscape and maritime archaeology, little communication has historically been made between these two sub-disciplines, each having distinct research agendas and avenues of publication. The separation between maritime and terrestrial archaeology creates an imbalance within the discipline, especially as most coastal and island communities in the past would have been based upon aspects of both environments (Crumlin-Pedersen 2010, 14; Westerdahl 2011, 311).

The agenda of maritime archaeology has recently been questioned, and vital new approaches that emphasize the social dimensions of the sea have arisen (Chapman and Gearey 2004; Van de Noort 2004, 2006; Farr 2006; Crumlin-Pedersen 2010). Much of this research has been developed by successfully bringing together maritime and landscape-based approaches in order to develop a critically aware social maritime archaeology. Key to this change has been Westerdahl's influential paper, which called for a refocus of maritime archaeology toward the "maritime cultural landscape" (1992). Westerdahl's concept of the maritime cultural landscape aims to incorporate all aspects of the human utilization of maritime space, including boats, landing places, settlement, fishing, hunting, and all of the attendant features and material culture of maritime communities (1992, 5; 2011, 337). Westerdahl's work had the effect of creating a more unified discipline where maritime and land-based archaeology share common themes and research questions (Flatman 2011, 311).

Recent developments within island archaeology have also highlighted the ways in which seascapes share many similarities with landscapes (Broodbank 2000; Robb 2001). The publication of a dedicated "seascapes" edition of *World Archaeology* marked an important recognition of the importance of the maritime social landscape within land-based archaeology (Cooney 2003). Another landmark in the move toward the widening appreciation of maritime issues within mainstream archaeology was the discovery in 1992 of the Dover Boat (Clark 2004a). The multidisciplinary approach adopted by this project and the emphasis placed upon the social significance and context of the boat (Clark 2004b, 3; 2010, 187) has contributed to a widening appreciation of maritime perspectives in mainstream reports and papers (Adams 2007, 219; Strachen 2010). Equally, the discovery and publication of the Dover Boat has brought about a renaissance of research into the entangled histories of prehistoric communities of the English Channel/Manche-Mer du Nord region (Marcigny and Talon 2009; Needham 2009; Philippe 2009; Lehoërff 2012).

If we are to attempt to discuss the use of the sea by coastal and island communities, it is essential that the approaches and themes explored within the complementary fields of landscape archaeology, maritime archaeology, and maritime anthropology are considered alongside one another in accounts of the past, as well as being brought to bear on studies of the present. Only by bringing together these fields of research can we provide a rich and meaningful understanding of engagements with the sea. In order to accomplish this task, we must consider a variety of available archaeological resources, including the configuration of the prehistoric coastline, the archaeological evidence for boats, the identification of landing places, the evidence for fishing and hunting, and systems of wayfaring. Only by exploring such themes can we begin to understand potential relationships between archaeological sites on land and the prehistoric use of the sea. Likewise, it is only through recognition of the ongoing nature of the relationship of humans with the ocean that we can appropriately understand the ways in which people continue to be at home on the waves.

Chapter Summaries

Cobb and Ransley open the volume with a chapter that combines the observations of both an archaeologist and an anthropologist. While drawing on the authors' individual field studies—in the archipelagos of Mesolithic western Scotland and modern-day Kerala, India, respectively—the chapter explores the key premise of the volume: that people have always been just as much at home at sea as on land. Indeed, their discussion problematizes the notion of any fundamental distinction between the two "scapes"—land and sea—and proposes a more integrated, Ingoldian view of the world that captures the meshwork of living in a world simultaneously earthy and watery.

Howard explores the processes through which Scottish fishermen come to know particular marine places or, rather, how these places simultaneously come into being through the purposeful labor, social encounters, and historically situated movements of fishermen. Places like Wullie's Peak emerge via the shared experiences, conversations, stories, and interactions among fishermen, both in and around these locations on the ocean as well as in the pubs and homes of the men for whom the places are salient. Drawing on Gibson's (1979) notion of "affordances"—a concept later employed by Ingold to establish the mutually constituting nature of people and places—Howard evocatively describes the day-to-day activities of Scottish fishermen as a process that "makes" the grounds that concurrently shape their activities, social encounters, and experiences of place.

Klokler and Gaspar's chapter explores the archaeological evidence from shell mounds along the Brazilian coast, particularly in the southern region of Santa Catarina, where populations built mounds up to eight thousand years ago. Rather than inferring a dumping ground for the remnants of feasts or the waste from temporary settlements, Klokler and Gaspar use the archaeological evidence to paint a picture of populations who were relatively sedentary, wide-ranging in their resource exploitation (partly through the use of maritime technologies) and who exhibited complex sociopolitical organization within, and among, groups. The evidence points to the importance of large bodies of water (such as lagoons and bays) in the establishment of stable territorial settlements and denser, more complex population structures than previously depicted.

Wickham-Jones's chapter, like so many in the volume, challenges us to see human encounters with land and sea as part of the same experience. Meandering over the Scottish mainland, around the islands of Skye and Orkney, and the ocean in between, Wickham-Jones stresses the dynamism of these spaces over the past ten thousand years and the fuzzy nature of the boundary as changing ocean levels have altered topography: coasts have emerged and retreated, mountains have sunk into the sea; for the peoples of the past, nothing was fixed. Following from this, she explores how the experience of being on land is informed by historical, social, and material experiences originating at sea, and vice versa, blurring the distinction between the two. For the archaeologist, this viewpoint is significant as it challenges the dominance of present paradigms, which were founded on dry-land research. If we are to understand the lives of our ancestors, we must broaden our understanding of their world by apprehending the changing and fluid nature of their experience.

Elixhauser explores orientation and wayfaring within the partly frozen waters of East Greenland. The chapter examines strategies adopted by the Iivit in finding safe passage through ice and the communication of this information by crew members. Issues of orientation and wayfinding are recurrent themes of communication, not only among boat drivers and passengers but also with other East Greenlanders encountered along the way. The chapter examines the importance of gestures, silences, and other modalities of nonverbal communication. For Elixhauser, just as for numerous authors in this anthology, communication goes beyond information transmittance between sender and receiver; it is a creative process that engages all of the senses.

Simonetti's chapter takes us beneath the surface of the water on the Chilean coast, where a group of Chilean and Argentinean underwater archaeologists explore a Pleistocene site discovered during the process of building a gas station. Simonetti explains that due to the physical challenges posed by diving, individuals dive in groups of two or three at a time. The chapter focuses on how these people communicate what they observe. The role of gestures is key to Simonetti's description, but he is careful not to suggest that divers have an image in their heads that they convert to an external picture using hand-signals. Rather, gestures both represent and transfer embodied knowledge among people in a way that does not reach the level of verbal language (speech) or even image (picture); the gestures themselves are the ideas being conveyed. Though not explicit in the link, Simonetti's description of gestures as a process of both knowing and becoming fits well with the Ingoldian notion of meshwork, where the focus is on the generating force of perpetual movement rather than on the information gleaned through a knowledge of static points. In this way, Simonetti's chapter problematizes the distinction between the underwater environment and the shore, encouraging us to see "how we inhabit together, through movement, a fluid world."

Robinson explores a prehistoric seascape that has been buried beneath alluvium as result of changes in sea level, long-term sediment transportation, and storm events. The chapter examines the exceptional prehistoric archaeology of Tremadoc Bay in northwest Wales, demonstrating that the significance of this impressive range of monuments and material culture can only be understood in reference to models of the configuration of the ancient coastline. Using Westerdahl's concept of the "maritime cultural landscape" (1992, 2011) the archaeological record of Tremadoc Bay is used to rethink the significance of this evidence for the study of its prehistoric maritime and coastal communities.

James evokes the worldview of the Yan-nhaŋu of Northern Australia, whose intimate knowledge of winds and other ecological features and events informs movement among the Crocodile Islands in the harvest of resources. As James says, "The synchronous relationship of the ancestors with their environment present in myths continues to shape the patterns of Yan-nhaŋu people's behavior as they harmonize their travels with the time and tides of their maritime homelands and the edicts of ancestral laws." James draws on the pioneering anthropological work of Donald Thomson, who described the use of fish traps and explored the complex intersection of marine technology, ecological knowledge—terrestrial, marine, and celestial—harvesting strategies, language, ritual, kinship, and cosmology. For example, for Yan-nhaŋu, the moon represents an ancestral figure that is perpetually sacrificed to atone for his drowning of two sons in a fish trap. Modern day fish traps are deployed according to the cycles of the moon, and various other harvesting practices coincide with the movement of celestial bodies; the cycles of plant, animal, and marine life; and the coming together of people within and among social groups. The generative nature of the movement of people and seasons and winds and creatures—again—evokes the "meshwork" that appears and reappears in the chapters of this volume.

Guilfoyle, Anderson, Reynolds, and Kimber present the results of a community-led research program documenting and interpreting the cultural seascapes of the Recherche Archipelago. Like that of Robinson (in this volume), this chapter draws on Westerdahl's concept of the maritime cultural landscape in an attempt to reconstruct the past maritime landscape of the archipelago. The chapter adopts a multidisciplinary approach to the archaeological record, modeling the process of postglacial sea level changes and documenting the human responses to these events over the last ten thousand years. This reconstruction of the ancient coastline of the archipelago allows the authors to place newly discovered sites, identified via fieldwork, back into an ancient maritime context. The scope of this chapter is chronologically wide, covering traces of human activities from prehistory to post-British colonial settlement. The strength of this research lies in its inclusive approach, allowing different perspectives to be voiced while sharing a single goal—to learn how to best understand, manage, and protect a shared natural and cultural landscape.

The role of women at sea is addressed in the richly ethnographic chapter provided by Willson and Tryggvadóttir. Challenging the popular Icelandic notion that women working in the fishing industry are anomalies or curiosities, Willson and Tryggvadóttir explore the experiences of contemporary large-vessel Icelandic seawomen, who must elude stereotypes of their own inadequacy before their male peers consider them equal seafarers. These women challenge stereotypes, not by styling themselves as "men," nor by explicitly driving a "feminist" agenda through asserting that "women," as a category, belong at sea. Rather, through hard work, persistence, strategy, and cleverness, successful seawomen establish themselves as known and trusted individuals.

Tejsner's chapter positions the life worlds of Greenlander Qeqertarsu-armiut in relation to broader Western narratives about climate change. He takes as a point of contrast the paternalistic depiction of all Greenland Inuit—like many indigenous or subaltern populations—as being particu-larly vulnerable to an inaccurately broad definition of climate change, the metaphor for which is melting sea ice. Tejsner describes the intimate as-sociation of the Qeqertarsuarmiut with their local environment, in which ice changes, tides flow and ebb, animals and sea creatures emerge, vanish, and reappear in their habitats, on their plates, and through their stories, in a continuous flow of life which the people influence as informed and stra-tegic agents. Tejsner provides an alternative discourse to that of "risk," a challenge to the notion that climate change is unproblematically linked to melting sea ice, with Greenlanders posited as helpless subjects in a global narrative.

Swift's contribution problematizes the characterization of the onboard environment of professional Filipino seafarers as being the "shop-floor" rather than "domestic" sphere of the village where men's families reside. Drawing on fieldwork in both locations, Swift describes an all Filipino-crewed car carrier as displaying features that might be associated with the nurturing, safe, and feminine space of "home," while in the union-run Seamen's Village in the Philippines, the business of the shipping companies plays out in the day-to-day work and social activity of the sea-farers' families. Challenging the characterization of Filipino workers as passive colonial subjects who have taken to seafaring as a stepping-stone to land-based work, Swift depicts them as upwardly mobile agents who have deliberately carved out professional positions in a global labor net-work that operates—at least in part—at sea. Rather than leaving their homes to enter a hypermasculine workplace, the Filipino seafarers are at home at sea.

Boucquey and Campbell take us to Carteret County in North Caro-lina, US, where conflict between commercial and recreational fishers is underpinned by similarities and differences in the experiences, practices, and motivations of the people of each sector. Both value the process of engaging with the natural world and meeting the challenges of overcom-ing an evasive prey. Professionals catch and sell fish in order to support their families, thus forming a core part of their identity and their links to heritage and place. Conversely, recreational fishers tend to make links be-tween their experiences of fishing and quality childhood time spent with male family members, being necessarily engaged in a leisure pursuit. By richly illustrating the overlaps and distinctions between the experiences of the two sectors, Boucquey and Campbell stress that successfully mitigating conflict between recreational and professional fishers will require not just careful resource allocation, but attention to the key ideological differences that inform the ongoing conflict.

Stacey and Allison explore the maritime-orientated livelihoods of the Sama-Bajau of Southeast Asia. Taking a wide chronological view of this group, the authors delve into the Sama-Bajau's history, dispersal, and settlement from the eleventh century to the present. Specifically, they examine the dependence of these specialist communities upon the highly biodiverse island, coral reef, and oceanic environments of the region and how they have responded to the social, economic, and environmental changes of the contemporary world. The chapter explores the concept of maritime nomadism through a detailed consideration of the livelihood strategies of the Sama-Bajau. It considers the negative connotations that have been associated with this group, connotations that largely result from a misunderstanding of the social complexities of their migratory maritime-orientated livelihoods. The authors argue for a more culturally informed approach to conservation initiatives in the region and for a reconsideration of the role of the Sama-Bajau within such initiatives.

King explores the territoriality of commercial shark fishermen in Australia and the genesis of particular boundaries among and between men and places at sea. While informal territoriality has generally been depicted in contrast to the formal regulations and classifications of fisheries managers and scientists, King argues that distinguishing too rigidly between formal and informal management arrangements ignores the mutuality of the two systems. Rather, she argues, perceptions of the ocean are invested with the encounters and salient categories found both at sea (with other fishermen) and on land (with fishermen, managers, and others). Indeed, in the course of their duties, and particularly their efforts at comanagement, fisheries managers encounter the social dynamics and territorial disputes of fishermen, which are subsequently incorporated into formal management structures.

Tanya J. King is a maritime anthropologist who focuses on the social and ecological implications of environmental policy implementation in Australia. She lectures in environmental anthropology at Deakin University, and is a director of the national women's commercial fishing organization, Women in Seafood Australasia, or WISA. Her publications include "'A Different Kettle of Fish': Mental Health Strategies for Australian Fishers, and Farmers" (2015).

Gary Robinson is a senior lecturer in archaeology at Bangor University in North Wales. His main research interest is the prehistoric archaeology of maritime and coastal communities in western Britain and Ireland. He completed his PhD at the Institute of Archaeology, University College London (PhD 2006), where his interest in British prehistory was first encouraged. His doctoral thesis explored the prehistoric archaeology of the Isles of Scilly, and he has continued to research prehistoric island and coastal communities in Western Britain and Ireland.

References

Acheson, J. M. 1981. "Anthropology of Fishing." *Annual Review of Anthropology* 10, no. 1: 275–316.

Adams, J. 2007. "Joined-up Boats: Maturing Maritime Archaeology." *Antiquity* 81, no. 311: 217–20.

Arlinghaus, R., S. J. Cooke, J. Lyman, D. Policansky, A. Schwab, C. Suski, S. G. Sutton, and E. B. Thorstad. 2007. "Understanding the Complexity of Catch-and-release in Recreational Fishing: An Integrative Synthesis of Global Knowledge from Historical, Ethical, Social, and Biological Perspectives." *Reviews in Fisheries Science* 15, no. 1–2: 75–167.

Barber, M. 2010. "Coastal Conflicts and Reciprocal Relations: Encounters between Yolngu People and Commercial Fishermen in Blue Mud Bay, Northeast Arnhem Land." *The Australian Journal of Anthropology* 21, no. 3: 298–314.

Barrett, J. C., and I. Ko. 2009. "A Phenomenology of Landscape: A Crisis in British Landscape Archaeology?" *Journal of Social Archaeology* 9, no. 3: 275–94.

Basso, P. 1984. "Stalking with Stories: Names, Places and Moral Narratives Among the Western Apache." In *Text, Play and Story: The Construction and Reconstruction of Self and Society.* Edited by E. Bruner, 19–55. Washington: Proceedings of the American Ethnological Society.

Beddington, J. R., D. J. Agnew, and C. W. Clark. 2007. "Current Problems in the Management of Marine Fisheries." *Science* 316, no. 5832: 1713–16.

Bowen, E. 1972. *Britain and the Western Seaways.* London: Thames and Hudson.

Breslow, S. J. 2014. "Tribal Science and Farmers' Resistance: A Political Ecology of Salmon Habitat Restoration in the American Northwest." *Anthropological Quarterly* 87, no. 3: 727–58.

Broodbank, C. 2000. *An Island Archaeology of the Early Cyclades.* Cambridge, UK: Cambridge University Press.

Brück, J. 2005. "Experiencing the Past? The Development of a Phenomenological Archaeology in British Prehistory." *Archaeological Dialogues* 12, no. 1: 45–72.

Castree, N. 2010. "Neoliberalism and the Biophysical Environment 1: What 'Neoliberalism' is, and what Difference Nature Makes to it." *Geography Compass* 4, no. 12: 1725–33.

Chapman, H., and B. Gearey. 2004. "The Social Context of Seafaring in the Bronze Age Revisited." *World Archaeology* 36, no. 4: 452–58.

Cicin-Sain, B., and A. Tiddens. 1989. "Private and Public Approaches to Solving Oil/Fishing Conflicts Offshore California." *Ocean and Shoreline Management* 12, no. 3: 233–51.

Clark, J. G. D. 1977. "The Economic Context of Dolmens and Passage Graves in Sweden." In *Ancient Europe and the Mediterranean: Studies Presented in Honour of H.O'Neil Hencken*. Edited by V. Markotic, 35–49. Warminster: Aris and Phillips.

Clark, P., ed. 2004a. *The Dover Bronze Age Boat*. London: English Heritage.

———. 2004b. "Introduction." In *The Dover Bronze Age Boat*. Edited by P. Clark, 1–3. London: English Heritage.

———. 2010. "Afterword: The Wet, the Dry and the In-between." In *Carpow in Context: A Late Bronze Age Logboat from the Tay*. Edited by D. Strachan, 179–90. Edinburgh: Society of Antiquaries of Scotland.

Cooke, S. J., and I. G. Cowx. 2006. "Contrasting Recreational and Commercial Fishing: Searching for Common Issues to Promote Unified Conservation of Fisheries Resources and Aquatic Environments." *Biological Conservation* 128, no. 1: 93–108.

Cooney, G. 2003. "Introduction: Seeing Land from the Sea." *World Archaeology* 35, no. 3: 323–28.

Crumlin-Pederson, O. 2010. "'Archaeology and the Sea in Scandinavia and Britain: A Personal Account' by Ian Friel." *International Journal of Maritime History* 22, no. 2: 350–51.

Cummings, V., and A. Whittle. 2003. *Places of Special Virtue: Megaliths in the Neolithic Landscapes of Wales*. Oxford: Oxbow Books.

Davies, M. 1946. "The Diffusion and Distribution Pattern of the Megalithic Monuments of the Irish Sea and North Channel Coastlands." *The Antiquaries Journal* 26, no. 1–2: 38–60.

Drengson, A. R., and B. Devall. 2010. "The Deep Ecology Movement." *Trumpeter* 26, no. 2: 57–78.

Farr, H. 2006. "Seafaring as Social Action." *Journal Maritime Archaeology* 1, no. 1: 85–99.

Flatman, J. 2011. "Places of Special Meaning: Westerdahl's Comet, 'Agency' and the Concept of the 'Maritime Cultural Landscape.'" In *The Archaeology of Maritime Landscapes*. Edited by B. Ford, 311–30. New York: Springer.

Fleming, A. 1999. "Phenomenology and the Megaliths of Wales: A Dreaming Too Far?" *Oxford Journal of Archaeology* 18, no. 2: 119–25.

———. 2005. "Megaliths and Post-modernism: The Case of Wales." *Antiquity* 79, no. 306: 921–32.

Gibson, J. J. 1979. *The Ecological Approach to Visual Perception*. London: Houghton Mifflin.

Hilborn, R. 2007. "Defining Success in Fisheries and Conflicts in Objectives." *Marine Policy* 31, no. 2: 153–58.

Hirsch, E., and M. O'Hanlon. 1995. *The Anthropology of Landscape, Perspectives on Place and Space*. Oxford: Clarendon Press.

Ingold, T. 2011. *Being Alive: Essays on Movement, Knowledge and Description*. New York: Taylor & Francis.

Johnstone, P. 1988. *The Seacraft of Prehistory*. London: Routledge.

Kearney, R. E. 2002. "Recreational Fishing: Value Is in the Eye of the Beholder." In *Recreational Fisheries: Ecological, Economic and Social Evaluation*. Edited by Tony J. Pitcher and Charles E. Hollingworth, vol. 2, 17–33. Oxford: Blackwell Publishing Ltd.

King, T. J. 2005. "Crisis of Meanings: Divergent Experiences and Perceptions of the Marine Environment in Victoria, Australia." *The Australian Journal of Anthropology* 16, no. 3: 350–65.

Lehoërff, A., ed. 2012. *Par-delà l'Horizon, Sociétés en Manche et Mer du Nord, il y a 3 500 ans*. Paris: Somogy éditions d'art.

Marcigny, C., and M. Talon. 2009. "Sur les Rives de la Manche: Qu'en est-il du Passage de l'Âge du Bronze à l'Âge du Fer à Partir des Découvertes Récentes?" In *De l'Âge du Bronze à l'Âge du Fer en France et en Europe Occidentale (X^e–VIIe siècle avant J-C); la Moyenne Vallée du Rhône aux âges du Fer*. Edited by M.-J. Roulière-Lambert, A. Daubigney, P.-Y. Milcent, M. Talon, and J. Vital, 385–404. Dijon: Revue Archéologique de l'Est, Supplément.

McCormack, F. 2012. "Indigeneity as Process: Māori Claims and Neoliberalism." *Social Identities* 18, no. 4: 417–34.

McCrea-Strub, A., K. Kleisner, U. R. Sumaila, W. Swartz, R. Watson, D. Zeller, and D. Pauly. 2011. "Potential Impact of the Deepwater Horizon Oil Spill on Commercial Fisheries in the Gulf of Mexico." *Fisheries* 36, no. 7: 332–36.

McGrail, S. 1987. *Ancient Boats in North-West Europe: The Archaeology of Water Transport to AD 1500*. London: Longman.

———. 1988. "Assessing the Performance of an Ancient Boat: The Halsholme Logboat." *Oxford Journal of Archaeology* 7, no. 1: 35–46.

———. 1989. "The Shipment of Traded Goods and of Ballast in Antiquity." *Oxford Journal of Archaeology* 8, no. 3: 353–58.

Muckelroy, K. 1980. "Two Bronze Age Cargoes in British Waters." *Antiquity* 54, no. 211: 100–9.

Needham, S. 2009. "Encompassing the Sea: Maritories and Bronze Age Maritime Interactions." In *Bronze Age Connections: Cultural Contact in Prehistoric Europe*. Edited by P. Clarke, 12–37. Oxford: Oxbow.

Philippe, M. 2009. "The Canche Estuary (Pas-de-Calais, France) from the early Bronze Age to the Emporium of Quentovic: A Traditional Landing Place Between South-east England and the Continent." In *Bronze Age Connections: Cultural Contact in Prehistoric Europe*. Edited by P. Clarke, 68–79. Oxford: Oxbow.

Pinkerton, E., and R. Davis. 2015. "Neoliberalism and the Politics of Enclosure in North American Small-scale Fisheries." *Marine Policy* 61: 303–12.

Pomeroy, C., M. Hall-Arber, and F. Conway. 2015. "Power and Perspective: Fisheries and the Ocean Commons Beset by Demands of Development." *Marine Policy* 61: 339–46.

Renfrew, C. 1973. *Before Civilization: The Radiocarbon Revolution and Prehistoric Europe*. Harmondsworth: Penguin Books Ltd.

Richards, C. 1996. "Monuments as Landscape: Creating the Centre of the World in Late Neolithic Orkney." *World Archaeology* 28, no. 2: 190–208.

Robb, J. 2001. "Island Identities: Ritual, Travel and the Creation of Difference in Neolithic Malta." *European Journal of Archaeology* 4, no. 2: 175–202.

Robinson. M. E., W. Shimwel, and L. G. Cribbin. 1999. "Re-assessing the Logboat from Lurgan Townland, Co. Galway, Ireland." *Antiquity* 7, no. 3: 903–8.

Scarre, C. 2002. "Coast and Cosmos: The Neolithic Monuments of Northern Brittany." In *Monuments and Landscape in Atlantic Europe*. Edited by C. Scarre, 84–102. London: Routledge.

Smith, A. D. M., K. J. Sainsbury, and R. A. Stevens. 1999. "Implementing Effective Fisheries-Management Systems-management Strategy Evaluation and the Australian Partnership Approach." *ICES Journal of Marine Science* 56, no. 6: 967–79.

Strachan, D. 2010. *Carpow in Context: A Late Bronze Age Logboat from the Tay*. Edinburgh: Society of Antiquaries of Scotland.

Thomas, J. 1993. "The Politics of Vision and the Archaeologies of Landscape." In *Landscape, politics and perspectives*. Edited by B. Bender, 49–84. Oxford: Berg.

Tilley, C. 1994. *A Phenomenology of Landscape*. Oxford: Berg.

Ucko, P., and R. Layton, eds. 1999. *Archaeology and Anthropology of Landscape*. London: Routledge.

Van de Noort, R. 2004. "The Humber, its Sewn Plank Boats, their Contexts and the Significance of it All." In *The Dover Bronze Age Boat in Context: Society and Water Transport in Prehistoric Europe*. Edited by P. Clark, 90–8. Oxford: Oxbow Books.

———. 2006. "Argonauts of the North Sea: A Social Maritime Archaeology for the 2nd Millennium BC." *Proceedings of the Prehistoric Society*, vol. 72, 267–87.

Voyer, M., K. Barclay, A. McIlgorm, and N. Mazur. 2017. "Connections or Conflict? A Social and Economic Analysis of the Interconnections Between the Professional Fishing Industry, Recreational Fishing and Marine Tourism in Coastal Communities in NSW, Australia." *Marine Policy* 76: 114–21.

Westerdahl, C. 1992. "The Maritime Cultural Landscape." *The International Journal of Nautical Archaeology* 21, no. 1: 5–14.

———. 2011. "Conclusion: The Maritime Cultural Landscape Revisited." In *The Archaeology of Maritime Landscapes*. Edited by B. Ford, 331–44. New York: Springer.

Wright, E. V. 1986. "A Bronze Age Beach Capstan?" *Oxford Journal of Archaeology* 5, no. 3: 309–21.

Figure 1.1. Ashtamudi Estuary. Photo by the authors.

CHAPTER 1

Moving Beyond the "Scape" to Being in the (Watery) World, Wherever

Hannah Cobb and Jesse Ransley

Living on, in, and by Water

The different fishing places in the channel between the islands of Pattomduruthu and Pezhunthuruthu in Ashtamudi Estuary emerge through interactions between currents, fish, and fishermen (figure 1.1). In these waters, *koruvala*, small seine fishing nets, are often laid in shallow water where tidal eddies form, while crab fishermen look for areas of calm, slack water. *Pattavala*, lighter drift nets, are laid across running currents and as these currents shift with tidal flows and monsoon rains so do the fish, nets, fishing, and "places." This world emerges and is known through everyday practices and actions. As the seasons and weather change, it is a fisherman's depth of experiential knowledge of the estuary that enables him to keep catching fish. This knowledge is gained through doing—through moving from place to place, over many seasons, and feeling out when and where you should lay which net. In attentively but intuitively feeling the wind on their bodies and the water and currents through the boat, paddle, and net, as one fisherman is alert to adjusting the speed of the boat and the other to the rhythm of feeding the net over the side, both apply their knowledge of the world and replenish it. As one boatman suggests, "You learn by doing it." For as you learn the mechanics of hauling and casting nets, you also become sensitised to the wind and weather, and their connection to the water and even the lake bed beneath. Multiple forms of perception are combined in this process—a freshening wind is heard as well as felt and approaching rain is smelt as well as seen—and through it you begin to know the world. It is even through the simple skills of moving about the boat, of balance, of your body learning to react to and anticipate the boat's response to your shifts in weight, as well as the currents, winds, and its own momentum, that the world around you emerges.

This description of fishing the Keralan backwaters, in addition to the many diverse examples in this volume, illustrates something of the fluid relationships experienced by those who live and work on, in, and around any body of water, in both the past and the present. The watery world is temporal and multidimensional, and those who live and work in it are attuned to it through their bodies, through everyday practices, and through the materiality of life.

In this volume and elsewhere, the term "seascape" is increasingly used by both archaeologists and anthropologists to conceptualize the experience that we articulate above (e.g., Cooney 2003; Ford 2011).[1] Its use reflects a need to consider the *inhabitation* of watery places and to recognize marine zones as lived spaces. In this endeavor, the seascape moves us closer to a more seamless perspective and away from the idea of human activity as an intrusion into the marine environment. It is, therefore, undoubtedly a useful heuristic concept. However, as an archaeologist and an anthropologist working in temporally and geographically diverse locales, it is the problems rather than strengths of this conceptualization of watery places that we have most frequently discussed. As we talked through our very disparate research areas, in the backwaters of present day Kerala in southwest India and the island archipelagos of Mesolithic western Scotland, it became clear that the term "seascape" did little to convey the relationship between the humans and the bodies of water in either area.

Consequently, in this chapter, we argue that the term is highly problematic, for while it is employed in an attempt to incorporate both land and water into theorizations of a seamless lived space, in reality it continues to juxtapose land and sea through its opposition to "landscape," and underlines, as well as extends, a reliance on the metaphor of "scapes."

To move beyond the seascape, then, we present examples from our different research areas to demonstrate how in daily life, in being in the world, land and sea are always intermingled and always connected in a way that defies the simple realm of one "scape" or the other. By drawing upon examples from both anthropology and archaeology, we highlight the ways in which being in the world occurs *within* a world of sky, water, and earth, of wind and weather, and not *upon* surfaces, be they sea or land. We live in a world in process, in flux, where places, things, and people are not fixed, but rather all are extended into and disclosed in the temporal, social world—a world that is not easily reduced to a "scape."

Landscapes and Seascapes

It is necessary to begin an examination of *sea*scapes by thinking first about *land*scapes, since the term grew in response to, and as a development of, traditional conceptions of landscape. While the very land-based excerpt below might seem somewhat incongruous, we will go on to explain why we think it is not merely relevant, but fundamental to how we, as archaeologists and anthropologists, interrogate and apply the notion of the seascape in our work.

> The landscape, I hold, is not a picture in the imagination, surveyed by the mind's eye; nor, however, is it an alien and formless substrate awaiting the imposition of human order . . . neither is the landscape identical to nature, nor is it on the side of humanity against nature. As the familiar domain of our dwelling, it is with us, not against us, but it is no less real for that. And through living in it, the landscape becomes a part of us, just as we are part of it (Ingold 1993, 154).

This excerpt represents one of a range of fascinating works that appeared in the first half of the 1990s that explicitly sought to challenge the pervasive understandings of landscape as an external and passive medium, upon which human action is imprinted (e.g., papers in Bender 1993; Ingold 1993; Tilley 1994). Such approaches argued that it was only in modernity, and particularly as a facet of capitalism, that a conception of landscape had arisen in which it was understood as a palimpsest of history, solid, stratified, permanent, and sure. In response, and influenced by developments outside their disciplines in the 1980s (e.g., Cosgrove 1984; papers in Cosgrove and Daniels 1988), archaeologists (most famously Tilley 1994) and anthropologists (notably Ingold 1993) drew upon phenomenological approaches to explore alternative ways of perceiving landscape (Tim Ingold's words, above, encapsulate this perspective).[2] Through such approaches, landscape is understood not as a two-dimensional external object against which people act; rather, it is conceptualized as a process situated in interactions, in movement and activities, so that both people and places emerge through their relations with one another, "a network of related places, which have gradually been revealed through people's habitual activities and interactions" (Thomas 2001, 173). In such a reformulation, landscapes are not static and fixed but historically and culturally contingent.

Twenty years on, such counter-modern approaches to past and present landscapes are ubiquitous in the literature (just some of the key texts include Ingold 1993; Gosden and Head 1994; Tilley 1994; Lemaire 1997; Thomas 2001; Brück 2005; Bender 2006; Johnson 2006; and numerous authors within Bender 1993; Hirsch and O'Hanlon 1995; Ucko and Layton 1999; and more recently, David and Thomas 2010). While some studies of landscape do remain concerned with the land as objectified and commoditized, it is in challenging these ideas that many more recent publications have been able to develop alternative, nuanced interpretations of the past (e.g., Edmonds 1999; Conneller 2005) and, in building upon these, presenting exciting broader conceptualizations of the way people dwell in the world (e.g., Ingold 2011). Hence, this chapter takes this work as a starting point and draws particularly on Ingold's reconceptualization of landscape as taskscape—as inherently temporal, social, and political and existing through the continually embodied actions and reciprocal interaction of both animate and inanimate (Ingold 1993, 163–64). This, we argue, enables us to decipher the complicated ways that the biographies of people, places, and things become entwined, enacted, experienced, and remembered in both the past and the present.

It is this rich body of literature about the *land*scape that prompted the rise of disciplinary concern with the *sea*scape. Such a fixation with landscape represents a view of the past that for many archaeologists is simply "the past on dry land." Frequently, accounts of the past have stopped at the water's edge, unless they were developed by underwater archaeologists, when accounts of the past-submerged invariably stopped at the water's surface. This view has perpetuated the idea of islands as isolated (Terrell, Hunt, and Gosden 1997), of various coastal regions as marginal and peripheral, and ultimately it has reinforced and been reinforced by modern, Cartesian dualistic understandings of the world. Thus, land has been conceptualized as existing in opposition to water, in the same dualistic framework as culture versus nature and subject versus object. (The problems with such dualisms more broadly are discussed in Thomas 2004.)

This, then, is where the seascape comes in. The notion seeks to replace our dualistic "land versus water" view of the world with a more seamless perspective, which attempts to capture the fluid relationship that those who live and work on and around any body of water experience in reality (Cooney 2003). But does the notion of the seascape really do this? Does it deliver, in this sense? To explore this, let us return to the quote with which we began this section. The point Ingold is making about landscape is clear, so let us replace the word "landscape" with "seascape" to explore whether the term seascape can be understood in the same way:

> The [seascape], I hold, is not a picture in the imagination, surveyed by the mind's eye; nor, however, is it an alien and formless substrate awaiting the imposition of human order . . . neither is the [seascape] identical to nature, nor is it on the side of humanity *against* nature. As the familiar domain of our dwelling, it is *with* us, not against us, but it is no less real for that. And through living in it, the [seascape] becomes a part of us, just as we are part of it. (Ingold 1993, 154, with amendments by the authors)

The first part of this altered excerpt undoubtedly and precisely articulates the idea that the seascape has been invoked to express that which is, as Cooney argues, "contoured, alive, rich in ecological diversity and in cosmological and religious significance and ambiguity . . . [through which] people in coastal areas actively create their identities, sense of place and histories" (Cooney 2003, 323). In these terms, we can understand the maritime environment according to Ingold's conception of landscape—not as culture versus nature, or in this case land versus sea, but as dynamic, temporal, and social.

The term has evidently catalyzed a challenging of the land/sea division in our accounts of the past and the present. However, let us return to Ingold's last sentence: "And through living in it, the landscape becomes a part of us, just as we are part of it" (1993, 154). This formulation is extraordinarily useful. In this short sentence lies the idea that places, things, and people are not fixed, but rather all are extended into and disclosed in the temporal, social world. People, things, and places emerge and are understood and negotiated through biography, narrative, memory, and simply being in the world. However, it is in the face of this understanding that the notion of the seascape starts to fall short. If we were to argue that the seascape "becomes a part of us, just as we are part of it," then we are faced with the notion that the objects, smells, experiences, and memories of the maritime environment ultimately can and will extend far beyond the limits of the sea itself. Consequently, this raises the question: Where does the seascape stop? And it is in asking this question that a fundamental problem with the term is revealed.

Ultimately, and problematically, the term "seascape" still asks us to define the limits of the maritime environment and then draw a line between what is maritime and what is not. In turn, the term perpetuates exactly the kind of reductive and atomized objectification and division of land and sea that it was intended to challenge. Moreover, without the embodied engagements with the world present in phenomenological approaches, the notion easily becomes narrowed to sketches of cognitive or symbolic seascapes imposed upon a passive, external, and objectified landscape of land and sea. From this perspective, places do not occur in the flows of interactions between persons, things, and materials, but exist in a solidified, external world where meanings are added to them.[3] Notably, even within the *World Archaeology* "Seascapes" volume in which Cooney introduced his notion of the seascape, this problem was evident. For example, Barber described the archaeology of Maori South Island fishing as reflecting a worldview without "hard and fast distinction between land, sea, animals, people and gods" (2003, 435). Yet he presented this solely as a "rational" understanding, a conception of land and sea as united, which is reinforced through "ritual behaviour" but not reflecting reality (Cooney 2003, 434). Meanwhile, McNiven wrote of the seascapes of the indigenous Australian "Saltwater People" as "spiritscapes engaged through ritual performance"

(2004, 329) and of coastal "ritual sites" as part of "formalized liminal zones for spiritual engagement with the sea" (2004, 344).

To move beyond these problems, we propose a shift away from the drive to atomize and categorize people's experience of the world as existing in a landscape *or* a seascape. In discussing examples from our two very different case studies, we will illustrate how the complicated relationships between people, places, and things may be extended inland and out to sea in a variety of different ways—ways that ultimately defy the classificatory boundaries implied in the term "seascape."

Where Does the Seascape Stop?

Turning first to the Mesolithic northern Irish Sea basin, there is ample evidence for the diverse relationships between people and the maritime environment. Although issues with preservation, such as the presence of raised beaches and substantial inland peat coverage, inevitably skew the record, many of the approximately fifteen hundred Mesolithic sites in the area are found by the coast or in the coastal hinterland. Evidence from sites such as the Oronsay shell middens indicates that people were engaged in deep-sea fishing, while also moving regularly between different islands and peninsulas and exploiting the differing resources that these offered (e.g., Mellars 1987). Consequently, as a range of recent accounts have argued, the centrality of the sea must have been fundamental to Mesolithic life ways, and in turn the sea must inevitably have played an important symbolic role in Mesolithic cosmologies (Pollard 1996; Warren 1997, 2000, 2005; Pollard 2000; Cummings 2003; Cobb 2005, 2006, 2008; Wickham-Jones 2005).[4]

Indeed, the concept of seascape undoubtedly provides a framework for thinking through such direct interactions with the maritime environment. However, it may also be productive to consider how different types of materials and material practices in the Mesolithic resonated with specific understandings of the world to extend and incorporate them elsewhere. Taking such a perspective may enable us to view the material record in a very different light.

An interesting example of this is represented in the extensive spread of Mesolithic material around Gallow Hill (Donnelly and MacGregor 2005) and the nearby Littlehill Bridge (MacGregor and Donnelly 2001) on the Ayrshire coast. Here, on the edge of a hill on the raised beach to the north of the once lagoonal and estuarine area at the mouth of the Water of Girvan (Donnelly and MacGregor 2005), both field walking and more targeted excavation work have revealed extensive surface scatters of Mesolithic material, a series of mixed, unstratified Mesolithic deposits, *in situ* scattered lithic material and open-site activity including pits, hearths, areas of burning, stake holes, and several sub-oval, shallow sided scoops (MacGregor and Donnelly 2001, 5).

Radiocarbon dates and the accumulations of material in this area, extending over approximately a square half-kilometer, suggest that it may have been revisited over a period of at least fifteen hundred years in the late Mesolithic. I have suggested in more detail elsewhere (Cobb 2008) that the repeated activity at this specific locale indicates that it had come to represent a potent place. Part of this potency must simply have been engendered through its reuse and thus its temporal connections to the past. However, this site conceptually connected people and places across the Firth of Clyde and the northern part of the Irish Sea in a number of ways. By the later late Mesolithic, a wide range of raw materials were being brought to the site, including some of the few definitively Mesolithic examples of worked pitchstone outside of the Isle of Arran (Donnelley and MacGregor 2005, 50). We may envisage these materials themselves as visceral reminders of journeys, places, and people across, entwined with, and connected by the sea. In addition, the location site and the visual connections it affords must equally have enhanced the physical and mnemonic connections it elicited across the seascape. Indeed, from here, there are superb views both inland over the Midland Valley and out to the Firth of Clyde, the northern Irish Sea, the islands of Arran and Ailsa Craig (which can clearly be seen from the Antrim Coast), and much of Argyll and Bute, as well as the edges of the Southern Uplands.

While this site may have acquired a potency from its use over time, and as a hub for bringing together a series of material and visual connections across the seascape itself, the critical point here is that these connections would have been extended back out into the world, far beyond what may conventionally be defined as the seascape. The excavators, for example, have pointed to a focus on specialized blade and microlith production (Donnelley and MacGregor 2005, 58), and the repair of microlithic tools (Donnelley and MacGregor 2005, 56). This is significant because, as Finlay (2000, 2003) has argued, through their composite nature, lithic technologies, and especially microlithic tools, may have been multiply authored and thus acted to bring together different identities and different parts of the world in their creation. These in turn would then be extended out into the world as the tool was used, further affecting and transforming the user or users of the tool and the animal or substances that were possibly encountered. The critical point here is that one does not need to be on the sea, or by the sea, or in a maritime environment at all, to be affected or transformed by a tool which itself encompasses elements or identities related to the sea. Thus the swift kill of a deer, far from the sea, deep within the forests of the Scottish Southern Uplands, may nonetheless have recalled the affects of the potency of Gallow Hill and Littlehill Bridge, and their connections to the past and the present, to the sea and people over the sea. As such, it is clear that applying the traditional remit and divisions implied in the term "seascape" may work more to restrict our interpretations of past understandings of identity and the world, rather than to allow us to explore how connections to the sea may have extended far beyond this.

Neither Seascape nor Landscape

Just as applying the term "seascape" artificially binds interpretations of the past, it also atomizes conceptions of watery worlds in the present. The village of Munruthuruthu, our second case study, is another place that falls between, and therefore challenges, the notions of landscape and seascape. It is situated on the fringes of an estuarine lake system. The Kallada River flows north of it and feeds into the estuary to its west, and with the largest lake, Ashtamudi (after which the estuary is named), between it and the Western Indian Ocean. It is threaded with small channels, canals, and waterways, with interconnected ponds and pools, and is a center of local boat building (figure 1.2) (Ransley 2009, 2012). It is very much a watery world, but though the estuary is connected to the sea, it is not part of a "maritime" one. The people of Munruthuruthu, the inland fishermen, city-commuters, laborers, and boat-builders alike make a clear distinction between their world and that of the nearby coastal fishing villages.

There are, of course, interactions between Munruthuruthu and coastal villages. Fish-sellers move through the village waterways selling marine species alongside estuarine lake ones, though marine fish are compared unfavorably with lake fish. As was documented in the case study, Lali, a sand-transporter from Munruthuruthu, purchased a second-hand coastal fishing boat in Chavara to dismantle to provide timber for repairs to his own boat. The timbers he did not use, he sold on. The *thalamaram* (stem piece) from the coastal boat was incorporated into a new boat, and other timbers went into, at the author's count, four other village boats. Yet, as well as illustrating material connections, Lali's purchase highlights the distinctions between Chavara and Munruthuruthu. The coastal boat had endured a fire, informing the belief that it was "unlucky"—no one wanted to go to sea in it—so it was sold at cut price to an inland boatman who made no such connection. Though there are links to the sea, the world of Munruthuruthu could not be described as part of a *seascape*, but neither is it a *landscape*.

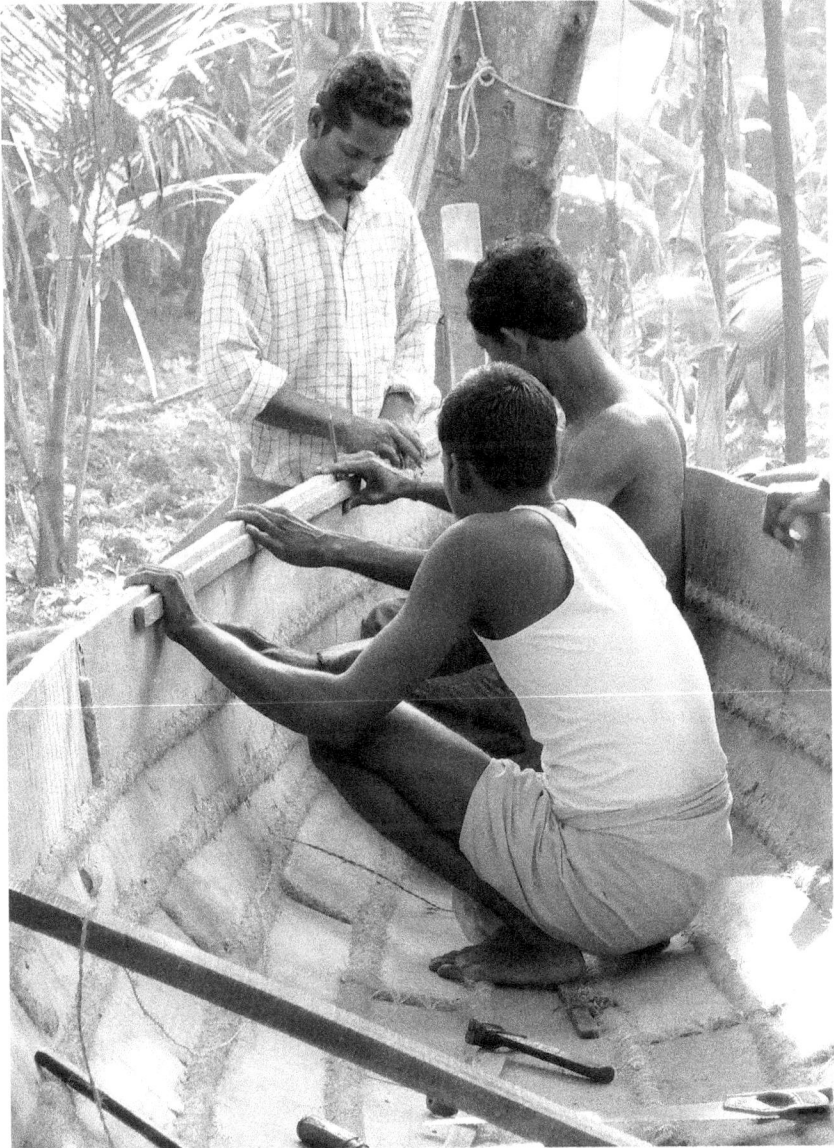

Figure 1.2 Local boat builders. Photo by the authors.

The watery between-ness of Munruthuruthu is part of the everyday, deeply embedded in the regular rhythms and pragmatic living of village life. The physical boundary between land and water is mutable and constantly renegotiated. People regularly, and unaffectedly, remake land and water. The paddy field becomes a coconut grove, as mud is collected from the paddy's bed and raised up around new palms, simultaneously making land and the channels between. The coconut grove becomes a prawn pond, as the revetment is built up and the channel is widened. The intricate network of channels and canals that weave through the village are subject to change, to widening, in-fill, or reopening. The older generation has made the land their houses stand on, collecting mud from the lake and infilling paddy fields. Mud collecting is still a profitable livelihood. Men cut mud from shallow areas of the lake bed with their feet, dive down, and scoop it into their boats, transport it into the village, and deliver it to coconut groves, fields, and revetments. In this way, parts of the village are made from the lake and the two categories are blurred.

Similarly, water itself keeps shifting in an active environment that is constantly re-establishing balance. In some places, it is hard to determine where the lake edge is, where the land ends or begins. Prawn ponds and channels blend into the lake and small tidal or seasonal rises in water level submerge revetments and areas of reclaimed land. Physically, land dissolves into water and water is absorbed into land (figure 1.3).

This boundary is also permeable and indistinct in people's experience of and movement through the world. People move in and out of water habitually as they move around the village, wading channels and getting in and out of boats. Daily chores, washing clothes for example, as well as work such as mud collecting and sand mining, move them in, under, and through water. Fishermen sit in their boats at lakeside teashops to eat and people climb in and out of the *kadathu* (small ferry) to cross the river. Discussions are held from boat to land, people call out across rivers and gather news from boats as they pass. Munruthuruthu does not end at the water's edge (if one could even be defined), but incorporates land and water, blended and intermingled, as lived space. Munruthuruthu is neither a *land*- nor *sea*scape, and perhaps it is both.

In Munruthuruthu, the world is conceived through the categories of village and, to the west, *kayal* (lake). Most watery occupations and activities—such as mud collecting, sand mining, and transporting coconuts or livestock—happen within a short distance of home. However, fishermen and sand-transporters, like Lali, travel kilometers into and across the wider estuarine lake when they work, where they must employ a different set of knowledge and skills. As such, the boundary between village and *kayal* is not the somewhat ephemeral shoreline, but the boundary between the area they work in, know, and experience, and the area within which their friends and neighbors move. Different skills and equipment are required to paddle, pole, and sail longer distances, skills that can only be acquired and tested through experience of storms and sudden changes in wind or tide. Similarly, knowledge of different places, of the lakebed, of

Figure 1.3. Land and sea blurred. Photo by the authors.

currents and confluences, of tidal flow and wind patterns are not needed nor acquired in the village. According to Lali, this experiential division is about half a kilometer from the shoreline. As he describes it, the boundary of Munruthuruthu emerges through being in the world, through the embodied skills and knowledge involved in everyday activities.

Yet, this boundary does not bind Munruthuruthu. The "edge" of the village reflects patterns of activities that occur, move, and change in time. As the description of fishing at the beginning of this chapter suggests, places move as the seasons and weather, the tidal flows and currents, change. It is far easier, therefore, to identify when you are *in* the lake or *in* the village, in the midst of the multiple confluences of boats, nets, fish, sand, bodies, water, mud, and wind through which places emerge, rather than to identify the border between them. Hoeppe describes a similarly ephemeral border between spatial categories of *kilakkuppuram* (outside in the east) and *patinnaruppuram* (outside in the west) among fishermen in a coastal village to the north, ephemeral because these categories are also constituted through doing, through the activities of "being a fisherman" (Hoeppe 2003, 6; 2007, 23ff).[5] The village edge, then, is an elastic, experiential boundary, one that is unidentifiable, blurred, close-up but emerging through the flow of materials, skills, and knowledge in a dynamic environment, the tangle of multiple lines of movement and life that accumulate over time.

Thus, the distinction between village and lake does not make Munruthuruthu a bounded place. Rather than turning "the pathways along which life is lived into boundaries within which life is contained" (Ingold 2008, 1796–97), it unfolds and is revealed across time and space as people move through and inhabit the world. Rather than existing as an external entity, it occurs in the comings and goings of humans and other organisms, in the jumbles of interactions between persons, things, and the weather-world (Ingold 2007). The paths of cashew factory workers taking their bus out of Munruthuruthu or the civil servants catching the ferry into the city each day, and all the entanglements of their lives, are interwoven into Munruthuruthu just as much as those of Lali and the inland fishermen. Life is not lived bounded, as implied by the term "seascape," but rather it is in the open, and it is where this bundle of life paths, of activities, and actions meshes that Munruthuruthu emerges.

Watery Worlds against Bindings

Despite its useful disruption of a false conceptual boundary between land and water, the notion of seascape creates its own classificatory boundaries, and leaves places like Munruthuruthu marooned in between land and sea. So rather than coining a new term (*estuarine*scape?!) to supplement the binary pairing of *sea*scape and *land*scape, drawing from the nuances of the case studies presented here, we suggest that there is a need to move beyond the "scape." The metaphor of the "scape" functions to atomize people's experience of the world in order to categorize them according to our own conceptual frameworks. In both cited examples, it is very clear that understandings of watery worlds are produced through work and movement, doing and knowing, through dwelling and being in the world. In this way, the "location" of Munruthuruthu is not maritime, nor land, it is simply lake and village, a watery world; similarly, the watery worlds of Mesolithic Ayrshire were not bound to the coast but extended through microliths, as the residues of watery assemblages, far in land.

Returning to Ingold's argument that "through living in it, the landscape becomes a part of us, just as we are part of it" (Ingold 1993, 154), we have sought to demonstrate that this argument applies as much to the sea as to the land—as to any watery world. From the Keralan backwaters to the Mesolithic of the Irish Sea, to simply you or I, waiting to cross a busy road in a busy city, thinking of the sea, we are entwined with the sea and we carry it with us in memories, materials, persons, and practice far beyond the bounds of the waves and the coast.

Cooney argues that the seascape is "contoured, alive, rich in ecological diversity and in cosmological and religious significance and ambiguity" (Cooney 2003, 323), but what we have sought to demonstrate in this chapter is that this is as much the case *by* the sea as it is *far from it*, where the water, the shore, the dunes, and the mud are just as present in memories, materials, and actions. The sea and the water and all of its connections do not stop at an easily definable line, but rather, as we have seen in Munruthuruthu, what is land and what is water are continually in flux. There, as in Mesolithic Scotland, we argue, there is ultimately no easily discernible place where landscape stops and seascape starts. Instead, the effects and the experiences of inhabiting the sea have the potential to resonate throughout daily life, wherever this is lived. As a result, we reject the term "seascape," which, while aiming to explore the holistic, wide-reaching experience of the watery world, nonetheless continues to contrast it with landscape. In contrast, we suggest that Ingold's notion of the "taskscape"[6] is more useful—this provides a perspective of the enmeshed, experiential, and temporal dynamic of being in the world that does not require a conceptual restriction to the categories of land and sea. Ultimately, we propose that it is simply in escaping from the bindings of the "scape" altogether, and in exploring the *specificity* of the being in the watery world wherever, that will enable us to fully understand the inhabitation of the sea in the past and the present.

Hannah Cobb is a Senior Lecturer in Archaeology at the University of Manchester, UK. Her research focuses on two areas: interpretive approaches to contemporary archaeological practice, and the Mesolithic and Neolithic of western Scotland. In the latter, Hannah's work examines the intersection between material culture, landscape, and identity, and explores the insights that a New Materialist approach may bring. She is one of the editors of *Reconsidering Archaeological Fieldwork* (2012).

Jesse Ransley is an ethnographer of seafaring and oceans, particularly the Indian Ocean past and present. She works on embodied knowledges, the materiality and temporality of oceans, and the broader philosophical question of how we conceive maritime space, studying subjects from traditional boatbuilding and watery landscapes to lascars, piracy, and maritime heritage ethnographies. She is currently a British Academy Postdoctoral Fellow at the University of Southampton based in the Centre for Maritime Archaeology. Her publications include *People and the Sea: A Maritime Archaeological Research Agenda for England* (2013) and "The Backwater Boats of Kerala: Identity, Place, and the World of Munruthuruthu" (2012).

Notes

Hannah Cobb wishes to thank the Royal Anthropological Institute and the University of Manchester who supported the fieldwork that formed the basis for the Mesolithic case study in this chapter. Jesse Ransley wishes to thank the Royal Anthropological Institute, INTACH UK, and the Nehru Trust who supported the fieldwork that formed the basis of the Keralan case study; and, as ever, Renu Henry for her help, friendship, insight, and support throughout the fieldwork, and Mohanan, Nakulan, and the people of Munruthuruthu for their welcome, patience, and tireless explanations. We would also like to thank those who made some interesting and insightful comments when this was originally presented as a conference paper at the European Association of Social Anthropologists in Bristol in 2009.

1. It is also worth noting that other terms frequently used to express this concept include "maritime landscapes" and "maritime cultural landscapes." In this chapter, we address the term "seascape" most specifically.
2. Influenced particularly by Merleau Ponty's (2002) *Phenomenology of Perception*.
3. Ford's recent definition of "a true seascape" in direct opposition to "landscape" and as distinct from "maritime cultural landscapes" is perhaps the best illustration of this configuration of the idea: "A true seascape is constructed of the factors that allow an individual to perceive his or her location out of sight of land" (2011, 4).
4. The most recent, nuanced, and rich discussion of this for the Mesolithic can be found in Leary (2013), although this is focused on Doggerland rather than the area discussed here (Western Scotland).

5. Hoeppe describes "being a fisherman" and "doing the work of the west" as a performative identity (2003, 6), citing Astuti's work (1995), and paralleling Busby's study of a Keralan fishing village much further south (2000). However, the key point here is that the constitution of place and identity, of "being a fisherman," is similarly about doing, about the confluences of materials, people, and skills in a dynamic environment.
6. And more recently, we find the concept of the meshwork (Ingold 2011) incredibly useful—see Elixhauser, Böschen, and Vogel (2018) for a discussion of this.

References

Astuti, R. 1995. *People of the Sea: Identity and Descent among the Vezo of Madagascar.* Cambridge, UK: Cambridge University Press.

Barber, I. 2004. "Sea, Land and Fish: Spatial Relationships and the Archaeology of South Island Maori Fishing." *World Archaeology* 35, no. 3: 434–48.

Bender, B., ed. 1993. *Landscape: Politics and Perspectives.* Oxford: Berg.

———. 2006. "Place and Landscape." In *The Handbook of Material Culture.* Edited by C. Tilley, W. Keane, S. Kuchler, M. Rowlands, and P. Spyer, 303–14. London: Sage.

Brück, J. 2005. "Experiencing the Past? The Development of a Phenomenological Archaeology in British Prehistory." *Archaeological Dialogues* 12, no. 1: 45–72.

Busby, C. 2000. *The Performance of Gender: An Anthropology of Everyday Life in a South Indian Fishing Village.* London and New Jersey: Athlone Press.

Cobb, H. L. 2005. "Midden, Meaning, Person, Place: Interpreting the Mesolithic of Western Scotland." In *Investigating Prehistoric Hunter-Gatherer Identities in Palaeolithic and Mesolithic Europe.* Edited by H. L. Cobb, S. Price, F. Coward, and L. Grimshaw, 69–78. Oxford: British Archaeological Reports (International Series 1411).

———. 2006. "Mutable Materials and the Production of Persons: Reconfiguring understandings of identity in the Mesolithic of the northern Irish Sea basin." *Journal of Iberian Archaeology* 9: 123–36.

———. 2008. "Media for Movement and Making the World: An Examination of the Mesolithic Experience of the World and the Mesolithic to Neolithic Transition in the Northern Irish Sea Basin." PhD dissertation. Manchester, UK: University of Manchester.

Cooney, G. 2003. "Introduction: Seeing Land from the Sea." *World Archaeology* 35, no. 3: 323–28.

Conneller, C. 2005. "Moving Beyond Sites: Mesolithic Technology in the Landscape." In *Mesolithic Studies at the Beginning of the 21st Century.* Edited by N. Milner and P. Woodman, 42–55. Oxford: Oxbow.

Cosgrove, D. 1984. *Social Formation and Symbolic Landscape.* London: Croom Helm.

Cosgrove, D., and S. Daniels, eds. 1988. *The Iconography of Landscape: Essays on the Symbolic Representation, Design and Use of Past Environments.* Cambridge, UK: Cambridge University Press.

Cummings, V. 2003. "The Origins of Monumentality? Mesolithic World-Views of the Landscape in Western Britain." In *Mesolithic on the Move. Papers Presented at the 6th International Conference in the Mesolithic in Europe, Stockholm, 2000.* Edited by L. Larsson, H. Kindgren, K. Knutsson, D. Loeffler, and A. Akerlund. 74–81. Oxford: Oxbow Books.

David, B., and J. Thomas, eds. 2010. *The Handbook of Landscape Archaeology.* Walnut Creek: Left Coast Press.

Donnelly, M., and G. MacGregor. 2005. "The Excavation of Mesolithic Activity, Neolithic and Bronze Age Burnt Mounds and Roman-British Ring Groove Houses at Gallow Hill, Girvan." *Scottish Archaeological Journal* 27, no. 1: 31–69.

Edmonds, M. 1999. *Ancestral Geographies of the Neolithic: Landscapes, Monuments and Memory.* London: Routledge.

Elixhauser, S., S. Böschen, and K. Vogel. 2018. "Meshworks and the Making of Climate Places in the European Alps: A Framework for Ethnographic Research on the Perceptions of Climate Change." *Nature and Culture* 13, no. 2: 281–307.

Finlay, N. 2000. "Microliths in the Making." In *Mesolithic Lifeways: Current Research in Britain and Ireland.* Edited by R. Young, 23–31. Leicester: Leicester University Archaeology Monograph 7.

———. 2003. "Microliths and Multiple Authorship." In *Mesolithic on the Move. Papers Presented at the 6th International Conference in the Mesolithic in Europe, Stockholm, 2000.* Edited by L. Larsson, H. Kindgren, K. Knutsson, D. Loeffler, and A. Akerlund. 169–76. Oxford: Oxbow Books.

Ford, B. 2011. "Introduction." In *The Archaeology of Maritime Landscapes.* Edited by B. Ford, 1–11. New York: Springer.

Gosden, C., and L. Head. 1994. "Landscape: A Usefully Ambiguous Concept." *Archaeology in Oceania* 29: 113–16.

Hirsch, E., and M. O'Hanlon, eds. 1995. *The Anthropology of Landscape: Perspectives of Place and Space.* Oxford: Clarendon Press.

Hoeppe, G. 2003. "The Work of Fishing and the Moral Constitution of Space in Kerala (South India)." People and the Sea II Conference, Amsterdam.

———. 2007. *Conversations on the Beach: Fishermen's Knowledge, Metaphor and Environmental Change in South India,* vol. 2. New York: Berghahn Books.

Ingold, T. 1993. "The Temporality of the Landscape." *World Archaeology* 25, no. 2: 152–74.

———. 2007. "Earth, Sky, Wind, and Weather." *Journal of the Royal Anthropological Institute* 13, no. 1: S19–S38.

———. 2008. "Bindings Against Boundaries: Entanglements of Life." *Environment and Planning A* 40: 1796–1810.

———. 2011. *Being Alive: Essays on Movement, Knowledge and Description.* London: London.

Johnson, M. 2006. *Ideas of Landscape.* Oxford: Blackwell.

Leary, J. 2013. "Northsealand: A Study of the Effects, Perceptions of and Responses to the Mesolithic Sea-level Rise in the Southern North Sea and Channel/Manche." PhD dissertation. Manchester, UK: University of Manchester.

Lemaire, T. 1997. "Archaeology Between the Invention and Destruction of the Landscape." *Archaeolgical Dialogues* 4: 5–21.

MacGregor, G., and M. Donnelly. 2001. "A Mesolithic Scatter from Littlehill Bridge, Girvan, Ayrshire." *Scottish Archaeological Journal* 23, no. 1: 1–14.

McNiven, I. 2004. "Saltwater People: Spiritscapes, Maritime Rituals and the Archaeology of Australian Indigenous Seascapes." *World Archaeology* 35, no. 3: 329–49.

Mellars, P. A. 1987. *Excavations on Oronsay: Prehistoric Human Ecology on a Small Island*. Edinburgh: Edinburgh University Press.

Merleau-Ponty, M. 2002. *Phenomenology of Perception: An Introduction*. London: Routledge.

Pollard, J. 2000. "Ancestral Places in the Mesolithic Landscape." *Archaeological Review from Cambridge* 17, no. 1: 123–38.

Pollard, T. 1996. "Time and Tide: Coastal Environments, Cosmology and Ritual Practice in Early Prehistoric Scotland." In *The Early Prehistory of Scotland*. Edited by T. Pollard and A. Morrison, 198–210. Edinburgh: Edinburgh University Press.

Ransley, J. 2009 "The Backwater Boats of Kerala: Identity, Place and the World of Munruthuruthu." PhD dissertation. Southampton: University of Southampton.

———. 2012. "The Backwater Boats of Kerala: Identity, Place and the World of Munruthuruthu." In *Beyond Boundaries: Proceedings of the 3rd International Congress on Underwater Archaeology, IKUWA 3*. Edited by J. C. Henderson, 247–56. Frankfurt am Main, DE: Römisch-Germanische Kommission.

Terrell, J. E., T. L. Hunt, and C. Gosden. 1997. "The Dimensions of Social Life in the Pacific: Human Diversity and the Myth of the Primitive Isolate." *Current Anthropology* 38, no. 2: 155–95.

Thomas, J. 2001. "Archaeologies of Place and Landscape." In *Archaeological Theory Today*. Edited by I. Hodder, 165–86. Cambridge, UK: Polity Press.

———. 2004. *Archaeology and Modernity*. London: Routledge.

Tilley, C. 1994. *A Phenomenology of Landscape: Places, Paths and Monuments*. Oxford: Berg.

Ucko, P. J., and R. Layton, eds. 1999. *The Archaeology and Anthropology of Landscape: Shaping your Landscape*. London: Routledge.

Warren, G. M. 1997. "Seascapes: Navigating the coastal Mesolithic of Western Scotland." *Assemblage* 2: 97–104.

———. 2000. "Seascapes: People, Boats and Inhabiting the Later Mesolithic in Western Scotland." In *Mesolithic Lifeways: Current Research in Britain and Ireland*. Edited by R. Young, 97–104. Leicester: Leicester University Archaeology Monograph 7.

———. 2005. *Mesolithic Lives in Scotland*. Stroud: Tempus Pub Ltd.

Wickham-Jones, C. R. 2005. "Summer Walkers? Mobility and the Mesolithic." In *Mesolithic Studies at the Beginning of the 21st Century*. Edited by N. Milner and P. Woodman, 30–41. Oxford: Oxbow.

CHAPTER 2

Working Grounds, Producing Places, and Becoming at Home at Sea

Penny McCall Howard

The sea around Scotland is thick with places like Wullie's Peak, the Wall of Death, the Sound of Music, the Burma, the Whiting Tow, and the Caol Mor.[1] These places are invisible from the sea's surface and are not related to any point on land. I draw on ethnographic participant observation to explore why these places have become significant to the fishermen[2] who have created them, and how fishermen have developed the affordances of these places into productive fishing grounds. I describe the deep subjective connections and sociable work practices that result in places at sea being named. I highlight the combined importance of the material affordances of grounds and the endless discussion of them within the context of particular forms of social organization and subjective experiences of labor. Finally, I draw out what this materially grounded and labor-centered sea-going ethnography can contribute to the anthropology of places and human–environment relations.

In this chapter, I examine the creation of places through their "historically experienced transformation" and "the practice of social relations" in the particular environment of the sea. This analysis is based on eighteen months of participant observation in 2006 and 2007 on the west coast of Scotland, primarily in the nephrops or "prawn" fishery around Skye, Lochalsh, and Wester Ross on a body of water known as the Inner Sound. During this time, I lived on a small boat in six different harbors; I worked as paid relief crew of a 10m prawn trawler; I also went out fishing on three other prawn trawlers, three prawn creel boats, and one crab creel boat. I engaged with fishermen, exfishermen, and their families on the pier, in local seafood processing factories, in the pub, and in their homes. I interviewed representatives of fisheries associations and government and attended government consultations on fisheries as well as the annual UK fishing trade show. Most quotes in this article are drawn from my daily ethnographic field notes, recorded according to methods recommended in Emerson, Fretz, and Shaw (1995). I used Atlas.ti to catalogue my field notes and interview notes, which totalled 250,000 words. My research continued informally until 2011, because I returned to the area and remained in contact with people I worked with.

Wullie's Peak

It was four o'clock one February morning, the first of a five-day fishing trip on board the *Friendly Isle,* a small 10m, two-person fishing trawler I was working on as relief crew paid by a share of the catch.[3] A spell of poor winter weather had kept the fleet tied up, but now there was a break and word of "a good fishing" up north. Alasdair, the boat's skipper and owner, started the engine with a warm roar and turned on our electronic GPS (global positioning system) chartplotter, depth sounder, and radar, which all chirped and beeped as they warmed up. After we cast off all the lines, Alasdair made the engine roar in reverse, forward, and reverse again, as he narrowly but artfully missed the other impatient skippers also maneuvering their boats in this small space between piers. Within ten minutes, almost all the boats were away, charging north on a flood tide, wheelhouses lit only by the glow of LCD (liquid crystal display) screens.

"We'll tow up to Wullie's Peak[4] before we turn south and head for Portree to land,"[5] explained Alasdair. "Who is Wullie?" I asked. "I don't know," said Alasdair. "It's just what it is called." On the GPS chartplotter, I scrolled north from the small icon indicating our position and asked Alasdair to show me the location of Wullie's Peak, which was already marked (figure 2.1). The sky started to lighten at about 5:30 a.m. It was perfectly grey and calm. I put the kettle on for a cup of tea and woke Alasdair to tell him that we were near Wullie's Peak and ten minutes away from where he wanted to shoot the net (figure 2.2).

Wullie's Peak is one of many significant places at sea regularly discussed by trawler fishermen. Five months after I first learned about Wullie's Peak, skipper James "the *Iris*"[6] explained to me how it had been named. James was a friendly and easygoing man who relished "good craic"[7] and had been fishing full-time since 1966. Trawling a few miles south of Wullie's Peak on his family-owned fishing boat, James smiled and chuckled as he told me the story:

> Wullie "the *Sincerity*" used to steam to that peak every morning to shoot his net. He worked out of Gairloch. You would shoot the net and start just south of the peak because it was shallow right out to Staffin. When you would call

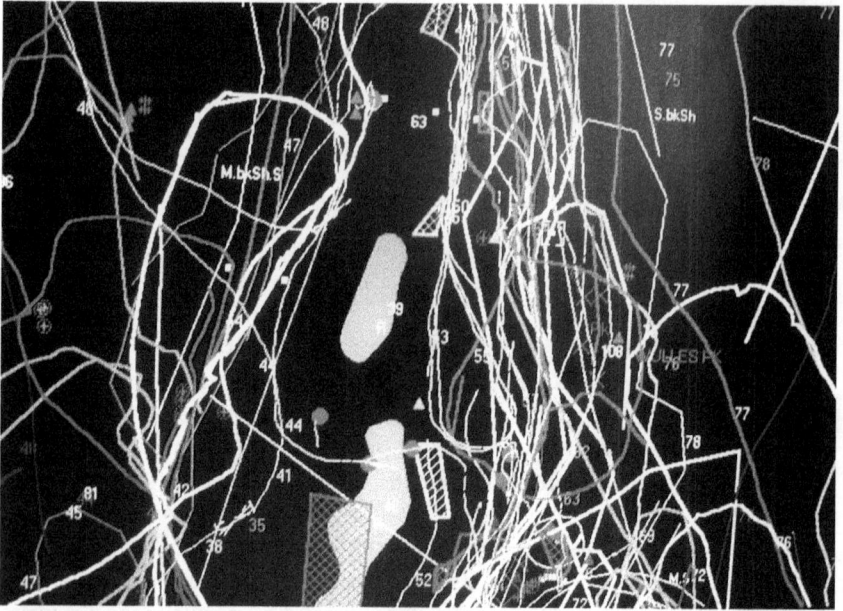

Figure 2.1. Wullie's Peak on the chartplotter (toward the right). The lines are the GPS-plotted traces made by the trawler while it was towing. Dots, crosses, hatches, and triangles represent "fasteners," or obstacles, on the seafloor. Numbers indicate the depth of the water. Photo by the author.

> Wullie on the radio to say, "Where are you this morning?" It would be, "Oh, I'm at the Peak." *Every* morning! He was here for fifteen years around the 1970s, and then he retired. The boat was sold and it ended up in Ireland, that would have been '82, '83.

Wullie was from Fraserburgh, one of the many fishermen from along the Moray Firth on the east coast of Scotland who worked mainly on the west coast (figure 2.3). They kept their fishing boats in Gairloch, driving through on a Sunday night, and driving home again on a Friday or Saturday (see also Knipe 1984). Despite the fact that he was not from the west coast and did not live there permanently, Wullie's work and his participation in the community of west-coast fishermen earned him a legacy that extended over thirty years and to those who had never heard his story.

When Wullie was starting his mornings "at the Peak" in the 1970s, trawling for langoustine or "prawns"[8] was a new fishery. The fishery had started experimentally on the east coast of Scotland in the 1950s and gradually new markets were developed as more fishermen tried catching the prawns they had previously ignored (Mason 1987). In the 1960s, some west-coast fishermen started fishing for the new prawn markets using creels (a low-cost baited trap), then east-coast fishermen like Wullie

Figure 2.2. The view of Wullie's Peak out of the wheelhouse window. Photo by the author.

started to explore and "open up" new west-coast prawn trawl grounds. In the area around Skye, I was told that Portree fisherman Johnny Ferguson on the *Silver Spray* was the first to convert to trawling in 1971 (although he was killed in a car accident soon after), followed by Tommy and Alfie Corrigal on the *Iris* in 1973 (the father and uncle of James "the *Iris*"). Wullie, the Corrigals, and their contemporaries[9] experimented with new prawn trawl fishing gear on these new grounds, regularly "blootering"[10] their nets on as-yet uncharted hazards on the seafloor. Together, these men "opened up new ground," developed techniques for working it, and a new vocabulary to talk about it.

The example of Wullie's Peak shows that the creation of significant places does not need a multigenerational history; it does not even need the people involved to be from that area. Fifteen years of working these grounds and discussing them with other fishermen was enough for them to be named after Wullie. Retsikas makes a similar observation for places on land in East Java, the creation of which was:

> Not contingent on some primordial quality that place has in and of itself, as nationalist ideologies of the modern era would have it. Rather . . . the power of place, that is, its capacity to inhabit us, stems from the practice of social relations, as well as its historically experienced transformation. (2007, 969)

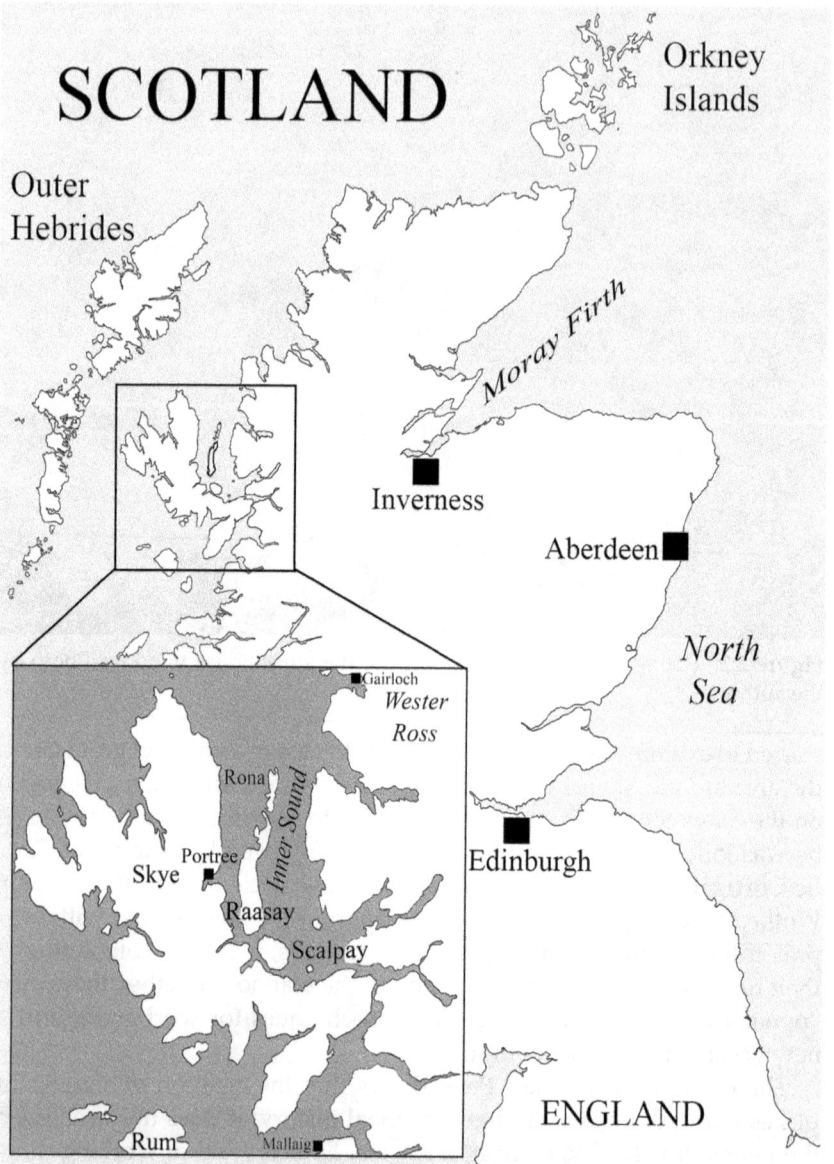

Figure 2.3. A map of Scotland. Most of my research took place in the area between Mallaig, Gairloch, and Portree on the west coast. Created by the author.

Places, Grounds, and Affordances

Wullie's Peak was one of many places within the "grounds" that fishermen "worked." The word "ground" was most commonly used by fishermen to describe an area where fishing was generally practiced, as in, "just north of the bridge there is a big expanse of prawn ground." It was the useful area, the worked-in and lived-in area, the area that was contested at sea and discussed on the radio, on the pier, and in the pub. Grounds had particular characteristics relative to the kind of work that was undertaken there. Fishing for mackerel, Lachie's ground was the entire volume of the sea; but for most fishermen when I talked with them, the ground was the parts of the seafloor that was a habitat for particular species of prawns and crabs. What linked these often quite different kinds of places was the productive labor that took place there.

The affordances of grounds were not static, and they were inextricably and historically connected to broader market conditions and the labor expended there: new affordances were developed with new markets as fishermen reshaped the affordances of grounds through their work, developing new tools in order to make grounds more productive for themselves.[11] The ongoing historical production of grounds meant that they were places with which people formed strong bonds and which came to be expressive of their personalities. As I will describe, names for these grounds and specific parts of them were also developed through the sociable practice of fishing in them.

The concept of "affordances" that I draw on here to describe the development of grounds was coined by ecological psychologist James Gibson to describe the "complementarity of the animal and the environment" (1979, 127). Gibson explains:

> An affordance is neither an objective property nor a subjective property; or it is both if you like. An affordance cuts across the dichotomy of subjective-objective and helps us to understand its inadequacy. It is equally a fact of the environment and a fact of behaviour. It is both physical and psychical, yet neither. An affordance points both ways, to the environment and to the observer. (1979, 129)

Grounds are both "a fact of the environment" and "a fact of behavior," both "subjective" and "objective." Anthropologist Tim Ingold has developed Gibson's description of affordances and draws on it in describing how places are constituted:

> A place owes its character to the experiences it affords to those who spend time there—to the sights, sounds, and indeed smells that constitute its specific ambience. And these, in turn, depend on the kinds of activities in which its inhabitants engage. It is from this relational context of people's engage-

ment with the world, in the business of dwelling, that each place draws its unique significance. (2000, 192)

There are three important aspects to this description of how places are formed: the specificity of the "kinds of activities," the role of movement, and the materiality of affordances in places. At sea, the "relational context of people's engagement" is particularly important. The limitations of the human body mean that people almost always experience the sea from a boat or from the shore, especially in cold or temperate climates. The same location at sea is experienced very differently if one is "dwelling" on an oil tanker or in a canoe, or if one is engaged in a sail boat race or in catching prawns. People may also have distinctive roles in these activities that affect their experience: as skipper or as cook, for example. The affordances that people seek, and therefore the places that become significant to them, are similarly diverse and dependent on their particular activity.

The influence of specific forms of activity on the experience of places at sea has been described by anthropologists working in a wide variety of field locations: on board a scientific research vessel off South America (Goodwin 1995); in a lagoon in the Solomon Islands (Lauer and Aswani 2009); and in the coastal Canadian Arctic (Tyrrell 2006; see also Elixhauser, and Simonetti, this volume). Goodwin describes a "convergent diversity" of method and intention that means scientists on the same ship "probing exactly the same patch of sea, each will in fact see something quite different there" (1995, 246). Lauer and Aswani similarly emphasize the importance of "context-specific activities" in generating knowledge at sea (2009, 323). In contrast to these careful ethnographies, some social theorists, and a few anthropologists, have used the sea as a "theory machine," drawing on scientific or aesthetic descriptions of its form as metaphors to illustrate and develop particular concepts—for example the "flow" of trade (Helmreich 2011). The popularity of such approaches makes it particularly important to attend to the huge diversity of human activities and experience in living and working at sea.

Anthropologists have also examined the importance of movement in constituting places, demonstrating that the "correspondence between persons and place" is "not rooted in deep histories of sedentary habitation rather it is predicated on short histories of mobility" (Retsikas 2007, 983). Amith also examines the historical processes of "place making and place breaking" during migration (2005). Both authors focus on origins and destinations. Retsikas's discussion of the "transformability of person and place" (2007, 983) emphasizes the *results* of migration and the creation of new settlements and hybrid persons. I will draw on Ingold's insight that an organism's perception of its environment relies on the "intentional movement of the whole being (indissolubly mind and body) in its environment" and therefore "what we perceive must be a direct function of how we act" (2000, 166). Thus, in focusing on movement, I will attend to what happens along the way and how the labor of movement itself can result in the creation of significant places. These connections are demonstrated in the word "tow" itself, which is used both as a verb referring to the activity of trawling and as a noun describing places where trawling is regularly carried out.

The experience of movement and activity in and among places is important to understanding them, at sea and on land. However, to understand *why* places are created, we must return to the ethnography of grounds and places at sea to explore the materiality, history, and economic context of the affordances that people seek and how these change over time.

Grounds were developed when they had an affordance that fishermen sought. For those working in a commercial fishery, this required both a viable market for the type of sea creature that could be caught there and a practical means of transporting it in bulk and in good condition to that market. Over time, specific techniques and tools were developed to extend the perception and reach of the human body so that people could find, feel, "get in to," and reliably travel between particular grounds (Howard 2013, 2017). This included constant tinkering and development of new nets, new sounding and navigation systems, and a lot of dogged persistence and willingness to risk damage to your gear on unknown obstacles. Trawlers described "cleaning" grounds, removing rubbish and boulders from them, and making them easier to work. Cleaner grounds had the potential to be more productive as less time was likely to be spent clearing and repairing the net, with more time spent actually fishing. Some fishermen talked about their role in removing prawn predators, such as skate. Grounds were only productive at the right light, tide, and season, which fishermen had to experiment with and identify. Grounds were made up of regularly used tows that were not wilderness areas at all; they were areas with promising affordances that had been further developed and modified to make particular kinds of work there more productive: the fishermen's equivalent of a farmer's field. Understanding places through their affordances emphasizes the role of the fisherman in developing grounds rather than simply discovering them. In a fairly profound way, fishermen saw their work as actually *making,* or at least contributing to, the productivity of grounds.

Such a view contrasts radically with the normative subject "fisherman exploiting the seas" that frames public policy and opinion on fisheries in Scotland and beyond (Nightingale 2011, 124). Such perceptions draw on longer-standing notions that fishing, hunting, and gathering are extractive activities in which people simply discover and collect organisms in their environment. This has a thematic link to Povinelli's ethnography of the labor-action of Belyuen Aboriginals (1993), despite other vast gulfs between these societies. Povinelli describes the role of labor-action as the "process by which space becomes 'country'" (Stanner quoted in Povinelli 1993, 136), "country" being the Aboriginal equivalent of the "grounds" I describe. Specifically, "land use also creates and refashions the preexisting features of the countryside that are then put to use" (Povinelli 1993, 146). The result of these interactions is the "mutual constitution of humans and country" (Povinelli 1993, 6) because the "health of the countryside and of human groups depends upon the mutual, positive action of each on the other" (Povinelli 1993, 31).

In both Australia and Scotland, interpretations of labor that deny the productivity of Aboriginal hunter-gatherers and of Scottish fishermen can be used to dispossess both groups from the environments they are materially, socially, and historically connected to and on which they rely for their livelihoods. In Australia, a denial of the productivity of Aboriginal labor was combined with the myth of *terra nullius* to rationalize violent colonization and their ongoing dispossession. In Scotland, many people began fishing full-time as a result of their dispossession from farming land (Howard 2012a), and these fishermen continue to refer to these Clearances in the ongoing debates about establishing marine parks and other regulations that may exclude them from the grounds they have developed at sea.

One important difference between the Belyuen and Scottish fishermen is the extent to which they have had to contend with commercial pressures in deciding what grounds to open up, what affordances to develop, and whether these efforts were considered a success. Scottish skippers assessed the difference between a good day and a "waste" based on these commercial pressures. Catching a net full of squat lobsters or jellyfish or kelp was "no use" on a commercial fishing boat as there would be no market for them. "A lack of prawns" would put any skipper in a foul mood. A day or two of poor catches was tolerable but would inspire frantic comparison with others. Before long, paranoia, self-doubt, and depression would creep in. The subjectivities of commercial fishermen were shaped by their economic context and also delicately balanced between the material affordances of grounds and the market conditions in which they had to operate. The "education of attention" (Gibson 1979, 254) of new fishermen took place in the context of the search for prawns and assessment of whether that search had been successful. They were trained in "feeling the ground" and in obsessively comparing their catch with that of others, constantly experimenting with new gear and new techniques, and assessing the effects of light, tide, and season in the constant process of opening up new ground. The result of each tow was critically important: Were you "catching"?

Grounds were "opened up" and their affordances only came into being through fishermen's labor in making them productive. The experience of fishermen in developing and enhancing the affordances of grounds made for particularly strong personal attachments to them: not just to "work" a bit of ground but to understand that it is your own initiative, labor, attention, and experience that were responsible for "opening it up," "cleaning" it, and *transforming* it into ground. In the following sections, I will show how the labor of developing affordances—essential to the creation of places within grounds—is a thoroughly social process. Places acquire power and meaning, coming to inhabit the very people who inhabit them, through the conversations and social relations generated in the process of transforming them into productive grounds.

Place and Subjectivity

Place names originated from individual experience and conversations and were shared through the collective work of developing affordances. The Peak became Wullie's through his work there, and through the "good craic" and the playful radio conversations he shared with other trawler skippers working in the area. The fact that this peak was Wullie's also told you something about the man: in a community of trawler skippers in which risk-taking was often glorified, he was a man of habit. No doubt, he was teased about being at the Peak *"every* morning!" Despite this, he persisted for fifteen years. That was enough for the place to be named after him and for him to be remembered by this place. Thus, part of the "sediment of relatedness" (Povinelli 1993, 137) that is generated by working in an environment is the names that reflect and subsequently reinforce individual and collective experience and subjectivities.

Fishermen poured themselves into opening up and working grounds, which they often saw as an expression of their effort, skill, and very being. I was told, with admiration, about Graeme, a young and successful hired skipper who "prided himself on trying to work an edge: a lot of people would just go up and down in the clean because they are too afraid of the edge." "Buckie" John was a hired skipper who prided himself on being a "grafter" (a hard worker) who would "go for quality" (large prawns), which meant working short tows on harder ground and lots of time spent mending damage to nets. Like Graeme, "not minding the ground" was an important part of "Buckie" John's identity: he enjoyed the challenge of working hard and rocky ground and was proud of the effort and skill required to do so.

Ruaridh "the *Accord*" had been fishing on the Inner Sound for forty years, and the strong relationship he developed with the ground he worked was described to me as follows:

> The Back of Kyle is Ruaridh's back garden, it is his cabbage patch. Do not try to fish in Pabay Corner[12] when he is about, he will show you the red light,[13] back you into a corner, and force you onto a nasty bit of ground or to haul up.[14] He is superb at that and good for him! If you go to steal brussels sprouts out of someone's garden, you should expect to get the back of the hand.

Graeme and "Buckie" John were brave enough to always "work an edge." Ruaridh was set in his ways and had the authority and the boat maneuvring skills to keep others out of the grounds that he preferred to work. Such strong attachments to grounds grew out of people's histories of developing the affordances of particular grounds through exploration, experimentation, and skilled technique. These histories could develop into a territorial attachment that could flare into conflict between fishermen using different techniques (such as trawlers or creel fishermen, both targeting prawns)[15] or hailing from different ports. One creel boat skipper complained about creel boats from another port, saying, "They want the ground to be theirs only. They aggressively defend it. But I have as much right to be there as anyone else!" A trawler skipper, frustrated at finding creels blocking what he saw as his fishing ground, complained, "Next year, I'm not going to bother with the fishery officer; I'll just go straight through and clear them myself. They can't just keep taking more and more ground! We are losing ground all the time!" Indeed, such relationships could also mean that people never came in contact with each other at sea because "we are on different ground." But in either case, the relationship between fishermen and the grounds they worked was strong and distinctive. Grounds afforded fishermen crabs, prawns, and a livelihood; and through their history of developing these affordances, fishermen also developed personal identities and social histories in these places (King, this volume).

Subjectivity describes the complex relationship between people's inner states and their lived experience (Biehl, Good, and Kleinman 2007, 464); and in this case, fishermen's experience of working in and transforming places as they tried to make a livelihood in commercial fishing. Places do not just reflect persons; people also incorporate significant places into their subjectivities. This was the case for those working the Wall of Death, a well-known but difficult tow in the Inner Sound located on a steep rocky bank. Towing at the Wall of Death was a badge that skippers like Buckie

John and Graeme wore proudly. The Wall of Death was named for a popular Scottish fairground attraction where motorcyclists ride around the inside of a bowl that rises to perfectly vertical walls, while the audience looks down on them from above. The popular meaning is explained quite well in the promotional material for a National Theatre of Scotland production titled *Wall of Death: A Way of Life*, which described the "unique thrill . . . the smell of the Castrol R, the noise, and the death-defying performance" of this experience (National Theatre of Scotland 2010, 1). Not everyone wished to take the risks of trawling at the Wall of Death. As we successfully trawled there, "Buckie" John told me of failed attempts to tow there by other, more experienced, trawler skippers. One man "tried to follow us on the Wall of Death with his big heavy gear, and he got stuck right away," and another "got a boulder and stopped towing on the Wall of Death. He got so many fasteners[16] he would have to haul his net back two, three times in a tow." In contrast, John seemed to enjoy and even relish this particular challenge.

James "the *Iris*" speculated that the Wall of Death was named by a skipper known as "Loopy" who "would tow up there and was always blootering his nets. After one time too many, he said, 'That place is just the wall of death!' and the name stuck. That would have been the 1980s sometime." Loopy's frustrated comment, possibly over the radio, possibly on the pier, was repeated by other trawl skippers in the area with enough frequency and amusement that it stuck.

Trawl skipper Alasdair had worked up and down the west and east coast of Scotland and explained, "You'll find these crazy names for tows all over, and they are all like that. Everyone knows them. There are probably several Walls of Death around Scotland." For example, there is another Wall of Death "at the back of Rum,"[17] an island south of Skye. Many of the place names given to tows by fishermen celebrate and lament the labor and difficulty of working them. Alasdair told me how he had "once spent a whole evening discussing the frightening names that fishermen give to places, and renaming them with nice names like Primrose Valley and Sunny Delight." This amusing exercise in the pub only reinforced the fact that such names never stuck because they did not resonate through the experiences and subjectivities of the skippers who worked there.

In addition to the individual effort and skill described above, working on the Wall of Death also required the development of a new tool—the hopper net—to transform this previously inaccessible area of the seafloor into prawn ground (Howard 2017). Ruaridh "the *Accord*" described how in the 1970s, "we didn't have the ground charted then. . . . We just stayed on the Whiting Tow,[18] which was clean." As Retsikas put it, the relationships between place and persons are not due to "some primordial quality" of place, but are directly reflective of the development of social relations in the course of transforming a location into productive grounds. The collective effort of this transformation is undertaken by individuals (in social contexts), and thus the names and places that signify this transformation also reflect the development of individual subjectivities.

Sociability and the Development of Affordances

Although fishermen on boats appear to work in small, isolated workplaces, it was clear that that they shared an "environment of joint practical activity" (Ingold 2000, 167), a very high level of communication, and tight social networks. These practices facilitated the ongoing collection of information over large areas of the coast. Understanding the details of fishermen's daily working practices is key to understanding the emergence and subsequent naming of significant places.

The best catch for the west-coast inshore prawn trawlers I worked on was usually from the tow that began just as the sun was coming up. Tows were typically two to four hours long and the number of prawns caught per tow declined during the day, although the catch sometimes improved in the last hours of daylight. Between November and January, the time between sunrise and sunset was very short; but in the summer days, sunlight could last over seventeen hours long, plus at least an hour of twilight at sunrise and sunset. Most inshore prawn trawlers had only two or three crew and no refrigeration. The boats needed to tie up overnight in order for the crew to get some rest and to land the catch with a buyer, but this also added daily travel time between the harbor and the fishing grounds. Skippers and crew worked extraordinarily long hours with very little rest—often from 3 a.m. until 10 p.m., and were back on the water at 3 a.m. the next morning.

Trawler skippers spent most of their waking hours onboard steering the boat from a chair in the wheelhouse, and on the telephone and radio talking to other skippers (figure 2.4).[19] One skipper explained, "If you are trawling, you *always* have to be thinking about where the prawns are and how to get them." Their fishing gear was always moving. Skippers constantly tried to make sense of the smallest clues they received from their own fishing gear and from the actions of other fishermen. They analyzed their accumulated experience in order to understand the changing effect of tide and light in particular grounds. They watched the depth sounder and their GPS chartplotter carefully, using them to record their fishing experiences (Howard 2017). As Povinelli described in relation to the Belyuen, there is a "constant querying of why an event occurred . . . people's

Figure 2.4. Skipper on the phone in the wheelhouse. The black box on the far left encloses the chartplotter, which he is watching carefully. Photo by the author.

strategy is to note all events, comment on their possible significance and then wait and see if some connection develops" (Povinelli 1993, 32).

"The first tow of the day is a sentinel, and you have to get it right in order to have a really good day," explained trawler skipper Alasdair. While an experienced and reliable crew member was often trusted to take the boat from the harbor to the place of the first tow, the skipper always took the first tow himself and sent the crew (like me) back to their bunks. The first tow was a quiet time of the day for assessment and discussion of the weather, the engine, the set-up of the trawl, the actions of other fishing boats, seafood buyers, fishing crew, and, most importantly, of the possibilities for a successful day's fishing. Alone in the wheelhouse with the sun rising and the crew asleep, skippers often spent the whole first tow on the radio or phone with other skippers, getting the news from the previous night (who landed how much and where) and the morning (where others were fishing compared to the day before, and what this might mean about the current affordances of different prawn grounds). This was the time of day that Wullie would be "at the Peak" chatting away on the radio to the other skippers around him. At this time of day, skippers talked just to keep each other company until it was time to "go put the kettle on" and have yet another cup of tea. A few hours later, they woke the crew, ate breakfast, and hauled up, emptied, and reset the net—a clattery, complicated, and potentially dangerous process that took at least half an hour.

Once the catch was on deck, the skipper would immediately try to assess how much they had caught and how successful the tow had been. Skippers' reactions to the result of that first tow ranged from giddy delight to a mood dark enough to silence the chattiest crew and make them creep gingerly through the wheelhouse. With the boat wallowing in the sea and the net only half on board, skippers also needed to make an immediate decision whether to reset the net there or to move elsewhere. An important factor was what they had learned during their first round of morning conversations. Once the net was back in the water, the skipper might assist the crew in sorting through the catch (figure 2.5); but if they did this, their ability to steer the boat and strategize about where to go next would be hampered. If the catch was particularly good, they would want to do their best to replicate that success. If the catch was particularly poor, they would try to determine if the problem was with their own fishing gear, or if everyone in the area was doing poorly. Skippers constantly used all possible social connections to try to track the productivity of fishing grounds in the whole area.

Figure 2.5. Sorting through or "picking" prawns. Photo by the author.

After the catch from the first tow had been brought onboard and assessed, the phone would really start to ring. Many skippers would spend
the next hour on the phone comparing catches and speculating. I kept
track of this process one morning, and by 9 a.m., the skipper of the boat
I worked on had gathered information directly from ten boats and indirectly from about ten others, all from different (though nearby) ports
along the coast. He was able to get information on sea conditions and
catches along a sixty-mile stretch of coastline, and from enough different
sources that he could cross-reference to ensure it was reasonably accurate.
That morning there was a long northwest swell running. When I mentioned this, the skipper absent-mindedly replied, "Yes, no one can figure
out where it is coming from." I was taken aback as we were the only ones
on the boat, yet we were also a part of a workplace spread out across the
sea's surface, and the fishing fleet was a "community of practice" integral
to the skill of the trawler skipper (Pálsson 1994).

It is not simply the activity that they undertook in a particular place,
but also the material results of that activity that mattered so desperately
to these skippers and made the difference between a good and a bad day.
The results of this activity were initially measured in volume, with the
skipper anxious for the crew's first count of how many baskets of "bulk"
were caught in the tow, information that was immediately reported to
whomever they were in regular communication with. Once the crew had
sorted through the catch, the number of baskets of each size of prawns and
the number of stones[20] of small prawn "tails" were each carefully tallied;
in some cases they noted in a logbook, but in any case, were remembered, compared, and discussed (figure 2.6). Masters of mental arithmetic,
skippers would then convert that volume into weight and multiply by
price to get an approximate value. Even after a long absence, if I encountered a fisherman in the grocery store or on the pier and inquired how
they were doing, their reply of "poor, poor" or "not too bad" did not refer
to themselves or their families, but to the state of their catches.

The importance of the material affordances of places is something that
Lauer and Aswani also emphasize in their study of the Roviana Lagoon
(2009). Here, the critical attribute of "mana" is demonstrated through "a
person's or thing's efficacious qualities manifested in tangible outcomes"
and "concrete results" (Lauer and Aswani 2009, 324). The "outcomes of
everyday human activities" are important and expertise is acknowledged
through "fishing prowess" (Lauer and Aswani 2009, 318). Povinelli (1993)
describes a similar focus on the material results of subsistence hunting
and fishing, indicating that this is seen as critical across a wide variety of
human activity. What is different is that while Belyuen Aboriginals and
people living around the Roviana Lagoon emphasized *what* they caught,

Figure 2.6. The results of one tow sorted into baskets of large and medium prawns and tails. Photo by the author.

Scottish commercial fishermen were more focused on the *value* of what they caught (Howard 2017). Market relations do have a very significant effect on how intentions are formed and productivity is assessed.

The carefully pitched banter between skippers would begin early in the morning and continue through the day, and it would not be unusual for skippers to speak to each other four or five times a day. When I was on board the *Iris*, the skipper James spent the entire day speaking on the telephone or radio. As I sat in the wheelhouse after shooting the net in the morning, I realized I would have to plan ahead and jump in with my questions during any gaps between the continuous stream of radio and mobile phone calls. Nonetheless, James was nostalgic about a time (in the 1970s and 1980s) when "everyone spoke to each other." He explained:

> It was more fun then. There was a lot more communication on the radio. It was a much more interesting job, better craic! There's certain ones now that will speak all right. But some, you won't hear from them for a week, until their catches are poor. Then they will call you wondering how you are doing!

Astonished at James's evaluation, I asked why he felt this was the case. "Everyone's worried that someone will get a prawn or two more than them," he replied. James felt that the pressure of competition had ruined the sociability of fishing. Market pressures had shaped sociability, subjectivities, and naming practices in subtle ways. The "community of practice" that skippers were part of was now a competitive one that included many members who were calculating how to gain the most information they could while revealing the least to others. One new crew member told me about the complete concentration his young ambitious skipper had on this task:

The skipper was constantly gathering information. During the day, it was by phone. If he wasn't ringing some other boat, they were ringing him. The mobile phone played this damn song really loudly, and you would hear the ringing over the whole boat. You would hear the song in your head even when it wasn't ringing; that's how much it went off. I would hear it in my sleep! If someone rang him, it was usually because they were trying to get information from him. So first thing, he would immediately ask them how they were doing. If there was going to be an exchange of information, then he wanted to be getting his fair share.

This aforementioned skipper often spoke to the skipper I worked for. One day, I woke up from a nap to find my skipper muttering in the wheelhouse. Irritation mixed with dry humour as he reported that:

Graeme called with twenty questions, "How many prawns do you have? What are their names? What are their shoe sizes?" Then he says, "Oh! Call waiting! Sorry I've got to get that!" And he hangs up without sharing anything!

I will have to remind him that it is a two-way street. For him it is all about sharing when you are doing poorly, then he tends to clam up if he is doing well. I'm irritated but I'm trying not to be.

The feverish gathering of information I have described took place within particular groups of fishermen: in this case, the skippers of small prawn trawlers who shared a common purpose and tools for achieving it. Only on rare occasions did prawn trawler skippers speak to the skippers of prawn creel boats, even those from the same village. In contrast, trawler skippers who had never met could spend significant amounts of time speaking to each other, and in many cases might know each other for years by radio before actually meeting in person.

The conversations described above took place on mobile phones. All fishing boats also carried a Very High Frequency (VHF) radio to communicate between boats, and it was understood that everyone would listen in on the conversations that others had, no matter what channel they were on. Consequently, the VHF radio was often a place for raising general grievances or indirectly broadcasting information to other skippers, including complaining about prawn and fish buyers. One particularly religious skipper read a bible passage on the VHF at 10 a.m. every morning that he fished. The development of the mobile phone did mean that skippers could have private conversations—although rumors constantly circulated about which skippers might have scanners to secretly listen in to others. Real secrets were only exchanged by text message or in person.

Despite the apparent isolation of a fishing boat, trawling is not an individual process: the information gained through tows is always put in the context of the discussion, observation, and analysis of the affordances of everyone else's tows. Human labor is "collectivised" and takes place in "populated environments" (Reed 1996, 124) within a community of practice characterized by friendship, mutual aid, frustration, endless speculation, scrutiny, and lies. The discussions that take place about developing the affordances of these populated environments directly contribute to the naming of significant places there, as I will demonstrate in the next section.

Naming Places

The constant communication among trawler skippers incorporated an intense scrutiny and discussion of each others' actions in relation to particular places at sea:

> Graeme keeps calling me. He is having a canary because he doesn't know what Ruaridh is doing. Two days in a row now, Ruaridh has been up to the Caol Mor in the morning, and back to the Crowlin in the evening.
> It must be working because he has done it two days in a row. And it's the ebb[21] he is at the Crowlin, and that has got John going too because he thinks that the Crowlin is no good on the ebb. Maybe I will nip by later this evening to see what Ruaridh is landing.

The Crowlin and the Caol Mor are both "tows": places named because trawling there is found to be consistently productive, although that productivity can vary considerably according to season, light, tide, and other factors. The Caol Mor and the Crowlin are both also names of nearby geographic features (the Crowlin Islands and the Caol Mor narrows). However, when trawler skippers used these names, it was quite clear that they were talking about the tow itself, which was relatively close to but quite distinct from the original features the names were taken from.

The subject of the conversation above, Ruaridh, was a well-established fisherman whom Graeme, John, and this skipper all respected and would speak to on a regular basis. Their intense curiosity about Ruaridh's actions could only be resolved by determining how many and what size of prawns Ruaridh was actually landing, which would be assessed through a deliberately casual and friendly visit that evening. In addition to this kind of cooperative scrutiny, the conversations among skippers about places could also include deception. Information about wrecks, boulders, and other dangerous hazards on the seafloor was regularly shared among skippers who would mark it on their GPS chartplotters (figure 2.7). But sometimes a particularly good fishing spot could be reported as a hazard in order to keep others away. I asked one skipper whom he would tell if he got a good catch: "Well, I would get on the radio and tell lies, and then I

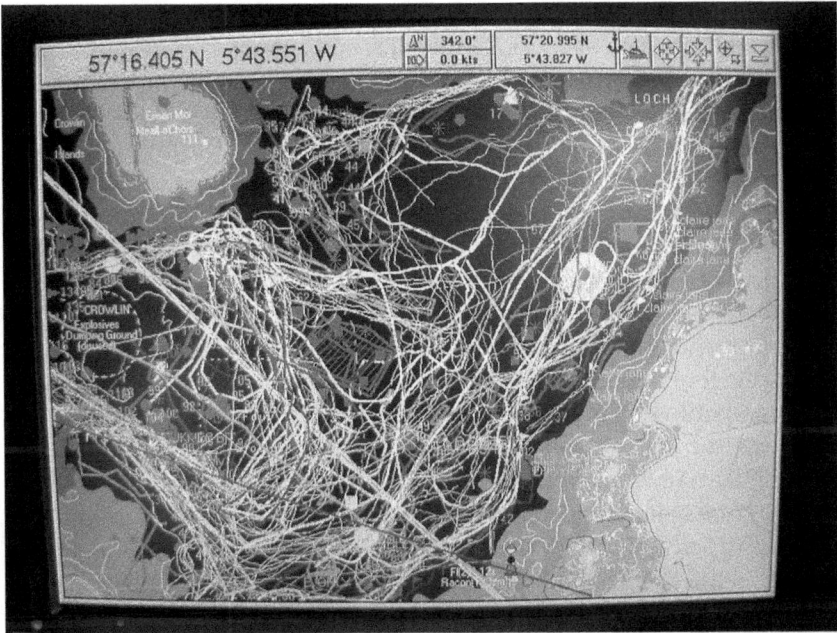

Figure 2.7. GPS chartplotter image for the Back of Kyle. The marks are hazards and the solid lines are tows. Photo by the author.

would call Graeme and tell him the truth. But people would be able to see you working back and forth in one place, and they could tell."

During my research, I counted fifty-seven place names at sea that covered approximately thirty miles of the Scottish west coast extending north and south of the Isle of Skye. None of these places are readily marked by terrestrial features visible from the surface. Angus Martin (1981) produced nine pages of place names at sea during the herring ring-net fishery around the Mull of Kintyre in southwest Scotland from the 1830s until the 1970s. He hypothesised that:

> the process of naming was probably advanced by the fishermen's unfailing curiosity to know where a successful crew had hauled a catch. Thus:
> "Where did ye get them last night?"
> "Oh, MacNair's Tree," or "The Flat Rock," or "South o' the Deer Shed."
> (Martin 1981, 140)

Such names are also a feature of fisheries seascapes in Iceland and Canada. In northern Canada, Tyrell describes how "Arviarmiut talk endlessly about the sea" and "through long-term use and habitation the sea becomes filled with meaningful named places that are a part of the on-going conversations among Arviarmiut" (2006, 232, 225). It is interesting to note, however, that the Arviat names Tyrell describes refer only to immediately visible features such as rocks, sandbanks, and islands.

The living development of place names is an example of language as "practical, real consciousness" (Marx 1998 [1845], 49) that *"arises* from the social demands and needs of the material world and also, through human cooperation and activity, *contributes* to the transformation of that world" (Holborow 2006, 6). In Scotland, the names for particular places at sea arise out of the practical activity of working collectively to develop the affordances of these places, and the sociability of fishing skippers involved in this process. Like language in general, these place names mark what is important and notable in an environment shared by a group of people as they seek common affordances, and allow them to work collaboratively (and competitively) in these places (Patterson 2009).

It was during the collective labor of developing the affordances of places that names were brought into social circulation through conversation. Names emerge from the need to carry on a conversation about a place, to scrutinize and discuss the actions of others in a place, and to gather as much information as possible to inform one's own decisions. They emerge through radio and telephone conversations that start before the sun comes up and continued long into the night. A place name is an abstract cultural term to describe the raw material of an environment. A name is developed through the process of laboring in and developing the affordances of that environment.

There is consequently only a very small and slippery distance between a conversation, a story, and a place name that "sticks." In James's account of the naming of Wullie's Peak (and the Wall of Death), there is a clear conversation-like story attached to the process that is repeated by enough other skippers that it sticks. I experienced this vertiginous transition once. A man from Mallaig, speaking to me about place names at sea, informed me that "Mallaig men" all call Camustianavaig "Bicycle Bay" because that was where skipper James Manson caught a brand-new bicycle in the trawl net. Trawl skipper Alasdair had told me a story about catching a brand-new bicycle in that bay some years ago while he worked for the same skipper. He had never mentioned that his experience, that story, had become a name that circulated among the fishermen of at least one (relatively large) port. Experiences were discussed, stories were told, and the most memorable, amusing, and resonant stories were repeated enough times to name the places that they featured.

Naming is also a form of appropriation useful to the mobile activities of trawler (or ring-net) skippers—a way of asserting their presence in and connection to a place from which they were usually physically absent. The easy way in which Graeme, Ruaridh, John, and Alasdair discussed the features of the Caol Mor and the Crowlin clearly showed that they regarded these places as "their" grounds, no matter where they happened to be when they were discussing them. This was something that creel fishermen vigorously contested, as one creel boat skipper told me in the pub one evening: "There are no such thing as recognized tows, they are always changing! What does a tow mean? Any piece of ground you have trawled once? And how is anyone else to know?!" These place names were not only generated by and connected to particular communities of practice, they also were historically specific and changed as fishing techniques, affordances, and social relations changed. As I will discuss in the next section, places could also be lost or replaced.

Places Change

Places have been transformed by work that connected them to new practices, places, economies, and political realities. One tow was named "the Burma." The name was inspired by the World War II soldiers who labored in very difficult conditions to build the Burma Road; as James told me, "You were always picking up boulders" on that tow. The naming of Wullie's Peak was directly linked to the establishment of a fleet of small prawn trawlers based around Gairloch and Skye, which was dependent on the opening of a new market for prawns and new capital investment in fishing boats, and grew with tourism-related demand from Spain, cut-throat competition among Spanish seafood buyers to expand their supplies, the development of air transportation networks, the demise of the herring and white-fish fisheries, and the subsequent concentration of fish quota into the hands of a few (Howard 2012a and 2017).

Until 1984, it was illegal to trawl in the Wall of Death. Many trawlers did work in the area, but the furtiveness of fishing illegally made it considerably riskier to work on the more challenging parts of these grounds. Trawling had been banned in waters fewer than three miles from shore since the 1800s; but in 1984, the rapidly expanding and valuable international market for prawns persuaded the UK parliament to abolish this restriction with the new *Inshore Fisheries Act (1984)*. Subsequently, the number of small prawn trawlers around the Inner Sound increased significantly, as did the time that people spent working, or attempting to work, tows like the Wall of Death. Shifting political and economic relations significantly affected the formation of these places (Bender 1993; Gupta and Ferguson 1997) through regulating the access that people had to these locations and the rewards they would get for developing their affordances. As Carrier discusses for the Jamaican seascape, "larger forces, springing from outside the locality at issue, can have a crucial role in defining the landscape" (2003, 13). The spatial connections generated through the process of gaining access to and developing the affordances of these places meant that places were necessarily "extroverted," and were "a constellation of social relations meeting and weaving together at a particular locus" (Massey 1994, 154, 142).

I have focused on the *creation* of places through the development of affordances, but of course these affordances could change through ecological shifts or changes in fishing practices—there is a history of at least seven thousand years of human habitation of the seascape and shores of the Inner Sound (Hardy and Wickham-Jones 2002). Most skippers working in the Sound today would not know places like the Pol Doine and the Clarach, even if they fished there or passed through them. These places were made through a different kind of fishing, in which men speaking Gaelic would row out "of an evening" in small wooden boats to catch herring and "haddies," and children would be sent around the village to drop some of the catch off at the houses of the elderly and widowed. Eighty-six-year-old Johnny "Beag" used to participate in this fishery alongside his main job of driving a lorry. He described the different taste of herring from each nearby sea loch, and told me about the Pol Doine, a fishing place off the coast that was "noted for haddock," although "there is not a haddie to be found round this area now." The Pol Doine is likely located in the Caol Mor tow, but I never heard any working fisherman use the term. For people like Johnny who remember these fishing places where there are no longer any fish, these places are not simply in the process of being forgotten, but places whose memory marks a sharp difference between the past and present, and a deep sense of loneliness and loss.

James told me with relish about a tow called The Sound of Music. But trawlers couldn't fish there any longer due to the establishment of the British Underwater Test and Evaluation Centre in the 1970s to test torpedoes and nuclear submarines. All fishing was banned on the range itself, but creel fishing was allowed, and had flourished, in a buffer zone which would be located in approximately the same place The Sound of Music had been. I worked in this location on a few different creel boats, but they never referred to it by this name.

Changes in fishing techniques and markets and the presence (or absence) of the fish themselves have meant that people now seek different affordances from the same locations, which have in turn become different places. The names and characteristics of these places are still half-remembered, but new place names now feature in the conversations about these locations, and fishermen discuss and speculate about new features relevant to their new affordances. Gordillo argues that "places are eminently *relations* between social actors and that these relations dissolve these places' appearance of fixity" (2004, 6). Here, I have described the relations of places as involving the subjective labor and experience of developing the affordances of a place, the conversations that take place during this process, the way in which these conversations are incorporated into collective practices and repeated, and the legal, political, and economic frameworks that regulate access to a place and make its affordances more (or less) desirable. These are not just local relations: global narratives and events can become part of the experience of a particular place.

One day, fishing with Dickie on the *Iona*, I asked him why he had chosen to fish for prawns. He sighed, and then patiently replied: "You have to understand that the fisheries we have now have to do with the fisheries in the past. It is not by choice that we are at the prawns, but we were forced to them because everything else ran out." The history of fishing in the Inner Sound is a history of constant social, economic, technical, and ecological change (in which fishermen have played an active role) and the development of different affordances in response to the needs of a global seafood market and local ecological conditions. Theirs is a "*selected* and *transformed* environment" (Reed 1996, 125—his emphasis). As Dickie admonished me, history is important.

Conclusions: The Metabolism of Places

The history of places at sea is not just the history of activities conducted in particular locations. The histories of the places created through work at sea, and the memory of their replacement, provide a detailed history of the forms of work, social relationships, and kinds of persons that have made their livelihoods at sea in the Sound. It draws in the history of the whole development of fishing in Scotland, the demise of the whitefish and herring, the rise of prawns, the successive development of technologies to work and extend human sensitivity and perception into the depths of the sea, the acceleration of the international economies of trade in seafood, the participation of people in distant wars, and the replacement of one language by another.

The anthropological literature on place has emphasized that places, particularly those at sea, are associated with the practice and results of particular activities (Goodwin 1995; Lauer and Aswani 2009) and with movement from one place to another (Amith 2005; Retsikas 2007). I have combined this understanding with Ingold's and Gibson's analysis of affordances to show that the creation and naming of places is generated through the labor of developing the affordances of places. The activities undertaken in places depend on the affordances people seek and the material results of their attempts to find and develop such affordances. Place names are not merely descriptions of a location or its features, but emerge from people's experience of collectively developing affordances and can incorporate global events and local history. Rather than locations, places are relations (Gordillo 2004), and the same location can become a different place over time and for different groups of people.

Ingold points out that it is only in the "context of practical activity" that the affordances of ground are developed (2000, 166). Objects or places "take on their significance—or in Gibson's terms, they afford what they do—by virtue of their incorporation into a characteristic pattern of day-to-day activities" (Ingold 2000, 168). While this is undoubtedly true, Ingold's treatment of "activity" glosses over the importance of the material results of affordances. Grounds are not significant simply because activities take place there, but because they are places where particular activities are found to be, or made to be, productive, and the process of working there may physically change the place and the affordances it offers. Thus, I question whether the language typically used in the anthropological literature on human–environmental relations ("engagement," "activity," "practice") and the qualifications usually attached to this language ("practical engagement," "lived-in," "dwelling") are sufficient to describe the types of relationships involved in creating and maintaining places. Both Ingold and Gibson effectively deploy the concept of affordances in the course of their thought-provoking efforts to understand how people and other organisms *perceive* their environments. To apply their analysis of affordances to understanding *why* places are established, it is also important to include clearly the physical and material affordances of environments, and the metabolic relation that people and other organisms have with them (Foster 2000; Howard 2017). While the analysis in this chapter is based on place-making at sea, I also hope that it can contribute to more materially grounded understanding of human–environment relations across the breadth of human experience.

Penny McCall Howard has a PhD in anthropology from the University of Aberdeen, and is the National Research Officer of the Maritime Union of Australia. She previously worked as crew and a skipper on passenger vessels in the United States. Her academic research develops a labor-centered approach to human-environment and human-machine relations and shows how the ecology of places, the techniques people practice, and the subjectivities they enact are significantly affected by market pressures and class relations. Her book, *Environment, Labour and Capitalism at Sea:*

Working the Ground in Scotland, was published by Manchester University Press in 2017.

Notes

This chapter is based, in part, on a chapter in Howard, Penny McCall. 2017. *Environment, Labour and Capitalism at Sea: "Working the Ground" in Scotland.* Manchester: Manchester University Press. Reprinted with permission.

1. "Caol Mor" is Gaelic for "wide waist," as in a wide passage between two islands.
2. I did not encounter any women working on board Scottish fishing boats, although I was told of a few. I will use the indigenous term "fishermen" when referring to Scotland, and "fishers" when referring to the global industry.
3. See Howard 2012a for an explanation and analysis of share systems.
4. A "peak" is a steep, shallow area, like an underwater mountain or hill.
5. To "land" means to take the prawns ashore to sell them to a shellfish buyer.
6. Fishing skippers who owned their own boats frequently had the name of their boat incorporated into how people referred to them, for example, James "the *Iris*" and Wullie "the *Sincerity*."
7. "Craic" is a Scots word referring to good entertaining conversation.
8. Those working in the nephrops fishery universally refer to their catch as "prawns." However, these shellfish are not the same species as those more widely referred to as prawns. They are *Nephrops norveigicus,* which have two claws and look like a small elongated lobster. Regulatory agencies and government refer to them as nephrops. They are also called Norway lobster and marketed as "langoustines" or "scampi" (usually sold as breaded and frozen tails).
9. James listed nine trawl skippers and their boats who were working out of Gairloch at that time. Eight were from the east coast (from Peterhead, Buckie, Fraserburgh [the *Broch*], and Avoch [*Achie*]). One boat was from Gairloch (Fred on the *Stroma*). Portree is not far from Gairloch by water, and James and his father would have worked similar grounds to these boats.
10. "Blootering" a net means to seriously damage it on an obstacle on the seafloor.
11. I do not make any significant distinction between the meaning of "work" and "labor." However, I generally use the indigenous term "work" in ethnographic description and "labor" when referencing existing literature which uses the term.
12. The Back of Kyle and Pabay Corner are both names for fishing grounds.
13. If you can see the red (port side) navigation light of another boat, you must give way to them. It was considered a skill to maneuver to deliberately "show the red light" to other boats and gain the right of way.
14. "Haul up" means to pull the net up to prevent it from becoming damaged or tangled, which would result in a significant waste of time and possibly damage.

15. For more on creel fisheries, see Nightingale 2010.
16. A "fastener" is an obstacle that could snag a net.
17. "At the back of" usually meant the exposed side of an island. On the west coast, this is usually the west or Atlantic Ocean side.
18. The Whiting Tow was "opened up" before the prawn fishery began, in an earlier phase of the fishing industry when it was a place to catch whiting. The place and name were adapted into the prawn trawl fishery, although whiting is no longer caught there.
19. In contrast to skippers, the crew tend to spend long hours in factory-like conditions processing the catch. For a detailed account of the working experience of crew, see Howard (2012a; 2012b).
20. A stone is 14 pounds or 6.35 kilos.
21. Ebb tide, which in this situation meant a significant sea-current running south.

References

Amith, J. 2005. "Place Making and Place Breaking: Migration and the Development Cycle of Community in Colonial Mexico." *American Ethnologist* 32, no. 1: 159–79.

Bender, B. 1993. *Landscape: Politics and Perspectives*. Oxford: Berg.

Biehl, J., B. Good, and A. Kleinman. 2007. *Subjectivity: Ethnographic Investigations*. Berkeley: University of California Press.

Carrier, J. 2003. "Biography, Ecology and Political Economy: Seascape and Conflict in Jamaica." In *Landscape, Memory and History: Anthropological Perspectives*. Edited by P. Stewart and A. Strathern, 210–28. London: Pluto Press.

Emerson, R., R. Fretz, and L. Shaw. 1995. *Writing Ethnographic Fieldnotes*. Chicago: University of Chicago Press.

Foster, J. B. 2000. *Marx's Ecology: Materialism and Nature*. New York: Monthly Review Press.

Gibson, J. J. 1979. *The Ecological Approach to Visual Perception*. London: Houghton Mifflin.

Goodwin, C. 1995. "Seeing in Depth." *Social Studies of Science* 25: 237–74.

Gordillo, G. 2004. *Landscapes of Devils: Tensions of Place and Memory in the Argentine Chaco*. Durham, NC: Duke University Press.

Gupta, A., and J. Ferguson. 1997. "Culture, Power, Place: Ethnography at the End of an Era." In *Culture, Power, Place: Explorations in Critical Anthropology*. Edited by A. Gupta and J. Ferguson, 1–29. Durham: Duke University Press.

Hardy, K., and C. Wickham-Jones. 2002. "Scotland's First Settlers: The Mesolithic Seascape of the Inner Sound, Skye and Its Contribution to the Early Prehistory of Scotland." *Antiquity* 76: 825–33.

Helmreich, S. 2011. "Nature/Culture/Seawater." *American Anthropologist* 113, no. 1: 132–44.

Holborow, M. 2006. "Putting the Social Back into Language: Marx, Vygotsky, Volosinov and Vygotsky Reexamined." *Studies in Language and Capitalism* 1: 1–28.

Howard, P. M. 2012a. "Sharing or Appropriation? Share Systems, Class and Commodity Relations in Scottish Fisheries." *Journal of Agrarian Change* 12, no. 2–3: 316–43.

———. 2012b. "Workplace Cosmopolitanization and the 'Power and Pain of Class Relations' at Sea." *Focaal: Journal of Global and Historical Anthropology* 62: 55–69.

———. 2013. "Feeling the Ground: Vibration, Listening, Sounding at Sea." In *On Listening*. Edited by A. Carlyle and C. Lane, 61–66. Devon: Uniformbooks.

———. 2017. *Environment, Labour and Capitalism at Sea: "Working the Ground" in Scotland*. Manchester: Manchester University Press.

Ingold, T. 2000. *The Perception of the Environment: Essays in Livelihood, Dwelling and Skill*. London: Routledge.

Knipe, E. 1984. *Gamrie: An Exploration in Cultural Ecology*. Lanham, MD: University Press of America.

Lauer, M., and S. Aswani. 2009. "Indigenous Ecological Knowledge as Situated Practices: Understanding Fishers' Knowledge in the Western Solomon Islands." *American Anthropologist* 111, no. 3: 317–29.

Martin, A. 1981. *The Ring-Net Fishermen*. Edinburgh, UK: John Donald Publishers.

Marx, K. (with F. Engels). 1998 [1845]. "The German Ideology." In *The German Ideology: Including Theses on Feuerbach and Introduction to the Critique of Political Economy*. Amherst, MA: Prometheus Books. 27–568.

Mason, J. 1987. "Scottish Shellfish Fisheries." In *Developments in Fisheries Research in Scotland*. Edited by R. S. Bailey and B. B. Parrish, 88–98. Farnham, Surrey, England: Fishing News Books.

Massey, D. 1994. *Space, Places and Gender*. Minneapolis: University of Minnesota Press.

National Theatre of Scotland. 2010. *Wall of Death: A Way of Life*. Retrieved 1 February 2011. www.nationaltheatrescotland.com/content/default.asp?page=home_WallofDeath.

Nightingale, A. 2011. "Beyond Design Principles: Subjectivity, Emotion, and the (Ir-)rational Commons." *Society and Natural Resources* 24, no. 2: 119–32.

Pálsson, G. 1994. "Enskilment at Sea." *Man* 29, no. 4: 901–27.

Patterson, T. C. 2009. *Karl Marx, Anthropologist*. Oxford: Berg.

Povinelli, E. 1993. *Labor's Lot: The Power, History, and Culture of Aboriginal Action*. Chicago: University of Chicago Press.

Reed, E. 1996. *Encountering the World: Toward an Ecological Psychology*. Oxford: Oxford University Press.

Retsikas, K. 2007. "Being and Place: Movement, Ancestors, and Personhood in East Java, Indonesia." *Journal of the Royal Anthropological Institute* 13, no. 4: 969–86.

Tyrrell, M. 2006. "From Placelessness to Place: An Ethnographer's Experience of Growing to Know Places at Sea." *Worldviews* 10, no. 2: 220–38.

CHAPTER 3

Reexamination of Brazilian Mounds
Changed Views of Coastal Societies

Daniela Klokler and MaDu Gaspar

The history of Brazilian archaeology is intrinsically linked to the shell-site research. The first archaeological studies in the country were done in these sites during the nineteenth century, encouraged by the emperor D. Pedro II, who was particularly interested in science. The mound shape, composition, and location in low-lying areas helped to make shell mounds and middens the focus of other archaeological sites.

Studies show that sites range widely in size, from small accumulations that barely appear on the ground to shell mounds up to thirty meters high. Large-scale shell mounds are exclusively found in the region between south-central São Paulo state and the north of Rio Grande do Sul state (figure 3.1), and these larger sites cluster chronologically at approximately four thousand years ago. Small shell mound–sites occur along the coast, especially in northern Paraná state. Their average maximum thickness is around six meters, and they share several characteristics with larger sites. Their settlement, shape, and content bear extreme similarities.

While shell sites abound along most of the Brazilian coast, the southern coast of Santa Catarina state has been the focus of a large number of archaeological studies (figure 3.1). Radiocarbon dates indicate that the expansion of the coastal populations that built shell mounds started at around eight thousand years ago while the most recent sites were active until about one thousand years ago (Gaspar 1998; Lima et al. 2004).

Shell sites are usually located near large bodies of water (seas, lagoons, rivers) and have a mounded shape and intricate stratigraphy composed of alternating layers of shell and bones, with large numbers of hearths, burial pits, and post holes. Even sites located farther away from the coast have evidence that their builders exploited marine resources. A recurring presence of high numbers of human remains along with the absence of habitation

Figure 3.1. Map of the Brazilian coast with areas with concentration of sites (dots) and region with concentration of studies. Created by the authors.

structures indicate that some sites were used exclusively as graveyards (Fish et al. 2000; Klokler 2008, 2014; Gaspar et al. 2013; Gaspar et al. 2014).

Changes in theoretical perspectives and improvements of methodological strategies dramatically altered the perception of these fisher-gatherer societies since the first researchers became interested in shell sites in the 1800s. A shift in focus, now more concerned with particular societies rather than the characterization of individual sites, has uncovered rich information about their lives and deaths, both of which were intrinsically connected to the coastal and maritime (or aquatic) environments. Discoveries from recent decades have led archaeologists to reassess their perceptions and challenge earlier assumptions about settlement, subsistence, and social relationships, highlighting the need to understand these communities in a different manner to societies that exploit more terrestrial resources.

Living by the Coast: Its Specificities

Studies of maritime societies demonstrate the many ways in which they differ from societies focused on terrestrial resources: choice of settlement location, technology, resource procurement, territoriality, mobility, intra- and inter-group relationships, population size, and organization, among others. Within Brazilian archaeology, until recently, shell mound research rarely explicitly analyzed the groups who built these structures with shell and bones as aquatic societies or aquatic hunter-gatherers. We advocate that research that highlights the intimate link between shell mound groups and aquatic resources can significantly advance interpretation of their way of life.

Maritime ecosystems can be very productive environments, particularly inshore and at upwelling zones. Oceanic upwelling increases the nutrients in the water, thereby attracting more animals to the area. Inshore areas, including estuaries and beaches, are generally richer in resources than the open sea and deep-sea areas (Yesner 1980, 1998; Reitz 1988). In some areas, there are conditions that facilitate the clustering of resources.

Shellfish beds are the sources that readily come to mind when researchers mention easy access, low mobility, and high-density resources for human populations. However, a myriad of species of crustaceans and fish also inhabited inshore/coastal areas. In addition, marine and terrestrial mammals are found in these maritime microenvironments as resources that were used by prehistoric groups.

Aquatic resources are associated to high productivity, high sustainability, and high predictability. Reliance on resources that are predictable, diverse, and nutrient-rich would have enabled aquatic hunter-gatherer societies to have higher mean population densities (Ames 2002, 46).[1] Areas with a higher degree of richness and productivity of resources could not only support large populations but also more sedentary occupations.

Studies indicate that sedentary populations tend to have higher growth rates, leading to the search of new sources of food (Benfer 1990; Fitzhugh 2002). Time is invested in gathering and transportation. The high degree of sedentism supported by the existence of a huge variety of highly renewable available resources within the same region, concentrated in certain points, suggests that aquatic resources also create conditions for enlargement of social groups. Benfer (1990) and Hayden (1994) argue that the adoption of sedentism implies changes and added variety in social life, leading to a higher degree of social complexity.

Water bodies (seas, rivers, and lagoons) provide a particular type of proprietary relationship with resources, a relationship that is different to the relationship usually established with land. Having made some investment in the exploitation of aquatic resources, certain property relationships can arise in relation to some spaces. Wessen's (1982) study of the Ozzette site found differences in household status and access to resources, hinting at the existence of resource ownership. Hayden (1996, 52) reinforces that among the Lillooet on the Northwest Plateau, "the largest and most productive fishing location in the region" was accessible to anyone in regular times, even people that did not belong to the group. On the other hand, "smaller fishing sites which were highly productive, but which required special facilities such as platforms for effective exploitation, were owned by individuals or families" (Hayden 1996, 52).

The technology used to exploit aquatic resources is specifically adapted to aquatic conditions, demanding the development of an assemblage different to that of terrestrial hunting (Acheson 1981). The artifact toolkits of aquatic hunter-gatherers are usually distinct, but few studies focus on them. Walker (2000) argues that a certain dismissive attitude toward shellfishing and fishing remains a problem in technological studies. Bowdler's study (1976) is an important assessment of the influence of modifications in fishing techniques in promoting change in gender strategies, economic decisions, and access to food items.

Initially, the study of site catchment areas concentrated on the potential of terrestrial resources, and later on agricultural aspects (Vita-Finzi and Higgs 1970; Gibbon 1984). McGovern (1980) highlights that when the object of analysis involves coastal economies, researchers must establish the type of transportation the societies used. As Blair notes (2010), most studies on mobility focus on pedestrian movements, and it is important to think about the intricacies of resource procurement, mobility, and overall use of space in the context of coastal societies and aquatic resources. While in the past it was proposed that marine resources were seasonal complements to terrestrial ones (Jarman, Bailey, and Jarman 1982, 46), research has repeatedly shown that coastal societies could have subsisted mainly on aquatic resources. Kelly (1995) suggests that the reduced mobility of coastal hunter-gatherer groups, facilitated by the exploitation of marine resources, triggered a chain of events leading to increasing sociopolitical complexity.

Movement by aquatic societies is greatly influenced by the use of boats. For Blair, "canoes contribute to prehistoric resource extraction and mobility in profound and complex ways by both changing the structure of human space, effectively shrinking space and time-distance relationships . . . changing the relationship between people and their material culture" (2010, 44). Use of vessels suggests the need to redraw site catchment area estimates. On the other hand, Jarman et al. (1982, 35) propose that the availability of transportation, such as boats, could promote the intensification of exploitation of nearby areas, instead of necessarily augmenting the catchment area.

In fact, even small-scale vessels such as canoes could increase the "catchment" range. By traveling larger distances, groups were able to meet other communities more often, thus increasing their networks. In addition, vessels allowed the transportation of dramatically larger hauls, supporting larger communities and enabling intensification (Ames 2002). Whitaker and Byrd (2012) show that later intensification in the use of red abalone in Central California was connected to a shift in procurement strategies due to the use of boats.

The coastline presents an excellent communication channel, facilitating contact among different communities through coastal navigation (which may have traditionally involved great risk and sophisticated knowledge). Lévi-Strauss (1983) has emphasized the importance of exchange in the institution and development of social life. The coastline provides beneficial conditions for social exchange through comprehensive networks and, in that way, for the circulation of information and acquisition of new habits.

Abundant and renewable resources such as those provided by the sea enable a smaller area to maintain a stable population. Moreover, the way in which some of these resources present themselves—sometimes in large quantities for restricted periods of times (temporally aggregated resources)—can allow for simultaneous exploitation by distinct communities. This has a great impact in the circulation of information and formation of regional networks. Groups that exploit aquatic resources have a tendency to structure themselves in a cooperative way, exploring the resources together with nearby groups. This is especially so in the case of fish that arrive in large schools during short periods every year.

The expression of territoriality is distinct among these societies; according to McCay (1978, 399), fishing rights occur over space, and not specific resources. Godelier (1984), Cordell (2000), and Diegues (2001), in discussing Brazilian traditional fishing groups, remind us that the notion of sea tenure grants access, control, and use of resources found in determined areas of the coast. King (this volume) illustrates how informal territorial rights to ocean spaces can be generated via social and political connections between individuals. Cordell highlights how these traditions are connected to "the construction and maintenance of a social identity and a sense of place" (2000, 31).

All these particularities demonstrate that to fully understand the shell mound societies, researchers have to go beyond merely establishing that the groups inhabited coastal areas and subsisted by consuming aquatic resources. We need to build a perspective that contemplates and comprehends these societies as a whole.

As Gaspar and colleagues assert, "Knowledge of wind, tides, nets, and boats are not generally part of the researcher's universe and these, along with regional particularities, must be taken into account in order to understand the daily life of coastal groups" (2011, 190). A clearer understanding of life by the sea will lead to a deeper comprehension of aquatic hunter-gatherers.

Putting the "Coast" in Coastal Societies

A review of archaeological evidence about aquatic hunter-gatherers shows how the framework of knowledge has been transformed during the past decades, specifically via advances in method and theory.

For the last century, archaeologists have commonly described shell mound societies as small nomadic bands that would come seasonally to the littoral areas (Ferreira Penna 1876; Rauth 1962; Beck 1974). Authors believed the groups lived in the high plains or more generally in the countryside and went to the coast during specific seasons—namely summer—to fish and gather mollusks. In the late 1970s, after analyzing studies that showed how marine environments can be resource-rich, researchers admitted the possibility that *sambaqui* builders could have had stable communities that lived most of their lives by the sea (Schmitz 1987; Schmitz, Barbosa, and Ribeiro 2015).

Radiocarbon dates and the analysis of shell mound profiles from Southern Brazil indicate that the sites had been continuously active over long intervals of time. The twenty dates obtained in the Jabuticabeira II indicate that it was constructed over at least eight hundred years. Less systematic information from other sites confirms the recurrence of long periods of activity without evidence of abandonment. The spatial order of the shell mounds, always grouped in zones of lagoons, bays, and deltas, indicate that these large water bodies provide conditions for sedentary life and territorial stability.

Figuti (1993) is one of the few authors that explicitly mentions specificities of maritime communities in terms of settlement location, duration, and subsistence strategies, and is the first researcher to identify fishing as the main activity for these groups. Faunal research initiated by Figuti (1992, 1993) demonstrated that fish were always more important resources for these groups than shellfish. His initial results were later confirmed by studies from Figuti and Klokler (1996), Klokler (2001, 2008), and Nishida (2001, 2007). The characterization of shell mound builders as fishers changed the academic perspective of these groups. Isotopic studies confirmed what faunal analyses demonstrated: that mollusks were probably a supplement to the diet (DeMasi 1999, 2009; Klokler 2008, 2014). Analyses show that, generally, the favored species were captured from areas neighboring the sites and excursions in the deeper ocean were rare. The resources more frequently recovered (from a site constructed over fifteen hundred years) were available throughout the year (Table 3.1). No longer treating the communities as small hunger-stricken bands, but as larger sedentary organized societies, studies of these groups underwent a major transformation.

Regarding aspects of territoriality of fishing groups, the study by Gaspar, Klokler, and DeBlasis (2011) shows that this activity by traditional communities is generally restricted to a lagoon or a narrow strip close to the shore, as there are great differences in value, size, and technology between inshore (lagoon) and offshore (ocean) fishing boats. To the north, in São Paulo State, Diegues (2001) found a similar trend: fishermen preferred to fish in estuaries and coastal lagoons, but feared open seas and the *passagem da barra* (beyond the mouth of the estuary), due to the possibility of storms and other potentially fatal dangers.

Table 3.1. Schedule of resources along Santa Catarina coast (modified from Farias 2001).

	Winter						Summer					
	Nov	Dec	Jan	Feb	Mar	Apr	May	Jun	Jul	Aug	Sep	Oct
Mullet							X	X	X			
Whitemouth Croaker	X	X	X	X	X	X	X	X	X	X	X	X
Bluefish	X										X	X
Catfish	X	X	X	X	X	X	X	X	X	X	X	X
Little mullet	X	X	X	X	X	X	X	X	X	X	X	X
Shrimp	X	X	X									X
Crab	X	X	X	X	X	X	X	X	X	X	X	X

The organization of the fishing, namely the resources concentrated on certain periods of the year, provides a pathway for the understanding of the space–time distribution of Brazilian shell mounds. In Santa Catarina, the margins of the Garopaba do Sul lagoon were intensively occupied. Furthermore, the archaeological study of the prehistoric fisher-gatherers' territory in the state of Rio de Janeiro indicates a superposition of resource catchment areas, precisely on large water reservoirs. This spatial arrangement was construed as an indicator of cooperative sociability among the builders of different shell mounds (Gaspar 1991, 1996). The way that the resources are exploited is beneficial for cooperative sociability among fishermen and the common exploitation of the environment. As the fishermen by the lagoon join their nets, they are quite aware of the fact that together they become better equipped to catch fish (Gaspar et al. 2011).

Gaspar (1991), Gaspar and DeBlasis (1992) and Afonso and DeBlasis (1994) tackled questions about the formation of these shell sites by considering the sites as artifacts, amenable to analysis similar to ones reserved for tools. The idea that shell mounds were intentionally built and not inadvertent accumulations of trash was confirmed with studies based on zooarchaeology. However, a question remains: If shellfish were not a dietary staple, why accumulate large amounts of shells (figure 3.2)?

The goals behind the building of structures in predominantly coastal plains were first analyzed by Gaspar (1994) and viewed as an integral part

Figure 3.2. View of Figueirinha site (note house to the right) located in southern Santa Catarina State. Photo by MaDu Gaspar.

of the group's identity. Site formation processes studies (Figuti and Klokler 1996; Klokler 2001, 2008, 2014; Nishida 2007; Villagran 2010) detailed the behavior behind the stages of mound building activities, demonstrating that shell valve accumulation was not accidental but planned, as Gaspar previously suggested. These building efforts would be significantly helped by the use of boats for transportation of large quantities of faunal remains.

The vast majority of sites investigated contain great quantities of human remains (sometimes in the hundreds). The recurring presence of human remains and the formation of small mounds on top of burial sites suggest that site construction was directly related to funerary rituals (Klokler 2001, 2008, 2014). The latter have indications of being a long process that involved the staging of feasts at the end of the mourning period.

The monumentality of the mound is no accident, but a result of massive, repeated depositional episodes over a lengthy period of time, eventually becoming a marker of territoriality on the landscape (Fish et al. 2000). The use of boats would help not only the capture of large amounts of fish for the feast but also their transport to the sites where funerary rituals were being performed, including the Jabuticabeira II and Amourins sites (Gaspar et al. 2013; Klokler 2014).

Funerary feasting, as well as being a lavish and joyous occasion, could also be a privileged arena for display of solidarity and intergroup cooperation (Dietler and Hayden 2001). The evidence for funerary feasting at Jabuticabeira II and Amourins, with use of foods neither rare nor exotic, is suggestive of these communal events as ways to improve cooperative behavior among the groups, as the food items could have been easily captured by most of their members (Klokler 2014). We believe that social distinctions could have been minimized through the use of these common resources. The feasts analyzed in some detail by Klokler (2008) in the Jabuticabeira II site hints at the cooperative nature of these events and support the hypotheses suggested by Gaspar in Rio de Janeiro.

Kneip (2004), based on a study of settlement patterns of clusters of sites located in southern Santa Catarina, suggested that settlements were organized and grew around water reservoirs such as bays and lagoons and areas with an intersection of ecosystems. DeBlasis and colleagues (2007, 48) even allude to a lagoonal (surrounding the lagoon) configuration of the settlements.

The use of watercraft by shell mound groups was generally accepted among archaeologists and attested by Fairbridge's comment (1976, 355) that "direct access to both the local shellfish bed and to more distant banks that were accessible by canoe seems to be the rule." For settlements located on islands, very little work focused on evidence of the use of vessels until recently (Amenomori 2005; Calippo 2010). According to Gaspar (1991), there are strong indicators that groups used boats, and this is a fundamental point in understanding the exploitation of resources in terms of catchment area size and intensity of exploitation near sites. Studies by Tenório (1999, 2006) with groundstone artifacts, particularly axes and "grinding surfaces" located in Rio de Janeiro, lead a growing interest in these tools and their possible uses in boat making. More recently, Belém's research (2012) also signals the possible use of the commonly found axes in the manufacture of canoes.

Lithic studies highlight the importance of plants for these groups (Tenório 1999). Archaeobotany research (Scheel-Ybert 1998) and the analysis of plant materials from wetsites are unveiling large quantities of seeds and fruits and basketry elements (Peixe, Melo and Bandeira 2007). Rita Scheel-Ybert (2002) has demonstrated through paleoethnobotany analysis the use of plant foods by these populations and suggested the practice of horticulture with the management of tubers (especially *Discorea*) and fruit (*Sapotaceae*). Due to the low probability of tuber remains being preserved, and their ubiquity in Brazilian sites, it is likely that tubers regularly contributed to the diet of these populations (Scheel-Ybert 2003). Scheel-Ybert's (2002) analysis of macroscopic plant remains has also identified stability of the regional plant communities, another factor that supports the long-term settlement and subsistence of *sambaqui* groups.

Physical anthropology research demonstrates that in individuals living on shell mounds, osteoarthritis was more prevalent in the upper limbs (Neves 1984; Mendonça de Souza 1995). Osteoarthritis is often used as a marker of activity intensity and results suggest that individuals walked shorter distances, which could be evidence of smaller terrestrial resource catchment areas (Scheel-Ybert et al. 2009). Moreover, higher frequencies of osteoarthritis in upper limbs might be indicative of activities such as swimming and rowing.

In addition, the aquatic hunter-gatherers of the southeastern and southern Brazil made elaborate sculptures in stone and bone, objects that are impressive in their beauty and figurative balance (figure 3.3). Researchers recovered just over 240 statuettes from forty sites (Prous 1974). They are polished pieces, ranging in size from 10–43 cm. The majority of these examples present a small oval cavity in the ventral part of the object. Some objects are easily recognizable as depicting animals and suitable for zoological identification, allowing the determination of the species. Skate, shark, whale, porpoise, sole, mullet, bluefish, spadefish, kingfisher, penguin, albatross, owl, vulture, bat, armadillo, tortoise, anteater, agouti, turtle, alligator, and various felines are among the animals portrayed.

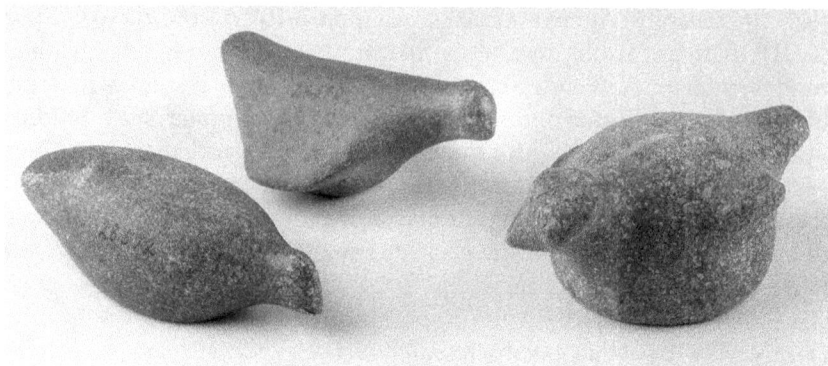

Figure 3.3. Examples of bird zooliths. Photo from the Museu Nacional-Universidade Federal do Rio de Janeiro archives; reproduced with permission.

For Prous, the analysis of these artifacts indicates that there is an ideological confluence[2] in the area in which the statuettes occur—from Rio Grande do Sul to São Paulo (1991, 223). This is evident in theme repetition and compliance with strict stylistic rules. The author provides examples of his findings by comparing two identical sculptures found more than one thousand kilometers away from each other.

This way of manufacturing indicates that there was a communication network running all along the southern and southeastern coast of Brazil. For the shell mound builders, the coast was a natural pathway that enabled the flow of people and ideas along a vast extension, leading to the dissemination of social practices inside the social-cultural system and contact between different cultures. Meanwhile, that contact might have reinforced social traditions and exposed the population to distinct practices and new social behaviors.

Living by the Sea, from the Sea

As the latest research advances attest, Brazilian archaeologists have come around to acknowledging the intrinsic characteristic of aquatic societies and their importance in shell site studies. Archaeological work in large shell mound sites face limiting factors as it demands time, large teams, and great sums of money. Nevertheless, there is commitment to the continuation of studies; projects are refocusing on previously studied sites and their collections with interesting results. New avenues should be explored further, namely site function, regional approaches, and especially ethnoarchaeological studies, in projects that involve greater integration of different disciplines.

Aquatic hunter-gatherer societies left indelible marks on the Brazilian territory, their communities stimulating interest in generations of archaeologists. As such, today's researchers have a clearer image of their life ways. These societies were making extensive use of coastal resources in dense, largely sedentary communities that had contact with neighbors with whom they shared catchment areas. Funerary feasts were occasions to demonstrate the strict ties to their environment and moments to express their solidarity. The festivities allowed further regional integration among groups. At the same time, it was during these events that many large mounds were created and maintained.

Shell mounds have come a long way since being seen as amorphous aggregates of shell, accumulated haphazardly. Today, researchers understand these sites as elements of an anthropic landscape, active participants in the transmission of messages of territoriality and power. The societies that inhabited the Brazilian coast and built shell mounds manipulated their surroundings through the construction of structures that resisted time and space. They are full of social meaning that researchers need to continue examining.

Daniela Klokler is an archaeologist whose research interests include shell mound societies, the relationship between humans and animals, and ritual practices. She is an associate professor at the Archaeology Department at the Universidade Federal de Sergipe, Brazil, and is the research co-coordinator for the Museu de Arqueologia de Xingó. Her publications include the edited volume, *The Cultural Dynamics of Shell Middens and Shell Mounds* (Roksandic et al. 2014).

MaDu Gaspar is an archaeologist who focuses on "Sambaquis" in the Southeast and South Brazilian Coast. She lectures archaeology as Professor at the Museu Nacional/ UFRJ (Universidade Federal do Rio de Janeiro) postgraduate program in Archaeology. She is a researcher at CNPQ (Conselho Nacional de Desenvolvimento Científico e Tecnológico [National Research Council]). Her publications include "Sambaquis Shell Mounds," in the *Encyclopedia of Global Archaeology* (2014).

Notes

We would like to thank Tanya King and Gary Robinson for the invitation to be part of the volume, Ian McNiven for the suggestion of our name, and all researchers who devoted their work to study shell sites in Brazil and helped inform us about the early settlement of our coast by aquatic hunter-gatherers.

1. Ames (2002) differentiates "aquatic" from "maritime" hunter-gatherers. To him, the latter suggests focus on exploitation of marine environments both coastal and pelagic. Shell mound groups were more focused on inshore resources.
2. In the sense the concept and representation rules were shared by the sambaqui builders from southern Brazil.

References

Acheson, J. M. 1981. "Anthropology of Fishing." *Annual Review of Anthropology* 10, no. 1: 275–316.

Afonso, M., and P. DeBlasis. 1994. "Aspectos da Formação de um Grande Sambaqui: Alguns Indicadores em Espinheiros II. Joinville." *Revista do Museu de Arqueologia e Etnologia* 19, no. 4: 21–30.

Amenomori, S. N. 2005. "Paisagem das Ilhas, As Ilhas da Paisagem: A Ocupação dos Grupos Pescadores-coletores Préhistóricos no Litoral Norte do Estado de São Paulo." PhD dissertation. São Paulo: Museu de Arqueologia e Etnologia, USP.

Ames, K. 2002. "Going by Boat: The Forager–Collector Continuum at Sea." In *Beyond Foraging and Collecting: Evolutionary Change in Hunter-Gatherer Settlement Systems.* Edited by B. Fitzhugh and J. Habu, 19–52. New York: Kluwer Academic/Plenum Publishers.

Beck, A. 1974. *O Sambaqui Enseada I.* Florianópolis: Universidade Federal de Santa Catarina.

Belém, F. 2012. "*Do Seixo ao Zoólito-A Indústria Lítica dos Sambaquis do sul Catarinense: Aspectos Formais, Tecnológicos e Funcionais.*" Masters dissertation. São Paulo: Museu de Arqueologia e Etnologia, Universidade de São Paulo.

Benfer, R. A. 1990. "The Preceramic Period Site of Paloma, Peru: Bioindications of Improving Adaptation to Sedentism." *Latin American Antiquity* 1, no. 4: 284–318.

Blair, S. E. 2010. "Missing the Boat in Lithic Procurement: Watercraft and the Bulk Procurement of Tool-stone on the Maritime Peninsula." *Journal of Anthropological Archaeology* 29, no. 1: 33–46.

Bowdler, S. 1976. "Hook, Line, and Dilly Bag: An Interpretation of an Australian Coastal Shell Midden." *Mankind* 10, no. 4: 248–58.

Calippo, F. 2010. *Sociedade Sambaquieira, Comunidades Marítimas.* PhD dissertation. São Paulo: Museu de Arqueologia e Etnologia, USP.

Cordell, J. C. 2000. "Remapping the Waters: The Significance of Sea Tenure-based Protected Areas." Keynote Address at the Third Conference on Property Rights, Economics, and Environment. Aix-Marseille: Centre d'Analyse Economique de l'Université d'Aix-Marseille. Retrieved 29 December 2018 from http://nupaub.fflch.usp.br/sites/nupaub.fflch.usp.br/files/remapping.pdf.

DeBlasis, P. A., A. Kneip, R. Scheel-Ybert, P. Giannini, and M. D. Gaspar. 2007. "Sambaquis e Paisagem: Dinâmica Natural e Arqueologia Regional no Litoral Sul do Brasil." *Arqueologia Sudamericanca/Arqueologia Sul-americana* 3, no. 1: 29–61.

DeMasi, M. 1999. "Prehistoric Hunter-gatherer Mobility on the Southern Brazilian Coast: Santa Catarina Island." PhD dissertation. Stanford: Stanford University.

———. 2009. "Aplicações de Isótopos Estáveis de 18/16o, 13/12c, e 15/14n em Estudos de Sazonalidade, Mobilidade e Dieta de Populações Pré-históricas no sul do Brasil." *Revista de Arqueologia* 22, no. 2: 55–76.

Diegues, A. C. 2001. "Traditional Fisheries Knowledge and Social Appropriation of Marine Resources in Brazil" (presentation). MARE Conference: People and the Sea, 30 August to 1 September. Amsterdam: Centre for Maritime Research.

Dietler, M., and B. Hayden. 2001. "Digesting the Feast: Good to Eat, Good to Drink, Good to Think; An Introduction." In *Feasts: Archaeological and Ethnographic Perspectives on Food, Politics, and Power*, 1–20. Tuscaloosa: University of Alabama Press.

Fairbridge, R. W. 1976. "Shellfish-eating Preceramic Indians in Coastal Brazil, Radiocarbon Dating of Shell Middens Discloses a Relationship with Holocene Sea Level Oscillations." *Science* 191, no. 4225: 353–59.

Farias, M. 2001. "A Pesca e a Sazonalidade no Camacho—SC: Um Estudo de Modos de Vida em Deslocamento." Masters dissertation. Florianópolis: Universidade Federal de Santa Catarina.

Ferreira P., and D. Soares. 1876. "Breve Notícia sobre os Sambaquis do Pará." *Arquivos do Museu Nacional* 1: 85–99.

Figuti, L. 1992. "Les Sambaquis COSIPA (4200 à 1200 ans BP): Étude de la Subsistance chez les Peuples Préhistoriques de Pêcheurs-ramasseurs de Bivalves de la Côte Centrale de l'État de São Paulo, Brésil." PhD dissertation. Paris: Museum National d'"Histoire Naturelle, Institut de Paleontologie Humaine.

———. 1993. "O Homem Pré-histórico, o Molusco e o Sambaqui: Considerações Sobre a Subsistência dos Povos Sambaquianos." *Revista do Museu de Arqueologia e Etnologia* 5, no. 3: 67–80.

Figuti, L., and D. Klokler. 1996. "Resultados Preliminares dos Vestígios Zooarqueológicos do Sambaqui Espinheiros II (Joinville, SC)." *Revista do Museu de Arqueologia e Etnologia* 12, no. 6: 169–88.

Fish, S., P. A. DeBlasis, M. Gaspar, and P. Fish. 2000. "Eventos incrementais na construção de sambaquis, litoral sul do estado de Santa Catarina." *Revista do Museu de Arqueologia e Etnologia* 22, no. 10: 69–87.

Fitzhugh, B. 2002. "Residential and Logistical Strategies in the Evolution of Complex Hunter-Gatherers on the Kodiak Archipelago." In *Beyond Foraging and Collecting: Evolutionary Change in Hunter-Gatherer Settlement Systems*. Edited by B. Fitzhugh and J. Habu, 257–304. New York: Kluwer Academic/Plenum Publishers.

Gaspar, M. 1991. "Aspectos da Organização de um Grupo Pescadores, Coletores e Caçadores: Região Compreendida entre a Ilha Grande e o delta do Paraíba do Sul, Estado do Rio de Janeiro." PhD dissertation. São Paulo: Faculdade de Filosofia, Letras e Ciências Humanas/ Universidade de São Paulo.

———. 1994. "Espaço, ritos funerários e identidade pré-histórica. *Revista de Arqueologia*, São Paulo 8, no. 2: 221–31.

———. 1996. "Território de Exploração e Tipo de Ocupação dos Pescadores, Coletores e Caçadores que Ocuparam o Litoral do Estado do Rio de Janeiro." *CLIO-Série. Arqueológica, Recife* 1, no. 11: 153–74.

———. 1998. "Considerations About the Sambaquis of Brazilian Coast." *Antiquity* 72: 592–615.

Gaspar, M., and P. A. DeBlasis. 1992. "Construção de sambaquis." *Anais da VI Reunião Científica da Sociedade de Arqueologia Brasileira* 2, no. 6: 811–20.

Gaspar, M., D. M. Klokler, and P. A. DeBlasis. 2011. "Traditional Fishing, Mollusk Gathering, and the Shell Mound Builders of Santa Catarina, Brazil." *Journal of Ethnobiology* 31, no. 2: 188–212.

Gaspar, M., D. Klokler, R. Scheel-Ybert, and G. Bianchini. 2013. "Sambaqui de Amourins: Mesmo Sítio, Perspectivas Diferentes. Arqueologia de um Sambaqui 30 Anos Depois." *Revista del Museo de Antropología* 6, no. 1: 7–20.

Gaspar, M., D. Klokler, and P. A. DeBlasis. 2014. "Were Sambaqui People Buried in the Trash? Archaeology, Physical Anthropology, and the Evolution of the Interpretation of Brazilian Shell Mounds." In *The Cultural Dynamics of Shell Middens and Shell Mounds: A Worldwide Perspective.* Edited by M. Roksandic, S. Mendonça de Souza, S. Eggers, M. Burcell, and D. Klokler, 91–100. Albuquerque: University of New Mexico Press.

Gibbon, G. 1984. *Anthropological Archaeology.* New York: Columbia University Press

Godelier, M.. 1984. *L' idéel et le matériel: pensée, économies, sociétés.* Paris: Fayard.

Hayden, B. 1994. "Competition, Labor, and Complex Hunter-Gatherers." In *Key Issues in Hunter-Gatherer Research.* Edited by E. S. Burch and L. J. Ellana, 223–39. Oxford: Berg Press.

———. 1996. "Feasting in Prehistoric and Traditional Societies." In *Food and the Status Quest: an Interdisciplinary Perspective.* Edited by Polly Wiessner and Wulf Schiefenhovel, 127–48. Oxford: Berghahn Books.

Jarman, M. R., G. N. Bailey, and H. N. Jarman. 1982. *Early European Agriculture.* Cambridge: Cambridge University Press.

Kelly, R. 1995. *The Foraging Spectrum: Diversity in Hunter-Gatherer Lifeways.* Washington, DC: Smithsonian Institution Press.

Klokler, D. 2001. "Construindo ou Deixando um Sambaqui? Análise de Sedimentos de um Sambaqui do Litoral Meridional Brasileiro: Processos Formativos. Região de Laguna-SC." Masters dissertation. São Paulo: Museu de Arqueologia e Etnologia, Universidade de São Paulo.

———. 2008. "Food for Body and Soul: Mortuary Ritual in Shell Mounds (Laguna—Brazil)." PhD dissertation. Tucson: Department of Anthropology, University of Arizona.

———. 2014. "A Ritually Constructed Shell Mound: Feasting at the Jabuticabeira II Site." In *The Cultural Dynamics of Shell Middens and Shell Mounds: A Worldwide Perspective.* Edited by M. Roksandic, S. Mendonça de Souza, S. Eggers, M. Burcell, and D. Klokler, 151–62. Albuquerque: University of New Mexico Press.

Kneip, A. 2004. "O Povo da Lagoa: Uso do SIG para Modelamento e Simulação na Área Arqueológica do Camacho." PhD dissertation. Sao Paulo: Museu de Arqueologia e Etnologia, Universidadede Sao Paulo.

Lévi-Strauss, C. 1983. *Structural Anthropology.* Vol. 2. Translated by Monique Layton. Chicago: University of Chicago Press.

Lima, T., K. D. Macario, R. M. Anjos, P. R. S. Gomes, M. M. Coimbra, and D. Elmore. 2004. "The Earliest Shellmounds of the Central-South Brazilian Coast."

Nuclear Instruments and Methods in Physics Research Section B: Beam Interactions with Atoms 223–24: 691–94.

McCay, B. J. 1978. "Systems Ecology, People Ecology, and the Anthropology of Fishing Communities." *Human Ecology* 6, no. 4: 397–422.

McGovern, T. H. 1980. "Site Catchments and Maritime Adaptations in Norse Greenland." *Anthropology UCLA* 10, no. 1/2: 193–210.

Mendonça de Souza, S. 1995. "Estresse, Doença e Adaptabilidade: Estudo Comparativo de Dois Grupos Pré-Históricos em Perspectiva Biocultural." PhD dissertation. Rio de Janeiro: Escola Nacional de Saúde Pública, Fundação Oswaldo Cruz.

Neves, W. 1984. "Estilo de Vida e Osteobiografia: A Reconstituição do Comportamento Pelos Ossos Humanos." *Revista de Pré-História* 6: 287–91.

Nishida, P. 2001. "Estudo zooarqueológico do sítio Mar Virado, Ubatuba, SP." Masters dissertation. São Paulo: Museu de Arqueologia e Etnologia, USP.

———. 2007. *A coisa ficou preta: estudo do processo de formação da terra preta do sítio arqueológico Jabuticabeira II.* Unpublished PhD thesis. Universidade de São Paulo.

Peixe, S., J. Melo Jr., and Dione Bandeira. 2007. "Paleoetnobotânica dos Macrorestos Vegetais do Tipo Trançados de Fibras Encontrados no Sambaqui Cubatão I, Joinville—SC." *Revista do Museu de Arqueologia e Etnologia* 3, no. 17: 211–22.

Prous, A. 1974. "Catalogue Raisonné des Sculptures Préhistoriques Zoomorphes du Brésil et de l'Uruguay." *Dédalo* 11–127.

———. 1991. *Arqueologia Brasileira.* Brasilia: Editora UnB.

Rauth, J. W. 1962. "O Sambaqui de Saquarema, S.10.B. Paraná-Brasil." *Boletim da Universidade do Paraná.* Curitiba: Conselho de Pesquisas, Imprensa da UFPR.

Reitz, E. 1988. "Faunal Remains from Paloma, an Archaic Site in Peru." *American Anthropologist* 90, no. 2: 310–13.

Scheel-Ybert, R. 1998. "Stabilité de l'Ecosyème sur le Littoral Sud-Est du Brésil à l'Holocène Supérieur (5 500–1 4000 ans BP). Les Pécheurs-Cueilleurs et le Milieu Végétal: Apports de L'Anthracologie." PhD dissertation. Paris: Université de Montpellier II.

———. 2002. "Mise en Évidence par l'Analyse Anthracologique de la Stabilité de la Végétation sur le Littoral Brésilien Pendant l'Holocène Supérieur." *Quaternaire* 13, no. 3–4: 247–56.

———. 2003. "Relações dos Habitantes de Sambaquis com o meio Ambiente: Evidências de Manejo de Vegetais na Costa Sul-sudeste do Brasil durante o Holoceno Superior." In *Atas do IX Congresso da Associação Brasileira de Estudos do Quaternário e II Congresso do Quaternário de Países de Línguas Ibéricas.* Retrieved 24 May 2018 from http://www.museunacional.ufrj.br/arqueologia/docs/papers/rita/ABEQUA2003.pdf.

Scheel-Ybert, R., S. Eggers, V. Wesolowski, C. C. Petronilho, C. H. Boyadjian, M. D. Gaspar, M. Barbosa-Guimarães, M. C. Tenório, and P. DeBlasis. 2009. "Subsistence and Lifeway of Coastal Brazilian Moundbuilders." *Treballs d'Etnoarqueologia* 7: 37–54.

Schmitz, P. I. 1987. "Prehistoric Hunters and Gatherers of Brazil." *Journal of World Prehistory* 1, no. 1: 53–126.

Schmitz, P. I., A. Sales Barbosa, and M. B. Ribeiro. 2015. *"Temas de Arqueologia Brasileira: 1980: edição histórica"*. Goiânia: Ed. da PUC Goiás; IGPA.

Tenório, M. C. 1999. "Os Fabricantes de Machado da Ilha Grande." In *Pré-história da Terra Brasilis*. Edited by M. C. Tenório, 233–46. Rio de Janeiro: Ed. UFRJ (Federal University of Rio de Janeiro).

———. 2006. "Os Amoladores-polidores Fixos." *Revista de Arqueologia* 16, no. 1: 87–108.

Villagran, X. S. 2010. *Estratigrafias que Falam: Geoarqueologia de um Sambaqui Monumental*. São Paulo: Editora Annablume-FAPESP.

Vita-Finzi, C., and E. S. Higgs. 1970. "Prehistoric Economy in the Mount Carmel Area of Palestine: Site Catchment Analysis." *Proceedings of the Prehistoric Society* 36: 1–37.

Walker, K. J. 2000. "Material Culture of Precolumbian Fishing: Artifacts and Fish Remains from Coastal Southwest Florida." *Southeastern Archaeology* 19, no. 1: 24–46.

Wessen, G. C. 1982. "Shell Middens as Cultural Deposits: A Case Study from Ozette." PhD dissertation. Pullman: Washington State University.

Whitaker, A. R., and B. F. Byrd. 2012. "Boat-based Foraging and Discontinuous Prehistoric Red Abalone Exploitation along the California Coast." *Journal of Anthropological Archaeology* 31, no. 2: 196–214.

Yesner, D. R. 1980. "Maritime Hunter-Gatherers: Ecology and Prehistory." *Current Anthropology* 21, no. 6: 727–50.

———. 1998. "Origins and Development of Maritime Adaptations in the Northwest Pacific Region of North America: A Zooarchaeological Perspective." *Artic Anthropology* 35: 204–22.

CHAPTER 4

Seamless Archaeology

The Evolving Use of Archaeology in the Study of Seascapes

Caroline Wickham-Jones

Interaction with the sea is a fundamental part of human existence and has been so since the Paleolithic. Archaeology plays an important role in providing evidence of this relationship—especially as it existed during prehistory—and in helping to understand how it has developed over the millennia. The aim of this chapter is to provide a critical review of the role of archaeology in the study of seascapes. The intention is to move from the "safe" academic reliance on excavated physical remains to the more challenging realm of perception, where the ambiguities of the human relationship with the sea provide a powerful means of broadening our horizons.

Background

Settlement by the sea, the ability to cross water, and the exploitation of marine and littoral resources are all attested from the earliest times; humans, from the *Homo erectus* populations of at least one hundred thousand years ago, have appreciated the benefits of "a day at the sea-side" (Erlandson and Fitzpatrick 2006, 6). However, the development of communities that practiced a specialized marine economy seems to have been more recent, taking place in the Early Holocene. The reasons for this are complex and involve access to and availability of coastlands, ameliorating climate and environment, and the intensification of both technology and population (Wickham-Jones 2014). From this time (known in Europe as the Mesolithic) onward, many communities around the world have occupied the seascape in a way that only really diminished within the twentieth century (and indeed still lingers in some places).

That there is a clear distinction between land and sea in many societies is not in doubt; yet, the boundary between land and sea, so obvious and important to the twenty-first century Westerner, is a recent one, which relies on our technological and geographical experiences. The comfortable primacy of dry land is a concept that drives much archaeological study; nevertheless, it can provide a biased view of human attitudes in the past. At the same time, archaeology does provide physical evidence, which offers valuable information relating to past human interaction with the sea. A brief account of two pertinent projects undertaken by the author—positing the discussion into the ever-shifting paradigm of archaeological analysis—will be the starting point for this chapter.

From Dry Land to Wetsuit: An Archaeological Career in the Twentieth and Twenty-First Centuries

For this chapter, the concept of "seascape" is defined as an area that in-cludes adjoining and interacting tracts (of variable size) of land and sea. In the 1980s, the island of Rùm archaeology project (Wickham-Jones 1990) was strictly bounded by the coastline of the roughly circular island of Rùm (figure 4.1). The coast provided a neat and convenient boundary that was rarely tested (or crossed), though there was one (unsuccessful) attempt to locate potentially submerged archaeology in the shallow wa-ters of Kinloch Bay directly below the main early prehistoric settlement site. The rest of the survey work and excavation took place on dry land, strictly within the confines of the island and, while the potential value of coastal and marine resources were considered, the significance of the sea and of other islands for the early inhabitants of Rùm was only discussed as background to their life on land.

Nevertheless, archaeological understanding of the importance of the surrounding seas for the prehistoric (and subsequent) settlers of the west coast of Scotland was developing, with the result that the next major field project (undertaken in collaboration with Karen Hardy, ICREA at the Departament de Prehistòria, Barcelona) was conceived specifically as a "seascape project." "Seascape" in this sense was used in opposition to landscape in order to emphasize that the coast was not seen to be a bound-ary, but rather as a fluid filter that has helped to define individual activities and approaches (in both past and present). The Scotland's First Settlers (SFS) project included archaeological survey and excavation around the Inner Sound (figure 4.2): on the Island of Skye, the Scottish Mainland (especially the Applecross Peninsula), and the islands in between (Hardy and Wickham-Jones 2009). Fieldwork was, nevertheless, specifically land-

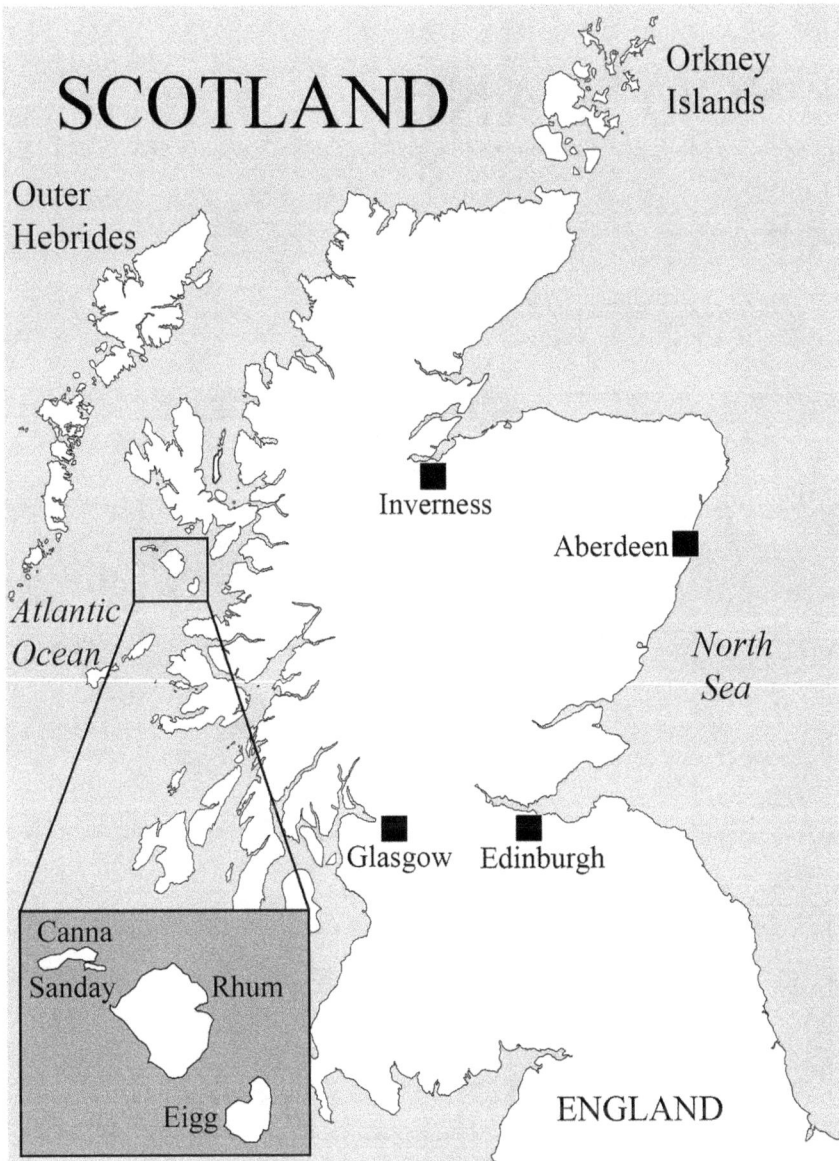

Figure 4.1. Map of Scotland: location of the Island of Rùm. Created by the author.

based; the sea was largely considered as a unifying medium for life on land, rather than as the potential setting for community activity in its own right. This project will form the basis for Case Study One. At the time of writing, this author's research (in collaboration with colleagues at various

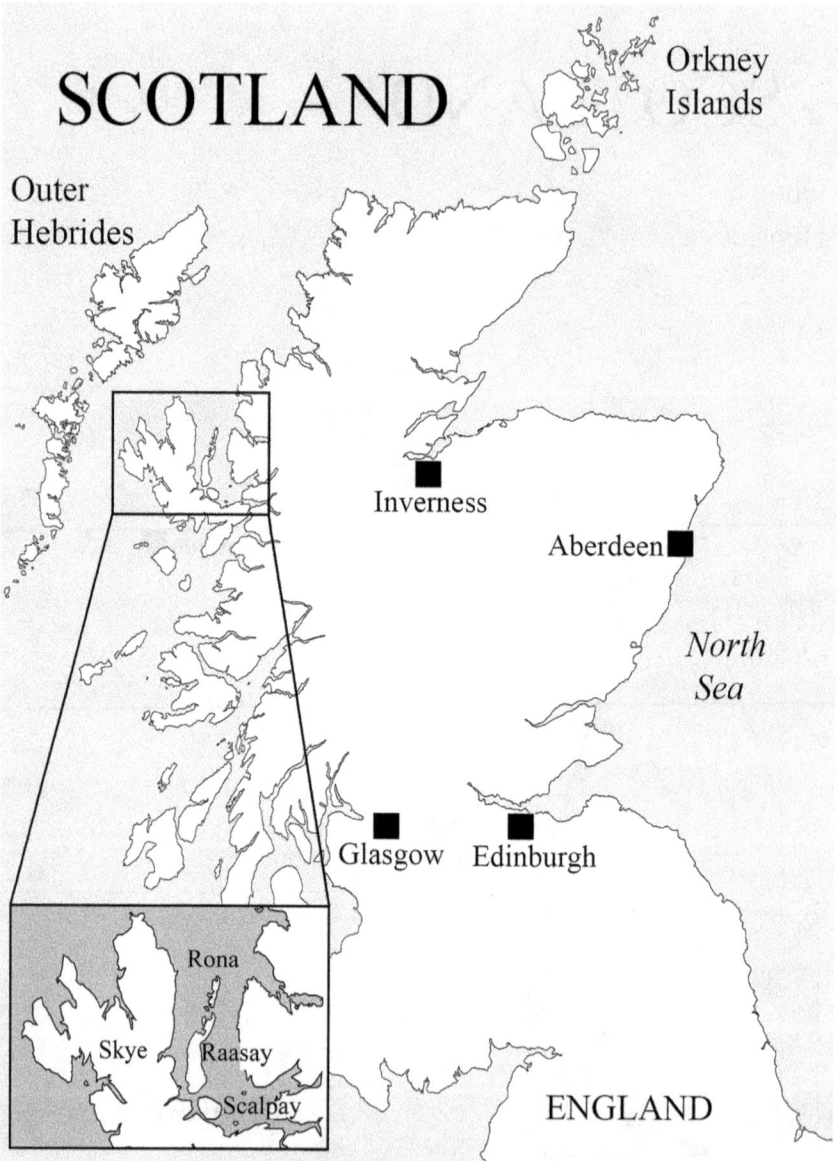

Figure 4.2. Map of Scotland: location of the island of Skye and the islands of the Inner Sound. Created by the author.

British universities) is examining the submerged landscape of Orkney (figure 4.3; Wickham-Jones et al. 2017).

Since the completion of SFS, the archaeological point of view has been further expanded. However, current sea level is an unstable filter through

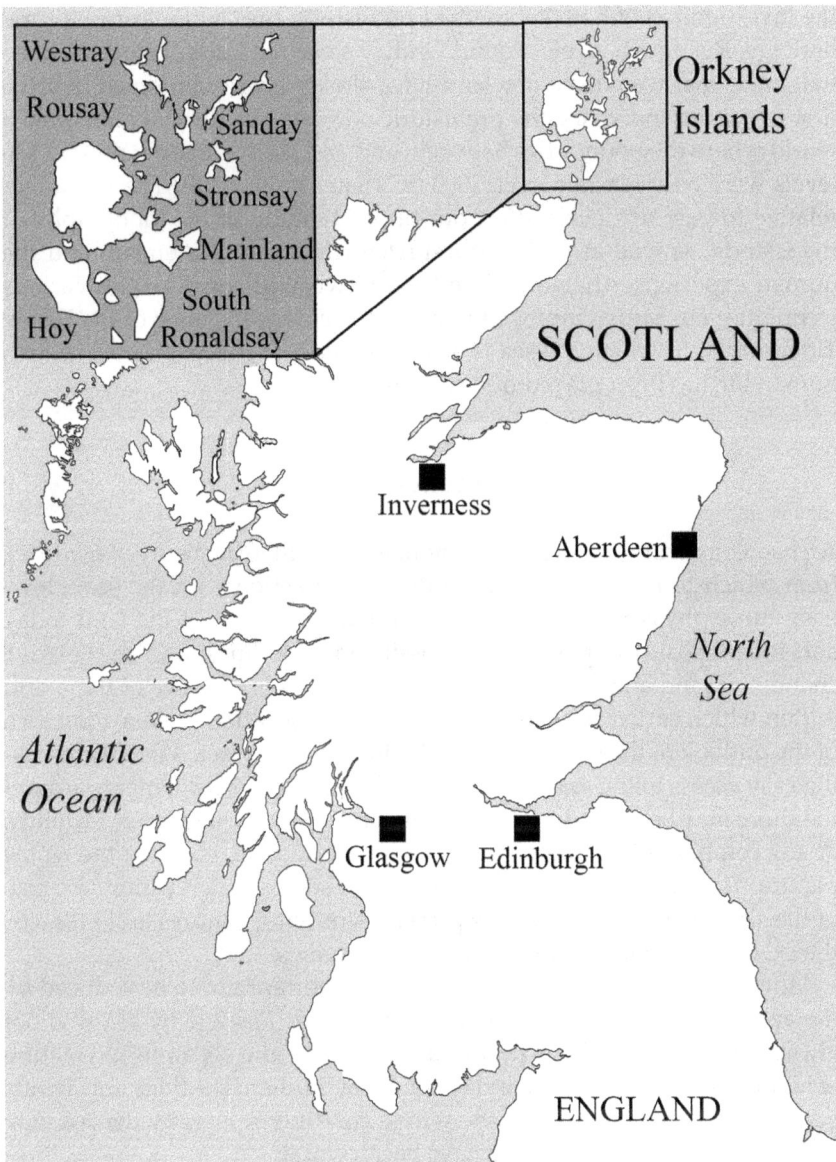

Figure 4.3. Map of Scotland: location of the archipelago of Orkney. Created by the author.

which to plan and interpret archaeological fieldwork. The Rising Tide is a multidisciplinary project that includes work on the changes in relative sea level around Orkney over the past ten thousand years, characterization of the submerged landscape, modeling of the prehistoric population, and the investigation of both submerged prehistoric sites and marine cultural heritage. Rising sea levels around Orkney since the Early Holocene mean that areas that were once dry land have slowly been submerged. For the first five thousand years, the prehistoric occupants of Orkney inhabited a world where the boundaries between land and sea were fluid; present sea levels were only reached circa 2000 BC (Bates et al. 2013). These changes relative to past sea levels affect our understanding of the topography of the islands, as well as their natural resources, early settlement, and the human experience thereon. Case Study Two will consider the various techniques currently employed in order to achieve the aims of the Rising Tide project, in which the sea is as much a part of the arena upon which human life has been played out as is the land.

The Evidence: Physical

Archaeology works from physical remains, and there is plenty of evidence from which to infer and analyze human interaction with the sea. However, these physical remains can be biased. The shape of the land today and in the past, the positions of fossilized shorelines, and the relative changes of land and sea can all add up to a complex picture of the world within which earlier settlement took place. Site location gives a good idea of the outlook of the communities who inhabited an area: Were they seeking easy access to the sea or flat land and fresh water? Settlements around the shore may be related to shelter, transport, resources, defense, visibility, or any combination of these, but it is also important to consider the whole picture. The physical remains of individual sites are also telling: the size of the site, the type of structures present, surviving features and artifacts, the existence of boundaries, or links to other sites.

However, with regard to location, it is important not to be seduced by the apparently obvious and deceptively simple. Passage by sea was not always possible, nor easy. The sea can both unite and separate; navigation is highly skilled and a simple day's journey in the right tides and winds could become a death trap in the wrong conditions. Sites by the sea may have been isolated, just as they have been central.

Another potentially biasing factor includes whether or not the evidence is simply a reflection of the preferred locations of archaeological work in the twenty-first century. Does the surviving archaeology merely reflect the loss of earlier coastal lands due to rising sea levels? It is also important to remember that the present landscape and environment is not always an accurate reflection of conditions in the past. While we are all familiar with the way in which pollen and other paleoenvironmental research demonstrate the different vegetation patterns of earlier times, other aspects of the landscape have changed as well. Tides and currents, for example, are not stable, though work to model paleo-tides and currents at times of lowered relative sea level is in its infancy (Uehara et al. 2006).

In archaeology, material culture is never complete; even so, it provides valuable clues relating to the activities that may have taken place. Even where full excavation is not possible, detailed prospection can establish an idea of the original extent and nature of a site. In addition to basic information relating to the functions and organization of a site, the analysis of material culture can probe deeper. For instance, the acquisition of raw materials from afar provides a strong indicator for mobility, including sea travel (e.g., Clarke and Griffiths 1990). Nonetheless, one may ask: Was transport direct, or were goods exchanged across a network? Exotic goods can suggest imports and interpersonal links. The survival of boats and their associated technology tends to be more common in the periods since prehistory, but there are examples from earlier times, such as the Bronze Age, as well (including Andersen 1986; Burov 1996; Mowat 1996). Recent work has highlighted the hitherto neglected possibility of prehistoric beachhead landing sites in northern Britain (Bradley et al. 2016).

In addition to the artifactual evidence, there is usually an environmental assemblage comprising anything from pollen and a few carbonized plant remains to a wide variety of microfossils, large quantities of shell, together with fish, bird, and animal bones, as well as beetle carapaces and snail shells. Environmental material provides an important context for any site, but it can also result from the deliberate accumulation of material, such as the waste material of a shell midden, or it may be an accidental import, as when plant remains are bought in on footwear. Nevertheless, it provides an important indicator of the human relationship with the environment. Fish bones may come from deep or offshore waters; shellfish may have been harvested in nearby shallow bays; crustaceans, sea mammals, and birds may have been exploited (Milner 2009a, 2009b; Parks and Barrett 2009).

The interplay of physical evidence provides information relating to the range of activities undertaken, and the size and types of environment across which people operated, but it does require interpretation. This evidence can be self-explanatory when it relates to recognizable technology. For example, boats (both wrecks and hulks) such as the Bronze Age log boat from Carpow (Strachan 2004) have already been mentioned, but they are accompanied by a wide suite of sites: beacons, slipways, harbors, yards, and mooring posts to mention but a few (figure 4.4).

Indeed, the archaeological evidence ranges in scale from monumental to humble (figure 4.5). Fishing, though largely transient in terms of today's

Figure 4.4. Landing place on the shore, Orphir, Orkney: the slip cleared for small boats is hardly noticeable except for the line of stones that demarcates it at either side. Photo by the author.

Figure 4.5. North Ronaldsay, Orkney: the simple mooring posts in the foreground are dwarfed by the tower of the late eighteenth-century Old Beacon in the background. Photo by the author.

technology, was once more physical as the many fish traps and weirs that dot the coastline attest. The sea could also be a source of energy: tidal mills, for example, once dotted the shoreline, but are rarely recognized today (though they provide a curiously satisfying class of monument in an age of marine renewables). It is also important to note that the human relationship with the sea was not always directly functional. It could also be tied to spiritual practice and ritual: prehistoric tombs were often located to be seen from the sea; or they were sited in the liminal zone between different environments such as at the junction of hill land and farm land, or along the shore; in Scotland, rock art may have been located as a marker along routeways including the sea (Bradley 1997); in highland Scotland in historic times, it was not unusual for coastal congregations to access their parish church by sea.

Another aspect of the human–sea relationship that has left a notable mark is that of war and defense. From the earliest times—when the coastal location of a site could offer both local defense and control (figure 4.6)—to recent times—when the material paraphernalia of distant wars litters our shores (figure 4.7)—many sites by the sea provide evidence of conflicts,

Figure 4.6. The Iron Age Broch tower at Mousa, Shetland: many brochs are sited along waterways that are still well used today. These towers served purposes that covered defense and display as well as control of passing trade and people. Photo by the author.

Figure 4.7. Martello Tower at Hackness, Hoy, Orkney: despite its strategic position and several potential military flashpoints, since it was built in 1813, the guns of this tower were never fired in anger. Photo by the author.

some of which were fought out well away from the site in question. Sites like these point to a much wider network of human activity than that evidenced by their immediate environs.

The Evidence: Intangible

In some cases, the physical evidence may be less direct in its meaning and it is important to remember that the human experience comprises more than physicality. Emotional reaction and other intangible forces can be as much a driver of human choice as material opportunity. Archaeological interpretation, therefore, needs to be made on as wide a basis as possible.

Images of boats, for example, provide evidence for the habitation of the sea. This may appear to be straightforward and obvious, but the location and abundance of a class of images that may best be described as graffiti suggests that the meaning can be deeper and more detailed than is at first apparent (Westerdahl 2013). While people may not be depicting the sea itself, there are many examples where they use material culture in order to express the relationship between themselves and the water, the prime motif being that of the boat: the medium on which human survival (and, in the case of a seafaring community, wealth) is dependent. Boats scratched onto the walls of a small chapel at Kilchattan on the Hebridean island of Luing may date to the Viking or Medieval period; but interestingly, they are likely to have been covered by plaster and thus not visible to those who frequented the chapel, suggesting that their presence had a deeper meaning, perhaps saying something about the importance of boats, fishing, and marine journeys to the community there (figure 4.8; Atkinson and Hale 2012). The depictions of European vessels on Easter Island Moai have been documented and interpreted as a commentary on the period of early contact with outsiders (Pollard, Paterson, and Welham 2010). In Orkney, two Martello towers contain twentieth-century graffiti, including abundant names of both naval vessels and fishing boats; local wisdom suggests that this records the desire of the crews to mark the existence of their craft. In addition, there are more formal depictions, including tombstones such as that of Alexander MacLeod, carved circa 1528 and bearing among other things a fine depiction of a local galley, or *birlinn*, at Rodel in the Outer Hebrides. This indicates considerable pride in the wealth and connections of the medieval family and highlights the central role of the sea.

In order to understand past interaction with the sea more fully, it is also necessary to work with other disciplines. The impact of changing

Figure 4.8. Pre-Reformation graffiti of a *birlinn* and fishing boats on a wall in the twelfth-century chapel of Kilchattan, Luing, Argyll. Photo by the author.

sea levels on our understanding of coastal topography and ecology has been noted above, but this is not just a straightforward matter of evolving coastlines. Eroding and emerging terrain was, in many cases, self-evident to the people who lived through the change from generation to generation. How, specifically, did the landscape change? How did people make sense of the evolving landscape around them? What part did this play in local story and myth, and in subsequent ethnoarchaeology? In some places, there is a suggestion that past coastal change may still be echoed in local oral tradition, as in Orkney, where there is a rich collection of stories that includes several depicting different coastal conditions and inundations (Muir 1995; Bates et al. 2013). Additionally, oral history recorded in Orkney depicts a wealth of interaction with the sea over the past century, providing interesting background context to the archaeology of recent decades (see Towsey 2002). Further back in time, there may be hints at a complex ethnoarchaeology that has since disappeared: the construction of the sophisticated monumental center of Neolithic Orkney along a fragile peninsula that was vulnerable to rising sea levels is one notable example (Wickham-Jones 2015). Just how did the architects of Neolithic Orkney respond to the influx of sea into the adjacent Loch of Stenness between 3500 and 1500 BC (Wickham-Jones et al. 2016)?

In addition to the spoken word, the written word is relevant. Local and national archives contain a wealth of information that sheds light on the human relationship with the sea, shaping the resulting archaeological record. Written accounts include merchants' records, commercial material, weather and lighthouse records, personal diaries, and travelers' accounts. Surprising detail can reward those with patience and time to browse old documents: the records in the Orkney Archive that relate to the Orkney Oyster Fishery of the early twentieth century provide information on stocking numbers and methods, as well as the complex reasons behind the eventual decline of the industry.

Other local traditions shed light on relationships with the sea that were once practiced across more widespread communities. For most people today, the sea is a uniform, fluid surface, very different to the variations of dry land. This is amply illustrated in the UK by the Ordinance Survey maps, which contrast the wealth of detail available for the land with the unbroken blue of the expanse of sea that surrounds it. Yet there are clues that the waters' surface, apparently featureless and indistinguishable to modern landlubbers, once held deeper meaning and importance for those who made their life upon the waves or lived along the shore. Firstly, the knowledge of place names at sea, though diminishing, should be evidence enough. Those who live close to the sea are often aware of a few remarkable places that merit naming: a difficult strait perhaps or the choppy waters of a tidal rip, though they may not pay heed to the full implication that the perceptual division between land and sea, so obvious from their window, may once have been less apparent. In the islands of the north of Scotland, good fishing grounds are known as "Fishing Hands." The fishing hands of Fair Isle have been recorded (Eunson 1961); they are all named and they demonstrate clearly the way in which the surface of the sea could be perceived as a solid landscape, an area to be divided, named, and used. Other locations at sea have been known to figure in ferry trans-shipping times, economic documents, and burial certificates. To sailors, they were well known. The nomenclature of the sea reflects our past engagement with it, though without the testimony of the written archive or oral history it is hard to make sense of the earlier naming of the waters.

The Evidence: New Lines

The current emergence of studies relating to submerged sites and landscapes is significant. In the UK, increasing awareness of the now-submerged Doggerland area, which once joined Britain to the continent (Gaffney, Thomson, and Fitch 2007), and of the peoples who once lived there (Fitch, Gaffney, and Thomson 2007) is not simply a product of developing technology. It is a carefully researched extension of existing archaeology. While the refinement of remote sensing techniques is undoubtedly important, its application to archaeology coincides with our increasing understanding of the ocean floor (and perhaps the need to explore new frontiers). Nevertheless, this work also comes at a time of cultural introspection; and for Britain, as a self-consciously island nation, the submergence of Doggerland between twelve- and eight-thousand years ago—in the millennia immediately after the last Ice Age (Gaffney, Fitch, and Smith 2009)—serves to develop Britain's sense of place in Europe.

There is also the environmental aspect of our understanding of Doggerland: it appeases Britain's conscience over the exploitation of the sea and rising sea-levels as well as providing an element of thrill through the introduction of information relating to the Storegga tsunami (Bondevik et al. 2003), which hit the northern coasts of the UK a little over eight thousand years ago with devastating effects on the coastal population. Indeed, some research suggests that the Storegga tsunami may have played an important role in the final submergence of the remains of Doggerland (Weninger et al. 2008). Doggerland can be comforting with its suggestion that we have seen rising sea levels and coastal change before, and yet it can be alarming with its reminder that Britain is not as safe a haven as we would like to think.

Doggerland is not a new discovery (Reid 1913), but recent work has served to bring it to life. Sophisticated data analysis, together with improved modeling techniques, has given shape to the land (Gaffney, Thomson, and Fitch 2007). Doggerland is no longer represented as a blank space, a uniform land bridge between Britain and Europe; rather, it now has topography: hills and valleys, rivers, lakes, and saltmarshes. The current vision of the early terrain highlights a landscape that must have been majestic and provoked a strong emotional reaction in those who knew it. Recent work in Orkney suggests that the earliest exploratory groups to penetrate the natural harbor of Scapa Flow were confronted by a narrow cliff-lined entrance that gave on to a wider body of water full of low-lying islands and shallow bays (figure 4.9). From a low-lying skin boat, it must have appeared awesome. Indeed, at the heart of our understanding of Doggerland lies a whole new style of interaction with the sea: that of the twenty-first-century archaeologist.

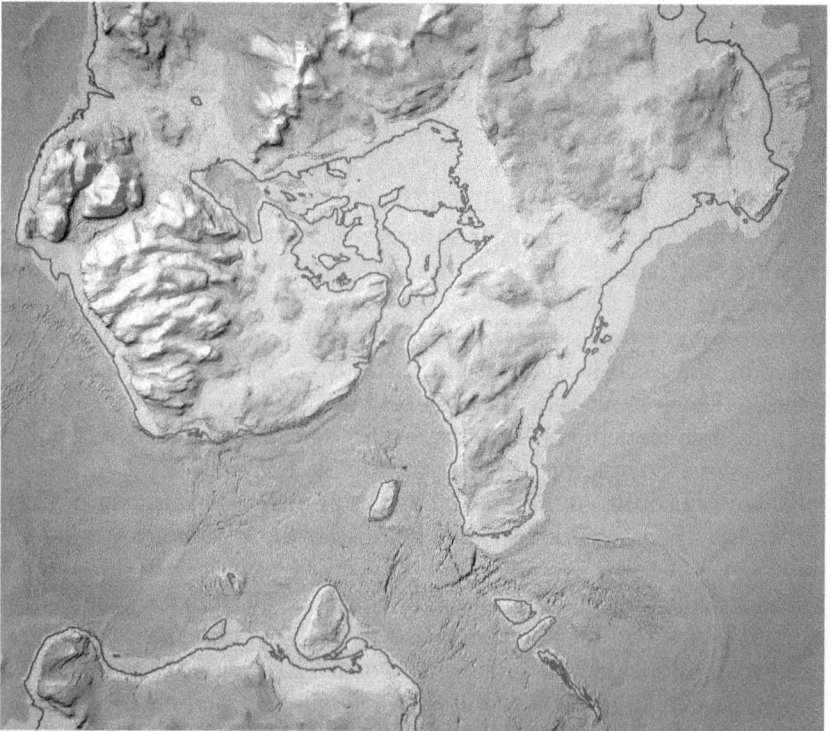

Figure 4.9. GIS (geographic information system) reconstruction of how the area of Scapa Flow may have appeared to the first exploratory groups to reach Orkney over ten thousand years ago. Lower relative sea levels mean that Scapa Flow becomes a land-locked bay of islands entered through narrow cliffs. It must have been a dramatic experience for those who arrived in small skin boats. Created by the author.

Case Study One: Scotland's First Settlers

The Scotland's First Settlers project took place between 1998 and 2004, and was fully published in 2009 (Hardy and Wickham-Jones 2009). It comprised archaeological survey and excavation around the waters and islands of northwest Scotland. At the heart of the project lay the stretch of water known as the Inner Sound, which lies between the island of Skye and the Scottish Mainland (see figure 4.2). The survey work covered all adjacent coastal areas, whatever the nature of the terrain. In practice, a variety of landscape was covered, from the flat grassy surfaces of raised beaches to rocky cliffs and outcrops, and steep, boggy boulder fields.

The overall aim of the project was to look for evidence of the earliest (Mesolithic) foragers, or settlers, of this part of western Scotland. The techniques employed included archaeological field survey and excavation (on land) as well as documentary work; the collation of local information; work on past environmental change including pollen, soil, and geophysical analysis; the analysis of changing sea levels; raw material analysis, specifically related to lithic and bone tools; and the detailed analysis of the environmental data such as the shells, fish bones, and land fauna from midden sites. Work targeted two specific manifestations of early prehistoric sites: the shell midden and the lithic scatter. In addition, the main focus was on sites within caves and rock shelters, although open-air sites were also recorded.

In common with much archaeological work, the results did not quite match anticipation, though the overall product was highly satisfactory. In some cases, there was less archaeological information than expected; this was perhaps most obvious with regard to early settlement: only twenty-one Mesolithic sites were recorded. In other cases, the end result exceeded expectation: 129 new sites were recorded; twenty-four historic sites. There were several examples where midden lay under rock fall; though inaccessible to the survey teams, this is likely closest in date to the immediate post-glacial period and may well explain the lack of visible early sites. At the same time, the focus on caves, rock shelters, and lithic scatters or open middens to the exclusion of upstanding built remains, such as shielings and abandoned farmsteads, means that the record of historic occupation is under-represented, and it is likely to be further biased by the fact that much of it will lie under current settlement.

Nevertheless, the field survey provided a richer record of change through time than foreseen and this enabled the analysis of a deeper pattern of use and meaning around the research area. The early-Prehistory focus on marine resources, including lithic material, was supplemented by the need for fertile land suitable for farming and hence the introduction of agriculture. Sporadic evidence of metalworking occurred in later prehistory; but in general, there were few sites from this period and evidence for the settlement of the area is poor until around AD 1,000, after which a variety of activities including bronze- and iron-working were recognized. In the early historic period, activity focused on settlement with some likely preaching and religious sites, while the later historic material included many smaller sites, suggesting the importance of local craftwork, with fishing once again rising in prominence. The use of specific caves and rock shelters in the later historic period suggests the need for concealment, perhaps related to the turbulent political history of the time. In recent times, the archaeological evidence continues to confirm the value of marine resources and the use of local caves and rock shelters as sheds and dens.

It is notable that the results of the Scotland's First Settlers project relate to life rather than death: there is no evidence for death and burial. In part, this is a gap in the evidence itself; there is as yet no clear information relating to Mesolithic burial patterns in Scotland. It is also a reflection of the survey techniques. Burial is only likely to have been picked up where it took place in a cave or rock shelter; and in the later periods, there were extant cemeteries, which were not recorded.

Down the millennia the varied topography of the Inner Sound has supported a growing population that made use of land, sea, and the different conditions afforded by the islands and coasts. The resources of the sea were clearly important, particularly in Prehistory and again in more recent centuries, and it is obvious that the sea has facilitated, rather than hindered, movement around the area. Nevertheless, the overriding assumption was made that the human populations of the area focused on dry land as their literal "terra firma." While this is likely to be true in recent historic periods, it is harder to prove for Prehistory, especially for the period before farming. It would be interesting to explore—with the benefit of hindsight—the possibility that the earliest settlers in the area were as at home at sea as they were on land. This, of course, may well have contributed to the apparent dearth of physical remains from this period.

Case Study Two: The Rising Tide

The work of the Rising Tide project is still ongoing, so the final results are not available (Bates et al. 2016 illustrates results specific to one small area; and Wickham-Jones et al. 2017 considers some more general questions of scale). Nevertheless, it is worthwhile examining the approach of this multidisciplinary geoscience project, which aims to investigate past sea level change, early settlement, and marine heritage in Orkney (see figure 4.3). The Rising Tide set out to eschew the boundary created by water level.

It has posited that the sea, whatever its height, provides as much of a backdrop for human activity as the land. At the same time, the land is not a fixed entity; the area of dry land at any one time is dependent upon relative sea level height and may change, as indeed it has in the past.

In order to provide a comprehensive view of past human activity and its changing context, various strands of research are combined. Sediment coring and microfossil analysis combine with an investigation of paleo-shoreline features to reconstruct the gradual rise of relative sea level since the start of the Holocene. Remote survey, comprising primarily sonar and seismic survey techniques, is employed to reconstruct the submerged landscape and locate potential archaeological sites. Diving is used to ground-truth the targets recorded by remote survey and to search for other archaeological material. In addition, intensive field walking is undertaken along the intertidal zone in order to record archaeological features, including material that runs into the sea. Environmental analysis, including the extraction of cores, takes place both below water and on land to provide a record of the changing environment through the millennia. Aerial photography provides information on potential submerged sites suitable for further survey or ground-truthing. Local information and the ethnoarchaeological record, including oral history and archive sources, have been examined for material relating to the changing environment and history of the area. Finally, the record is bought together using GIS in order to combine information from different sources, and modeling can be applied to push interpretation further.

The preliminary results are promising. Research indicates that relative sea levels approached their present heights around Orkney circa 2,000 BC. The submerged landscape includes both paleoenvironmental deposits—indicative, for example, of former lacustrine areas—and archaeological material. While the precise interpretation of remains has proved difficult due to the collapse of stone-built structures through time and inundation, detailed data collection and analysis that includes context as well as shape has helped to build up a record of the submerged landscape. Material suitable for environmental analysis has been found in all zones, including frequent deposits of intertidal peats, and there is a rich record of structural material on the foreshore, some of which extends under water. Finally, the ethnoarchaeological record has yielded a rich repository of material, including old stories, recent memories, and information from local archives.

Slowly, the project is building a picture of the land- and seascape history of Orkney, including in-depth insight into specific locations. GIS modeling of the past landscape highlights the considerable topographical change experienced by previous settlers of the archipelago (see figure 4.9). The Orkney that greeted the first exploratory groups some ten thousand years ago was a very different place to that of the early farmers some six thousand years ago, and both differ from today. To date, the upstanding cultural material in Orkney spans from the Neolithic past to recent wartime remains and relates to the changing nature of the human relationship with the sea down the millennia. This relationship includes activity on land (such as settlement and agriculture), on the foreshore (such as moorings and slipways), and on the water (such as aquaculture and fishing). The flexible history of past sea level change means that the evidence for any one of these activities may well be bound into a palimpsest with others. This palimpsest holds no distinction between land and sea: for instance, early settlement evidence may well lie below the evidence for more recent remains relating to aquaculture.

Definitions: The Past in Orkney

The case studies illustrate how the sea and its seascapes have meant different things to different people (or even the same people) through time. This fluidity is an important aspect of the study of the human relationship with the sea; there is no overarching set of rules. Orkney, for example, has been defined by its surrounding seas through the Ages. The seas around Orkney have served multiple purposes: shelter, food, marketplace, transport, work, and defense.

Throughout the human history of the area, Orkney has always been an island, but not always an archipelago. The sea provided the highway for the arrival of the earliest settlers, but local currents and shores have changed. Sea level rise over the early millennia may have provided a catalyst to the loss of homes on land (Bates et al. 2013), but it also provided the means for survival: in the Early Holocene, easy access to productive waters facilitated human survival and were supplemented by resource-rich and ever-changing coastal environments (see Schmitt et al. 2006; Statham, Skidmore, and Tranter 2008; and Hasegawa, Lewis, and Gangopadhyay 2009 for comparable examples further afield). The sea can be a homeland in the broadest possible sense; it was both provider and protector. Later, with the arrival of farming, life became more specialized. Farming communities eschewed the sea to focus on the land, though it was never completely ignored. Over the last thousand years, the use of the sea for food has fluctuated, from the specialized export of fish that took place in the Norse Period (Barrett 1997), and the intense activity of the herring fisheries in the late nineteenth and early twentieth centuries (Coull 1996; Rorke 2005), to the reduced trawler fleets of the early twenty-first century that are balanced by a thriving trade in luxury seafood.[1]

The seas around Orkney remain at the heart of transport systems to the present day. This reached its maximum expression during the Norse Period when the sea facilitated a network that stretched from Byzantium to Vinland. In the nineteenth century, a more complex and wider communication network operated to make the sea an axis of opportunity for those who lived on the islands. Whether they were looking for employment on a whaling boat, passage to the Arctic, or entry into the merchant navy, the ships entering the flourishing port of Stromness and other harbors of Orkney held the key to a wider world for those who lived in the archipelago.

For the early Norse inhabitants of the islands, Orkney provided an ideal base from which to venture out and raid the wealthy settlements of Scotland and Ireland. The Sagas relate that the use of the islands as a center for piracy had become a problem (Pálsson and Edwards 1978, section 4); there is also evidence of piracy existing around the islands in the seventeenth and eighteenth centuries (Thomson 2008, 264–75). At other times, aggression has been replaced by defense, most notably during the first half of the twentieth century when Scapa Flow provided an easily defended base for the Grand Fleet during World War I and for the Home Fleet in World War II. In both cases, the defense of the fleet extended beyond the immediate environs of the islands to play a crucial role in the protection of the UK as a whole. The strategic value of Orkney lies at the heart of the way in which it has been defined by the seas that surround it, and includes aggression and defense as well as support in wider networking activities.

Definitions: The Present in Orkney

Even today, there is no single definition of the role of the sea for the archipelago. Perceptions of Orkney depend not only on the individual but also on specific needs: any one individual may hold different views at different times. For some, Orkney is remote, a safe haven away from the trauma and stress of twenty-first-century metropolitan centers (Liptrot 2016). For others, it lies at the heart of things, a thriving center of culture and innovation that points the way forward for modern life.

For many, Orkney is defined as a center for the marine renewable energy industry. Strong currents, accessible waters, and a flourishing scientific and technological industry have combined to provide ideal conditions for the development and trial of marine energy generation, something that many see as the most viable economic future for the islands (figure 4.10). Others, while not so specialized, still define Orkney as a place where work is articulated through the seascape. Employment is provided by the

Figure 4.10. Renewable energy device at the Falls of Warness, Orkney. Photo by the author.

offshore oil industry, local ferries, fishing and shellfish industries, and recreation, scientific, and technical boats. Even in the twenty-first century, the sea still provides the workplace for many Orcadians. In addition, despite depleted stocks and diminishing returns, the harvest of the sea remains important. Local fish is prized, fish farms flourish, and the shellfish industry thrives. Twenty-first century Orkney is not self-sufficient, but the sea is an important element of the local larder.

Harvesting and work aside, the seascape also provides a place of leisure for all who live in or visit Orkney. Diving and sailing are enjoyed alongside traditional pastimes such as beach visits and recreational fishing. Many appreciate the beneficial value of the sea views and coastal walks, the sea being integral to relaxation. This is taken a step further by those for whom the seascape has become intimately bound with tourism. Orkney is a popular destination for the cruise industry. Some come simply to see the islands, themselves defined by the presence of the sea. Others come to participate in sport such as diving or bird watching; and many come to visit the remains of past populations—those who, like them, had their own relationship with the sea and lived by its shores. The sea characterizes even the basic act of reaching Orkney: there is water to be crossed before you arrive. Orkney, for visitors, is defined by her seas.

Finally, there is the place of education. Orkney is home to branches of two universities (Heriot Watt and the University of the Highlands and Islands), and there is a thriving research community, driven by the interest of the waters that surround the islands. Some focus on the natural world (marine species, plants, habitats), others on mechanics (wave energies, currents, and marine technology). A recent trend has seen the arrival of teams researching the human relationship with the sea, via past remains and present stories. For many of those who live here, intellectual life is defined by their relationship with the sea and the material it contains.

Moreover, this rich tapestry is reflected in local literature. There are collections of memories and stories old and new (Muir 1995, 1998; Schei and Moberg 2007). There are novels and picture books, handbooks and technical volumes (Towsey 2002; Arthur 2004; Brown 2014). Perhaps, more than anything, a visit to one of the local bookshops serves to illustrate the depth and range of the ways in which the relationship between people and the sea may be defined.

Conclusions

With such variety, the precise nature of the human relationship with the sea can be hard to pin down, especially in archaeological publications. Archaeologists search for clear-cut categories, taking the fragile and incomplete remains of the past and using them to extrapolate the predominant trends of life. But for those who study the physical articulations of people and the sea, such well-defined categories tend to be frustrated by the highly dynamic nature of the physical and mental spaces in which they work.

The human relationship with the sea is challenging. Archaeologically, it is important, at many levels, from the basic provision of a secure lifestyle to more subtle cognitive and emotional manifestations. The archipelago of Orkney, for example, is generally considered to be peripheral in the twenty-first century; and yet in the past, it was central, for example during the Norse control of the islands in the eleventh to thirteenth centuries. Our understanding of this relationship impacts both the physical interpretation that we do and our emotional perception of the societies concerned.

In order to continue the development of rich and sophisticated archaeological study, it is essential to develop a more nuanced mindset concerning the interplay of land and sea (figure 4.11). The rigid boundary of today was not shared by many peoples of the past (and indeed some of the present, as this volume illustrates). In fact, changes in sea level mean that the clear physicality of this boundary is a phantom. Ironically, the

Figure 4.11. Orkney, a place of water and land. The only true archaeology is seamless. Photo by the author.

current acceleration of relative sea level changes may induce a more "normal" viewpoint and thus, perhaps, assist a more balanced understanding. Archaeology has an important role to play in this; it provides the means to uncover the physical evidence together with the discipline to analyze it. The application of seamless archaeology is essential if we wish to understand fully the complexities of the world and its inhabitants.

Caroline Wickham-Jones is an archaeologist specializing in the earliest, post-glacial settlement of Scotland and the relationship between people and the land in which they live. She lives in the islands of Orkney where much of her research is based. Her current research focuses on the impacts of environmental change due to rising sea levels. She is an Honorary Research Fellow in the Department of Archaeology at the University of Aberdeen. Her publications include *The Landscape of Scotland, a Hidden History* (2009) and *Between the Wind and the Water: World Heritage Orkney* (2015).

Note

1. See Orkney Shellfish website, http://www.shellfish.co.uk/; Jollys of Orkney website, http://www.jollyfish.co.uk/.

References

Andersen, S. H. 1986. "Mesolithic Dug-Outs and Paddles from Tybrind Vig, Denmark." *Acta Archaeologica* 57: 87–106.

Arthur, E. 2004. *Bring Deeps*. London: Bloomsbury.

Atkinson, D., and A. Hale. 2012. "From Source to Sea: ScARF Marine and Maritime Panel Report." Scottish Archaeological Research Framework, Society of Antiquaries of Scotland.

Barrett, J. 1997. "Fish Trade in Norse Orkney and Caithness: A Zooarchaeological Approach." *Antiquity* 71: 616–38.

Bates, M., C. R. Bates, S. Dawson, S. D. Huws, N. Nayling, and C. R. Wickham-Jones. 2013. "A Multi-Disciplinary Approach to the Archaeological Investigation of a Bedrock Dominated Shallow Marine Landscape: An Example from the Bay of Firth, Orkney, UK." *International Journal of Nautical Archaeology* 42, no. 1: 24–43.

Bates, C. R., M. Bates, S. Dawson, S. D. Huws, J. E. Whittaker, and C. R. Wickham-Jones. 2016. "The Environmental Context of the Neolithic Monuments on the Brodgar Isthmus, Mainland, Orkney." *Journal of Archaeological Science: Reports* 7: 394–407.

Bondevik, S., J. Mangerud, S. Dawson, A. Dawson, and O. Lohne. 2003. "Record-breaking Height for 8000 Year Old Tsunami in the North Atlantic." *EOS: Transactions American Geophysical Union* 84, no. 31: 289–93.

Bradley, R. 1997. *Rock Art and the Prehistory of Atlantic Europe*. London: Routledge.

Bradley, R., A. Rogers, F. Sturt, and A. Watson. 2016. "Maritime Havens in Earlier Prehistoric Britain." *Proceedings of the Prehistoric Society* 82: 125–59.

Brown, G. M. 2014. *The Masked Fisherman and Other Stories*. London: Hachette.

Burov, G. M. 1996. "On Mesolithic Means of Water Transport in Northeastern Europe." *Mesolithic Miscellany* 17, no. 1: 5–15.

Clarke, A., and D. Griffiths. 1990. "The Use of Bloodstone as a Raw Material for Flaked Stone Tools in the West of Scotland." In *Rhum, Mesolithic and Later Sites at Kinloch, Excavations 1984–1986*. Edited by C. Wickham-Jones, 149–56. Edinburgh: Society of Antiquaries of Scotland (Monograph Number 7).

Coull, J. R. 1996. *The Sea Fisheries of Scotland: A Historical Geography*. Edinburgh: John Donald.

Erlandson, J. M., and S. M. Fitzpatrick. 2006. "Oceans, Islands, and Coasts: Current Perspectives on the Role of the Sea in Human Prehistory." *Journal of Island and Coastal Archaeology* 1, no. 1: 5–33.

Eunson, J. 1961. "The Fair Isles Fishing Marks." *Scottish Studies* 5: 181–98.

Fitch, S., V. Gaffney, and K. Thompson. 2007, "In Sight of Doggerland from Specu-lative Survey to Landscape Exploration." *Internet Archaeology* 22. Retrieved 16 May 2018 from https://www.researchgate.net/publication/255542619_In_sight_of_Doggerland_From_speculative_survey_to_Landscape_Exploration.

Gaffney, V., S. Fitch, and D. Smith. 2009. *Europe's Lost World*. York: Council for Brit-ish Archaeology, Research Report 160.

Gaffney, V., K. Thomson, and S. Fitch. 2007. *Mapping Doggerland*. Oxford: Archaeopress.

Hardy, K., and C. R. Wickham-Jones, eds. 2009. *Mesolithic and Later Sites Around the Inner Sound, Scotland: The Work of the Scotland's First Settlers Project 1998–2004*. Scottish Archaeological Internet Reports 31, The Society of Antiquaries of Scotland.

Hasegawa, D., M. R. Lewis, and A. Gangopadhyay. 2009. "How Islands Cause Phytoplankton to Bloom in their Wakes." *Geophysical Research Letters* 36, no. 20.

Liptrot, A. 2016. *The Outrun*. Edinburgh: Canongate Books.

Milner, N. 2009a. "Mesolithic Middens and Marine Molluscs, Procurement and Consumption of Shellfish at Sand." In *Mesolithic and Later Sites Around the Inner Sound, Scotland: The Work of the Scotland's First Settlers Project 1998–2004*. Edited by K. Hardy and C. R. Wickham-Jones, section 3.12. Scottish Archaeological Internet Reports 31, The Society of Antiquaries of Scotland.

———. 2009b. "Consumption of Crabs in the Mesolithic, Sidestepping the Evi-dence." In *Mesolithic and Later Sites Around the Inner Sound, Scotland: The Work of the Scotland's First Settlers Project 1998–2004*. Edited by K. Hardy and C. R. Wickham-Jones, section 3.13. Scottish Archaeological Internet Reports 31, The Society of Antiquaries of Scotland.

Mowat, R. J. C. 1996. *The Logboats of Scotland*. Oxford: Oxbow (Monograph 68).

Muir, T. 1995. *Orkney Folklore and Sea Legends*. Kirkwall: Orkney Press.

———. 1998. *The Mermaid Bride and Other Stories*. Kirkwall: The Orcadian Ltd.

Pálsson, H., and P. G. Edwards, trans. 1978. *Orkneyinga Saga: The History of the Earls of Orkney*. London: Penguin Books.

Parks, R., and J. Barrett. 2009. "The Zooarchaeology of Sand." In *Mesolithic and Later Sites Around the Inner Sound, Scotland: The Work of the Scotland's First Set-tlers Project 1998–2004*. Edited by K. Hardy and C. R. Wickham-Jones, section 3.11. Scottish Archaeological Internet Reports 31, The Society of Antiquaries of Scotland.

Pollard, J., A. Paterson, and K. Welham. 2010. "*Te Miro o'one*: The Archaeology of Contact on Rapa Nui (Easter Island)." *World Archaeology* 42, no. 4: 562–80.

Reid, C. 1913. *Submerged Forests*. Cambridge, UK: Cambridge University Press.

Rorke, M. 2005. "The Scottish Herring Trade 1470–1600." *Scottish Historical Review* 84, no. 2: 149–65.

Schmitt, L., S. Larsson, C. Schrum, I. Alekseeva, M. Tomczak, and K. Svedhage. 2006. "Why They Came: The Colonization of the Coast of Western Sweden and its Environmental Context at the End of the Last Glaciation." *Oxford Journal of Archaeology* 25, no. 1: 1–28.

Schei, L. K., and G. Moberg. 2007. *The Islands of Orkney*. Edinburgh: Colin Baxter Photography Ltd.

Statham, P. J., M. Skidmore, and M. Tranter. 2008. "Inputs of Glacially Derived Dissolved and Colloidal Iron to the Coastal Ocean and Implications for Primary Productivity." *Global Biogeochemical Cycles* 22, no. 3: GB3013.

Strachan, D. 2004. "A Late Bronze Age Logboat from the Tay Estuary at Carpow, Perth and Kinross." *Tayside and Fife Archaeological Journal* 10: 58–63.

Thomson, W. P. L. 2008. *The New History of Orkney*. Edinburgh: Birlinn.

Towsey, K. 2002. *Orkney and the Sea*. Kirkwall: Orkney Islands Council.

Uehara, K., J. D. Scourse, K. J. Horsburgh, K. Lambeck, and A. P. Purcell. 2006. "Tidal Evolution of the Northwest European Shelf Seas from the Last Glacial Maximum to the Present." *Journal of Geophysical Research* 111, no. C9: 1–15.

Weninger, B., R. Schulting, M. Bradtmöller, L. Clare, M. Collard, K. Edinborough, J. Hilpert, O. Jöris, M. Niekus, E. J. Rohling, and B. Wagner. 2008. "The Catastrophic Final Flooding of Doggerland by the Storegga Slide Tsunami." *Documenta Praehistorica* 35: 1–24.

Westerdahl, C. 2013. "Medieval Carved Ship Images Found in Nordic Churches: The Poor Man's Votive Ships?" *International Journal of Nautical Archaeology* 42, no. 2: 337–47.

Wickham-Jones, C. R. 1990. Rhum, Mesolithic and Later Sites at Kinloch, Excavations 1984–1986. Edinburgh: Society of Antiquaries of Scotland (Monograph Number 7).

———. 2014. "Prehistoric Hunter-gatherer Innovations: Coastal Adaptions." In *The Oxford Handbook of the Archaeology and Anthropology of Hunter-gatherers*. Edited by V. Cummings, P. Jordan, and M. Zvelebil, 694–711. Oxford: Oxford University Press.

———. 2015. *Between the Wind and the Water: World Heritage Orkney*. Oxford: Windgather Press. Revised Edition.

Wickham-Jones, C. R., M. Bates, C. R. Bates, S. Dawson, and E. Kavanagh. 2016. "People and Landscape at the Heart of Neolithic Orkney." *Archaeological Review from Cambridge* 31, no. 2: 26–47.

Wickham-Jones, C. R., R. Bates, S. Dawson, A. Dawson, and M. Bates. 2017. "The Changing Landscape of Prehistoric Orkney" In *Ecology of Early Settlement in Northern Europe: Conditions for Subsistence and Survival; The Early Settlement of Northern Europe*. Vol. 1. Edited by P. Persson, F. Riede, B. Skar, H. M. Breivik, and L. Jonsson, 393–413. Sheffield: Equinox Publishing.

CHAPTER 5

Moving Along

Wayfinding, Following, and Nonverbal Communication across the Frozen Seascape of East Greenland

Sophie Cäcilie Elixhauser

The inhabitants of the Tasiilaq region, East Greenland, inhabit a fjord system located just south of the Arctic Circle (figure 5.1). Most residents identify as Inuit, or Iivit in the East Greenlandic language, and they also call themselves Tunumeeq[1] (East Greenlanders). During two thirds of the year, frozen or partly frozen waters surround the Iivit. Ice is a constant topic of conversation and observation. Many Iivit, especially those from the villages, frequently travel on and through the ice in order to visit relatives and friends, the hospital in Tasiilaq, or to go fishing and hunting. To do so, they use a variety of means of transport, including the boat. Finding a safe way through the ice in a boat requires much skill and experience, especially during the changing of seasons when the ice can be unpredictable. Issues of orientation and "wayfinding" are recurrent themes of communication, not only among boat drivers and passengers but also with other East Greenlanders encountered along the way.

This chapter describes communication processes among the Iivit traveling the East Greenlandic seascape, and examines the importance of gestures, silences, and other modalities of nonverbal communication. Exploring Iivit practices of "wayfinding"—leading, following. and communicating about navigation through ice-covered waters—I will show that communication takes place not only through face-to-face encounters, but is often achieved by observing others (e.g., through peripheral vision) while moving alongside each other and adjusting ones' movements accordingly. This style of communication is connected to the strong value of personal autonomy among the Iivit, informing East Greenlanders' encounters with, and understandings of, the seascape.

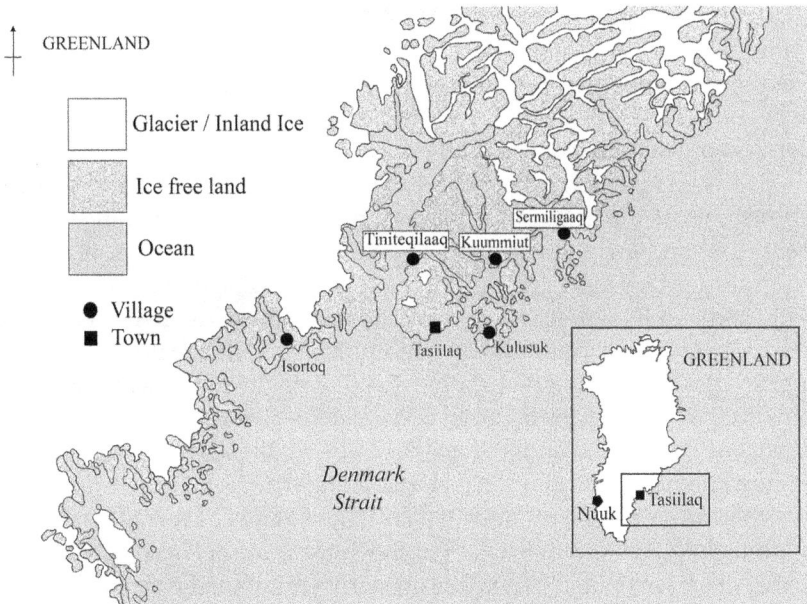

Figure 5.1. Map of the Ammassalik region in East Greenland. Created by the author.

To set the scene for the ethnographic analysis, I will begin by introducing the Tasiilaq region and its people. After defining my use of the term "communication," I will sketch some important characteristics of Iivit everyday communication and the importance of the value of personal autonomy. By means of ethnographic examples, I will then exemplify practices of orientation and the communication of travel routes. I will particularly highlight the ways orientation and wayfinding are taught to an apprentice "wayfinder," focusing on the role of gestures and silences. The process of navigating through difficult icy passages often involves the intimation of a leader, although this appointment is contingent upon the social and environmental context of the encounter. Finally, I will explain how communication and personhood between the Iivit and the ways Iivit move about in the East Greenlandic Sea and fjords are mutually constituted.

Traveling the Tasiilaq Region in East Greenland

The Greenlandic east coast is a sparsely populated region with around 4,000 inhabitants. Of these, 3,500 of them live in the fjord system of the Tasiilaq district. Due to a cold sea current bringing along huge amounts of ice from North Greenland and the North Pole region, which makes navigation for long periods of the year extremely hazardous and often impossible, the population of the east coast did not have sustained contact with southerners until the late nineteenth century. Contrary to West Greenland, where colonization began in the early eighteenth century, colonization in East Greenland started as recently as 1894.

The Tasiilaq region, which was formerly called the Ammassalik region, forms part of the grand municipality of Sermersooq, spanning areas in both East and West Greenland. It consists of the small town of Tasiilaq with around two thousand inhabitants, and five villages with between one hundred and five hundred people. The regional centre of Tasiilaq serves as a hub for people from the surrounding villages, due to its economic opportunities as well as its educational and social institutions. Research for this chapter took place between 2005 and 2008, and intermittently since then, both in Tasiilaq and in the village of Sermiligaaq, which lies around eighty kilometres north of Tasiilaq (figure 5.1).[2]

Apart from a small number of Danish and West Greenlandic residents, who mainly reside in Tasiilaq, the inhabitants of the Tasiilaq region are mostly East Greenlandic Iivit. The formerly seminomadic people live from wage labour for the public institutions and some local private companies, and to a lesser extent from fishing and hunting. Though nowadays, not all Iivit travel on a regular basis, as was the case in former times, being *en route* is still a highly appreciated condition and a theme people often engage with in everyday life. In the past, East Greenlanders' seminomadic lifestyle implied movements within the wider region during approximately half of the year. Travel was "not a transitional activity between one place and another, but a way of being," as Claudio Aporta (2004, 13) has written with regard to Canadian Inuit. Though the contemporary situation in East Greenland binds large parts of the population to the settlements during the week, traveling is still widely practiced and valued, though often confined to the evenings, weekends, or holidays (Elixhauser 2015). Exceptions in this regard are professional hunters and fishermen who spend much of their time *en route*, out on the sea.

Means of transport include motorboats, the supply ship that services the regional villages once a week during summer, helicopters, dog sleds, and snow scooters, depending on the season and travel purpose. This chapter focuses on boat journeys. Vessels are either small open craft with an outboard motor, or bigger cabin boats. Most boats are equipped with a VHF (Very High Frequency) radio system, and the more modern ones have a GPS (Global Positioning System) device. But before I take a closer look at my ethnographic material from East Greenland, I will briefly define my use of the term "communication."

Communication as a "Joint Movement" of Cotravelers

Following Finnegan, my view of communication is "not confined to linguistic or cognitive messages but also includes experiences, emotion and the *un*spoken" (Finnegan 2002, 5—original emphasis). Communication is a creative process that occurs in a particular moment of activity, as opposed to the transport of static data between minds. Much like Simonetti (this volume), my view of communication goes beyond the preoccupation with information transmittance between sender and receiver that—firmly anchored in Saussurean structuralism—has shaped much current discussion. Communication entails the manifold modes of persons interacting and living, both near and distant—through smells, sounds, touches, sights, gestures, embodied engagements, and material objects (Finnegan 2002, 5). Communication is a relational phenomenon that—apart from the communicating parties and other human actors—involves the broader contexts and settings of the communicative encounter. As Ingold has explained, "There is no 'reading' of words or gestures that is not part of the [person's] practical engagement with his or her environment" (1997, 249).

Movement is intrinsic to communication, and the movement of communication always involves the movement of people. For Iivit travelers, every conversation involves the communicant moving about, be it through a gesture, turning head, or averted gaze, or through more obvious mobile practices such as walking or traveling with a boat or other means of transport. Hence, communication can be regarded as a joint movement of various cotravelers, be they human or animals.[3] Communication implies following the movements of others and reacting and adjusting one's own movements. Communication, thus, does not happen in addition to peoples' activities of moving, but as an aspect of them (Ingold and Vergunst 2008).

Accordingly, the sea- and landscapes people pass through while being on the move are not merely settings for communicative encounters or a background to human action. They come into being while people *move along* them and, as van Dommelen describes, they have to be regarded as "the outcome of particular processes of engagement between people and the world in which they live" (1999, 278). These issues have been discussed in various contributions from landscape studies, archaeology, and environmental anthropology, questioning the sharp divide between the natural/material and human/social dimensions of landscape or environment (e.g., Hirsch and O'Hanlon 1995; Ingold 2000; Árnason et al. 2012). I will now introduce some widespread communicational modalities and the importance of the value of personal autonomy.

Everyday Communication and
the Value of Personal Autonomy

Iivit interpersonal relationships are based on a particular carefulness in approaching other people and beings. This is expressed through manifold implicit and subtle modalities in ways of speaking and in communicating without words such as through gestures, facial expressions, bodily postures, and silences. These communicational patterns point to the high value placed on personal autonomy in interpersonal encounters, which is expressed through the concept *nammeq*, a term frequently used by the Iivit to denote that something is up to a person (Elixhauser 2011). Contrary to a view of autonomy in the sense of complete individual freedom, however, this kind of autonomy expressed by *nammeq* is not tantamount to a complete independence from others. As similarly reported from various small-scale societies around the globe, many of which are subsumed under the label "hunter-gatherers," this autonomy is closely embedded in relationships with others (e.g., Myers 1986; Bird-David 1987). It refers to a kind of knowledge which is not given in advance, but which a person needs to find out for him- or herself, by being observant and attentive.

Most Iivit are very cautious both in speaking about another person's opinion or experience—unless they are able to reproduce an exact quote of this person—and in interfering with it by telling others what to do (cf. Briggs 1998 regarding Canadian Inuit). These practices seem to imply an inappropriate intrusion on another person's autonomy. Likewise, I have rarely experienced Iivit attributing any general statement to collective opinion or sentiment (except when referring to the past). As has been reported for other Inuit groups, I found among the Iivit a particular relevance of what another person has *said*. If a person says something, he or she has to take responsibility for the uttered words and for the possibility that others might pass them on. Moreover, I often had the impression that verbal utterances are perceived as particularly powerful in themselves, aside from the specific meanings of the words (see Holm 1911, 88). This is linked to the ideal of staying indifferent and not showing one's anger, as Fienup-Riordan explains with respect to the Yupiit in Alaska:

> Just as the mind is powerful so it is also vulnerable, and hasty words can do great damage. From this reticence to hasty verbalization it followed that value was placed on a person's ability to retain equilibrium in tense situations. (1986, 264)

Communication among the Iivit is characterized by manifold cues that indicate opinions and tensions, or point to confrontational situations. These may be of a verbal kind with respect to patterns of speech or of a nonverbal kind such as ways of looking, turning one's body, gestures, or silence. Silence, nevertheless, does not mean that communication is broken or interrupted. On the contrary, these quiet moments may themselves be a meaningful way of communicating that a person does not want to speak about a particular issue. Hence, silence has similar communicative functions to speech (Jaworski 1993). With regard to patterns of speech, humour and teasing provide an important means in East Greenland to address issues that cannot be formulated in a serious way. They offer room for interpretation and choice for the addressee to decide how he or she wants to understand a particular statement, and therefore have a face-saving function.

This carefulness not to intrude into another person's autonomy, via speech, gaze, and so on, is taught to children from a very early age. It is not very common in East Greenland to scold a child or to give explicit verbal instructions on how to behave. This was already observed by the first ethnographers in the region at the beginning of the twentieth century (Holm 1911, 63; Thalbitzer 1941, 600), and—with some exceptions—it is still more or less applicable to the contemporary situation, at least for what I have encountered in Sermiligaaq and for some families in Tasiilaq and other settlements in East Greenland. Being present at many adult interactions as silent but attentive observers, children learn through looking and paying attention. Initial phases of observation are followed by supervised participation and a period of unsupervised self-testing. Children are not prevented from making mistakes and are often left to resolve quarrels without the interference of their parents (cf. Briggs 1998 on Canadian Inuit).

Yet, children in East Greenland are not generally free in deciding about all kinds of issues that concern them, and they have to follow their parents' or other family members' expectations once in a while. For example, a parent might decide if a child may accompany him or her to visit somewhere, or if the child has to stay behind during boat trips or longer absences; parents tell their children to do their homework, to be in time for school, or to brush their teeth. These explicit rules and guidelines are often (yet not in all cases) related to one or another of the official regulations that structure modern life in a Greenlandic settlement. Nevertheless, parents do not always strictly enforce such regulations, and sometimes orders are formulated as suggestions instead of telling children what to do (cf. Robert-Lamblin 1986, 145). Children are confronted with a variety of expectations that are communicated in a rather implicit way. Some of these are introduced through stories, others through a certain way of joking and sarcasm, or "morality play" as Briggs (1998) has called it. Yet, all in all, a child, just as any other person, is perceived as an autonomous agent who is capable of making decisions by him- or herself (*nammeq*), and is often asked about his or her own opinion (Gessain 1969, 35–36; cf. Bodenhorn 1997; Briggs 2001). The learning processes of an apprentice, as for instance with regard to navigating ice-covered waters, are quite similar to the education of children, as I will explain below.

Communicating Travel Routes and Orientation

Most journeys along the East Greenlandic seascape are very social, and East Greenlanders often meet others during their trips. People converse while driving side-by-side, during brief halts in the fjords, or while taking breaks along the coastline or at a popular lookout. Apart from basics such as destination or starting point, topics of exchange often relate to the surrounding sea- and landscape, including the animals and people encountered, and issues of orientation and wayfinding.

Ingold writes that in hunting and gathering societies, "wayfinding depends upon the attunement of the traveler's movement in response to the movements, in his or her surroundings, of other people, animals, the wind, celestial bodies, and so on" (2000, 242). This statement closely parallels my experience in East Greenland. A number of ethnographers working in different northern areas have expressed their amazement about the Inuit ability to find the way during periods of bad visibility, and have drawn attention to the range of senses (beyond simply vision) involved in orientation (e.g., MacDonald 1998, 160–91). During bouts of boat travel with Iivit, not only did my companions rely heavily upon different senses and capacities to find their way through the sea—including touch, taste, hearing, smell, vision, and speech—different senses and parts of the body were also highly relevant in communicating wayfinding with fellow boat passengers and other people encountered along the way. In order to illustrate communication practices related to wayfinding and orientation, I will give a description of a trip I undertook in late spring 2007 (field diary, 3 June 2007):

> I was searching for a boat lift from Tasiilaq to Sermiligaaq. I had heard from a friend that a group of young men were about to commute back to the village. Gedion,[4] the owner of the boat, belongs to a family I know well, and had agreed that I may join the trip. In the small region, with dense social networks, word on who plans to travel where is quickly spread and it is not difficult to keep track of possibilities for boat rides.
>
> Down at Tasiilaq harbour, all of the passengers waited for Gedion and one of the other companions to arrive. The two came quite late, carrying the fuel they had bought at the gas station. Some other people were hanging out at the dock, and my companions discussed ice and weather conditions. Boat drivers and passengers just arriving at Tasiilaq harbour were questioned, as

well as other East Greenlanders in town who had recently returned from a boat trip. People were telling us that there is much ice in the fjords, which makes boat navigation difficult. On other occasions, when I had been arriving from a boat trip at Tasiilaq or Sermiligaaq harbour, I had been asked many times about routes and ice conditions: "Suminngaanii?" (Where are you coming from?) "Sigekkaaju?" (Is there much ice?)

We set off, accompanied by two other boats. The boat ride of eighty kilometers takes several hours, depending on the strength of the motor, the weight of the boat, and environmental conditions. Our boat carried a lot of weight, with seven people on board, luggage, and fuel. We were not sure if our attempt to reach Sermiligaaq would be successful that day. Shortly after embarking, we reached the trickiest part of our journey: the entrance to Kong Oscar Fjord outside of Tasiilaq. As expected, it was closed off by a large number of icebergs and ice floes. By chance, we encountered two other boats carrying East Greenlanders also trying to get through the ice. My companions and the people from the other boats exchanged some basic information on destinations and possible routes. Short questions and comments were shouted between the boats; yet more often, directions were pointed out using hand gestures. Gedion explained to me that the two other boats were trying to reach the villages of Kuummiut and Kulusuk.

At the outset, our group and the two other boats drove along the front of the icebergs searching the most accessible entrance point. Passage did not look promising and, without a word being said, the possibility of having to turn back toward Tasiilaq felt tangible. After having checked the ice situation, our group and one of the other motorboats landed at the foot of a small island of rocks in the middle of the fjord entrance. We tied up our vessels next to another empty boat and two brightly colored kayaks. The island is a common vantage point. Climbing up the rocks gave us a much better view of the situation of the fjord ice. We were overlooking the wider region, mountains and fjords scattered with icebergs—appearing like white dots—and on the other side the open sea. The men had binoculars with them to search out possible routes through the ice. On top of the island, we met some familiar faces from other settlements with whom my companions discussed the current ice situation. The small crowd was closely bunched as people looked around, sometimes pointing, gesticulating, or commenting. We also met four foreign kayak tourists who had hiked up the small, rocky island.

Climbing down again and getting back into the boat, we noticed that the third vessel heading for the neighboring village of Kulusuk had just found an entry point between the floating icebergs. The boat opened up a small trail within the frozen water for us to follow behind. Using the boat like an icebreaker, we navigated through the ice-covered waters. This was a challenge, since the passage cleared by the boats ahead of us quickly froze over. The boats ahead did not take the followers much into account. Most of the time, we followed the trail broken by the other boats; sometimes we found another, easier passageway. Though not explicitly traveling together, we were three boats traveling in a line, following the boat taking the lead, most of the time staying in viewing distance of each other. Our boat was the last one.

The ice was constantly moving, and within a very short time, the ice cover could change; passages were getting blocked or becoming more accessible.

Every now and again, one of my companions used a lance (hunting tool) to push aside some of the icebergs so that we could pass between them.

They did not talk much about what to do or which route to choose, apart from once in a while, gesticulating or dropping a few words. Everybody seemed to know, and actions and reactions occurred without discussion. At one point, we all climbed out of the boat onto the ice to lighten the boat's weight. The men pushed the boat over a large ice floe back into the open water. After an hour of straining work, all three boats had passed the difficult area and drove off in different directions. The rest of our journey went smoothly.

Boats commuting between the different settlements in the region often carry a substantial number of people. The groups usually consist of family members and relatives, and sometimes include other community members who needed a lift. Hunters and fishermen are habitually on tour either by themselves or in a team of two or three (or sometimes more). In contrast to groups of travelers commuting between different settlements, hunting and fishing parties are usually made up of regular hunting or fishing partners who are most often male relatives.

Encounters during hunting and fishing trips may result in shorter or longer halts, or just in noticing each other from a distance. Greenlandic hunters I have joined were never surprised to meet another boat appearing out of the fog or from behind an ice floe. My observations parallel those of Nooter, who writes, "It is evident that in many cases hunters paddling between the tall ice floes are well aware of the presence of other hunters some distance away" (1976, 41). Accordingly, when problems arise, such as the breakdown of an engine or difficulties in finding one's way through the ice, help can often be sought quite quickly. The awareness of the presence of others is created through various communicational means, such as direct encounters, recognizing others from a distance or from a lookout (sometimes using binoculars), or through communication via the VHF radio.

Travel routes and orientation are important topics of conversation, both among the passengers of a boat and with other East Greenlanders encountered on the way.[5] Briefly stopping during travel (or before starting a trip), the passengers exchange destinations and origin of travel, and sometimes routes and environmental conditions. Many of the encounters on the move take place along memorized trails and routes crisscrossing the wider region that the Iivit inhabit.[6] These routes form networks of exchange and communication. Having been used for a long time, they are regularly being talked about, for instance when telling the story of a recent trip or when telling stories from the olden days. They are thus part of the social and individual memory of the inhabitants (Elixhauser 2015; cf. Aporta 2004). People meet while moving along these trails, during activities at various hunting and fishing spots, or while taking a break at popular stopovers or lookouts.

The Importance of Gestures

When talking about directions, East Greenlanders, like most hunter-gatherers, do not refer to an independent set of variables such as the points on a compass. They use two sets of terms to assign directions, both of which are aligned to the surrounding environment. The first and most common set consists of four directions, indicated by the terms *sava, pua, qava,* and *ava,* plus varying suffixes, which are defined according to the direction of the coast stretching out to infinity. The second set of terms is only used within a restricted area, such as a fjord. Here, also, four directions are named—*kita, kangia, orqua, and kiala* (plus suffixes)—that refer to the mouth, the inward end, and the different sides of the fjord (Robbe 1977).

As my earlier example has illustrated, verbal indicators of directions and place-names used by communities of travel or other people encountered on tour are usually accompanied by gestures and facial expressions. Accordingly, pointing gestures and bodily movements play a prominent role in wayfinding and orientation, such as gestures showing directions or calling someone's attention to relevant environmental features or animals. Apart from arm movements, practices of showing the way also include movements with the head and facial expressions. These are not always accompanied by place-names or verbal indicators of direction. When pointing toward a specific direction, for example, other Iivit often knew where the person or group was heading, without verbal specification, as illustrated in the trip I have described. The passengers of the other boats we encountered did not name the villages to which they were heading, yet their gestures and arm movements were well understood by my companions who all had an intimate knowledge of the wider region.[7]

The Iivit also know manifold gestures signifying animals (as well as means of transport, people, environmental features, and so forth). One of the gestures frequently used is an upward, outstretched fist, signifying a seal (figure 5.2). Figure 5.3 shows the gesture indicating the presence of a narwhal. Communication about animals while traveling is often linked to an exchange of information on locations abundant with seals, fish, or other animals. For example, in the summer months, many families who have the capacity (i.e., access to a boat) leave by boat for fishing and hunting on the weekends, or berry picking in the autumn. Sometimes larger numbers of boats gather at one of the particular fishing locations in the fjords, exchanging some words (or gestures) on their catch and possible

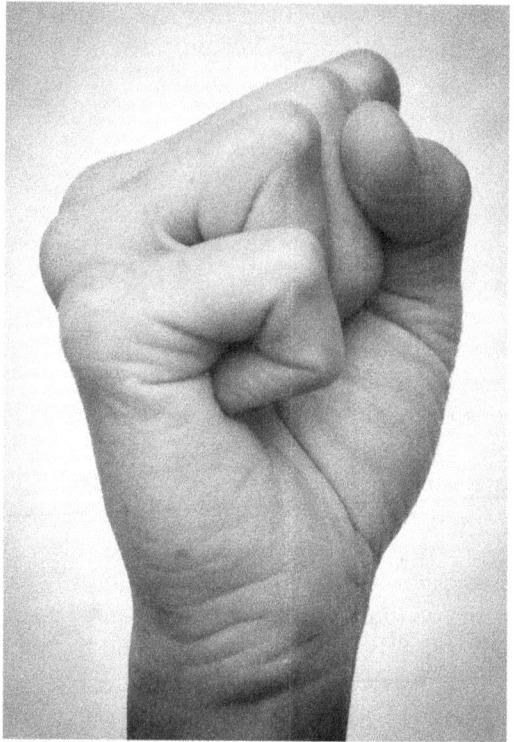

Figure 5.2. Gesture for a seal. Photo by the author.

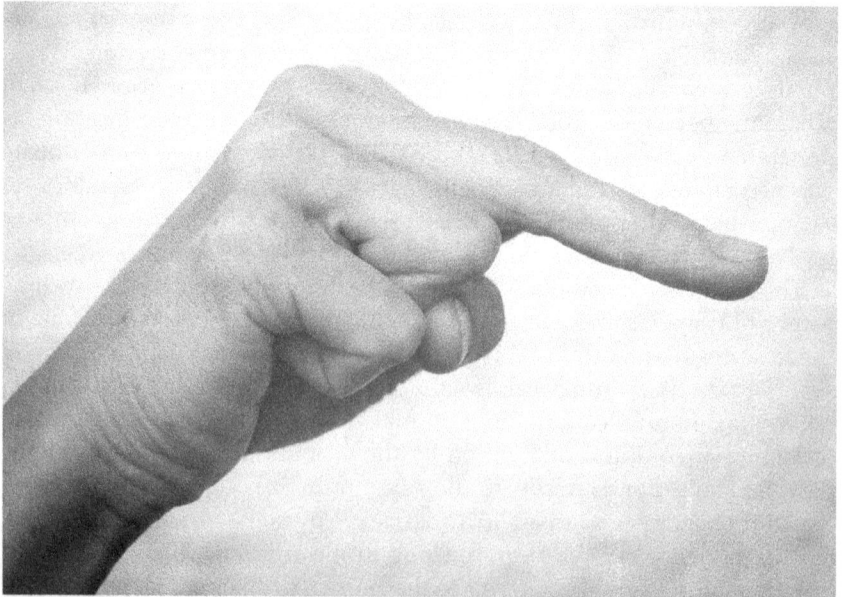

Figure 5.3. Gesture for a narwhal. Photo by the author.

fishing spots. Every settlement in the region has a few of these popular fishing (and hunting) spots nearby. The exact locations of these places often change, adapting to the movements of the fish. New locations are usually quickly communicated to other boats nearby, often using gestures. Talking about animals is thus closely connected to the wider topic of wayfinding and orientation.

Gestures or facial expressions used during processes of wayfinding, moreover, are often used to call attention to obstacles or other occurrences encountered along the way, such as weather events or the changing ice, the latter of which is particularly relevant during the change of the season (see the above story). Other obstacles may be passageways, physical barriers, other boats approaching, animals in the vicinity, and so on. When I asked about wayfinding procedures while traveling with East Greenlandic friends, the explanations given to me were often accompanied by movements of the arm, and sometimes comprised gestures alone. After having my attention drawn to something—an iceberg blocking the continuation of a particular travel route, for example—it was then my task to understand the significance and implication of what was being shown to me. Extensive verbal elaborations were rare and the gestures, in this context, were the appropriate and widely understood form of communication. This again resonates with a broad view of communication, as explained above, defined as "mutually recognized actions" (Finnegan 2002, 3).

The frequent use of gestures among the Iivit also implies that the persons communicating often look in the same direction, sharing the same visual field. This applies not only to communication among boat companions, but also to communication between passengers of different boats. As explained above, travelers are often aware of other boats in the vicinity, be they travel companions or just some other boat one has met on the way; communication between different boats is often characterized less by face-to-face confrontation than by driving *with* the other, side by side or after each other, and by attuning movements to the other, which implies attending to peripheral areas in the visual field.

Communicative Silences

When traveling with Iivit friends across the East Greenlandic fjords and sea, the general atmosphere often did not invite questioning or extensive talking. Being en route together habitually includes periods of silence. Indeed, sitting together not talking can be a very communicative moment (Jaworski 1993); and just like gestures, these silences are the communication in a given moment. They have to be seen as a sign of respect and of the welcoming acceptance of the other (be it people or environmental features). As Sejersen writes, this "active silence" correlates with a way of talking shared by many Greenlanders that has to be distinguished from the kind of silence that conveys a lack of interest (2002, 68). Moreover, Gessain has mentioned the importance of respecting the "silence of nature" in East Greenland, especially crucial for hunters (1969, 140). Accordingly, though during the initial months of my fieldwork I often felt like asking for explanations, I learned to be patient and to wait for the right moments to find out more. During situations of travel as well as in many other contexts of daily life, too much talking and questioning is often not appreciated by Iivit.

This was also most notably shown by Jean Briggs in her famous book *Never in Anger* (1970), in which she writes about her fieldwork with the Utkuhikhalingmiut Inuit (abbreviated "Utku" by Briggs) in Northern Canada. Similarly to my experiences in East Greenland, among the Utku anger is not usually directly expressed, but is disguised by various subtle and indirect ways of communication. Briggs gives the example of her being ostracized due to a misunderstanding—a situation in which she had lost her temper—explaining how she did not at first even notice. Only later did she come to realize that there had indeed been clear nonverbal signs of this ostracism, though she had not been familiar with them at this stage of her fieldwork.

Returning to the theme of wayfinding and travel, I want to refer to the work of Roepstorff, an anthropologist who has made similar observations regarding the importance of nonverbal communication while navigating ice-covered waters in west-central Greenland (2007, 192). He recounts a boat journey he took with a Greenlandic father and his son, during which the father nodded or pointed toward a specific direction that featured something to which the boy should pay attention. Without further explanation, the boy then had to find out for himself what was being pointed out take it into account in his planning of the way through the water. Through an "education of attention" (Gibson 1979; see also discussions in Ingold 2000; McCay, this volume; Howard, this volume), the boy learned to see specific phenomena that he formerly had not recognized or found important. Here we are dealing with a process of visual enskilment, of "learning to see" (Grasseni 2007; on enskilment in the Icelandic fisheries, see Pálsson 1994). Nuttall likewise remarks that becoming a hunter in Greenland is the result of "situated learning," or "learning in practice," to understand the territory, the movements and other habits of seals, and "the hunter's place in the wider social context" (2000, 42). These descriptions relate to some overall characteristics of children's education and processes of learning in East Greenland, as I have explained above. Children are often asked to pay attention to a procedure they are learning and to take the role of a silent, patient observer of the adults' way of doing things. Later on, they practice by themselves, often unsupervised.

Wayfinding and Leadership

Turning to a slightly different perspective, I will now relate the communication that accompanies wayfinding as it relates to leadership. During the spring or autumn, when the fjords are still partly ice-covered, boats meeting on their way that are heading in the same direction often try to keep together, especially around locations that are difficult to navigate. Usually, the most experienced boat driver goes ahead to form a path through the ice-covered waters, which the other boats then follow through (for example, see figure 5.4). This happened, for example, during the trip with Gedion and the other young men, in which our boat met up with two other boats at the entrance of Kong Oscar Fjord. For this difficult passage, one of the other boats took the lead, and our boat and another one followed behind. Usually, the selection of who goes first happens smoothly and in silence, depending on the skills, experience, and technical equipment of

Figure 5.4. Boats following each other in the Sermilik Fjord, June 2007. Photo by the author.

the people present. In the case of this trip, my companions in their early twenties had only little experience of wayfinding, while the driver of the boat going ahead had greater navigational skills. The three boats were of similar size and equipment. The leading boat managed to enter the icy passage first, and we others took the chance of an open trail to follow. Which boat would take the lead had not been much discussed; instead, it had depended upon the personal initiative of that specific boat driver at that moment.

I experienced the perspective of the leading boat, for instance, when joining an experienced hunter and boat driver called Nikolaj on a several-day-long hunting party in the Sermilik Fjord in spring 2005. The ice cover was still quite dense, but, as the first boat that year, Nikolaj had managed to navigate his way from Tasiilaq into the Sermilik Fjord. On the second day hunting out in the fjord, we had met several other local boats. Some of these meetings had been arranged via the VHF radio, but often we had met travelers or hunters by chance, along well-known routes or at locations favorable for hunting. In the evening, when trying to reach the nearby village of Tiilerilaaq, we experienced a challenging boat ride, which I described in my field diary as follows (field diary, 11 April 2005):

> We started heading back to Tiilerilaaq. The ice was getting denser and denser, and Nikolaj maneuvred the boat between the ice floes. Time passed, and I had long since lost my sense of orientation. The temperature had dropped significantly. Visibility was low and the ice was freezing quickly. Our boat acted like an icebreaker, and we needed its entire weight to break through the floes. After a while, some of the other boats we had met earlier in the day reappeared and silently fell into line behind our boat. Nikolaj stood behind the visor of his open motorboat, fully concentrating on the changing ice formations. His gaze focused on the surroundings, and at times, when driving over some layers of ice or breaking a path through the ice, his movements and the movements of the boat seemed to be one. The others followed our trail. Nikolaj did not look back at our followers, nor did he take them into account in any apparent way. Already, in previous days before, I had noticed the respect paid to him by the other hunters. Nikolaj is the expert when it comes to difficult navigational situations, as I was later told by other East Greenlanders.

In this incident of leading other boats through the ice, Nikolaj, thus, temporarily took over a leadership position. This example thus illustrates the existence of leadership of a temporary kind that is applicable only to specific situations, found today mostly with regard to subsistence and other so-called traditional activities. By and large, East Greenlandic society has long been characterized by a lack of formally organized leadership patterns, and the early ethnographic sources describe a situational leadership (Hughes 1958, 369). Petersen describes East Greenlandic society before the 1950s as "cemented not by leaders but by the reciprocity of free hunters" (1984, 639). Likewise, relying on fieldwork material from the beginning of the twentieth century, Thalbitzer writes that East Greenlandic society:

> knows neither lawfully recognized chiefs nor representative institutions. Only as an exception have there existed Eskimo chiefs, of whom tradition relates. It was a temporary occurrence, not hereditary condition. As a rule the hunter is head only of his own family, and has no authority over other families in the village. Custom, however, gives the oldest sealer in the village, or in the house, a certain degree of patriarchal authority, but this does not extend beyond the boundary of the village. (1941, 618)

With colonization, and the integration of Greenland into the Danish state, various formal leadership positions have developed in politics, the schools, and businesses and institutions. The contemporary situation reveals both situational as well as formal leaders, and the continuing importance of situational leadership in many arenas of everyday life influences the practices of formal leaders.

Nooter, a Dutch anthropologist who conducted fieldwork in Tiilerilaaq in the 1960s and 1970s, wrote a valuable book about leader- and headship and changing authority patterns in East Greenland (Nooter 1976). Nooter distinguishes the operation of situation-specific, shared-goal leadership from that of quasi-institutionalized, imposed-goal leadership. The East Greenlandic language does not offer an overall term for leader, akin for example to *umialik* in the Western Arctic (Alaska) (Nooter 1976, 7–9). The terms used among East Greenlanders are *piniartorssuaq* for a great hunter (as for example Nikolaj) and for situational leadership in tasks widely related to hunting such as wayfinding and boat navigation, and *naalanngaq*, which denotes a leader in an official institutionalized or formal context.

This distinction between situational and institutionalized leadership was also much in evidence during my fieldwork. The situation-specific, shared-goal leadership is the kind we find in situations of wayfinding as described above. Another example is breaking a trail for the first time in the year, which is always led by an experienced hunter (cf. Aporta's account of Canadian Inuit, 2004, 18). Also, the shamans (*angakkit*, pl.) were situational leaders in that their knowledge and practices in the shamanic realm were not tied to a position of influence and power in other areas of daily life. Sonne explains, "The men tacitly followed the advice of the oldest, most experienced hunter in matters of fishing and hunting, and the *angákoq* had no power except in religious matters bearing on the existence of the whole community" (1982, 24).

By and large, someone becomes a situational leader because he or she has demonstrated ability in some spheres, or has the best technical equipment, and many individuals have chosen to follow his or her suggestions (cf. Barth 1966, on the relationships among the boat crews of Norwegian fishing vessels). The leading position, which usually does not relate to other spheres of daily life, can easily be taken over by someone else the next time, if they perform better. Of course, some individuals are well known for particular skills and regularly take the lead. Yet, the choice to follow somebody is always voluntary, and giving orders or trying to convince others is not common, as I have found in a variety of contexts of daily life in East Greenland. Giving orders or telling somebody what to do is perceived as an improper intrusion into the other person's personal autonomy. Similarly, a situational leader usually proposes a way of doing that leaves the decision of whether to follow—or not to follow—to others. A skilled boat driver, for example, navigates the way he thinks is best, and other drivers decide themselves if they want to follow. I was often told "nammeq" ("that's up to you") when asking others about what to do. Accordingly, "power works by attraction rather than coercion," as Ingold has stated for hunting and gathering societies more broadly, and "the relationship between leader and follower is based not on domination but on trust," which is conditional upon respecting the followers' autonomy (Ingold 1999, 404; cf. Henriksen 1993, 44, for the case of the Naskapi in Canada).

Similar practices of leader- and followership are apparent in many realms of East Greenlandic society, from the education of children to various personal decisions made in daily life. In situations of wayfinding, such as the ones I have described as well as in other comparable situations, both positions are situational and voluntary: the leading position, based on initiative, skill, and equipment, and the position of the follower, who decides for each moment if he or she wants to follow or not. Here, we find many parallels with what has been observed in other formerly egalitarian and nonhierarchical societies such as the Tlicho Dene (Legat 2012) or the Naskapi (Henriksen 1993) in Canada.

Likewise, communication between the leading party and followers is characterized not so much by face-to-face exchanges, as by recognizing each other while driving *along*. The driver of the leading boat, just as his fellow passengers, usually does not look back, though he is aware of the presence of the boat(s) following, perceived through the corners of his eyes. Learning happens while following, through enskilment among followers who are not being explicitly instructed. Processes of learning, and of leading and following, are thus, to a large extent, based on peripheral vision, just as I have shown in my above descriptions of wayfinding. Communication in these situations entails noticing the movements of the other, be it an iceberg or a boat following, and mutually engaging with and reacting to the other's movements (see King 2007, on the mutually constitutive actions of Australian commercial shark boat skippers and their young deckhands).

Conclusions

Iivit practices of travel are based on a close engagement with other people, animals, and environmental features (as well as technological equipment used), and entail detailed observations of and learning processes about the sea and the surrounding environment. Building on the premise that communication may be understood as the movement of various cotravelers who attune their movements to each other, the orientation, wayfinding, and communication practices described in this chapter reveal some broader underlying social tenets among the Iivit.

My examples on learning and apprenticeship in relation to wayfinding and orientation have revealed the importance of gestures and silent observation, which, again, are often accompanied by peripheral vision, as people share the same visual field. Apprentices, such as my young boat companions, learn—and at the same time are taught—through following. This specific way of teaching, based on nonverbal communication, implies drawing attention to or suggesting something, be it through a pointing gesture or simply through driving ahead and proposing a path in the ice. Then the apprentice has to discover and test by him- or herself. In this way, learning to find the way through the East Greenlandic sea and fjords is closely connected to nonverbal modes of communication as well as particular practices of following and situational leadership. In other contexts of daily life, too, I have experienced that among the Iivit, imposing yourself on others and giving orders is not very popular. A situational leader proposes a way of doing, which leaves the decision of whether or not to follow to the discretion of any potential pupils. Iivit usually do not feel eligible to speak for another or to try to convince others of an opinion. This behaviour is perceived as an improper intrusion into the other person's personal autonomy.

People in East Greenland are careful in how they approach others, avoiding face-to-face encounters by moving side by side, allowing gestures and silences to speak for themselves, and not telling others what to do while leaving them to find out for themselves. This carefulness in communication that I observed in many contexts of daily life is not only related to the high value placed on personal autonomy, but also tells us something more fundamental about the notion of the person. A person in East Greenland is particularly vulnerable to the impacts of speech, gaze, and other face-to-face communicative modalities, which leads to various forms of circumlocution and indirectness. The ways the Iivit respect themselves and communicate among each other, as well as their movements through the East Greenlandic sea and fjords, are all based on similar premises and are mutually constituted.

Sophie Cäcilie Elixhauser is a social anthropologist affiliated with the University of Aberdeen and the University of Munich who currently manages an information and counseling center for binational families in Munich. She conducted long-term fieldwork in East Greenland for her PhD, focusing on human-environmental relations, perception and movement, interpersonal communication, and personhood among the Inuit. She further conducted fieldwork in the Italian Alps and the Philippines, dealing with perception of climate change, sustainability, and tourism/ travel. Publications include the book *Ethik in der angewandten Ethnologie: Eine Feldforschung zum Tourismus auf den Philippinen* (2006), and the journal article "Travelling the East Greenlandic Sea- and Landscape: Encounters, Places and Stories" (2015).

Notes

An earlier version of this chapter was presented at a panel on seascapes at the ASA conference 2009 in Bristol, and I thank the organizers Penny McCall Howard and Caroline Wickham-Jones and the participants for their insightful comments. I am most grateful to the people of East Greenland who have opened their homes to me, and who have taught me a whole lot. Many thanks go to Tim Ingold and Nancy Wachowich for their constant advice and help throughout the project. I acknowledge the University of Aberdeen's Sixth Century Studentship for funding my doctoral research project.

1. *Tunumeeq* stems from the noun *Tunu,* which is the Greenlandic name for East Greenland. *Tunu* literally means "backside" of the country.
2. I visited all the other settlements in East Greenland and several towns in West Greenland in the course of my research.
3. Studies of animal communication have shown that "communicative behaviour is not a human monopoly," and that many animals may express feelings and simple thoughts, which are reflected in the ways they communicate (Griffin 2001, xi).
4. Pseudonyms are used throughout this chapter.
5. Boat driving and orientation while traveling are men's tasks, and therefore women are involved to a much lesser extent in discussions and exchanges on wayfinding and travel routes. Women do join boat trips on a regular basis,

but they do not usually take up the driver's position, and rely on the men for orientation.

6. Routes used by local travelers exist for boat travel during the ice-free months of the year and for dog sled and, nowadays, snow scooter travel in the winter times.

7. In this context, people often additionally rely on indicators or clues such as what kind of people are traveling, the luggage on board, the time of day, and so on. For instance, assuming that a boat is heading for a settlement, given that there are so few settlements in the region, pointing in a certain direction is often easily understandable.

References

Aporta, C. 2004. "Routes, Trails and Tracks: Trail Breaking Among the Inuit of Igloolik." ["Les Routes, Sentiers et Traces Chez les Inuit d'Igloolik"]. *Études Inuit Studies* 28, no. 2: 9–38.

Árnason, A., N. Ellison, J. Vergunst, and A. Whitehouse, eds. 2012. *Landscapes Beyond Land: Routes, Aesthetics, Narratives.* New York: Berghahn.

Barth, F. 1966. *Models of Social Organization: Royal Anthropological Institute Occasional paper, 23.* London: Royal Anthropological Institute of Great Britain and Ireland.

Bird-David, N. 1987. "Single Persons and Social Cohesion in a Hunter-Gatherer Society." In *Dimensions of Social Life: Essays in Honor of David G. Mandelbaum.* Edited by D. G. Mandelbaum and P. Hockings, 151–65. Berlin: M. de Gruyter.

Bodenhorn, B. 1997. "'People Who Are Like Our Books:' Reading and Teaching on the North Slope of Alaska." *Arctic Anthropology* 34, no. 1: 117–34.

Briggs, J. L. 1970. *Never in Anger: Portrait of an Eskimo Family.* Cambridge, MA: Harvard University Press.

———. 1998. *Inuit Morality Play: The Emotional Education of a Three-year-old.* New Haven, CT: Yale University Press.

———. 2001. "'Qallunaat Run on Rails; Inuit Do What They Want To Do.' 'Autonomies' in Camp and Town." *Études Inuit Studies* 25, no. 1/2: 229–47.

Elixhauser, S. C. 2011. "Nammeq: Everyday Communication and Personal Autonomy in the Ammassalik Region, East Greenland." PhD dissertation. Aberdeen: University of Aberdeen.

———. 2015. "Travelling the East Greenlandic Sea- and Landscape: Encounters, Places and Stories." *Mobilities* 10, no. 4: 531–51.

Fienup-Riordan, A. 1986. "The Real People: The Concept of Personhood among the Yup'ik Eskimos of Western Alaska." *Études Inuit Studies* 10, no. 1/2: 261–70.

Finnegan, R. H. 2002. *Communicating: The Multiple Modes of Human Interconnection.* London: Routledge.

Gessain, R. 1969. *Ammasalik où la Civilisation Obligatoire.* Paris: Flammarion.

Gibson, J. J. 1979. *The Ecological Approach to Visual Perception.* London: Houghton Mifflin.

Grasseni, C., ed. 2007. *Skilled Visions: Between Apprenticeship and Standards*. EASA (European Association of Social Anthropologists) series. Oxford: Berghahn.

Griffin, D. R. 2001. *Animal Minds: Beyond Cognition to Consciousness*. Chicago: University of Chicago Press.

Henriksen, G. 1993. *Hunters in the Barrens: The Naskapi on the Edge of the White Man's World*. Newfoundland Social and Economic Studies No.12: Institute of Social and Economic Research, Memorial University of Newfoundland.

Hirsch, E., and M. O'Hanlan, eds. 1995. *The Anthropology of Landscape: Perspectives of Place and Space*. Oxford: Clarendon Press.

Holm, G. F. (1888) 1911. "Ethnological Sketch of the Angmagsalik Eskimo." In *The Ammassalik Eskimo: Contributions to the Ethnology of the East Greenland Natives*. Edited and Translated by W. Thalbitzer, 39, no. 1: 1–148. Copenhagen: Meddelelser om Grønland.

Hughes, C. C. 1958. "Anomie, the Ammassalik, and the Standardization of Error." *Southwestern Journal of Anthropology* 14, no. 4: 352–77.

Ingold, T. 1997. "Life Beyond the Edge of Nature? Or, the Mirage of Society." In *The Mark of the Social*. Edited by J. D. Greenwood, 231–52. Lanham, MD: Rowman and Littlefield Publishers.

———. 1999. "On the Social Relations of the Hunter-gatherer Band." In *The Cambridge Encyclopedia of Hunters and Gatherers*. Edited by R. Lee and R. H. Daly, 399–409. Cambridge, UK: Cambridge University Press.

———. 2000. *The Perception of the Environment: Essays in Livelihood, Dwelling and Skill*. London: Routledge.

Ingold, T., and J. L. Vergunst, eds. 2008. *Ways of Walking: Ethnography and Practice on Foot*. Aldershot: Ashgate.

Jaworski, A. 1993. *The Power of Silence: Social and Pragmatic Perspectives*. London: Sage Publications.

King, T. J. 2007. "Bad Habits and Prosthetic Performances: Negotiation of Individuality and Embodiment of Social Status in Australian Shark Fishing." *Journal of Anthropological Research* 63, no. 4: 537–60.

Legat, A. 2012. *Walking the Land, Feeding the Fire: Knowledge and Stewardship among the Tlicho Dene*. Tucson: University of Arizona Press.

MacDonald, J. 1998. *The Arctic Sky: Inuit Astronomy, Star Lore, and Legend*. Toronto: Royal Ontario Museum and Nunavut Research Institute.

Myers, F. R. 1986. *Pintupi Country, Pintupi Self: Sentiment, Place, and Politics among Western Desert Aborigines*. Washington, DC: Smithsonian Institution Press.

Nooter, G. 1976. *Leadership and Headship: Changing Authority Patterns in an East Greenland Hunting Community*. Leiden: E. J. Brill.

Nuttall, M. 2000. "Becoming a Hunter in Greenland." *Études Inuit Studies* 24, no. 2: 33–47.

Pálsson, G. 1994. "Enskilment at Sea." *Man* 29, no. 4: 901–25.

Petersen, R. 1984. "East Greenland before 1950." In *Handbook of North American Indians*. Edited by D. Damas, vol. 5 Arctic (Greenland), 622–39. Washington, DC: Smithsonian Institution.

Robbe, P. 1977. "Orientation et Repérage chez les Tileqilamiut (Côte est du Groenland)." *Études Inuit Studies* 1, no. 2: 73–83.

Robert-Lamblin, J. 1986. *Ammassalik, East Greenland: End or Persistence of an Isolate? Anthropological and Demographical Study on Change.* Meddelelser om Grønland, Man and Society 10. Copenhagen: Nyt Nordisk Forlag.

Roepstorff, A. 2007. "Navigating the Brainscape: When Knowing Becomes Seeing." In *Skilled Visions: Between Apprenticeship and Standards.* Edited by C. Grasseni, 191–206. Oxford: Berghahn.

Sejersen, F. 2002. *Local Knowledge, Sustainability and Visionscapes in Greenland.* Eskimology Scriptures 17. Copenhagen: Department of Eskimology, University of Copenhagen.

Sonne, B. 1982. "The Ideology and Practice of Blood Feuds in East and West Greenland." *Études Inuit Studies* 6, no. 2: 21–50.

Thalbitzer, W. 1941. *The Ammassalik Eskimo: Contributions to the Ethnology of the East Greenland Natives,* [in two parts, second part, second half-volume, number 4, "Social Customs and Mutual Aid."], 569–739. Copenhagen: Meddelelser om Grønland.

van Dommelen, P. 1999. "Exploring Everyday Places and Cosmologies." In *Archaeologies of Landscape: Contemporary Perspectives.* Edited by W. Ashmore and A. B. Knapp, 277–85. Oxford: Blackwell Publishers.

Victor, P.-É., and J. Robert-Lamblin. 1989. *La Civilisation du Phoque I: Jeux, Gestes et Techniques des Eskimo d'Ammassalik."* Paris: Éditions Raymond Chabaud & Armand Colin.

CHAPTER 6

Drawing Gestures

Body Movement in Perceiving and Communicating Submerged Landscapes

Cristián Simonetti

Underwater archaeology is an excellent discipline for studying perception and communication, especially given the particular characteristics and limitations of work around watery sites. Namely, this medium puts several constraints on visual perception and communication. Underwater archaeologists rely mainly on communication on the surface for sharing relevant knowledge. However, they manage to silently communicate while diving, in small groups, therefore never having a collective view of the whole landscape. This brings several questions about how underwater archaeologists are able to communicate knowledge about submerged landscapes.[1] Based on ethnographic work, and the analysis of audiovisual recordings of underwater archaeologists interacting on site, I show that experts rely, most of the time, on gestures to communicate about submerged landscapes. The material analyzed was collected in 2007 at a site located in the central coast of Chile, studying a well-established team of Chilean and Argentinean underwater archaeologists with whom I have been collaborating since 2006. This group has been together for more than ten years, working both in scientific and consultancy projects.

Challenging mainstream research on gesture, I argue that in representing the absent properties of the landscape, archaeologists do not convey mental, self-contained representations but open movements that are intrinsic to the constant flow of their thoughts. As they perceive the underwater landscape from a limited perspective, they draw it gesturally for others upon resurfacing. In turn, this gestural enactment emerges as an invitation that draws others' attention to the absent properties of the site. In this form of communication, knowledge is not static, but instead corresponds with the dynamic changes of a fluid environment. As such, understanding the relationship between perception and communication requires us to challenge the distinction between perception and imagination. Indeed, as archaeologists communicate knowledge of the submerged landscape, they also craft it, focusing on drawing its absent properties rather than providing a complete and accurate picture of it. It is likely that such skills have also been relevant to others, including the past inhabitants of the very sites that underwater archaeologists want to understand. Past and present, these individuals have made themselves at home along the fluid properties of the sea.

Drawing the Absent Landscape

Visibility underwater is tied to the amount of light that reaches a particular depth. Sunlight is progressively muted once it enters the water. As such, underwater sites are more obscure and, most of the time, hidden from a bird's eye view. In addition, in their interaction and communication under water, archaeologists are not able to use speech because divers depend on external breathing systems to survive. As a result, archaeologists have traditionally relied on gestures to communicate under water.

At the same time, SCUBA (self-contained underwater breathing apparatus), commonly used in archaeological diving, is limited by time constraints. Specifically, the external sources of air on which divers depend tend to be limited, and extended time underwater, at a certain depth, increases the risk of decompression illness. Due to the increase of pressure under water, divers tend to assimilate more nitrogen than in normal breathing. As a result, archaeologists have to stay at sea level for a considerable period of time after they have resurfaced to eliminate the nitrogen accumulated in their blood. For safety reasons, only after this period is completed are they in a condition to continue working under water. Therefore, a diver is able to carry out only a limited number of immersions per day. Moreover, when diving with equipment autonomous from the surface, archaeologists tend to dive in groups of at least two, so that in the case of an accident befalling one, others are present to assist.

These limitations have to be aligned with the requirements of a continuous process of interpretation conducted over time. Work must start somewhere, the divers knowing that each subsequent move is dependent on previous ones. As a result, depending on the site, the number of divers, and the limited technical resources, work tends to be organized in small groups of two or three that dive sequentially, one after the other. In order to accomplish the task, they need to coordinate the movements between each of the groups. Each resurfacing group needs to communicate what has been done, and together they have to agree on what to do next. Almost all the coordination relies on knowledge about a space they have not perceived together at the same time. Interestingly, they manage to discuss this information, which raises the questions of how archaeologists are able to share this knowledge and the conditions necessary for this to occur.

To accomplish their tasks, the team of underwater archaeologists with whom I work rely on hand drawings, using paper to convey spatial knowledge (see figure 6.1). However, in the initial stages of discussion, and in informal conversations, they tend to draw the submerged landscape by gesturing with their hands. This becomes critical when archaeologists have to locate the position and orientation of a site. Archaeologists depend on technologies like portable Global Positioning Systems (GPS), which help them calculate this position with respect to other landmarks in a coordinate system. Each time they start a new excavating season, they have to relocate it. This relocation may bring new challenges, namely the potential emergence of new objects and new sediment covering the site, both of which depend on the currents and the topography.

This may be illustrated with an example related to the drawing in figure 6.1, which shows the orientation of a submerged site of the Pleistocene. The Chilean-Argentinean team of underwater archaeologists found this site in 2005 in the course of a gas station development (see Carabias et al. 2014). The group needed to relocate the site, from which they had been absent for over two years. Specifically, the site needed to be located with respect to a platform already under construction. Together with governmental and private institutions, they worked on moving the platform so

Figure 6.1. Drawing on paper. Photo by the author.

that the site could be preserved and studied. After more than two years, in a highly dynamic underwater environment, most of the features previously visible had become barely recognizable, as new sediment had covered them almost completely.

At the outset of the relocation task, the position, extension, and orientation of a site is defined by a baseline, placed on the seabed across the site, which helps to organize the excavation and locate objects by triangulating them in two-dimensional space. Usually, a tape measure is used, both ends attached to the seabed, marked on the surface using buoys and positioned with a GPS. Divers manage to find their position by knowing the orientation of the baseline and by looking at the numbers on the tape. Deciding the orientation and extension of this baseline with regard to relevant landmarks is critical for the synchronization of tasks. The following sequence (figure 6.2) corresponds to an early interaction in which the archaeologist in charge, Diego (on the left), is working on the location and orientation of the baseline with two other members of the team, Damian (in the middle) and Renato (on the right).[2]

The previous day, Diego and Damian (who was new to the project) dived together to visually inspect the site. In the sequence, filmed the morning after this inspection, Diego, who has more experience, explains to Damian and Renato where the baseline will be placed in relation to a gas pipe, running perpendicular on the sea bed at the southwest end of the site (lines 1–5), and to the platform, visible on the surface, northeast from the site (lines 6–10). This platform is new to them. Two years ago, it was not there.

In trying to locate the site with respect to the pipe, Diego marks the beginning of the baseline close to it. And as he moves his hand to the left, he draws the orientation of the site in relation to the pipe (see line three). The line next to the hand represents the trajectory of the gesture, from right to left. Next, he specifies the location of the site with respect to the platform by pointing to the closest platform leg and drawing the potential orientation of the northeast end of the site with respect to this leg (see lines 6–8). Through hand gestures, Diego conveys spatial knowledge that would take an impossibly long time to communicate if he relied only on speech. Indeed, compared to speech, which unfolds in the form of sound, gestures are much better suited to conveying spatial knowledge synthetically (McNeill 1996, 2000; Kendon 1997). Although speech can locate and describe the shape of things in space, in the absence of gestures, speech is forced to increase the amount of description, often relying in abstract systems of measurement. Interestingly, Diego refers to the location and position of a site in a landscape full of features that are hidden from view, and where elements visible from the surface look very different under the water. For example, the legs of the platform have been placed with a pronounced in-

1. Diego	La orientación que tenía el sitio originalmente. *The original orientation of the site*	
2. Diego	desde:: tomado desde el extremo de la cañería. *from:: taken from one side of the pipe*	
3. Diego	es norte 270 grados practicamente. *is north 270 grades practically.*	
4. Renato	ya *ok* ((nod))	
5. Diego	Cachai. *Got it.*	
6. Diego	La plataforma está = *The platform is =*	
7. Diego	si tu te paras desde el extremo del sitio *if you stand from the end of the site*	
8. Diego	y avanzas hacia ese esa pata. *and you move to that that leg*	
9. Diego	en el fondo tiene norte 162. *essentially it has north 162.*	
10. Damian	((nods))	

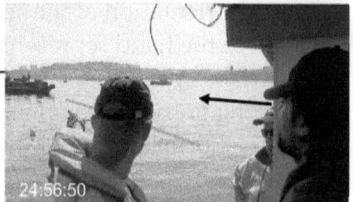

Figure 6.2. Drawing on the surface of the sea. Photos by the author.

clination to provide more stability to the station; depending on the depth, their position can vary significantly.

But archaeologists do not always have the absent site "in front" of them. When the surface of the sea that corresponds to the site is not visible, the archaeologists might draw it using their bodies along with objects at hand. The sequence in figure 6.3, capturing communication that occurred less

13. Diego   Antes de limpiar vamos a
               Before cleaning we are going to

14. Diego   desde el ⌐punt¬ donde realmente se tomó
               from the point where it was really taken

15. Diego   digamos la orientación y las medidas del sitio.
               lets say the orientation and the measures of the site.

16. Diego   Que coinciden además con el segundo punto.
               That corresponds with the second point.

17. Diego   El segundo ⌐punto¬ está en la ⌐orientación.¬
               The second point was in the orientation.

18. Diego   El segundo punto se ⌐marcó¬ acá.
               The second point was marked here.

19. Diego   El primero está ⌐pegado¬ a la cañería.
               The first one was next to the pipe.

20. Diego   Acá está la ⌐plataforma.¬
               Here is the platform.

Figure 6.3. Drawing with hand gestures and with a pencil. Photos by the author.

than a second after the sequence in figure 6.2, demonstrates this. At the end of the sequence in figure 6.2, the boat on which the archaeologists are standing starts turning to the left. Subsequently, the platform and the surface above the site are totally out of sight as the boat has turned 180 degrees. Even though Diego has managed to communicate the location of the site and started to move on to the instructions, he finds it necessary to start again. The initial drawing he set up on the surface of the sea with respect to visible and submerged landmarks is now gone. This tension is visible from line seventeen onward, when Diego talks about the points of the site that were positioned first and second. These two points correspond to the two ends of the site mentioned earlier (the first next to the pipe and the second next to the platform). What is evident from Diego's speech is that he begins locating the site again in line seventeen, this time not with respect to the surface of the sea and the platform but his hands and the pen he is holding. While talking about the two points of the site, Diego starts using his left hand to represent the baseline, while pointing with the pencil he is holding in his right hand (see the second picture). Suddenly, he switches the pencil from the left to the right hand, using it now as a baseline (see the third picture). Having drawn the baseline again, three iconic gestures help to index elements on this emerging drawing of the submerged landscape. The second point is marked using the right index finger (line eighteen). The first point, next to the pipe, is marked showing the location and orientation of the pipe (perpendicular to the baseline) by placing the right hand extended next to the left (line nineteen). Finally, the platform is located using the right hand with all the fingers pointing downward, resembling the legs of the platform (line twenty).

Drawing Attention beyond Hand Gestures

It is worth noting that as Diego draws the absent landscape, he also draws the attention of the other individuals in his vicinity. Damian and Renato seem to systematically follow the vanishing traces Diego leaves as his hands move. The sequence in figure 6.2 is an example of this: in line three, as Diego draws the orientation of the site, both Damian and Renato seem to follow the movement. This can be seen in how Damian moves his head and Renato leans forward, turning slightly to the right to have the moving hand in sight. Here, the arrows represent the direction in which Damian and Renato are gazing every time. Even though it is not entirely clear whether Renato is following the movement with his eyes—as the camera is almost behind him—he provides verbal and gestural confirmation in line four. The "ok" and the "nod" assure Diego that Renato is following his movements. Then, as Diego marks the leg, both Damian and Renato follow the movement (line six). And when Diego goes back to mark the northeast end of the site (line seven) and draw its orientation with respect to the leg (line 7–8), Renato again follows Diego's hand with his eyes. After that—and this unfortunately is not included in the transcript—Diego looks at Damian, who in line eight does not seem to follow the movement, and makes a call that is subsequently answered by Damian with a nod.

The idea of drawing gestures discussed here is an attempt to emphasize the ongoing crafting of knowledge, where the body allows our understanding of the world's properties to become visible by drawing along our listeners' lines of attention. This begets an understanding of perception and communication as processes unfold in movement. It also contains an understanding of the environments that humans and other organisms inhabit as constantly changing, in an endless flux of present and absent properties. In a watery medium like the sea, traces disappear as organisms carry out their daily actions. Like the lines archaeologists trace with their hands in the open air, the lines drawn by moving bodies, such as those of swimmers, divers, or boats, fade almost immediately as waves conduct and disturb the surface of the sea. In this, as in probably any other environment, knowledge depends necessarily on performance, as archaeologists rely not only in the information gathered via technologies and visual representations (such as maps, pictures, or drawings), but also on corporeal movement. In this, gestures are crucial for connecting experience, the knowledge generated in technologies and the particularities of each environment while moving forward between them. In this sense, knowledge of the sea is bound to those who corporeally enact it.

This view necessarily invites us to go beyond the emphasis on individual hand gestures of most gesture-centered approaches (see, e.g., McNeill 1985, 1996). In an attempt to establish the scientific study of gestures, these approaches have concentrated on acts of storytelling, but have neglected the entire body as it is socially and perceptually involved in its environment. For example, there has been a tendency to study iconicity in the absence of things by paying attention solely to the relationship between speech and gesture, which has resulted in an inaccurate division of gestures into iconic and deictic types (Goodwin 2002), a point returned to in the conclusion.

In addition, this approach has given rise to tentative questions about the role of gestures in cognition. This is visible, for example, in the widespread discussion on whether gestures serve thinking through lexical retrieval or communication (see Krauss 1998; Iverson and Goldin-Meadow 1998; Goldin-Meadow 1999; Iverson and Thelen 1999; Kita 2000). This discussion starts from the assumption that thinking is a process of the individual mind, which is constituted in isolation from perception and communication. Here, cognition is understood as a staged process in which information is internalized (input) perceptually and externalized (output) through communication. The following passage from Enfield, in his analysis of how Lao speakers use gestures for conveying kinship relationships, exemplifies this logic:

> In the absence of telepathy, communicating an idea to another person involves both internal (cognitive) and external (perceptive) processes. In order to make our inner states known, we must produce external representations which are perceptually available to others. . . . And in order to know the internal states of others we must perceptually access external representations and transform them into corresponding internal representations. (Enfield 2005, 65)

This tradition has a long history within cognitive science, which has influenced a big part of the contemporary work done in linguistic anthropology on spatial cognition (see Haviland 2000; Kita, Danziger, and Stolz 2001; Levinson 2003). This is related to the idea of "mental models" (see Johnson-Laird 1980; Collins and Gentner 1987). The idea of drawing gestures as proposed here aims to counter this staged understanding of the relationship between perception and communication. This view can be clarified with another example, namely Liddell's (1996) analysis of how an English speaker conveys spatial knowledge of a city from within his house by using objects. To do so, the speaker places a cap and a sugar bowl next to one another, and a knife in front of them. These objects stand respectively for a house, a building and a road. Suddenly, the person starts speaking about the top of the building. As he does so, he points not to the rim of the sugar bowl but significantly higher. Liddell concludes that the person is projecting a mental space, which is constituted by at least two other internal spaces. The first would correspond to the speaker's image of the real space while the second to the image of the arrangement of objects in front of him. The final projected space would be a blend of these two.

This is a perfect example of a staged understanding of perception and communication. In Liddell (2000), and the theory of conceptual blending that he relies on (Faucounnier and Turner 2002), the analogy between the sugar bowl, the gesture, and the actual building occurs inside the head as a step separate from perception and communication. It does not occur as the person moves the hand to point to the "top of the building." In this sense, the gesture does not draw the building. It only reflects the projected image previously stored inside. The analogical blending occurs at an internal disembodied and unemotionally conceptual level. However, this understanding gets complicated when examples like the one presented here are considered, where agents and the landscape are constantly moving. Imagine how many mental spaces the underwater archaeologists would need to hold in their minds when moving from the first drawing, on the surface of the sea, to the second drawing, using the pen, after the boat has turned 180 degrees. The idea of a blending of mental spaces is quite misleading.

This understanding of meaning belongs to a school of thought that goes back at least to the abstract understanding of signs, as defined by Saussure (1974). Its influences are still visible in most contemporary approaches that try to bridge the gap between language and perception. The very popular cognitive linguistic program lead by Lakoff and Johnson (1980, 1999), on which blending theory is based, is not the exception. As Cornejo (2007) has shown, even though this theory tries to close the gap between language and perception, the emphasis has been toward the conceptualization of embodiment rather than the embodiment of the language itself. Following Jackson (1983), things stand analogically for others not because they are integrated at an abstract mental level but because there is continuity between different experiential domains. Falling to the ground and falling morally are existentially connected because in both cases we feel our bodies going down. The understanding of gestures we are following here does not start from the idea that these are mere instantiations of what was previously inside. To the contrary, they constitute, along with speech, the very unfolding of our thoughts. Thinking is never separate from the trajectories of our body. Following the work of Farnell (1999) on gestures and body movement, it is necessary to move beyond discourses *about* and *of* the body and to consider instead how we talk *from* it. In the words of the philosopher Maxine Sheets-Johnstone, as we think in movement, "movement is not the medium by which thoughts emerge but rather, the thoughts themselves" (1981, 400).

From another point of view, namely a social understating of the mind, it seems impossible to imagine thoughts that do not serve a communicative purpose. Even in solitude, we sometimes find ourselves subtly following the trajectories of our thoughts, speaking and gesturing to an absent audience. At the same time, understanding others in interaction is not a passive reception of information but an active engagement, as participants attempt perceptually to follow a path together. Here, the individual mind is insufficient as a starting point for understanding the phenomena of language and communication (see Mead 1913; Wertsch 1985; Voloshinov 1986; Vygotsky 1986; Valsiner and Van der Veer 2000; Bakhtin 2006). Thinking is social and therefore communicative at its core, right from the start. As a result, it does not make sense to distinguish between thinking and communicational gestures, as each gesture is necessarily both at the same time.

It is important to mention that a large part of the discussion around the communicational versus the thinking role of gestures is based on an enquiry into why congenitally blind people gesture while giving directions. To start from a distinction between thinking gestures and communicational gestures is probably not the best answer. Here, it is necessary to take into account what Ingold describes as the interchangeability of our senses, a capacity to experience sensations traditionally regarded as visual with the other senses, which provides a sense of space for those who lack vision (2000, 243–88). Despite a reduced experience of space, blind people still inhabit a spatial world as they move around and feel their whereabouts in the company of others. Such experience can still be conveyed through corporeal movement. However, the particular way in which their knowledge of space is constituted is probably reflected in how they convey it gesturally. This coincides with Streeck's emphasis on how "gesture, as a media of human understanding, incorporates *haptic epistemology*, more than any other media of communication: it presents the world not as visible, but as handle-able" (2009, 150—original emphasis). This point may be missed by the studies that try to answer this presumption by quantifying and comparing the frequency with which blind and sighted people gesture in experimental conditions (see Iverson 1999). It is important to bear in mind that not only blind people gesture but also most sighted speakers in the absence of an interlocutor, which does not mean that, in those situations, our gesturing is purely at the service of our thinking. In the absence of an interlocutor, sighted speakers act as if they are facing an audience and not just exercising their thinking. Viewed from another angle, it could be argued that blind people's gesturing is a reflection of the fundamentally expressive character in which our thinking in movement is constituted from birth, beyond a conventionalized system of gestures.

From the perspective of corporeal movement in interaction, the social aspect of communication becomes evident. Other approaches to the study of gestures have started here. Particularly interesting is the work of Charles Goodwin (2000, 2002), and his notion of *coparticipation* that results from the mutual orientation that participants tend to accomplish in interaction. Regarding the notion of gestures we have been developing here, as archaeologists *draw* the absent, they necessarily *draw* their own attention and the attention of other participants in interaction. Their capacity to recreate analogically what is absent is developed as a collaborative perceptual accomplishment, a dance of coordinated movements that depends on the corporeal involvement of entire persons in interaction. From the perspective of this involvement, it is ultimately not clear where one intervention starts and the others end.[3] Participation occurs in-between. This is what Alfred Schütz described as the "mutual tuning-in relationship by which the 'I' and the 'Thou' are experienced by both participants as a 'We' in *vivid presence*" (1951, 79—emphasis added). This temporal horizon is fundamental for communication through meaningful movement. It allows for corporeal movements to become vanishing traces, which can be followed by others. In Sheets-Johnstone's words, "thinking in movement is a perpetual *dissolution and dilatation*, even a mutability, of here-now movements and a moving present" (1981, 405—emphasis added). In interaction, such dissolution and dilatation become social.

Here, the discussion follows a particular tradition of knowledge that has systematically challenged staged thinking by emphasizing the primacy of movement in the study of perception and communication (see, e.g., Merleau-Ponty 1962; Bergson 1970; Gibson 1979; Sheets-Johnstone 1999; Ingold 2000).[4] Just like the environment that the underwater archaeologists encounter, perception and communication are open rather than closed. Archaeologists have to take the *risk* of moving in order to start. And as in any form of movement where the particularities of the trajectory cannot be specified in advance, the analogical gesture has to be enacted. Neither perception nor communication is the result of the production of still images, both in the individual minds and in the immediate visual field shared by participants in interaction. In this sense, gesturing interactively in the absence of things resembles more the crafting skills of drawing than the generation of a sequence of cinematographic images.[5]

This later emphasis in the study of gestures is not surprising given how this scientific study, in "modern times," emerged after the development of audio-visual technology. Even though gestures allow synthetic conveying of more than one thing at a time, speakers still have to start somewhere in order to finish somewhere else. Both speech and gestures are temporal in that sense. If that is the case, then the in-between, the continuity and the openness of the movement that makes a gestural shape possible, becomes crucial.

It is worth noting that Streeck, in his remarkable book *Gesturecraft: The Manu-facture of Meaning* (2009), develops an argument similar to the one included here, which I came across after I conceived, wrote, and presented this article at the European Association of Social Anthropologists (EASA) in 2009, the conference from which this edited volume emerged. Fundamentally, I agree with the central argument in Streeck's book, particularly the invitation to move from resemblance to the manufacture of knowledge through ecologies of gestures, which justifies their being understood as a craft practice (similar to an action such as drawing or sculpting). However, Streeck seems to hold both sides of the argument. This is particularly evident in his use of Liddell's work to understand depiction through gestures. On the one hand, analogy occurs through gesture as a process in the making. At the same time, however, it becomes a process of the individual mind that results from the blending of mental spaces inside the head (Streeck 2009, 124). By staying close to the notion of embodiment in cognitive linguistics, he seems to hold both a continuous (though open-ended) and a punctuated understanding of the relation between knowledge and corporeal movement. But as Sheets-Johnstone (1999, 359) has suggested, the notion of embodiment has introduced a packaged understanding of the self that hardly accounts for the primacy of movement in its constitution.

This dual understanding can also be seen in how Streeck defines gestures. Even though he rightly denounces the portrayal of communication "as being *about*, but not *of* this world" (Streeck 2009, 83—original emphasis), for him gestures, as cultural entities, "are the product of invention and tradition, not biology" (Streeck 2009, 37). But how can gestures and culture be both embodied and of this world while at the same time be something not biological? In Streeck's view, to craft, fabricate, manufacture, or construct the world through gestures is to move the body, while, at the same time, taking distance from it, in an action that distinguishes us from all other species. This capacity, which is at the core of the modern constitution, is what ultimately justifies a staged understanding of what lies beneath our skin as well as outside it (Latour 1993; Ingold 2000). In this view, the world humans inhabit seems suddenly to be just a world of meaning divorced from material transformations. But this emerges in tension with the experience of a fluid environment, in which we can only "know as we go" (Ingold 2000, 229; see also Suchman 1987). In this, knowledge is neither discovered nor constructed but grows in the unfolding of a continuous process of becoming (see also Simonetti 2015).

Conclusions: Perception, Communication, and Imagination

Returning to the sequences discussed earlier, it is important to note that the gestural drawings produced by Diego in figures 6.2–6.3 fundamentally differ. The drawing in figure 6.3 is less dependent on the actual landscape it represents. Its orientation changes as the boat moves. Conversely, the drawing in figure 6.2 is bound to a specific surface right above the site; otherwise, any surface would serve as a replacement. As such, it seems that the level of iconicity becomes more salient in the drawing in figure 6.3 due to the lack of corresponding landmarks. Gestures and objects seem to stand more clearly for other things by resembling their form. However, from the understanding of gestures being proposed, the relationship between iconicity and pointing in both drawings emerges in a continuum.

Ultimately, it does not make sense to classify gestures into different types, such as iconic and pointing. Following Goodwin (2002), deixis and iconicity should be understood as different aspects of a gesture. In the sequences described above, pointing gestures index not only visible landmarks but also invisible ones. Moreover, in marking these points, the gestures seem to draw the trajectories divers would take if they were to follow these points. Similarly, gestures that are traditionally considered iconic also mark or point to the position of a particular object in space. Both pointing and iconicity follow a narrative that takes interacting participants on a journey through the different trajectories of a site, which coincides with how divers move underwater. Both perception and communication unfold along the lines of movement (see Ingold 2007a).

Embracing this perspective involves recognizing that ultimately all forms of gestures craft our experience of the world. They do not just point to a ready-made external reality independent of the observer. Rather, they outline the points of view and the trajectories of those who move in a particular environment. In this sense, perception and imagination go together, as it is ultimately impossible to draw the line that divides them. In the example cited above, as archaeologists interact on the subject matter of the submerged site, they recreate its properties using gestures that highlight more than what is visible. In fact, they mostly draw in its invisible properties. This craft is probably not limited to the specialized activity of planning an underwater excavation. Perhaps it is only more salient in this context. On land, archaeologists also find themselves interacting with sites full of absences, which they have to imagine in the midst of a perceptual exchange with the changing properties of soils, which vary constantly due to the weather (Simonetti 2015).

Following Murphy (2004) in his study of design practices among architects, it seems that imagination is not a process of the mind but a capacity that emerges in the collaborative encounters of participants as they rely on speech, gesture, and drawing. In this, a special kind of imagination is involved, what Murphy calls *"perceiving in the hypothetical mode"* (2004, 269—original emphasis). Even though this invitation to take imagination out of the brain coincides with the argument developed here, the particular context analyzed above necessarily pushes us to move beyond the context of design practices, where the tendency is to imagine (or design) things, into a "hypothetical mode," before materials are encountered (or constructed) (Ingold 2007b). In a working environment where the presence and absence of things fully intermingles, perception and imagination become part of a single process of finding your way in a constantly changing world. This blurs any absolute division between the processes so that imagination not only comes to the fore, but also allows an encounter with a fluid environment to take place. In other words, the "as if" becomes part of what "is."[6] This very merging is embodied by this chapter. By telling a story, using arguments, lines, and arrows on pictures, I have traced paths that enable the reader to follow an approach to perception and communication of submerged landscapes. I hope that in doing so, I have drawn the reader's attention to how we inhabit together, through movement, a fluid world.

Cristián Simonetti is an Assistant Professor at the Programa de Antropología, Instituto de Sociología, Pontificia Universidad Católica de Chile, and an Honorary Research Fellow at the Department of Anthropology, University of Aberdeen. He has worked on perception and communication, processes of enskilment and the use of technology. His research concentrates especially on how movement and bodily gestures relate to concepts of time in archaeology and other related disciplines, which is the topic of his monograph, *Sentient Conceptualizations: Feeling and Thinking in the Scientific Understanding of Time* (2017).

Notes

I wish to thank Diego, Renato, and Damian from ÁRKA: Maritime Archaeology for allowing me to follow their work. An earlier version of this chapter was presented in 2009 at a panel on seascape, organized by Penny McCall Howard and Caroline Wickham-Jones for the European Association of Social Anthropologists (EASA) in Bristol. I would like to thank those who organized the panel, as well as those who attended it and provided feedback. I am also grateful to Tim Ingold and Laura Siragusa for their very insightful comments and suggestions on earlier versions of this chapter.

 1. "Submerged landscape" is a standard term used in underwater archaeology to convey a particular section of the seabed where terrestrial animals used to walk and crawl freely, which is now, due to sea level rise, covered in water.
 2. The conventions developed by Jefferson for conversation analysis are followed here with some modifications (see Atkinson and Heritage 1984). Translations are included in italics. Text in parentheses provides contextual descriptions that are not visible in the pictures (e.g., nods). Still frames showing gestural strokes are connected to words using lines and boxes. Lines and arrows within pictures illustrate trajectories of hand movements and gazing directions respectively. Please note that the emphasis of the transcript is on gestures, so many aspects of speech that are relevant for conveying knowledge about absent landscapes have been intentionally left aside.
 3. Here, I am distancing myself from the emphasis on sequences in interaction on which conversational analysis rests. According to Ochs (2006), looking at

a transcript as a form of theory reveals that the analysis follows the model of adult communication, understood as the product of discrete sequential interventions, which is insufficient for understanding other communicational modalities and communication in general.

4. It is important to mention the existence of an unresolved tension between perception and imagination in some of these authors, particularly Gibson. It seems that in developing a theory of *direct perception,* imagination was left aside.

5. Ultimately, this presents a challenge to the staged objectivity of the scientific method from which Western science has traditionally aimed to progress. If knowledge results from collaborative interaction through open-ended gestures, then the trajectories of scientific exploration cannot be fully define before the world is encountered.

6. It is worth noting how the archaeologists in the examples above, just like Murphy's (2004) architects, are not using the conditional to talk about hypothetical scenarios but are mostly engaged in discussing present and absent things using past, present, and future tenses. Imagination primarily emerges in action.

References

Atkinson, J. M., and J. Heritage, eds. 1984. "Jeffersons's Transcript Conventions." In *Structures of Social Action: Studies in Conversation Analysis,* ix–xvi. Cambridge, UK: Cambridge University Press.

Bakhtin, M. 2006. "The Problem of Speech Genres." In *The Discourse Reader.* Edited by A. Jaworski and N. Coupland, 98–107. Oxon: Routledge.

Bergson, H. 1970. "The Cinematographic View of Becoming." In *Xenon Paradoxes.* Edited by W. C. Salmon, 59–66. Indianapolis: Bobbs-Merrill.

Carabias, D., I. Cartajena, R. Simonetti, P. López, C. Morales, G. Vargas, and C. Ortega. 2014. "Submerged Paleolandscapes: Site GNL Quintero 1 (GNLQ1) and the First Evidences from the Pacific Coast of South America." In *Prehistoric Archaeology on the Continental Shelf.* Edited by A. Evans, A. Flatman, and N. Flemming, 131–49. New York: Springer.

Collins, A., and D. Gentner. 1987. "How People Construct Mental Models." In *Cultural Models in Language and Thought.* Edited by N. Quinn and D. Holland, 243–65. Cambridge, UK: Cambridge University Press.

Cornejo, C. 2007. "Conceptualizing Metaphors Versus Embodying the Language." *Culture and Psychology* 13, no. 4: 533–46.

Enfield, N. J. 2005. "The Body as a Cognitive Artifact in Kinship Representations: Hand Gesture Diagrams by Speakers of Lao." *Current Anthropology* 46, no. 1: 51–78.

Farnell, B. 1999. "Moving Selves, Acting Bodies." *Annual Review of Anthropology* 28: 341–73.

Fauconnier, G., and M. Turner. 2002. *The Way We Think.* New York: Basic Books.

Gibson, J. J. 1979. *The Ecological Approach to Visual Perception.* London: Houghton Mifflin.

Goldin-Meadow, S. 1999. "The Role of Gestures in Communicating and Thinking." *Trends in Cognitive Science* 3, no. 11: 419–29.

Goodwin, C. 2000. "Action and Embodiment within Situated Human Interaction." *Journal of Pragmatics* 32, no. 10: 1489–522.

———. 2002. "Pointing as a Situated Practice." In *Pointing: Where Language, Culture and Cognition Meet*. Edited by S. Kita, 217–41. Mahwah, NJ: Erlbaum.

Haviland, J. 2000. "Pointing, Gesture Space and Mental Maps." In *Language and Gestures*. Edited by D. McNeill, 13–46. Cambridge, UK: Cambridge University Press.

Ingold, T. 2000. *The Perception of the Environment: Essays in Livelihood, Dwelling and Skill*. London: Routledge.

———. 2007a. *Lines: A Brief History*. London: Routledge.

———. 2007b. "Materials Against Materiality." *Archaeological Dialogues* 14, no. 1: 1–16.

Iverson, J. M. 1999. "How to get to the Cafeteria: Gestures and Speech in Blind and Sighted Children's Spatial Descriptions." *Developmental Psychology* 35, no. 4: 1132–42.

Iverson, J. M., and S. Goldin-Meadow. 1998. "Why People Gesture when they Speak." *Nature* 396, no. 6708: 228.

Iverson, J. M., and E. Thelen. 1999. "Hand, Mouth and Brain: The Dynamic Emergence of Speech and Gestures." *Journal of Consciousness Studies* 6, no. 11/12: 19–40.

Jackson, M. 1983. "Knowledge of the Body." *Man* 18, no. 2: 327–45.

Johnson-Laird, P. N. 1980. "Mental Models in Cognitive Sciences." *Cognitive Science* 4: 71–115.

Kita, S. 2000. "How Representational Gestures Help Speaking." In *Language and Gestures*. Edited by D. McNeill, 162–85. Cambridge, UK: Cambridge University Press.

Kita, S., E. Danziger, and A. C. Stolz. 2001. "Cultural Specificity of Spatial Schemas, as Manifested in Spontaneous Gestures." In *Spatial Schemas and Abstract Thought*. Edited by M. Gattis, 115–46. Cambridge, MA: MIT Press.

Kendon, A. 1997. "Gestures." *Annual Review of Anthropology* 26: 109–28.

Krauss, R. M. 1998. "Why do we Gesture when we Speak?" *Current Directions in Psychological Science* 7, no. 2: 54–60.

Lakoff, G., and M. Johnson. 1980. *Metaphors we Live By*. Chicago: University of Chicago Press.

———. 1999. *Philosophy in the Flesh: The Embodied Mind and its Challenge to Western Thought*. New York: Basic Books.

Latour, B. 1993. *We Have Never Been Modern*. Cambridge, MA: Harvard University Press.

Levinson, S. C. 2003. *Space in Language and Cognition: Explorations in Cognitive Diversity*. Cambridge, UK: Cambridge University Press.

Liddell, S. K. 1996. "Spatial Representations in Discourse: Comparing Spoken and Signed Language." *Lingua* 98, no. 1–3: 145–67.

———. 2000. "Blended Spaces and Deixis in Sign Language Discourse." In *Language and Gesture*. Edited by D. McNeill, 331–57. Cambridge, UK: Cambridge University Press.

McNeill, D. 1985. "So you Think Gestures are Nonverbal?" *Psychological Review* 92, no. 3: 350–71.

———. 1996. *Hand and Mind: What Gestures Reveal about Thought.* Chicago: University of Chicago Press.

———, ed. 2000. *Language and Gestures.* Cambridge, UK: Cambridge University Press.

Mead, G. H. 1913. "The Social Self." *Journal of Philosophy* 10, no. 14: 374–80.

Merleau-Ponty, M. 1962. *The Phenomenology of Perception.* London: Routledge and Kegan Paul.

Murphy, K. M. 2004. "Imagination as Joint Activity: The Case of Architectural Interaction." *Mind, Culture, and Activity* 11, no. 4: 267–78.

Ochs, E. 2006. "Transcription as Theory." In *The Discourse Reader.* Edited by A. Jaworski and N. Coupland, 166–78. Oxon: Routledge.

Saussure, F. 1974. *Course in General Linguistics.* Bungay: Fontana/Collins.

Schütz, A. 1951. "Making Music Together: A Study in Social Relationship." *Social Research* 18: 76–97.

Sheets-Johnstone, M. 1981. "Thinking in Movement." *The Journal of Aesthetics and Art Criticism* 39, no. 4: 399–407.

———. 1999. *The Primacy of Movement.* Philadelphia: John Benjamins.

Simonetti, C. 2015. "Feeling Forward into the Past: Depths and Surfaces in Archaeology." *Time and Mind* 8, no. 1: 69–89.

Streeck, J. 2009. *Gesturecraft. The Manu-facture of Meaning.* Amsterdam: John Benjamins.

Suchman, L. 1987. *Plans and Situated Actions: The Problem of Human-Machine Communication.* Cambridge, UK: Cambridge University Press.

Valsiner, J., and R. Van der Veer. 2000. *The Social Mind: Construction of the Idea.* New York: Cambridge University Press.

Voloshinov, V. N. 1986. *Marxism and the Philosophy of Language.* Cambridge, MA: Harvard University Press.

Vygotsky, L. S. 1986. *Thought and Language.* Edited and Translated by E. Hanfmann, G. Vakar, and A. Kozulin. Cambridge, MA: MIT Press.

Wertsch, J. V. 1985. *Vygotsky and the Social Formation of Mind.* Cambridge, MA: Harvard University Press.

CHAPTER 7

Exploration of a Buried Seascape
The Cultural Maritime Landscapes
of Tremadoc Bay

Gary Robinson

In 1985, Charles Thomas published *Explorations of a Drowned Landscape*, a volume that sought to address a problem identified over two centuries earlier: the effect of changes in sea level upon our interpretation of the archaeological record (Borlase 1756; Crawford 1927). Thomas used a combination of archaeological fieldwork, historic place-name evidence, and available sea level data to reconstruct the relationship between submerged and terrestrial archaeological sites and the ancient configuration of the Isles of Scilly. In this chapter, I take inspiration from the approach adopted by Thomas. However, while Thomas explored a landscape inundated by the sea, this chapter will explore a former seascape buried beneath coastal and estuarine sediments. The focus of this study will be Tremadoc Bay in northwest Wales and, in particular, the estuaries of the Arfon Glaslyn and Arfon Dwyryd (figure 7.1). This chapter will consider the archaeology of the Glaslyn and Dwyryd estuaries in relation to their original coastal contexts. Moreover, I will refocus our interpretation of this evidence toward the sea. It will be argued that the prehistoric archaeology of this region can only be understood and interpreted in relation to the wider cultural maritime landscape (Westerdahl 1992, 2011).

Tremadoc Bay is approximately 26 km long and 20.3 km wide. The Llŷn Peninsula forms the northern boundary of Tremadoc Bay, while Sarn Badrig, extending southwest for 19.5 km from Mochras Island, on the tip of Morfa Dyffryn, marks the southern extent (figures 7.2 and 7.3). To the east, the bay narrows into the broad estuaries of the Arfon Glaslyn and Dwyryd. These estuaries cut dramatically into the Rhinogydd Mountains of Snowdonia. The area surrounding Tremadoc Bay contains an exceptional number of prehistoric sites including ritual and funerary monuments,

Figure 7.1. Location map of the study area, Tremadoc Bay, Wales. Created by the author.

settlements, and artifact assemblages (Smith 2001, 2003). Many of these sites have been the focus of investigation since the nineteenth century, but research carried out has been piece-meal, only instigated in response to development and thus lacking in focus. While Tremadoc Bay is primarily a maritime landscape, no consideration of this important aspect has been taken into account in the interpretation of its prehistoric archaeology.

The appearance of the Glaslyn Estuary as a terrestrial landscape with little marine influence is misleading, considering what it would have been like in prehistory (figure 7.2). The main cause of this terrestrial appearance has been the reclaiming and enclosure of land within the estuary since the fifteenth century, and most significantly the construction of the Cob by

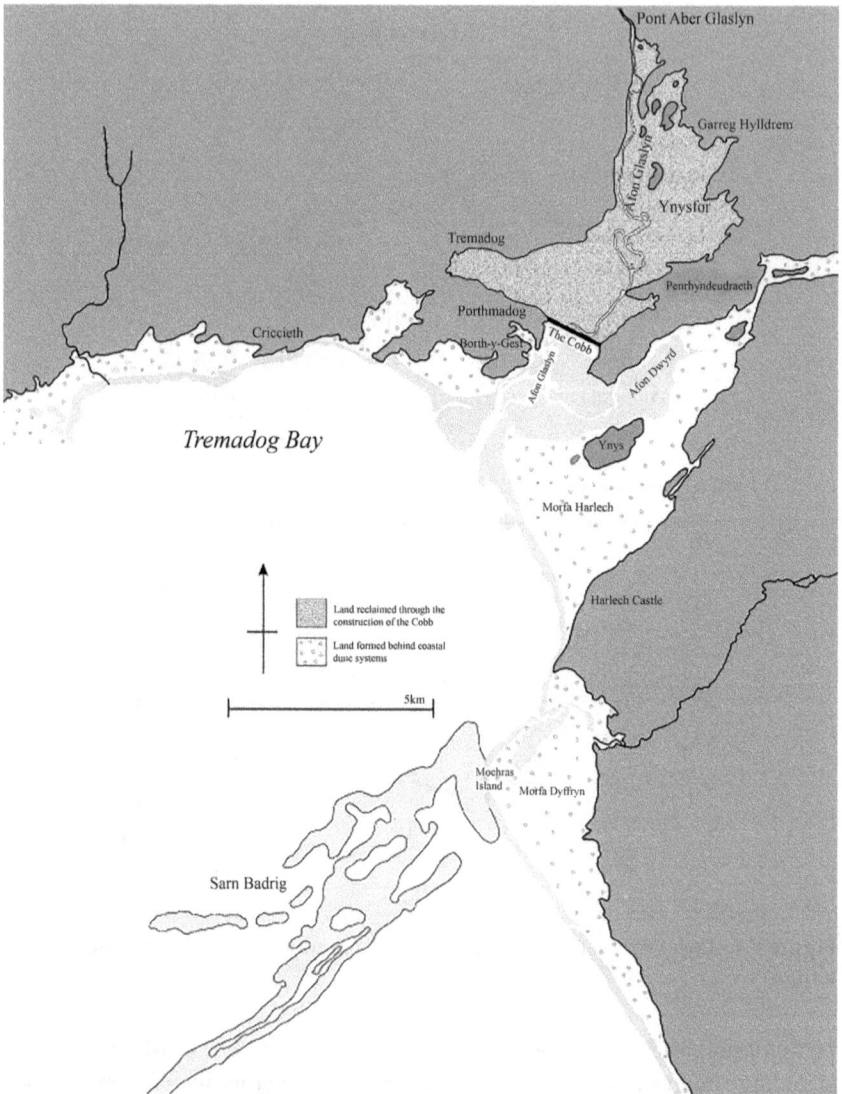

Figure 7.2. Map of Tremadoc Bay showing the location of places mentioned in the text. Created by the author.

W. A. Madocks in 1811 (Richards 1925). The Cob was constructed across the Afon Glaslyn to carry the railway and limits the tidal influence up to the village of Tremadog (figure 7.2). However, historical accounts note that before the construction of the Cob, the tide reached nearly to Pont Aber Glaslyn, and the whole of the Glaslyn Valley resembled the Mawddach and Dovey estuaries (Steers 1939, 212). During this time, the Glaslyn

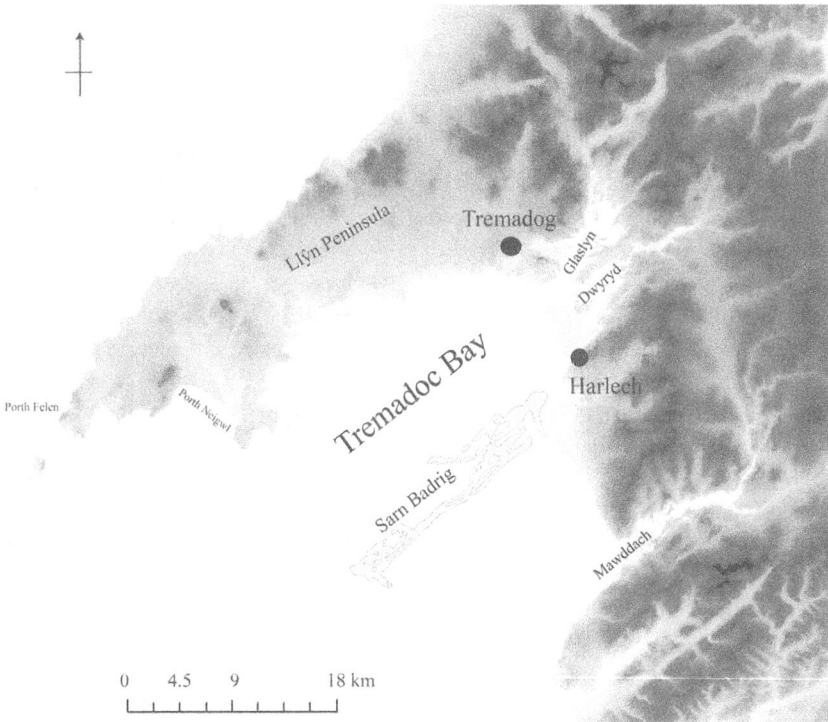

Figure 7.3. Tremadoc Bay and the estuaries of the Arfon Glaslyn and Arfon Dwyryd in relation to Sarn Badrig. Created by the author.

Estuary was used for marine transport. Jenkins notes that Porthmadog only came into existence during the nineteenth century, and that before the construction of the Cob, Borth y Gest and Aberglaslyn were the ports of the Glaslyn Estuary (1899, 327); the estuary was an important transport route to ship supplies and produce both into and out of the Glaslyn Valley (Owen 1943). Ashton notes that long before boats were built at Porthmadog, boats were constructed at Garreg Hylldrem and launched at Borth y Gest, at Abergafren and Borthwen in the Traeth Bach; and on the south of the Traeth at Tŷ Gwyn and at Glan-y-Mor (1920, 241). The Glaslyn estuary is dotted with small islands, the largest of which is Ynysfor. What is clear is that prior to the construction of the Cob, the lives of the communities of the Glaslyn were intimately connected to the sea.

The Dwyryd Estuary is a sand-clogged tidal estuary, partially blocked to the south by a substantial sand wedge known as Morfa Harlech (figure 7.2). Morfa Harlech is triangular in shape and measures some six kilometers north to south and five kilometers east to west along its northern edge. The morfa is low lying, most of it below ten meters Ordnance Datum

(OD), with the exception of the small islands, the largest being Ynys. The west side of the triangle is defined by a line of sand dunes that divide the morfa from the sea. Morfa Harlech has formed since the twelfth century AD. Today, the medieval castle of Harlech stands separated from the sea behind Morfa Harlech (Davidson 2012). However, historical and archaeological evidence demonstrates that when constructed, between AD 1283 and 1295, the castle had direct access to the sea via its Water Gate (Davidson 2012). The morfa has formed over as a result of sediment transported along Cardigan Bay via longshore drift. However, it is also likely that the instigation of the formation of the morfa may be a result of major storm events that deposited large quantities of sand along the North Wales coast, most notably at Newborough and Aberffraw, on the west coast of Anglesey and within the Menia Strait (Robinson 2016, 55). Dating of dune systems at Aberffraw suggests that this major depositional event is likely to have occurred during the twelfth and thirteenth centuries AD (Bailey et al. 2001). The origin of the sediment that forms Morfa Harlech is likely to be from the mobilization of a sand wedge previously located to the south of Sarn Badrig (Steers 1964, 132–36; May and Hansom 2003, 449–53).

I will argue that in order to interpret the coastal archaeology of Tremadoc Bay, it is essential that we understand its relationship to the ancient coastline. By viewing prehistoric sites in relation to the ancient coastline, we are forced to rethink the archaeological record, thus transforming our perception of Tremadoc Bay's significance in prehistory.

Past and Present Coastlines

The reconstruction of ancient coastlines is based on an understanding of a range of erosional and depositional marine processes. These processes are dynamic and interrelated and vary temporally from long-term changes in sea level to single storm events (Steers 1939; Ranwell 1959; Bailey et al. 2001; Rhind, Blackstock, and Hardy 2001; May and Hanson 2003).

Recent studies in North Wales have sought to explore sea-level change on a regional scale or on a site-specific basis. Such studies demonstrate greater regional variability than previously recognized (Larcombe and Jago 1994; Roberts 2006). One study conducted within the Menai Strait provides a detailed model of post-glacial sea-level change (Roberts et al. 2011). The model is derived from offshore borings within the northeast Menai Strait (Roberts 2006; Roberts et al. 2011). Analysis and dating of deposits, combined with detailed bathymetric and geophysical survey, have allowed a high-resolution model of the effect of sea-level change to be produced (Roberts et al. 2011). The quality of sea-level data from this single locality is unprecedented and has major implications for how we interpret the prehistoric archaeology of Tremadoc Bay. This demonstrates a rapid increase in sea level between 11000 cal BC and 5000 cal BC, with a marked decrease in the curve after 5000 cal BC (Roberts 2006; Roberts et al. 2011). Bell has mapped the effect of this sea-level change upon the coastline of Cardigan Bay (2007, 7–10, figure 1.4). He argues that during the Early Holocene, the coastline of Cardigan Bay was up to 35 m lower than today (Smith, Davidson, and Kenney 2002; Bell 2007, 2). By 7500 BC, sea level stood at -18 m and the Llŷn Peninsula and Anglesey were closed to the sea, but a third of Cardigan Bay remained dry land. After 6000 BC, marine influence extended inland up valleys, covering all of the areas of peat and estuarine sediments by 5500 BC (Bell 2007). As sea level continued rising after 5000 BC, larger areas of Cardigan Bay slowly became submerged.

During the Late Devensian, the Glaslyn and Dwyryd estuaries would have been the site of valley glaciers that flowed into the present inner shelf of Cardigan Bay. The modern course of the Afon Glaslyn and Arfon Dwyryd were over-deepened by erosive subglacial flows, and later infilled by a coarse-grained subglacial and proglacial infill sequence. Geophysical surveys carried out on a number of estuaries in Cardigan Bay concluded that all the valleys with the exception of the Glaslyn and Dwyryd could have been carved out during Pleistocene times, but that the much deeper buried valleys of the Glaslyn and Dwyryd, extending south of Porthmadog across Morfa Harlech, are probably of earlier origin (Blundell, Griffiths, and King 1969, 162–80). Depths to bedrock of up to 380 m were recorded for the Glaslyn and Dwyryd estuaries (Blundell, Griffiths, and King 1969, 171–75). In support of this interpretation, boreholes carried out within the Glaslyn Estuary during the late 1990s, in advance of road construction, identified only estuarine deposits. The implication of these findings for the context of prehistoric sites within the estuaries is that even with substantially lower sea levels during the Mesolithic (Roberts et al. 2011), the Glaslyn Estuary may have been subject to marine inundation earlier than previously thought.

Today, Sarn Badrig extends 19.5 km offshore and breaks the surface at low water (figure 7.3). The sarn is formed from lateral moraine deposited by glaciers that once extended from Snowdonia into the Irish Sea (Caston 1966, 407). Prior to mid-Holocene sea-level changes (circa 5,000 cal BC), when sea levels in Cardigan Bay were substantially lower than today, Sarn Badrig would have formed the southern limit of a flooded over-deepened glacial valley. To the south of Sarn Badrig, land would have extended out into Cardigan Bay, as demonstrated in the identification of submerged forests and peat deposits (Bell 2007). With rising sea levels after 5000 BC, sediment would have been mobilized and transported along the coastline of

Cardigan Bay, via longshore drift. Sarn Badrig would have acted as a formidable physical barrier to the movement of water and sediment between Cardigan Bay and Tremadoc Bay, and, as it would today, would have had an effect upon current and tidal circulation (Neill, Elliott, and Hashemi 2007, 1778). As a consequence, it can be assumed that a major depositional environment would have been created by the sarn and that a substantial sand wedge would have formed along its southern edge. When and how this sand wedge was eventually eroded is unclear, although this is likely to be the source of sediment that ultimately clogged up the estuaries of Tremadoc Bay and formed Morfa Harlech and Morfa Dyffryn.

In summary, although the estuaries of the Glaslyn and Dwyryd are today clogged by eluvium and terminated by substantial sand wedges and spits, during prehistory, they would have been substantial, deep coastal inlets containing numerous small islands and with areas of saltmarsh and peat mires along their shorelines. The appearance of the Glaslyn and Dwyryd Estuaries during prehistory would have resembled many Scottish lochs and as such would have provided a range of inshore environments for fishing, hunting, shellfish harvesting, and the landing of boats.

The Sea, Boats, and Landing Places

Boats are integral to coastal and island communities within western Britain. Callaghan and Scarre have recently simulated Neolithic seaborne movement within the Irish Sea, demonstrating the potential for boat journeys made between North Wales and Ireland throughout all seasons of the year (2009, 365). The presence of boats in western Britain is demonstrated by the colonization of off-shore islands, the movement of material culture, similarities in the forms of monuments, and evidence for fishing (Lynch 1989; Robinson 2013a).

A growing number of boats have been identified within the archaeological record for the British Isles, giving some indication as to the types of vessels that may have been in use within western Britain (McGrail 2001; Robinson 2013a). The Irish Sea, the Minch, and the Atlantic are cold, frequently changeable, and always unreliable. The coast of North Wales is exposed to the prevailing southwesterly wind and currents are strong and dangerous, particularly around the Llŷn Peninsula and Anglesey. Such sea conditions can be overcome through knowledge of the temporal cycles of tides and currents; coasting within sight of land along the North Wales coast during slack tides is unproblematic and relatively easily undertaken. Indeed, if one were to look for a barrier to movement, the mountains of Snowdonia would provide a more formidable obstacle to daily movement, trade, and contact. Nonetheless, crossings over the Irish Sea would have been challenging and boats operating within this environment would have had to be seaworthy. In general, skinboats are more seaworthy and sea-kind than their wooden counterparts and thus more suitable for operating along the western coasts of Britain. While no direct archaeological evidence exists for skinboats, they are clearly the most suitable vessels for transport on the sea, and the technology and skills for their manufacture are present within the archaeological record of Britain from at least the Mesolithic. Skinboats may have been the workhorse boat of prehistory (Robinson 2013a).

The importance of safe places to land boats would be critical, and the shelter offered by Tremadoc Bay would have been attractive to prehistoric communities. This interpretation is given weight by the discovery of planks from an Early Bronze Age sewn plank boat at Porth Neigwl (figure 7.3) on the southwest coast of the Llŷn Peninsula (Smith et al. 2017). The boat planks were discovered during the excavation of a Bronze Age burnt mound, where the planks had been reused to form a wooden water trough at the center of the mound (Smith 2008, 2009; Kenney 2013). Radiocarbon dating of one of the boat planks has produced an Early Bronze Age date of 1740–1520 cal BC (Smith 2009; Smith et al. 2017). Because of the shelter offered by Sarn Badrig and the Llŷn Peninsula, it is likely that the planks originate from a boat that had come to rest within Porthmadog Bay, but whether this was in close proximity to its discovery on the Llŷn or as flotsam washed out from the estuaries is unclear. However, the discovery of this boat highlights the importance of this bay as a landing place and as a locale of interaction between distant communities. Only a small element of this boat has so far been identified, and while clearly not in context, this discovery provides the first concrete evidence for the use of these boats along the coast of western Britain. The full sophistication of Bronze Age sewn plank boats is only now beginning to be appreciated (Van de Noort 2006, 2010).

These boats mark a major technological innovation in boat design and construction, creating strong seaworthy vessels potentially capable of crossing back-and-forth across the Irish Sea (Van de Noort 2010; Robinson 2013a). This discovery forces us to rethink Bronze Age connection along and across the Irish Sea. It is likely that this boat would have been used in the trade and exchange of copper ore and Bronze Age metalwork along the coastlines of the Irish Sea. The close proximity of the Llŷn boat with the Bronze Age copper extraction sites of Parys Mountain on Anglesey and the Great Orme, near Llandudno, is perhaps not surprising (Dutton and Fasham 1994; Jenkins and Timberlake 2001). These sites produced thousands of tons of copper ore during the Bronze Age, providing the raw

resources for the production, exchange, and trade in metalwork throughout Britain, Ireland, and Continental Europe.

The continued importance of these trade and exchange networks is
demonstrated by the discovery of a lead-stock anchor found off Porth
Felen on the west coast of the Llŷn Peninsula (figure 7.3). This anchor is
of a Mediterranean pattern, dates to the second century BC, and is unique
to British waters (Boon 1977). Further evidence of maritime contact with
the Mediterranean is demonstrated by the presence of imported pottery,
including amphorae and Phoenician red slip dishes at Dinas Emrys, near
Beddgelert (Savory 1960). The most likely route through which these imported goods would have reached Dinas Emrys would be via the Glaslyn
estuary, demonstrating the ongoing significance of the estuary as a landing place into the early centuries AD.

Landing places represent the interface between sea and land, invariably
created by people, for people using boats. They are at the center of coastal
and island communities and are thus a common focus and reference point
for the location of settlements and the construction of monuments (Robinson 2013a). Ilves (2012) has argued that boats "shape the shoreline," in that
access to the sea, and thus the launching and landing of boats, is central
to the daily life of coastal communities. Equally, it has been argued that
for coastal communities, landing places play an important role in the creation of social identity (Robinson 2007, 2013a). Access to the sea is a central structuring principle within the lives of coastal communities around
which other elements of their daily lives are constructed.

However, we should not assume that landing places were openly accessible to all communities along a coastline, nor that access to the sea and
its resources was necessarily common property. Durrenberger and Pálsson (1987) argue that historical and ethnographical discourse frequently
assumes as natural that the seas and their resources have always been
common property. However, their work demonstrates that this conception
is neither universal nor natural; it is not historically or ethnographically
supportable (Acheson 1981, 280–81; Durrenberger and Pálsson 1987, 510).
Landing a small boat on a coast would have been risky, especially during
the winter season, and access to the sea would therefore have depended
upon the availability of good landing sites. One could only get access
to the sea from the shore, which may have been controlled by particular coastal communities (Durrenberger and Pálsson 1987, 510). Such discussions of territoriality suggest that prehistoric landing places are not
purely functional spaces, but invested with issues of ownership, access,
and identity. In order to explore the importance of Tremadoc Bay during
prehistory in greater detail, I will now examine the available prehistoric
archaeological evidence.

Prehistoric Estuarine Settlement

The Glaslyn and Dwyryd estuaries are dotted with numerous small islands. The largest of these islands in the Dwryd estuary is Ynys, now land-
locked by the formation of Morfa Harlech. Other islands include Hir Ynys
and Ynysfor. These islands and the coastline around the estuaries appear
to have been the focus of human activity within Tremadoc Bay.

Evidence of Mesolithic (8000–4000 BC) activity within Tremadoc Bay
takes the form of assemblages of stone tools and shell middens. At present,
the largest clustering of sites occurs along the Llŷn Peninsula (Smith and
Walker 2014, 100, figure 1). Sites are predominantly located on the coast, frequently located on headlands, as at Pencilan Head where a collection of approximately seventy Mesolithic flints were found on the eroding headland
(Gwyn and Dutton 1996; RCAHMW 1960, 1964). Off the coast of the Llŷn
on Ynys Enlli (Bardsey Island), a number of Mesolithic assemblages have
been identified (Edmonds et al. 2004, 2009; Smith 2005, 41). The presence
of Mesolithic artifacts on an offshore island demonstrates the presence of
boats and the ability to make journeys into the sea.

The earliest dated evidence for Mesolithic occupation comes from Garreg Hylldrem (Robinson 2013b). At Garreg Hylldrem in the north of the
Glaslyn Estuary, a rock shelter containing a shell midden has produced a
series of Early Mesolithic radiocarbon dates. The rock shelter would have
been directly overlooking a tidal estuary during the Mesolithic (figure
7.4). The midden were comprised of a dark humic deposit that contained
marine shells. A variety of species were identified, including winkle (*Littorina sp.*), oyster (*Ostreidae sp.*), limpet (*Patella sp.*), mussel (*Mytilus sp.*),
and cockle (*Cardiidae sp.*). Winkles occurred in substantially larger numbers than the other marine mollusks represented. The midden produced
thirty-six pieces of heat-reddened flint. Five radiocarbon tests taken from
the shell midden returned dates ranging from 7036–6755 cal BC (Robinson
2013b, 5). A second midden identified within the rock shelter produced a
late Mesolithic date range of 5193–4942 cal BC (Robinson 2013b, 6). The
marine shell collection from this later midden was dominated by limpet
(*Patella sp.*) and mussel (*Mytilus sp.*) with occasional occurrence of winkle
(*Littorina sp.*), namely rocky and exposed shore species.

There is a marked variation in the size of shellfish brought to the rock
shelter, with numerous examples of exceptionally small specimens that
would have provided only minimal food value. Indeed, one would expect
that selective gathering would be reflected in the intentional selection of
larger specimens. Whether this variation in selection is a reflection of a
dwindling local resource, caused by over exploitation, or as indicator of
environmental changes taking place within the estuary is yet to be deter-

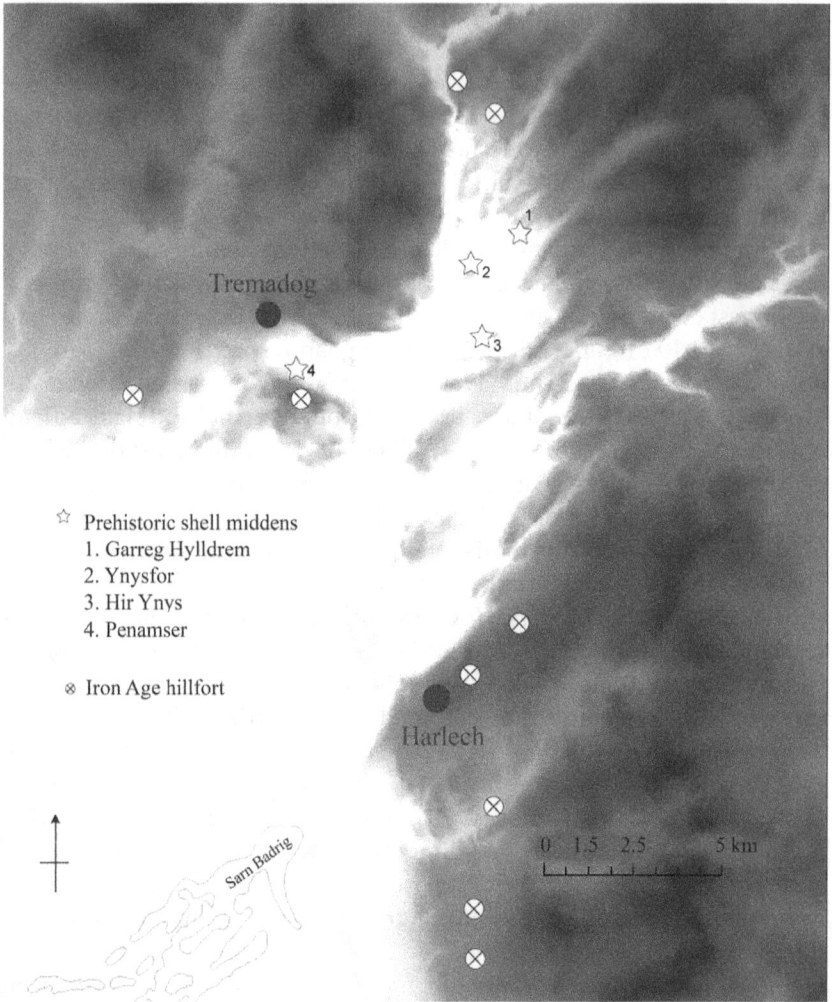

Figure 7.4. The distribution of prehistoric shell middens within Tremadoc Bay. Created by the author.

mined. However, it should be noted that the hand gathering of shellfish is not necessarily a rigorously selective procedure. Hand gathering of mussels may result in the collection of individuals at all stages of growth (Waselkov 1987, 100). The presence of small marks observed on the inside of a number of mussel shells has been identified as having been made by the boring sponge *Cliona celata*, (Dr. Clare Valentine, Natural History Museum, London, personal communication). The presence of these marks supports the idea that bunches of mussel shells were gathered, reflecting the incorporation of dead shells rather than selective collecting.

There is a strong coastal distribution of evidence to both Early and Later Mesolithic sites throughout Wales (Wymer 1977; Bell 2007) suggesting activity around coastal headlands and within estuaries and river courses. This is most clearly demonstrated at Prestatyn and Rhuddlan where a variety of lithic scatters, shell middens, and possible settlements have been recorded in close proximity to the large estuary that once existed there (Bell 2007; Quinell, Blockley, and Berridge 1994). The location of Garreg Hylldrem within such a locale is in keeping with our current knowledge of the Mesolithic evidence from Wales (Bell 2007).

Garreg Hylldrem appears to have been used sporadically by Mesolithic hunter-gatherers, perhaps as an overnight campsite for foraging and hunting forays into the estuary (O'Sullivan and Breen 2011, 45–46). The site was located in close proximity to the sea and could have been accessed by boat along the Afon Glaslyn. Evidence for the continued reuse of the rock shelter over a long period of time suggests the significance of this locale within the estuarine landscape. Such persistent places would have been invested with social memory, primarily reproduced through habitual practices and made through the very processes of their production. Therefore, we should not draw sharp distinctions between places, objects, and people, as all are implicated in the construction of individual and social biographies and memories.

Burial and ritual monuments dominate the archaeological record of the Neolithic and Early Bronze Age, with little evidence for settlement (Smith 2003). This lack of settlement is a defining feature of these periods and occurs throughout Britain. A small number of Early Neolithic (4000–3000 BC) houses have been identified in North Wales (Lynch and Musson 2001; Kenney 2007, 2008; Rees and Jones 2015), but these are rare. Similarly, evidence for Late Neolithic (3000–2400 BC) and Early Bronze Age (2400–1600 BC) houses is largely absent. When houses do occur, they are frequently found under later funerary monuments (Lynch 1993; Gibson 1999). These houses have variously been interpreted as temporary shelters or structures involved in funerary rites and other ritual activities. Settlement evidence for the Neolithic and Early Bronze Age is typified by scatters of stone tools, pottery, and midden deposits (Smith 2001).

The large number of stone tools found within Tremadoc Bay demonstrates a significant Neolithic presence (RCAHMW 1956, 1960, 1964; Bowen and Gresham 1967; Burrow 2003). A total of 157 Neolithic flint artifacts, including fragments of a core trimming flake, a knife, and a leaf-shaped arrowhead, were identified at Y Bryn, near the village of Tremadog (Smith 2013, 41). The context of the assemblage relates to a rocky knoll that would have been a small island within the estuary prior to the construction of the Cob (Hopewell 1995, 1).

The discovery of a barbed and tanged arrowhead within the rock shelter at Garreg Hylldrem, possibly associated with a burial (Robinson 2013a), suggests that the presence of Mesolithic midden material within the rock shelter was recognized during the Early Bronze Age as the residue of past occupation. Through the reuse of the rock shelter during the Bronze Age, links are made to an ancestral past and the significance of particular locales within the landscape is maintained. We can see similar activity in western Scotland, at sites such as Raschoille and the Oban caves, where earlier shell midden sites are revisited during the Bronze Age (Wickham-Jones 2007, 90).

During the Later Bronze Age and Iron Age (1600 BC–AD 43), we see the emergence of archaeological detectable settlement in the form of stone roundhouses (Ghey et al. 2007; Waddington 2013). However, these settlements are not found within the estuaries themselves, but within the uplands surrounding Tremadoc Bay (Waddington 2013, Plate 3.4). During the Iron Age (800 BC–AD 43), we see the development of defended settlements and hill forts. These sites are located on higher ground on the edges of the bay (Aldhouse-Green, Davies, and Lynch 2000, figure 4.1; Waddington 2013, plate 3.7). Entrance to the Glaslyn Estuary is marked by the hill fort of Moel y Gest, which stands above Porthmadog, while the hill fort of Pen y Gaer is located in the uplands overlooking the west of the estuary. Entrance to the Dwyryd Estuary is flanked by Byrllysg and Moel Goedog hill forts located on high ground above Harlech (figure 7.4).

Within the estuaries themselves, we see evidence of Later Bronze Age and Iron Age settlement focused on small islands within the estuaries (figure 7.4). Excavations during 2014 revealed a substantial shell midden on the island of Hir Ynys (Hudson 2014). The midden is associated with a large stone-built enclosure that encircles the summit of the island. Samples taken from the midden have produced Late Bronze Age radiocarbon dates of 1006–843 cal BC (Hudson 2014). The midden is comprised of substantial quantities of shellfish and pig bones. The shellfish present are dominated by sandy estuarine species, primarily oysters, cockles, and winkles. Similarly, on Ynysfor, a number of shell middens occur across the island, the largest being associated with a large enclosure assumed to date from the Iron Age. While no excavation has taken place on Ynysfor, erosion within the largest of the middens has exposed a midden deposit of similar composition to the one at Ynysfor. Erosion of this midden has also revealed the presence of high quality metalwork in the form of two bronze Romano-British bow brooches (Steele 2010). At the foot of Moel-y-Gest, near Penamser, a small shell midden was discovered during mitigation work by Gwynedd Archaeological Trust (Kenney 2014, 45–50). The location sits within the estuaries' southwest corner at five meters OD, a height that suggests a former shoreline. Cockleshells are the predominant species, but winkles and oysters are also present. Beneath the midden, a fire-reddened layer containing flecks of charcoal and burnt stone suggests the presence of a hearth. Samples of shell and charcoal provide a statistically combined radiocarbon date range of 590–335 cal BC.

These midden sites suggest long-term occupation and demonstrate exploitation of marine resources and the use of the estuaries as places of everyday working practice into the first millennium BC. Equally, the presence of settlement enclosures on islands within an active estuary suggests the importance of these locales during the late Bronze Age and Iron Age. Such locales would certainly have functioned to control movement within the estuaries and may indicate a closer demarcation of sea territory or access to landings during this period.

The Location of Early Neolithic Chambered Tombs

The Early Neolithic (4000–3000 BC) archaeology of Wales is characterized by the presence of chambered tombs. It has been noted that the distribution of these tombs is largely concentrated around the coastline (Lynch 2011). However, this distribution is not uniform, but occurs within discreet groupings (Cummings and Whittle 2003). In North Wales, three groups of monuments are located along the coast (Daniel 1950, 54–61, 86–92; Lynch 1969). One particular group of monuments occurs within Tremadoc Bay and has been described as the Llŷn-Ardudwy group (Lynch 1969, 109). This group occurs along the Llŷn Peninsula and around the village of Ardudwy (Robinson 2016, 58, figure 3.4). At Ardudwy, seven chambered tombs form a discreet cluster (figure 7.5).

Accounts of the landscape settings of these monuments have emphasized their location between the sea and the mountains, a pattern identified in other chambered tombs in Wales (Tilley 1994; Cummings and Whittle 2003; Nash 2006). This interpretation highlights the symbolic significance of views across the sea as a structuring principle in the monuments' settings. Justification for this interpretation draws on the fact that the chambers and long-cairns associated with these monuments all share a common east–west orientation, facing the sea and mountains (Cummings and Whittle 2003; Nash 2006, 141).

While this pattern is interesting and potentially significant, its interpretation ignores the agency of Tremadoc Bay as a locale of everyday working practice and experience, thus reducing the sea to a symbolic backdrop to life on land. If we consider the setting of this group of monuments in relation to the ancient coastline, we see a correlation with the southern shore

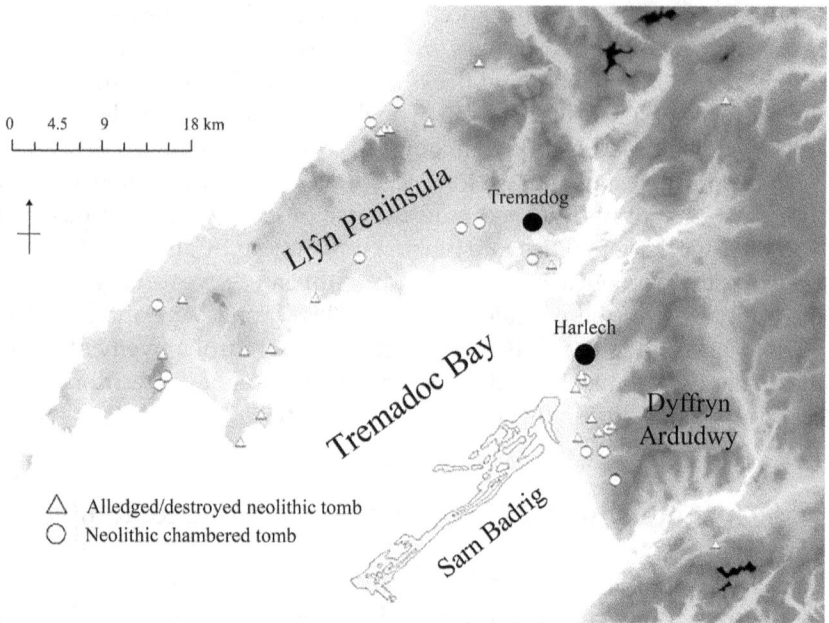

Figure 7.5. The distribution of Early Neolithic (4000–3000 BC) chambered tombs within Tremadoc Bay. Created by the author.

of Tremadoc Bay and in particular Sarn Badrig. This landscape setting emphasizes the sheltered bay, possibly an area of daily Neolithic activity in the form of shellfish gathering and the provision of a safe harbor for boats. Equally, the common orientation of these monuments, rather than a focus on the sea *per se*, is more likely related to inland topography, situated along Sarn Badrig, the former coastline of the bay.

A similar clustering of chambered tombs occurs along the southern slopes of the Llŷn Peninsula (Robinson 2016, 58, figure 3.4). Nash has argued that we should not consider the monuments found at Ardudwy and those on the Llŷn as a single group as the two clusters have a ten-mile corridor between them that has little or no evidence for Neolithic activity (Nash 2006, 155). While this observation is correct, it overlooks the point that the landscape settings of these monuments are related to a much wider sense of place, one that incorporates both land and sea. In this light, monuments are found on either side of Tremadoc Bay, marking entry and movement within the bay and access to the estuaries of the Glaslyn and Dwyryd.

If we look further up the coast of North Wales, a similar association between chambered tombs and bays and estuaries occurs. In Caernarfon Bay, chambered tombs are found at the outer edges of the bay, on the northern slopes of the Llŷn and along the eastern coast of Anglesey. On Anglesey, a high concentration of monuments occur in association with the Menai Strait, which until approximately 3000 cal BC would have been an estuary (Roberts 2006; Roberts et al. 2011; Robinson 2016, 58, figure 3.4). Further north again, the pattern is repeated in Penhryn Bay with monuments found on the western coast of Anglesey and on the Great Orme. A fourth group of monuments found within the Conwy Valley has an association with the Conwy Estuary (Cummings and Whittle 2003). The pattern identified is consistent: rather than monuments having general coastal settings, they are located in association with large bays and estuaries.

The Neolithic is a period that presents growing evidence for long-distance sea-borne movement. During the Mesolithic/Neolithic transition, the resources necessary for Neolithic farming must have been transported across the English Channel by boat (Case 1969; Rowley-Conwy 2011; Stevens and Fuller 2012). Indeed, the western seaways of Britain have long been considered crucial to any geographical understanding of the transition (Callaghan and Scarre 2009; Sheridan 2010; Garrow and Sturt 2011). Further weight has recently been added to this hypothesis, in that many of the earliest traces of Neolithic practices and material culture occur within and around western Britain and Ireland: early cow bones have been found in Ireland (Woodman and McCarthy 2003), early cereal pollen in the Isle of Man (Innes, Blackford, and Davey 2003), early pottery in western Scotland (Sheridan 2000), and a passage tomb of earlier Neolithic date in Devon (Sheridan et al. 2008).

Contact by sea throughout the Neolithic and Bronze Age is evident in the exchange and trade of stone and metal artifacts, but the nature of the boats used within such exchange networks remains unclear (Patton 1991; Waddell 1993; Peacock and Cutler 2010). There is ample evidence for Neolithic journeys from France to Britain in the form of smaller objects, such as jadeite and Breton axes (Clough and Cummins 1988; Sheridan 2007). However, the discovery at Maiden Castle of a large Neolithic saddle-quern of French provenance demonstrates evidence for the transportation of large stone objects during the Neolithic (Peacock and Cutler 2010). The quern from Maiden Castle weighs over sixteen kilograms and is the largest and heaviest artifact demonstrated to have crossed the channel in Neolithic times (Peacock and Cutler 2010, 122). The transportation by sea of large stone objects forces us to reconsider the types of boats in use during prehistory and the logistics of seafaring in this early period.

Indeed, during the Neolithic, coastal areas were clearly spaces where people, ideas, and cultural traits could encounter each other, which explains the similarities between chambered tombs of Wales, Ireland, and Scotland (O'Sullivan and Breen 2011, 74). The concept of places of encounter is loaded with social significance. The locations of chambered tombs with Tremadoc Bay mark out and inscribe territory and rights of access, while providing a visual marker of social identity and genealogy.

Late Neolithic and Early Bronze Age Monumentality

During the Late Neolithic and Early Bronze Age (3000–1600 BC), we see intense human activity within Tremadoc Bay (Lynch 1984). Above Tremadoc Bay, arranged around the ancient cliff line, we see a concentration of Late Neolithic and Early Bronze Age monuments that include burial cairns, standing stones, and stone circles (figure 7.6). This concentration of monuments emphasizes the estuaries of the Glaslyn and Dwyryd and stands at odds with the wider distribution of monuments within North Wales (Smith 2001). There are two, not incompatible, interpretations of this distribution pattern. First is that the monuments emphasize the continued importance of Tremadoc Bay during prehistory. The marking out of the bay through the placement of burial monuments, which contain the remains of past ancestors, creates a genealogy of landscape that links together past peoples, practices, and place. Monumentality is used as a means of legitimizing sea and land tenure, and access to the resources of the bay.

The second perspective holds that these arrangements of monuments may represent prehistoric trackways that lead from the coast into mainland Wales (Gresham and Irvine 1963; Lynch 1984). The cliffs that form the edges of the Glaslyn and Dwyryd estuaries are steep and difficult to negotiate, and the narrow gorge of Aberglaslyn would have been impassable by boat or on foot. The safe harborage of Tremadoc Bay therefore offers only two possibilities for landward movement. The first is from the village of Tremadog heading east following the northern cliff line of the Glaslyn Estuary. This overland route is marked out by numerous monuments, most notably by standing stones and cairns. The second route is via Llanbedr in the south of the bay, known as the Ardudwy trackway. Monuments here form a significant linear group set alongside an important trackway, which runs from the coast at Llanbedr to cross the mountains north of Moel Ysgyfarnogod, coming into the basin of Trawsfyndd and from there perhaps going east toward Bala, or south to the Mawddach (Bowen and Gresham 1967, 56–59). This arrangement of monuments has been interpreted as evidence of a prehistoric route that links the North Wales coast into the interior of Wales, potentially connecting with the River Severn. This implies that the trackway was part of a prehistoric net-

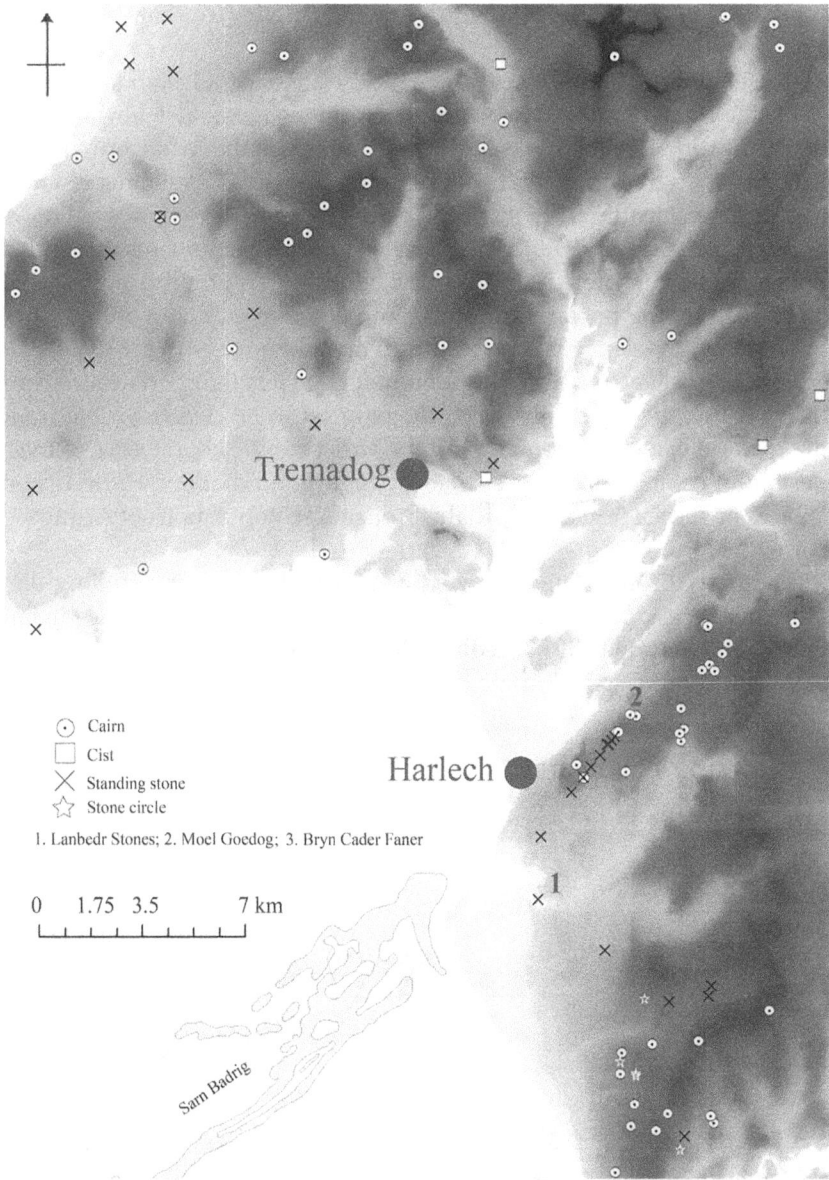

Figure 7.6. The distribution of Late Neolithic and Early Bronze Age (3000–1600 BC) ritual and funerary monuments within Tremadoc Bay. Created by the author.

work used to connect Ireland with mainland Britain (Gresham and Irvine 1963, 55; Sherratt 1996).

The beginning of this route is marked by a pair of tall standing stones at Llanbedr on the ancient foreshore of a former coastal inlet, now clogged up by the formation of Morfa Ardudwy, into which the Arfon Artro flows. When higher ground is reached, an impressive series of standing stones and cairns follow the ancient sea cliff before crossing the uplands of Snowdonia (figures 7.7 and 7.8). The concentration of monuments along this line might be interpreted simply as the builders' wish for the monuments to be seen by the maximum number of people in an area naturally frequented by travelers passing to and fro along the road (Lynch 1984, 34). However, the way in which the monuments cluster along certain stretches of the route, the care with which they are set to be clearly visible from the road only at certain points, and the variety and elaborateness of their design all combine to suggest that the high ground above Harlech was an area of special importance to the Bronze Age populations of Ardudwy (Lynch 1984, 34).

The Early Bronze Age is viewed as a period during which long-distance networks of interaction were important (O'Connor 1980; Needham, Parfitt, and Varndell 2006; Needham 2009). Beaker pottery is found across a wide area of Western Europe (Vander Linden 2007), and the raw mate-

Figure 7.7. The ring cairn of Moel Goedog 1 looking toward the northwest with Morfa Harlech and Tremadoc Bay visible in the foreground. Photo by the author.

Figure 7.8. The cairn circle of Bryn Cader Faner that stands at the head of the Ardudwy trackway. Photo by Ray Humpheys; reproduced with permission.

rials required for bronze were moved over long distances (Ottaway and Roberts 2008). Boats played a key role in proposed elite exchange and trade networks (Van de Noort 2006), and caches of bronze artifacts and tin ingots recovered from probable wreck sites off Salcombe in south Devon, from near Dover and from the sea floor at the mouth of the estuary of the River Erme, show that such cargoes were being transported in this region in the Bronze Age (Muckelroy 1980; Fox 1995; Needham, Parham, and Frieman 2012).

The importance of landing places within the wider debate of Bronze Age exchange networks has received little attention. Tremadoc Bay would have represented an ideal location from which boats could be safely launched and landed. It would seem no coincidence that the clustering of monuments along the Ardudwy trackway is found in direct associa- tion with the bay. Such monumentality represents a legitimization and control of access to the bay and goods transported along the trackway. Therefore, the significance afforded to the trackway, through the construc- tion of monuments, is directly related to the bay. The trackway and the monuments take on meaning from being part of this cultural maritime landscape.

Ritual Deposition

The Neolithic and Bronze Age of the estuaries is also marked out by high concentration of finds of stone tools and metalwork (RCHAMW 1964; Bowen and Gresham 1967; Morton-Williams 2015). The distribution of these finds is largely concentrated to the edges of the former estuaries, although it is likely that many of these artifacts are not in their original contexts of deposition, having being transported by the flow of rivers and the ebb and flow of tides (figure 7.9).

Within the reclaimed land of the Glaslyn Estuary, the majority of artifacts have been discovered through the digging of drainage channels in an effort to improve and reclaim land from the sea. In these instances, artifacts are found at shallow depth (less than 2 m) within estuarine and wetland deposits. No artifacts to date have been located within the central band of the estuary (figure 7.8). Within the Dwyryd Estuary, a similar pattern of distribution emerges. It would appear that in the majority of cases, stone and metal artifacts are being deposited within saltmarsh environments or within peat mires around the edges of the estuaries.

Neolithic artifacts include polished stone axes and perforated Late Neolithic mace heads and battle axes (figure 7.8). An unusual mace head from Nantmor, in the east of the Glaslyn, appears to be a Neolithic polished stone axe that has been reworked into a perforated mace head, with the blade set at a right angle to the shaft like an adze. Bronze Age metalwork found includes a wide chronological and typological range of artifacts, including flat axes, socketed axes, halberds, palstaves, daggers, shields, and gold torques (Bowen and Gresham 1967, 45–52, 109–28). The concentration of these artifacts within the estuaries cannot be solely accounted for by accidental loss and is suggestive of intentional deposition. Such deposition of artifacts within water has been well documented elsewhere in Britain and Ireland, usually in association with freshwater lakes and bogs (Cooney and Grogan 1994; Bradley 1998; Pryor 2001; Needham 1988). Within Tremadoc Bay, metalwork is found in association with peat and saltmarsh conditions around the edges of the bay and in particular within the estuaries of the Glaslyn and Dwyryd.

A Bronze Age shield discovered in 1890 close to the ancient cliff line near Harlech was found in an upright position within a peat mire on the edge of the present-day estuary. It is likely that the shield was thrown into a mire and was preserved in its original position of deposition (Bowen and Gresham 1967; Uckelmann 2011). A leaf-shaped, basal-looped spearhead, belonging to the Taunton Phase (1400–1300 BC), was recently discovered, eroding from intertidal peat deposits at Ardudwy (Morton-Williams 2015,

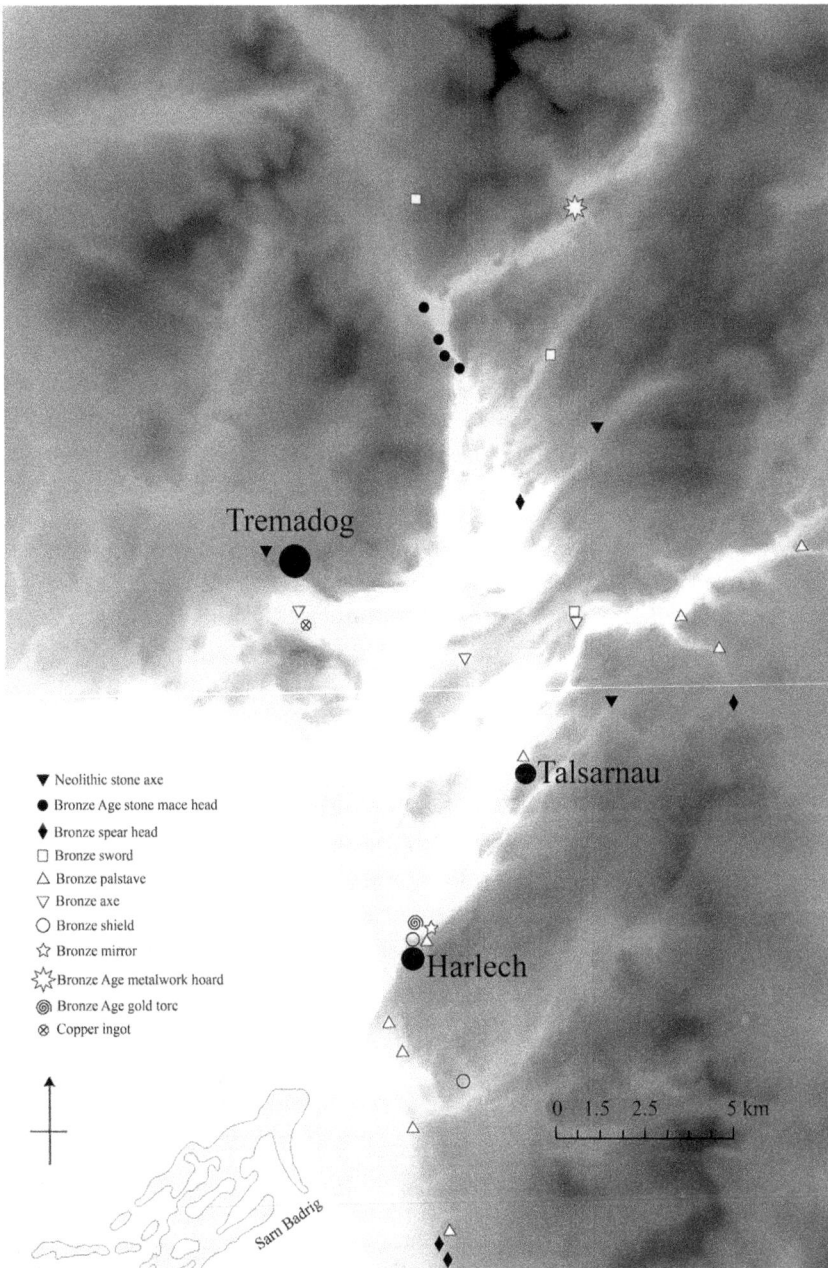

Figure 7.9. The distribution of Neolithic and Early Bronze Age (3000–800 BC) stone axes and mace heads and Bronze Age (2400 BC–AD 43) metalwork within the estuaries and coast of Tremadoc Bay. Created by the author.

43). The artifact shows no evidence of damage from movement in water and sand, so it can confidently be presumed that the artifact was originally deposited within coastal peat mire where it remained to be worn away by coastal erosion.

Other metalwork finds include a shield pattern palstave from Llanbedr, dating 1500–1300 BC (Grimes 1951). A hoard of bronze artifacts from near Harlech contained a large number of palstaves, only one of which survives. The surviving palstave is of a low-flanged type, dating to around 1300 BC. This palstave is an untrimmed casting, demonstrating that the object was new when deposited (Savory 1980, 46). Other metalwork finds from the area include three swords from the Cwm-Moch, datable to 1200–1100 BC (Bowen and Gresham 1967, 122, figure 48) and a leaf shaped sword from Bwlch-y-Fedwen, Penrhyndeudreath, dating to the Ewart Park metalwork phase, around 900 BC (Aldhouse-Green, Davies, and Lynch 2000, 180). A number of the artifacts identified from the estuaries have clear affinities with locations outside of the area, in particular Ireland. These include a copper-alloy flat axe from Penrhyndeudreath (Bowen and Gresham 1967, 47, figure 53) dated to around 1800 cal BC (Needham 1988, 238) and decorated with incised lozenges and lines that are typically Irish in style. Similarly, a gold torque dug up at Harlech in 1692 is a Tara type torque dated 1050–900 BC, and with clear Irish affinities (Bowen and Gresham 1967, 124, plate VI).

This clustering of metalwork directly associated with Tremadoc Bay demonstrates the importance of this maritime landscape during the Bronze Age. The destruction of valuable and rare resources via votive deposition suggests that the bay represented a powerful and ritually charged maritime landscape. Interestingly, a second clustering of metalwork is associated with the Ardudwy trackway (Morton-Williams 2015), suggesting a further link between distant places, landing sites, and networks of exchange.

The Cultural Maritime Landscape

The archaeological evidence from Tremadoc Bay shows that people have lived, traveled, and buried their dead in this maritime landscape. The former estuarine environment and its shorelines were the source of food and raw materials, a means of travel and communication, and a place to build communities. This landscape was more than an environmental larder of seafood; it was a landscape that should be considered a storehouse of cultural values and traditions. For those who inhabited and used this maritime landscape, it was a place where ideas about ancestry, community, belonging, and identity were constructed and enacted. People of the coastlines would have thought about and understood the maritime landscape in multiple ways, using their knowledge of the sea to define themselves.

Past archaeological research on coastal landscapes has largely remained landlocked, with little consideration given to the role of the sea. This chapter has attempted to refocus our attention toward the sea. This approach could—perhaps rightly—be accused of over-emphasizing the significance of the sea within accounts of prehistory. However, this emphasis placed upon the relationship between the archaeological record and the sea is intentional and necessary. This focus aims to redress the current imbalance within research and to sensitize us to the potential role that the sea may have played in prehistory. Central to the development of the themes and ideas explored in this discussion is the need for better archaeological data on coastal and island communities. Excavation and survey need to be alerted to the potential for archaeological evidence to reveal valuable sources of information on the economic and social basis of coastal communities and for the identification of the ephemeral traces of the record, such as skinboats and structures associated with landing places. It has been argued that the sea, like the land, would have held great significance to people in the past, and while providing challenges to its study, should be considered in archaeological accounts of British prehistory.

Acknowledgments

I would like to thank the following people for advice, information, and references; the author claims all responsibility for the how this information may have been interpreted: Ian Brooks, Frances Lynch, Dilwyn Griffith, Clive Hudson, Shân Hudson, Sarah Morton-Williams, Nigel Nayling, Mike Roberts, George Smith, and Geneviève Tellier.

Gary Robinson is a senior lecturer in archaeology at Bangor University in North Wales. His main research interest is the prehistoric archaeology of maritime and coastal communities in western Britain and Ireland. He completed his PhD at the Institute of Archaeology, University College London (PhD 2006), where his interest in British prehistory was first encouraged. His doctoral thesis explored the prehistoric archaeology of the Isles of Scilly, and he has continued to research prehistoric island and coastal communities in Western Britain and Ireland.

References

Acheson, J. M. 1981. "Anthropology of Fishing." *Annual Review of Anthropology* 10, no. 1: 275–316.

Aldhouse-Green, S., G. Davies, and F. M. Lynch. 2000. *Prehistoric Wales*. Stroud: Sutton.

Ashton, W. 1920. *The Evolution of a Coastline: Barrow to Aberystwyth and the Isle of Man*. London: Edward Stanford.

Bailey, S.D., A. G. Wintle, G. A. T. Duller, and C. S. Bristow. 2001. "Sand Deposition during the last Millennium at Aberffraw, Anglesey, North Wales as determined by OSL dating of Quartz." *Quaternary Science Reviews* 20, no. 5–9: 701–4.

Bell, M. 2007. *Prehistoric Coastal Communities: The Mesolithic in Western Britain*. Research Report 149. York: Council for British Archaeology.

Blundell, D. J., D. H. Griffiths, and R. F. King. 1969. "Geophysical Investigations of Buried River Valleys around Cardigan Bay." *Geological Journal* 6, no. 2: 161–80.

Boon, G. C. 1977. "A Greco-Roman Anchor-stock from North Wales." *Antiquaries Journal* LVII, no. 1: 10–30.

Borlase, W. C. 1756. *Observations on the Ancient and Present State of the Isles of Scilly*. Oxford: W. Jackson.

Bowen, E. G., and C. A. Gresham. 1967. *History of Merioneth*. Landysul: Gormerian Press.

Bradley, R. 1998. *The Passage of Arms: An Archaeological Analysis of Prehistoric Hoards and Votive Deposits*. Oxford: Oxbow Books.

Burrow, S. 2003. *Catalogue of the Mesolithic and Neolithic Collections at the National Museums and Galleries of Wales*. Cardiff: National Museums and Galleries of Wales.

Callaghan, R., and C. Scarre. 2009. "Simulating the Western Sea-ways." *Oxford Journal of Archaeology* 28, no. 4: 257–372.

Case, H. 1969. "Neolithic Explanations." *Antiquity* 43, no. 171: 176–86.

Caston, V. N. D. 1966. "Localised Sediment Transport and Submarine Erosion in Tremadoc Bay, Northern Wales." *Marine Geology* 3, no. 6: 401–10.

Clough, T. H., and W. A. Cummins. 1988. "List of Identifiers." In *The Petrology of Prehistoric Stone Implements from the British Isles*. Vol. 2. Edited by T. H. Clough and W. A. Cummins, 141–264. London: Council of British Archaeology.

Cooney, G., and E. Grogan. 1994. *Irish Prehistory: A Social Perspective*. Dublin: Wordwell.

Crawford, O. G. S. 1927. "Lyonesse." *Antiquity* 1, no. 1: 5–14.

Cummings, V., and A. Whittle. 2003. *Places of Special Virtue: Megaliths in the Neolithic Landscapes of Wales*. Oxford: Oxbow.

Daniel, G. E. 1950. *The Prehistoric Chambered Tombs of England and Wales*. Cambridge, UK: Cambridge University Press.

Davidson, A. 2012. "Harlech Castle Watergate." In *Reflections on the Past: Essays in Honour of Frances Lynch*. Edited by W. J. Britnell and R. J. Silvester, 417–31. Welshpool: Cambrian Archaeological Association.

Durrenberger, P. G., and G. Pálsson. 1987. "Ownership at Sea: Fishing Territories and Access to Sea Resources." *American Ethnologist* 14, no. 3: 508–22.

Dutton, A., and P. J. Fasham. 1994. "Prehistoric Copper Mining on the Great Orme, Llandudno, Gwynedd." *Proceedings of the Prehistoric Society* 60: 245–86.

Edmonds, M., R. Johnston, E. La Trobe-Bateman, J. G. Roberts, and G. M. Warren. 2004. Bardsey Island. *Archaeology in Wales* 44: 146–7.

———. 2009. "Ynys Enlli: Shifting Horizons." In *Mesolithic Horizons: Papers presented at the Seventh International Conference on the Mesolithic in Europe, Belfast, 2005.*" Oxford: Oxbow.

Fox, A. 1995. "Tin Ingots from Bigbury Bay." *Proceedings of the Devon Archaeological Society* 53: 11–23.

Garrow, D., and F. Sturt. 2011. "Grey Waters Bright with Neolithic Argonauts? Maritime Connections and the Mesolithic–Neolithic Transition within the 'Western Seaways' of Britain, circa 5000–3500 BC." *Antiquity* 85, no. 327: 59–72.

Ghey, E., N. Edwards, R. Johnston, and R. Pope. 2007. "Characterising the Welsh Roundhouse: Chronology, Inhabitation and Landscape." *Internet Archaeology* 23. Retrieved 16 May 2018 from http://intarch.ac.uk/journal/issue23/johnston_index.html.

Grimes, W. F. 1951. The Prehistory of Wales. Cardiff: National Museum of Wales.

Gibson, A. 1999. *The Walton Basin Project: Excavation and Survey in a Prehistoric Landscape 1993–7*. York: Council for British Archaeology.

Gresham, C., and H. Irvine. 1963. "Prehistoric Routes across North Wales." *Antiquity* 37, no. 145: 54–58.

Gwyn, D. Rh., and L. A. Dutton. 1996. *Coastal Erosion Survey: Aberdaron to Aberdyfi*. GAT Report 198. Bangor: Gwynedd Archaeological Trust.

Hopewell, D. 1995. "A487 Porthmadog By-pass: Proposed Roundabout West of Porthmadog, Archaeological Evaluation." GAT Report G1330. Bangor: Gwynedd Archaeological Trust.

Hudson, C. 2014. "Late Bronze Age Shell Midden." *CBA Wales/Cymru Newsletter* 50: 3.

Innes, J., J. Blackford, and J. Davey. 2003. "Dating the Introduction of Cereal Cultivation to the British Isles: Early Palaeoecological Evidence from the Isle of Man." *Journal of Quaternary Science* 18, no. 7: 603–13.

Ilves, K. 2012. "Do Ships Shape the Shore? An Analysis of the Credibility of Ship Archaeological Evidence for Landing Site Morphology in the Baltic Sea." *The International Journal of Nautical Archaeology* 41, no. 1: 94–105.

Jenkins, D. E. 1899. *Bedd Gelert: Its Facts, Fairies, and Folklore*. Porthmadog: Llewelyn Jenkins.

Jenkins, D. A., and S. Timberlake. 2001. "Prehistoric Mining: Geochemical Evidence From Sediment Cores at Mynydd Parys, Anglesey." British Archaeological Reports, S939. London: Archaeopress.

Kenney, J. 2007. "Parc Cybi, Holyhead: A Large Multi-phase Site in Anglesey." *Archaeology in Wales* 47: 71–78.

———. 2008. "Recent Excavations at Parc Bryn Cegin, Llandygia near Bangor, North Wales." *Archaeologia Cambrensis* 157: 9–142.

———. 2013. "Burnt Mounds in North Wales: Are these Ubiquitous Features Really so Dull?" In *Reflections on the Past: Essays in Honour of Frances Lynch*. Edited by W. J. Britnell and R. J. Silvester, 254–79. Welshpool: Cambrian Archaeological Association.

———. 2014. *Pwllheli to Blaenau Ffestiniog gas pipeline.* GAT Report 1136. Bangor: Gwynedd Archaeological Trust.

Larcombe, P., and C. F. Jago. 1994. "The Late Devensian and Holocene Evolution of Barmouth Bay, Wales." *Sedimentary Geology* 89, no. 3–4: 163–80.

Lynch, F. M. 1969. "The Megalithic Tombs of North Wales." In *Megalithic Enquiries in the West of Britain.* Edited by T. G. E. Powell, J. X. W. P. Corcoran, F. M. Lynch, and J. G. Scott, 107–48. Liverpool: Liverpool University Press.

———. 1984. "Moel Goedog Circle 1: A Complex Ring-cairn near Harlech." *Archaeologica Cambrensis* 133: 8–50.

———. 1989. "Presidential Address: Wales and Ireland in Prehistory; A Fluctuating Relationship." *Archaeologica Cambrensis* 138: 1–19.

———. 1993. *Excavations in the Brenig Valley: A Mesolithic and Bronze Age Landscape in North Wales.* Bangor: Cambrian Archaeological Society.

———. 2011. "Megalithic Studies in Wales: Some Thoughts on the Last Twenty Years." *Archaeology in Wales* 50: 3–12.

Lynch, F. M., and C. R. Musson. 2001. "A Prehistoric and Early Medieval Complex at Llandegai, near Bangor, North Wales." *Archaeologia Cambrensis* 150: 17–142.

May, V. J., and J. D. Hansom. 2003. *Coastal Geomorphology of Great Britain.* Peterborough: Joint Nature Conservation Committee.

McGrail. S. 2001. *Boats of the World: From the Stone Age to Medieval Times.* Oxford: Oxford University Press.

Morton-Williams, S. 2015. "Bronze Age Connections: An Investigation into the Prehistoric Trackways of the Mawddach and Dwyryd Estuaries." Masters dissertation. Bangor: Bangor University.

Muckelroy, K. 1980. "Two Bronze Age Cargoes in British Waters." *Antiquity* 54, no. 211: 100–9.

Nash, G. 2006. *The Archaeology of Death: The Neolithic Chambered Tombs in Wales.* Almerley: Logaston Press.

Needham, S. 1988. "Selective Deposition in the British Early Bronze Age." *World Archaeology* 20, no. 2: 229–48.

———. 2009. "Encompassing the Sea: Maritories and Bronze Age Maritime Interactions." In *Bronze Age Connections: Cultural Contact in Prehistoric Europe.* Edited by P. Clarke, 12–37. Oxford: Oxbow.

Needham, S., K. Parfitt, and G. Varndell. 2006. *The Ringlemere Cup: Precious Cups and the Beginning of the Channel Bronze Age.* British Museum Research Publication 163. London: British Museum Press.

Needham, S., D. Parham, and C. Frieman. 2012. *Claimed by the Sea: Salcombe, Langdon Bay and Other Marine Finds of the Bronze Age.* London: Council for British Archaeology Monograph.

Neill, S. P., A. J. Elliott, and M. R. Hashemi. 2007. "Inter-tidal Variability of Beach Levels in Tremadoc Bay, Eastern Irish Sea." *Continental Shelf Research* 28, no. 14: 1769–81.

O'Connor, B. O. 1980. *Cross-Channel Relations in the Later Bronze Age, Relations Between Britain, North-East France and the Low Countries during the Late Bronze Age and Early Iron Age, with Particular Reference to the Metalwork.* International Series 91. Oxford: British Archaeological Reports.

O'Sullivan, A., and C. Breen. 2011. *Maritime Ireland: An Archaeology of Coastal Communities.* Stoud: History Press.

Ottaway, B. S., and B. Roberts. 2008. "The Emergence of Metalworking." In *Prehistoric Europe: Theory and Practice.* Edited by A. Jones, 193–225. London: Routledge.

Owen, B. 1943. *Diwydiannau coll: ardal y ddwy afon, Dwyryd a Glaslyn.* Lerpwl: Gwasg y Brython ar ran Cyngor yr Eisteddfod Genedlaethol.

Patton, M. 1991. "Stone Axes of the Channel Islands: Neolithic Exchange in an Insular Context." *Oxford Journal of Archaeology* 10, no. 1: 33–43.

Peacock, D., and L. Cutler. 2010. "A Neolithic Voyage." *The International Journal of Nautical Archaeology* 39, no. 1: 116–24.

Pryor, F. 2001. *The Flag Fen Basin: Archaeology and Environment of a Fenland landscape.* Swindon: English Heritage.

Quinnell, H., M. P. Blockley, and P. Berridge. 1994. *Excavations at Rhuddlan, Clwyd 1969–73 Mesolithic to Medieval.* Council for British Archaeology Research Report no. 95. York: Council for British Archaeology.

Ranwell, D. S. 1959. "Newborough Warren, Anglesey. I: The Dune System and Dune Slack Habitat." *Journal of Ecology* 47, no. 3: 571–601.

RCAHMW (Royal Commission on the Ancient and Historical Monuments of Wales). 1956. *An Inventory of the Ancient Monuments in Caernarvonshire: Volume I.* London: Her Majesty's Stationary Office.

———. 1960. *An Inventory of the Ancient Monuments in Caernarvonshire: Volume II.* London: Her Majesty's Stationary Office.

———. 1964. *An Inventory of the Ancient Monuments in Caernarvonshire: Volume III.* London: Her Majesty's Stationary Office.

Rees, C., and M. Jones. 2015. "Neolithic Houses from Llanfaethlu, Anglesey." *PAST: The Newsletter of the Prehistoric Society* 8: 1–3.

Rhind. P., T. H. Blackstock, and H. S. Hardy. 2001. "The Evolution of Newborough Warren Dune System with Particular Reference to the Past Four Decades." In *Coastal Dune Management: Shared Experience of European Conservation Practice.* Edited by J. A. Houston, S. E. Edmondson, and P. J. Rooney, 345–79. Liverpool: Liverpool University Press.

Richards, W. M. 1925. "Dissertation on the History of Traeth Mawr and the Industrial Results of the Formation of the Embankment." PhD dissertation. Cardiff: University College of Wales.

Roberts, M. J. 2006. "Holocene Sea-Level Change in North Wales: The Evolution of the Menai Strait." PhD dissertation. Bangor: University of Wales.

Roberts, M. J., J. D. Scourse, J. D. Bennell, D. G. Huws, C. F. Jago, and B. T. Long. 2011. "Late Devensian and Holocene Relative Sea-level Change in North Wales, UK." *Journal of Quaternary Science* 26, no. 2: 141–55.

Robinson, G. 2007. *The Prehistoric Island Landscape of Scilly.* Oxford: British Archaeological Reports.

———. 2013a. "'A Sea of Small Boats': Places and Practices on the Prehistoric Seascape of Western Britain." *Internet Archaeology* 34. Retrieved 16 May 2018 from https://doi.org/10.11141/ia.34.2.

————. 2013b. "The excavation of a multi period rock-shelter at Garreg Hylldrem, Llanfrothen 2011–2012." *Archaeology in Wales* 52: 3–10.

————. 2016. "An Island Archaeology of Neolithic Ynys Môn (Anglesey)." In *Decoding Neolithic Atlantic and Mediterranean Island Ritual.* Edited by G. Nash and A. Townsend, 53–63. Oxford: Oxbow.

Rowley-Conwy, P. 2011. "Westward Ho! The Spread of Agriculturalism from Central Europe to the Atlantic." *Current Anthropology* 52, no. S4: 431–51.

Savory, H. N. 1960. "Excavations at Dinas Emrys, Beddgelert (Caern.) 1954–56." *Archaeologia Cambrensis* 109: 13–77.

————. 1980. *Guide Catalogue of the Bronze Age Collections.* Cardiff: National Museum of Wales.

Sheridan, A. 2000. "Achnacreebeag and its French Connections: Vive the 'Auld' Alliance." In *The Prehistory and Early History of Atlantic Europe.* Edited by J. Henderson, 1–16. International Series: 861. Oxford: British Archaeological Reports.

————. 2007. "Green Treasures from the Magic Mountains." *British Archaeology* 96: 22–27.

————. 2010. "The Neolithization of Britain and Ireland: The Big Picture." In *Landscapes in Transition.* Edited by B. Finlayson and G. Warren, 89–105. Oxford: Oxbow.

Sheridan, A., R. Schulting, H. Quinnell, and R. Taylor. 2008. "Revisiting a Small Passage Tomb at Broadsands, Devon." *Proceedings of the Devon Archaeology Society* 66: 1–26.

Sherratt, A. 1996. "Why Wessex? The Avon Route and River Transport in Later British Prehistory." *Oxford Journal of Archaeology* 15, no. 2: 211–34.

Smith, G. 2001. *Gwynedd Lithic Scatters Project.* GAT Report number 357. Bangor: Gwynedd Archaeological Trust.

————. 2003. "A Survey of Prehistoric Funerary and Ritual Sites in Meirionnydd, 2000–2001." *Journal of the Merioneth Historical and Record Society* 14, no. 2: 105–17.

————. 2005. "The North-west Wales Lithic Scatters Project." *Lithics* 2, no. 26: 38–56.

————. 2008. *Nant Farm, Neolithic site, Porth Neigwl, Llŷn: Preliminary Report on the Archaeological Rescue Recording, March 2008.* GAT Report number 745. Bangor: Gwynedd Archaeological Trust.

————. 2009. *Nant Farm, Prehistoric Burnt Mound, Porth Neigwl, Llŷn: Preliminary Report on Assessment Recording and Rescue Excavations.* GAT Report number 796. Bangor: Gwynedd Archaeological Trust.

————. 2013. "Lithics, Y Bryn." In *Balfour Beatty/Jones Brothers Joint Venture A487 Porthmadog, Minffordd and Tremadog Bypass Report on Archaeological Mitigation.* Edited by L. W. Parry, 40–43. GAT Report 1065. Bangor: Gwynedd Archaeological Trust.

Smith, G., A. E. Caseldine, C. J. Griffiths, I. Peck, N. Nayling, and D. Jenkins. 2017. "An Early Bronze Age Burnt Mound Trough and Boat Fragment with Accompanying Palaeobotanical and Pollen Analysis at Nant Farm, Porth Neigwl, Llŷn Peninsular, Gwynedd." *Studia Celtica* 51, no. 1: 1–63.

Smith, G., A. Davidson, and J. Kenney. 2002. *North Wales Intertidal Peat Survey.* GAT Report 450. Bangor: Gwynedd Archaeological Trust.

Smith, G., and E. Walker. 2014. "Snail Cave Rock Shelter, North Wales: A New Prehistoric Site." *Archaeologica Cambrensis* 163: 99–133.

Steele, N. 2010. "Report on the Ynysfor brooches (PRN 24144)." Unpublished Gwynedd Archaeological Trust Report for the Portable Antiquities Scheme. Retrieved 23 August 2016 from https://finds.org.uk/database/search/results/q/Ynysfor.

Steers, J. A. 1939. "Sand and Shingle Formations in Cardigan Bay." *The Geographical Journal* 94, no. 3: 209–27.

———. 1964. *The Coastline of England and Wales*. Cambridge, UK: Cambridge University Press.

Stevens, C. J., and D. Q. Fuller. 2012. "Did Neolithic Farming Fail? The Case for a Bronze Age Agricultural Revolution in the British Isles. *Antiquity* 86, no. 333: 707–22.

Thomas, A. C. 1985. *Exploration of a Drowned Landscape: Archaeology and History of the Isles of Scilly*. London: Batsford.

Tilley, C. 1994. *A Phenomenology of Landscape*. Oxford: Berg.

Uckelmann, M. 2011. "The Function of Bronze Shields." In *Bronze Age Warfare: Manufacture and Use of Weaponry*. Edited by M. Uckelmann and M. Mödlinger, 187–200. International Series Number 2255. Oxford: Archaeopress.

Vander Linden, M. 2007. "What Linked the Bell Beakers in Third Millennium BC Europe?" *Antiquity* 81, no. 312: 343–52.

Van de Noort, R. 2006. "Argonauts of the North Sea: A Social Maritime Archaeology for the 2nd Millennium BC." *Proceedings of the Prehistoric Society* 72: 267–87.

———. 2010. "The Humber, its Sewn-plank Boats, their Contexts and the Significance of it all." In *The Dover Bronze Age Boat in Context: Society and Water Transport in Prehistoric Europe*. Edited by P. Clark, 90–98. Oxford: Oxbow.

Waddell, J. 1993. "The Irish Sea in Prehistory." *The Journal of Irish Archaeology* VI 91/92, no. 6: 29–40.

Waddington, K. 2013. *Settlements of Northwest Wales: From the Late Bronze Age to the Early Medieval Period*. Cardiff: University of Wales Press.

Waselkov, G. A. 1987. "Shellfish Gathering and Shell Midden Archaeology." *Advances in Archaeological Method and Theory* 10: 93–210.

Westerdahl, C. 1992. "The Maritime Cultural Landscape." *The International Journal of Nautical Archaeology* 21, no. 1: 5–14.

———. 2011. "Conclusion: The Maritime Cultural Landscape Revisited." In *The Archaeology of Maritime Landscapes*. Edited by B. Ford, 331–44. New York: Springer.

Wickham-Jones, C. 2007. "Middens in Scottish Prehistory: Time, Space and Relativity." In *Shell Middens in Atlantic Europe*. Edited by N. Milner, O. E. Craig, and G. N. Bailey, 86–93. Oxford: Oxbow.

Wymer, J. J. 1977. *A Gazetteer of Mesolithic Sites in England and Wales*. London: Council for British Archaeology.

Woodman, P., and M. McCarthy. 2003. "Contemplating some Awful(ly Interesting) Vistas: Importing Cattle and Red deer into Prehistoric Ireland." In *Neolithic Settlement in Ireland and Western Britain*. Edited by I. Armit, E. Murphy, E. Nelis, and D. Simpson, 31–39. Oxford: Oxbow.

CHAPTER 8

Fish Traps of the Crocodile Islands

Windows on Another World

Bentley James

In 1938, the eminent Australian anthropologist, Donald Thomson, described a "new type of fish trap in North East Arnhem Land" and the cultural and ecological context in which it was being used (1938). Following Thomson, this chapter focuses on the fish traps of the inner and outer Crocodile Islands, Northern Australia, to show how fish traps refurbished for the first time in seventy years provide a window on ancestral relationships between people and place. Each place is a node in a preexisting ancestral network of sites, people's relationship to which anchor and embed each person in a kin-based social universe. A collaborative project to reanimate these fish traps revives highly endangered site-based knowledge, language, and ritual linked to their use. In contrast to stark changes wrought by settler-state colonialism, ancestral laws ordering relations between kin, ancestral sites, and practices continue to shape Yan-nhaŋu conduct with regard to their marine ecology. These marine people persist in their struggle to keep their island way of life, a way of life evolving over uncounted generations of intimate coexistence with the sea. The fish traps of the Crocodile Islands provide rare insight into recent Yan-nhaŋu precontact patterns of interisland travel, navigation, and local knowledge linked to a preexisting ancestral geography.

The *Betŋu*: Fish Trap at Murruŋga Island 1937

In the late 1930s, anthropologist Donald Thomson examined links between indigenous technology, ecological knowledge, and ancestral laws in his detailed recording of the material culture of North East Arnhem Land, in particular the construction and rituals of the fish traps of mainland Yolŋu people. I will build on these themes in his work, beginning with a fish trap he photographed at Murruŋga, the largest of the outer Crocodile Islands and home to the island-dwelling Yolŋu[1] people speaking the Yan-nhaŋu[2] language.

In 1993, I showed Yan-nhaŋu people of Murruŋga Thomson's photographs of the fish trap (figure 8.1). In response, they described an extensive and previously unrecorded system of ritual and ecological knowledge in which fish traps were integral to a seasonal round of interisland voyaging and marine resource utilization. I suggest that rituals and practices associated with the deployment of fish traps provided intergenerational transfer of what is now an endangered and distinctive local, site-based ontology or worldview. This view assumes a preexisting ancestral network of sites that anchor each person in a kin-based social universe bestowed by the Yan-nhaŋu ancestors with the *rom* (law). This distinctive metaphysics of essential and ancestrally bestowed connectedness is referred to and understood through the idiom of kinship. Everything is kin. Yolŋu people believe that their ancestors bestowed not only kinship, but the "'law'—the

Figure 8.1. Two men by a fish fence (*Betŋu*) in an estuary at Ga<u>d</u>atha, Wessel Islands, North East Arnhem Land. The man in the foreground is Laurie Baymarrwaŋa's father, Burrundjiŋu. The man in the background is the Wubulkarra man Badapat, Baymarrwaŋa's husband. Photo by D. Thomson, courtesy of the Thomson family and Museum Victoria, 1937 (TPH 774).

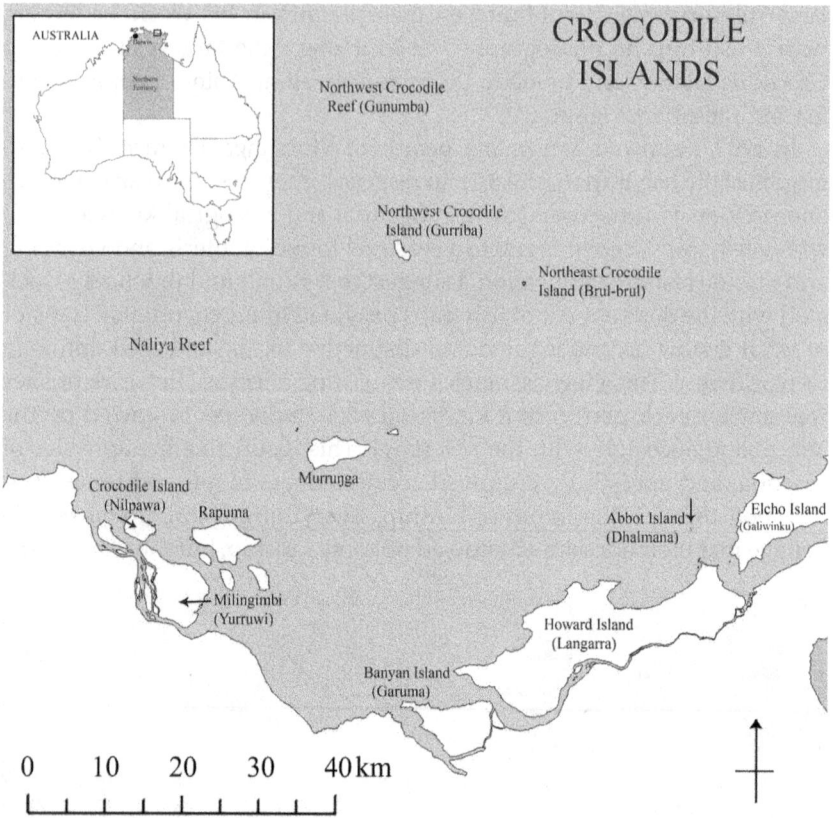

Figure 8.2. Map of the Crocodile Islands and surrounding Arafura Sea (Northern Territory, Australia). Created by the author.

precepts and practices that shape human social life—on the humans that follow them" (Keen 2004, 211). In this way, the fish traps present a window into a deeper understanding of life on the Crocodile Islands and a more profound appreciation of contemporary Yan-nhaŋu people's attachment to sea country and life on their island homelands (figure 8.2).[3]

The Sea Connects Us All

The sea is central to the Yan-nhaŋu way of life as a physical space and a mental map inscribed with ancestral meaning.[4] The exclusively marine geography of their estates structured patterns of ritual, travel, and marine resource management with a distinctively kin-based island-dwelling organization. This island-based pattern was in place by Pleistocene sea level stabilization and is potentially much older (Plumb 1965, 4; Woodroffe, Chappell, and Thom 1988, 262; Woodroffe and Grindrod 1991; Faulkner 2006). This way of life was all but wiped out by the coming of the mission. In more recent times, the familiar mechanisms of dispossession of land and marine resources via settler-state intervention increase the destructive force of persistent colonization. At this precipice, some Yan-nhaŋu and their kin, still resident at small island homelands, are partially shielded from the harshest state-imposed disciplines, as resources from their sea country continue to supplement their livelihoods.[5] Indeed, it is not too much to say that the sea continues to protect the last surviving Yan-nhaŋu people.

The Yan-nhaŋu are very properly Yolŋu people. That is, Yan-nhaŋu is a variety of Yolŋu language endemic to North East Arnhem Land. The six Yan-nhaŋu speaking clans (*bäpurru*) are grouped into patri-moieties: Dhuwa and Yirritja. These are two halves, or semi-moieties, of an ideational system that sees the world divided into two categories, fundamentally classifying every aspect of the Yolŋu universe. This metaphysical division classes all aspects of the physical and spiritual world as essentially/spiritually Dhuwa or Yirritja. This metaphysic underpins the Yolŋu worldview. The three Dhuwa and three Yirritja Yan-nhaŋu clans (*bäpurru*) each inherit distinct sites and estates. Each clan also inherits a dialectical variety slightly different—although mutually intelligible—which, as such, reflects a discrete and specific ancestral provenance. These differences and similarities at once differentiate the Yan-nhaŋu from, and link them with, their Yolŋu kin, in extended strings of relatedness across the wider region (Keen 1994).

Starting in the last four hundred years or so, Macassan sailors—probably *Sama-Bajau* from Celebes (Sulawesi)—began visiting the islands, seeking *bêche-de-mer* or *trepang* (sea cucumber) and other resources (McKnight 1976, 153–54, 158; Berndt 1977; see also Stacey and Allison, this volume for detailed discussion). Relations were generally characterized as good. Arriving with the northeast monsoon in December and leaving in March when the wind turned to the southeast, the Macassans brought with them new technologies, including the buoyant wooden dugout canoe quite distinct from the endemic *gal-gal* or *dirrka* bark canoe. Lloyd W. Warner, who visited the islands in the 1920s, speculates that this new dugout canoe technology may have increased regional travel by sea throughout the area (Warner 1937, 448–53). Contact with Europeans is often reported as starting in 1803 with Matthew Flinders' mapping of the north coast; however, the "Krokodillen Eÿlandts" appeared on Abel Tasman's charts as early as 1644 (Robert 1973, 175).

As previously alluded to, profound changes swept the islands in 1922 when the Methodist Overseas Mission (MOM) established a mission on the largest of the inner Crocodile Islands at Milingimbi. Throughout Australia, Christian missions were key tools of assimilation policy with the aim of making sedentary what the settler-state described as the "nomadic" inclinations of Indigenous people.[6] The subsequent corralling of people with highly mobile subsistence patterns had the predictably disastrous effects, as witnessed across Australia over the last century or so. The urgent need to curb the "native's" want to go "walkabout"—a settler expression to describe seasonal travel—was couched in terms of the moral responsibility to protect them, coupled with the oft-heard "it's for their own good."

At Milingimbi on the inner Crocodile Islands, year-round residence at the mission by an increasing number of geographically distant kin precipitated intense inter-clan violence. This fighting resulted in a steep numerical decline in the population of Yan-nhaŋu men. This decline had a profound effect on the political and ritual power of the Yan-nhaŋu, diminishing their control over resources. The past ninety-five years of missionization and increasing settler-state control have intensified the associated diminution of Yan-nhaŋu language use. As Yan-nhaŋu language became associated with the internecine conflict, it became an unused language within the new Milingimbi polity. This decline in the use of the endemic language of the islands curtailed the intergenerational transmission of, among other things, a detailed knowledge of the once-customary routines of interisland migrations and the procedures of fish trap deployment.

When I arrived in the Crocodile Islands in 1993, only three hundred words of the Yan-nhaŋu language had been recorded. Yan-nhaŋu was all but forgotten. As chance would have it, I met with an octogenarian on the outer islands who spoke Yan-nhaŋu. Over the next twenty years, we worked together to record some four thousand words and the intimate connections of myth and local knowledge therein. This gracious old lady, Laurie Baymarrwaŋa, sadly no longer with us, passed away in her ninety-seventh year. Together, we created a ranger program called the Crocodile Islands Rangers (CIR) to nurture and pass on the precious biological, cultural, and linguistic coordinates of a Yan-nhaŋu metaphysic. One of our projects was to restore the fish traps of the Crocodile Islands, as many had not seen a fish trap in use since the last were set in the 1940s. It was the process of refurbishing the fish traps that brought to light the many unrecorded stories and the enactment of this long-unseen ritual linked to the physical and spiritual deployment of fish traps. This was an emotional experience for an older generation as the intergenerational transmission of this local knowledge and its symbols, the revivification of its rituals, are held very dear and decreed by ancestral law.[7] I want to turn now to a brief introduction to the former practice of interisland travel, the fish traps of the inner islands, followed by fish traps of the outer Crocodile Islands.

Human occupation of Northern Australia dates back some sixty thousand years (Roberts, Jones, and Smith 1990). In addition to the enormous time-depth of this human endeavor, Klokler and Gaspar (this volume), remind us that ocean harvesters need to be understood in a different manner to societies that exploit terrestrial resources. In the North of Australia, a wide variety of fish trap styles indicates the significance of fish retrieval technologies to coastal indigenous people (see Roth 1901; Hale and Tindale 1933; McCarthy 1940; Akerman 1976; Smith 1983; Walters 1985a, 1985b; Trigger 1987). In coastal Arnhem Land, Thomson (1938) records fish traps adapted to fresh and salt water, streams, and estuaries, where weirs and palisades trap fish upstream on the returning tide[8] (see also Hale and Tindale 1933, 111; Altman 1987). There are seven named varieties of permanent fish trap on the Crocodile Islands. Three are made on the inner islands and four other kinds on the outer islands. Distinctive environmental conditions dictate the materials to be used in fish trap construction. The inner islands are deep grey anoxic mud, which is used in the three kinds of mud and grass fish traps. On Murruŋga in the outer islands, the four kinds of fish traps made use available rocks, timber, and fiber of various kinds. Today, fish traps have been outmoded by the ubiquitous nylon fishing line and a number of highly effective traditional fish spear types still in use. What is of special interest are the complex social relations and ritual life that surround the deployment of fish traps.

Thomson records that "tradition, handed on in mythology, furnishes the motive, the driving force, in all behaviour and practice, even in matters of material culture" (Thomson 1938, 195). Indeed, mythological narratives, rituals, and ecological relations comprise a powerful ideational engine at the heart of Yan-nhaŋu life. This system produces the actual physical behavior by which ecological relations are determined. In this way, the practices and symbols of human ecological relations are windows that reveal deeper metaphysical themes (Ellen 1982, 206). Anthropologist Ian Keen lived for some years on the Crocodile Islands in the early 1970s. He describes how Yolŋu "ancestral laws" shaped human and environmental ecological relations in four primary ways:

> Firstly, they framed the regional orders of law that provided the foundations of social order. Second, they were implicated in the ownership and control of access to land and waters and their resources. Third, people believed, on the basis of these doctrines, that they could tap ancestral and magical powers to enhance the supply of resources and their power to acquire resources. And fourth, many economic rights, obligations, prerogatives, and prohibitions were framed explicitly in terms of ancestral law. (Keen 2004, 210)

For Yolŋu people, these cosmological doctrines are understood to be the endowment of the *waŋarr* (creator/ancestor/spirits) (Williams 1986;

Keen 1978, 2004; Morphy 1984). The Yan-nhaŋu consider their language and culture, local practices and symbols as bestowed on them in the act of creation. It is this bestowal that furnishes the authority that binds them in perpetuity to their sacred sites and to their inescapable responsibility for the continuation of their associated practices. The fulfillment of this ancestral necessity grows more onerous. Despite the deceptive public rhetoric of the Australian state, its legacy of settler colonialism and continuity in punitive assimilation policies circumscribe the conditions under which the Yan-nhaŋu are able to pass on their life ways to a new generation.

Myth, Mobility, and the Timing of Seasonal Interisland Travel

The Yan-nhaŋu tradition of song and myth is still strong at Murruŋga. Songs, stories, and rituals are the vehicle for—and the repository of—local knowledge, ways of life embedded in language and metaphor gleaned by uncounted generations of subsistence by the sea. Up until recently, migratory voyaging provided access to the seasonally available marine resources on the islands. These resources and the journeys to access them have sustained the Yan-nhaŋu for millennia. For the Yan-nhaŋu, the power of ancestral forces can still be seen in the mighty movement of the currents and waves, the tides and seasons, and in the ever-changing moods of the sea.

Yan-nhaŋu myths depict fearless seafarers who braved monstrous crocodiles, sharks, deadly jellyfish, and a profusion of marine hazards on their journeys between the islands. Journeys were carried out on buoyant devices like the floating log (*wuḏuku*) and the insubstantial paper bark raft (*djutu*), although, these were rarely used for longer voyages, as truly gigantic crocodiles of six meters were, and are, still present. Thomson's field notes (1937) report the construction of more robust canoes made of sheets of eucalyptus tree bark and called *ḏirrka* at Murruŋga. These *ḏirrka* were capable of carrying ten people at a time. Made by sewing together layers of bark in a method called *barrwan-minḏapumaway*, the largest were up to four meters long. Thomson's field notes applaud their surprising seaworthiness and speed over rough water:

> the biggest of all are made at Mooroonga [Murruŋga] (yana:ngo matta, Yiritja, and Mandjikai malla) of two sheets of bark sewn together and in these the natives make journeys to Rabuma [Rapuma] and other islands of the Crocodile group, as well as to the mainland. (Thomson 1937, File No. 115)

There was also a smaller bark canoe, *gal-gal,* associated with travel over shorter distances between the islands and the transport of marine resources. As mentioned, these two types of bark canoe are quite distinct from the hollow log or dugout canoe (*lipalipa*) of Macassan origin. The following picture depicts the buoyant *lipalipa* at Milingimbi circa 1927 (figure 8.3).

The dugout canoe of Macassan design was typical of the way people made journeys between the islands in the last four hundred years or so. Today, Yan-nhaŋu people continue to travel between the twenty-seven inner and three outer islands in aluminum boats with motors. Two islands now have airstrips. Even in more modern sea craft, the journey by sea is still not to be taken lightly.

The reckoning of the seasons and their winds is at the heart of island time. Knowledge of the seasonal availability of local resources is captured in the expression *maŋutji bulthanaway* (literally, "quality of telling the eye") (see also Christie 1994). This way of seeing describes how attributes such as the flowering times of certain trees or the characteristic winds of a season may signify the availability or ripeness of resources on distant islands. For example, when the Kurrajong tree (*balgurr*) (*Brachychiton paradoxus*) begins to flower, Yan-nhaŋu or Mariŋa[9] men travel by dingy to Northwest Crocodile Island or Gurriba to gather the crested tern eggs (*djarrak*) (*Sterna bergii*) laid on the sand of the beach called *Balawarrga*.[10] The window of egg gestation is narrow and eggs must be acquired with alacrity or they, or more properly their contents, will have flown. Once at Gurriba while searching for eggs, the men will drink at the fresh water well (*Ganinygurra*) and sit by the fish trap *Nanḏuwurra* at *Nanḏuwa* as those of generations be-

Figure 8.3. Dugout (*lipalipa*) at Milingimbi, circa 1927. Reproduced with permission of the University of Sydney Archives (Warner/Webb collection Image 37_133 by Reverend T T Webb 1926–39 Yolŋu'-yulŋu ga marrtji wakirlil lipalipay).

fore have done. Here, they will sing the songs of the wind. These songs of the winds, the knowledge they impart, and these variable seasonal winds themsleves, still have great significance to the timely execution of interisland travel, to fishing, and to the collection of marine resources generally.[11]

Table 8.1 is an adapted seasonal calendar from the Murruŋga School that outlines the relationship between seasons and named wind directions on the outer islands.[12] In the past, the seasons of *rarranhdharr* and *dhuludur'* were known as "the hungry time" on the mainland, especially *dhuludur'*, as it is the height of the wet season and there was a scarcity of many food types during the heavy rains. *Rarranhdharr* is "the hot time"—*luku ga nhära*, which literally translates to "feet on fire"; it is at this time that Yolŋu from all over the region would customarily congregate at the inner island Milingimbi in what Warner called the "shellfish and ceremony season" (Warner 1937, 4). During the ceremonial season, large numbers of kin would assemble to gather and share in the abundant shellfish (*ŋa'kanyu*) (*Anadarra granosa*) and ritual cycad bread (*ŋathu*) (*Cycas media*) while practicing the most sacred of regional and local ceremonies (Warner 1937, 4). The yearly practice of these major rituals, focused as they were on fertility, was frowned on by the missionaries and largely came to an end, or had gone underground, by the late 1920s. Nevertheless, the ceremonies that were carried on in secret for the most part and are still practiced occasionally today are of enormous significance to the reckoning of a preexisting ancestral geography of sites and associated mythologies. Cessation of seasonal travel to the most distant islands was dictated by strong wind. Conversely, the gentle seasonal winds of *mayaltha* and *midawarr* coincide with an abundance of available marine resources on the outer islands. Figure 8.4 describes the winds and extent of cyclical travel around the islands circumscribed according to seasonal wind patterns.

Travel was restricted to the inner islands in the season *rarranhdharr* (August–September) and *dhuludur'* (October–December) by strong northerly winds. In *bärra'mirr* (January–February) and *dharratharramirr* (May–July), strong westerly winds and easterly winds respectively did not permit

Table 8.1. Seasonal calendar (adapted from James et al. 2003).

Month	Season	Wind direction	Wind name
March–April	*Midawarr*	Gentle southeast	*Djalataŋ*
May–July	*Dharratharramirr*	Strong east	*Bulwunu*
August–September	*Rarranhdharr*	Northwest	*Bärra*
October–December	*Dhuludur'*	North	*Luŋgurrma*
January–February	*Bärra'mirr*	West	*Bärra*
February–March	*Mayaltha*	Gentle northeast	*Dhimurru*

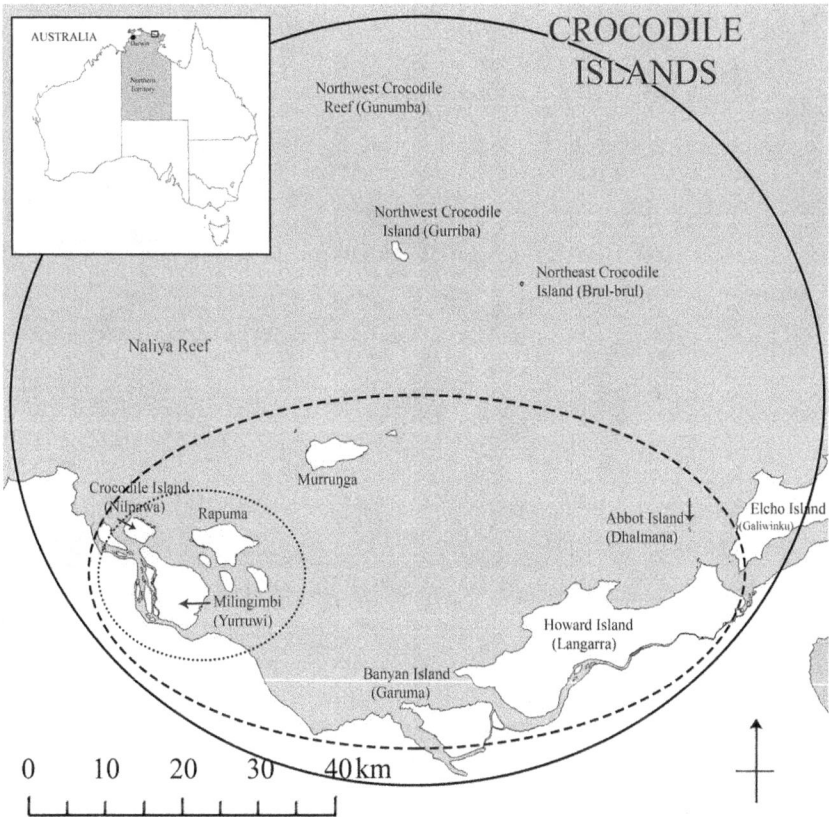

Figure 8.4. Seasons of interisland travel. Created by the author.

travel to the most distant islands. In *mayaltha* (February–March) and *midawarr* (March–April), travel throughout the entire domain was possible. The importance of seasonal reckoning in fishing success is critical. As such, it is part of a detailed knowledge of the geographical and biophysical circumstances of the islands at the very heart of local knowledge.

It is still possible to hear stories of the way the winds governed the planning of the seasonal round of island resource usage by speaking to members of an older generation. There is nothing quite like the profound and direct account of someone who has lived tooth and bone with the necessities and dangers of a life totally dependent upon the sea, such as the account I heard from Laurie Baymarrwaŋa, who was born on Murruŋga Island in 1917 (figure 8.5).

Baymarrwaŋa never spoke a word of English, but her stories were epic tales of high drama and narrow escapes. She survived generations of her kinsmen, the coming of the white man, internecine clan warfare, sorcery

Figure 8.5. Laurie Baymarrwaŋa (Baymarrwangga), 1917–2014. Photo by Salome Harris, May 2006; reproduced with permission.

and sickness, and the bombing of Milingimbi in World War II. Living day-to-day on the islands that she loved, she recounted with joy her experiences as a youth traveling throughout the islands by canoe to access seasonally available resources.

The following story, recorded by the late Laurie Baymarrwaŋa at Murruŋa, describes a time governed by the seasonal round of interisland travel, the lure of ripening fruits, and the cyclical reoccurrence of marine resources emerging with the changing seasons:

Yan-nhaŋu

Midawarr-yu galiyana djalkirri-yu, galiyana Yurruwi galiyana raŋan gudubunuma dhabakthana barrwan nhankara bundunha Rapumaŋurunha bayku-munu walima Murruŋa ŋurunha Murruŋa nhan'ku-munu

Midawarryunha nhan'ku Murruŋa räkay bulaŋgitj-nha dandathanabal garrana dandathanabal garrana dandathanabal garrana. Yalalaba Gadatha dhula ganitjirri bulaŋgitjinha ŋapurr garrana Gadathalili ŋumunkara gudubunuma räkay binkumunu Garaŋ-karaŋalili. Midawarryu dananah luŋdana dandathanabal djini-ku räkaygu, yo.

English

In Midawarr (the season of calm water), we would paddle the canoe from Milingimbi to Rapuma and from Rapuma to Murruŋa Islands (forty nautical miles to sea; see figure 8.2).

During March–April season, the Eleocharis sedge corm arrives, and they ripen at Murruŋa. Later, when the water at Gadatha is good, we would take the special Eleocharis corms from Gadatha to Garaŋ-Karaŋa (water hole). This is the time when we would all gather together on the islands and dig the Eleocharis corm, yes.

Moon, Tides, and the Morning Star

Local knowledge provides a blueprint for the timing of yearly migrations and seasonal behaviors linked to the lives and times of the key marine species. Calendar plants and winds continue to be important signifiers of the changing seasons and the reappearance of roving varieties of, among other things, animals and birds to feed and nest. More precise measurements of daily time are determined by reckoning the movements of the celestial bodies. Yan-nhaŋu of an older generation parse the time of day and night by the relative advance of the sun, the moon, and the stars.

The second planet Venus is called *Baṉumbirr* (Zorc 1986, 12; Rudder 1993; James and Baymarrwaŋa 2014, 213). The Yan-nhaŋu people say that the morning star *Baṉumbirr* is pulled into the sea below the horizon (*Baṉumbirr dhupthana*; see table 8.2, 4:00 a.m.) by the spirits of the mythical island of *Barralku* in the east. When in the sea, the star turns back into the iridescent blue starfish *Baṉumbirr* (*Linckia laevigata*) found on the reefs of Murruŋga. Any day, the blue starfish can be seen on the reef flats making their way to the west to rise into the sky again at days end. Keeping up with modern times, children at school are taught to read analogue and digital time; however, people living on the islands do not generally calculate time in the idiom of hours and minutes. A description of Yan-nhaŋu time corresponds more closely to that described by Rudder for Yolŋu elsewhere (1993, 247–49) (table 8.2).

These divisions of time may be further specified by adding suffixes equivalent to "past," as in, *baṉubal* (past the hour), or *garrana* (to). For example, past the time when the morning star dips below the horizon is called *Baṉumbirr dhupthana baṉubal*. At this time, in the season of *dharratharramirr* (May–July), the time of *rika* (the cold wind), no one gets

Table 8.2. Celestial movement and time (adapted from Rudder 1993).

Hours	Celestial phenomena	Yan-nhaŋu classification
6:00 a.m.	Sun coming up throwing out its light	*Guku girriyana baṉubal*
10:00 a.m.	Sun half up mid-morning	*Munubi gabiyana*
12:00 p.m.	Sun overhead midday	*Riya walirrway*
4:00 p.m.	Sun halfway down the sky, late afternoon	*Walirr rirrpirru*
6:00 p.m.	Sunset and the orange colours of its decline	*Wanbali*
8:00 p.m.	Evening Star emerges from the horizon	*Munuguba Baṉumbirr girriyana*
10:00 p.m.	Pleiades dips below the horizon	*Dhampthun munuguba*
12:00 a.m.	Milky Way in the middle of the night sky	*Guyulan miṯtji gulun riyaway*
2:00 a.m.	Milky Way decline	*Djeda munuguba*
4:00 a.m.	Morning Star in decline	*Baṉumbirr dhupthana*

out of bed until *Baṉumbirr dhupthana baŋubal* because the wind is still too cold at that time of the morning.[13]

The moon holds a powerful sway over the movement of the tides and therefore over the behavior of fish. Yirrijta Yan-nhaŋu mythology holds the moon to be the embodiment of a masculine ancestral entity. His monthly resurrection is the outcome of a recurrent immolation, as he is repeatedly burnt to death in his unending punishment for drowning his two sons in a fish trap. Tidal intensity, low-low and high-high tides, are signified by the appearance of a full or new moon; traps are configured in graduated layers to take full advantage of these different tidal phases.[14] For example, fish-trap deployment is influenced by the fact that one of the two daily low tides is lower than the other. For six months, from roughly *dhuludur'* (October) through *bärra'mirr* (February), the lower of these two tides occurs at night. From roughly April to September, (*Miḏawarr, dharratharramirr,* and *rarranhdharr*), this low-low tide occurs during the day, at which time people forage on the *märraṉdil* (reef). The subsequent tidal return signals the ascendency of the domain of fish and the reef flats are submerged.

The return and departure of turtle, dugong, and fish species that inhabit the islands is a primary interest of local knowledge, and at the homelands, it is the topic of morning conversation. At certain times of the year on the island of Murruŋga, fish make up 70 percent of the daily protein intake for all the people on the islands (James 2009, 243). One way Yan-nhaŋu classify fish is by the ecological niche that they inhabit (table 8.3). Some fish move from the *wiyaŋgul* (deep water and outer rocks) up the reef slope and onto the reef flat to feed as the tide rises, while others come after the tide is full. Others, mainly bottom feeders, move from channels or depressions from the *ŋarŋganabo* (inside reef) onto the reef flat and reef pools on a rising tide.

As a consequence, inshore bottom feeders and some surface-feeding, schooling fish that feed on the low tide are typically caught in fish traps. Seasonal changes in tidal phenomena mean that for some of the six months of the year, the traps may be deployed most effectively at night and are dependent on the availability of particular species of fish.

Table 8.3. Fish types by habitat (adapted from Davis 1982).

	Habitat	Yan-nhaṉu classification
1	fish that live near the surface	*garŋgiyabu*
2	fish that live near the bottom	*ŋoybu*
3	fish of the rocks and reefs	*dhuṉupalbu*
4	fish that live in the rivers	*mayaŋbu*
5	fish that live in freshwater	*rirrikulbu*

Fish Traps of the Inner Crocodile Islands

In the time before the coming of the missions, the king tides of the *rar-ranhdharr* (the hot, humid time) (August–September), on the full and new moon, and later in the season of the easterly winds *bärra'mirr* (January–February), opportunities for corralling fish on the extensive mud flats of the inner Crocodile Islands occur. The large tidal variations of the full moon and new moons produce the spring-tide range of about three meters that make the construction of mud and grass fish traps possible (figure 8.6). These traps were designed to catch *gapila* (butterfish, *Selenotoca multifasciata*), *garkuwi* (mullet, *Mugil cephalus*), and *ratjuk* (barramundi, *Lates calcarifer*), as well as *watjarrkali* (young barramundi), coming up onto the *ninydjiya* (mud flats) at these times to feed and spawn.

The temporary grass fish trap technique identified as *yinika lolo* (grass fish fence) can only be made at sites where there is enough grass and mud to allow such construction and, crucially, at such sites where fish congregate. At Milingimbi, there are vast areas of mud and grass that could potentially be used to make the *yinika lolo*, but there are only four sites around the island where the fish congregate. One of these sites is called *Djaluwa*.[15] At the king tides, people band together, preceding the returning tide, and manipulate the mud and grass into a progressing wall preventing fish from escaping. The relative bounty is then collected by spear or scoop and the stranded fish packed into bags by hand.

Figure 8.6. Grass and mud fish trap *yinika lolo*. Reproduced with permission of the University of Sydney Archives (Warner/Webb collection Image 37_133 by Reverend T T Webb 1926–39. Fish trap at Djaluwa).

The following translation by the late Laurie Baymarrwaṇa describes how as a girl she and her relatives would construct the l̲ol̲o (fish trap) with skillful manipulation of mud and grass, as a group with one intention, specifically gathered for the purpose:

Yan-nhaŋu	English
Gol̲'manana galkgalkmiyana ŋapurr manana nyindjiya gama manana nhaŋu nawuna djiliŋdjil. Gol̲'manana gama nawuna niŋgulkmiyana yinika. niŋgulkmiyana dhula niŋgulkmiyana djiniŋu mana niŋgulkmiyana balaŋu. Dhula ganatjirri nhaŋuba guya ŋurramana. Dhula bayŋu wapmiyaŋu bathiw, mewanthu, raŋanthu, barrawanthu. Gaŋul d̲andathul dana nhaŋu wala	Carefully pushing the grass and the mud like this [demonstrates with hands] we would carefully bend the [mangrove leaves] grass and mud wall. Pressing it this way and then that way to encircle the fish. When the fish were inside, we put them into bags of many kinds made of bark or fibers. Then we would take them to share.

The whole family would participate in such an enterprise, often producing enough food for everyone and excess for exchanges in requirement of obligations laid down in law. According to tradition, the estate owners and their ritual managers, for such sites where traps were constructed, would receive by law a share of the fish collected on their ancestral sites. Seasonal fishing events of this kind are remembered as joyful communal occasions filled with laughter (Warner 1937; Thomson 1938).

The mud and grass fish trap technology itself was not owned by a particular group. This made the mud fish traps different from those of the outer islands, as these were most definitely owned as objects of ancestral bestowal. I wish now to turn attention to the ancestrally inherited fish traps of the outer islands and look at some of the rules for their deployment.

Fish Traps of the Outer Crocodile Islands

Of the twenty-four fish traps present on Murruŋga Island, four kinds are discernible. Two of these are of great mythological significance. We will look at one of these called the Betŋu.[16] The redeployment of the Betŋu in 2010 provided new information about fish traps. The Betŋu is a variety of stone fish trap called gand̲amu that exists at a number of named sites around the islands. Gand̲amu stone fish traps are divided into two types. The stone weir fish traps include nine of the type named munathaŋa l̲ol̲o (enclosure on sand), and fifteen of the kind commonly referred to as mär-rand̲ilŋa l̲ol̲o (enclosure on the reef surface). Altogether, there are twenty-four fish traps present at Murruŋga.

Despite the many differences in these fish trap designs, the character of the geographical conditions necessary for their successful operation restricts their arrangement in the marine environment (Thomson 1938, 195). The fish traps of the outer islands exhibit a subtle synchronization with the temporal and spatial rhythms of the sea, tides, and nearby coastal ecosystem. At Murruŋga, fish traps are located—given topographic and bathometric prerequisites—next to permanent sources of fresh water and permanent campsites. Fish traps are found in close proximity to mixed species of fruiting trees and shrubs, shade, breezy hilltop viewing platforms, and other assets in the environment. People staying in the vicinity of the fish traps discard the seeds of fruits, creating fruiting trees around semipermanent camps and fresh water, making oases. Resources in close proximity to the fish traps are the outcome of interdependencies between people and environment, in which systems of human and natural ecology feed back into each other. The map of Murruŋga shows this clustering of permanent named campsites, fish traps, and fresh water wells in the land and seascape (figure 8.7).

The distribution of terrestrial resources and their periodical availability close to fish traps are additional economic drivers shaping the pattern of seasonal travel to and around the islands. Moreover, the distribution of these resources on the islands is itself the legacy of historical patterns

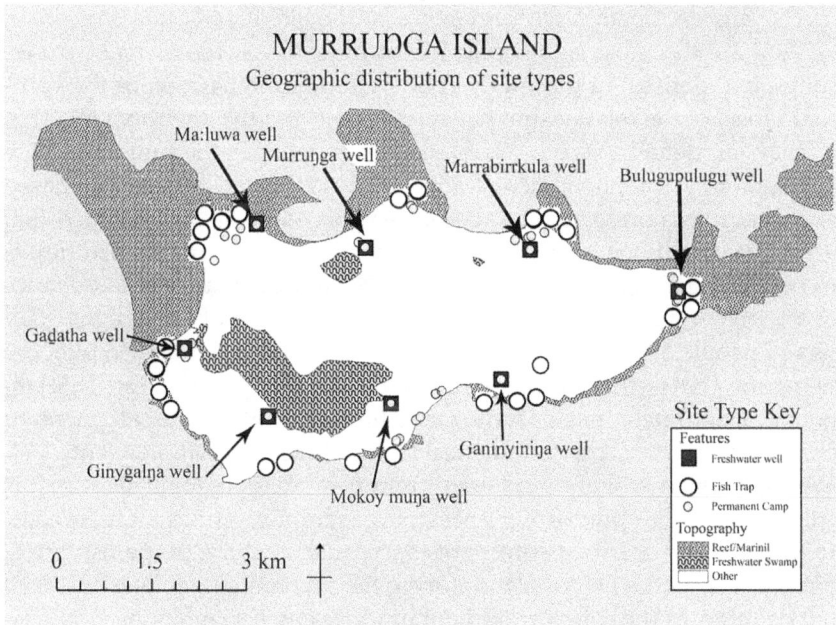

MURRUƉGA ISLAND
Geographic distribution of site types

Figure 8.7. Fish traps and fresh water wells of Murruŋga Island (James 1999).

of travel. The travels of the ancestors passed on in mythology reflect the patterns wrought over time by the travels of living people. Those who travel the seaways always follow the edicts of ancestral law to ensure their physical and spiritual safety.

Redeploying the *Betŋu* of Murruŋga

The Yan-nhaŋu elders proposed that the Crocodile Islands Rangers be brought in to refurbish the *Betŋu* in 2010 for the first time since 1937. During the collaborative refurbishment project, in the season of *midawarr*, young and old gathered at Murruŋga to discuss the upcoming reconstruction. Senior Rangers and children from the Crocodile Islands Junior Ranger program were invited to participate. There was a big meeting in which many things were discussed. The work was to be supervised by seniors from the owning Gurryindi clan and their kin. In particular, the ritual work was to be managed by the Malarra clan related to the Gurryindi owners as a mother's mother's group, and the classificatory mother's group for the site of the *Betŋu*. According to local custom, senior people direct the discussion, social organization, and timing of the fish trap work. During this process, nonagenarian Laurie Baymarrwaŋa gently directed proposals.

The process opened with reference to the site-based rituals of place, as they are the most significant. It was agreed that the *buŋgul* (rituals, songs, and dances) of place would be performed to harmonize the spiritual aspect of the relationship between people and the environment. That is, they are done to revive the relationships between the human participants, biophysical phenomena (tides, fish, and winds), and the site-based ancestral forces understood to be present. Secondly, it was declared that during preparations, no signal of the intention to prepare the fish trap is to be aired. This is so the spirits of the *Betŋu* are not alerted in advance of the preparations. This required the obligatory use of hand signs. Yan-nhaŋu people, like all Yolŋu, are not only multilingual, but also bimodal bilingual. That is, they grow up using an alternate sign language. This language of sign encompasses some many hundreds of signs for all phenomena in the universe and grammatical features to create complex sentences. Yan-nhaŋu sign is slightly different from post-mission Yolŋu sign, as it is still linked to the preexisting ancestral geography—it has signs specific to the sites and spiritual entities of place, such as those of the fish traps. Finally, once at the fish trap and during the preparation, no one must call out or laugh, as the spirits would not produce any fish and none would be caught in the trap. Laurie Baymarrwaŋa told the following story of when she was a girl using the *Betŋu*:

Yan-nhaŋu

Ŋatjili dananha malguda mananha bena daŋuniya, malguda, ganay, Murruŋga benaŋur yuwapi dulthana bilyana ŋayathana djapliŋu, dhaŋuniya, malguda, guŋgupul, dhirrpu, bena mananha nhaŋ"-kumunu. Ŋapurr baman garrana nirrpan. Wirrpalayinhaba nhaŋu Betŋu nhaŋ"ku nhaŋu-way guyaway. Ŋapurr garrana girri nhan"ku lolo, duŋupal, mulmu, raniya, bambitj, balku ŋarriyarriyaniŋ manapana dananha. Nhaŋ"kuway guyaway nhaŋu wirrpala-yirri ŋapurr dhabakthana nhama ganatjirri dukarryini. Liwmiya nyininha dananha dhabakthana rantana, rantana guya gurdaŋayini dhula gaypumayini nhani dananha garrana mananha dhabakthana guyaway Betŋu napurrunha

English

In the old days, we would customarily eat the many bush vegetables: *Cayratia trifolia, Nyphoides, Ampelocissus, Nyphoides violacea*. At the change of tide, we would leave these forest foods and go down to set up the *Betngu* at the fish trap site. We would repair the fish trap using rocks, local grasses, beach mistletoe, pandanus, sticks, and string. When the fish trap was completed, we would wait at the campsite until the tide was low. When the tide had receded, we would go to the fish trap and look for fish. At the *Betŋu* after the tide was out, we would spear the fish in the shallow waters of our fish trap.

At the site called Gadatha on Murruŋga, the *Betŋu* is arranged at the lowest point in a depression between two extended lateritic promontories. The rock wall is prepared while the young women collect shellfish and the boys fish by spear on the reef flat while they wait for the tide to return. On the stone-weir base, a *miṉḏal-buyubuma* (long loosely woven

Figure 8.8. The son of Baḏapat (Ranger Billy Boyman) takes his father's place, as does Buthan, the son's son (*marratja*) of Burrundjiṇu, 2010. Photo by Chiara Bussini; reproduced with permission.

mat)—usually made of the grass *mewana* (*Cyperus conicus*) or pandanus locally known as *ranyia* (*Pandanus spiralis*)—is secured by *bambitj* (body-length sticks) crossing at the top and pinned at the bottom with heavy stones. Photographs (from 2010) illustrate the refurbishment of the *Betŋu* at Murruŋga (see figures 8.1, 8.8, 8.9, 8.10).

In figure 8.1, standing at the *Betŋu* at Gadatha, the closer Yan-nhaŋu man, Burrundjiŋu, is the *djuŋaya* (senior ritual manager) in the mother's relationship to the site. The more distant man is the Wulbukarra man, Badapat, in the *mari* (mother's mother) relationship to the site (James 2009, 234). In the recent picture (figure 8.8), the son of Badapat (Ranger Billy Boyman) takes his father's place at the fish trap, as does Buthan, the classificatory son of Burrundjiŋu. The final two pictures (figures 8.9, 8.10) feature the *Betŋu* looking north. Upon completion of the fiber fence, the senior persons removed themselves to a secret site associated with the *Betŋu* to make the obligatory ritual incantations to the spirits of the fish trap. These rituals are of great significance for the proper deployment of the fish traps of the outer islands.

Ritual Past and Present

Rituals of the *Betŋu* are enacted according to ancestral precedent in order to harmonize the physical and numinous (spiritual) aspects of the fish

Figure 8.9. The *Betŋu* in the estuary at Gadatha on Murruŋga Island—North East Arnhem Land. Photo by D. Thomson, courtesy of the Thomson family and Museum Victoria, 1937 (TPH 773).

Figure 8.10. *Betŋu* looking north, 2010. Photo by Chiara Bussini; reproduced with permission.

trap, revivifying reciprocal relations and entreating the spirits to increase profitability.[17] Senior Yan-nhaŋu traditional owner Laurie Baymarrwaŋa told the following story on the occasion of this recent restoration of the *Betŋu* fish trap at Murruŋga:

Yan-nhaŋu	English
Betŋuŋa Yan-nhaŋumurru. napurrunha. gurrku wuna waŋa dhantan-dhu dhulamun walima yan waŋanha gurrku dhanakarra binam bayŋu dhana waŋanha Yannhaŋumurru. Lima rulku gurrku watana mananha git-kitthu bili ŋalapal̲ mit̲t̲ji barrŋarranha ŋumum lima git-kitthu rulka lima gurrku milima ŋarirri. D̲ilkurruwurru mit̲t̲ji dananha mananha guykthana dambu waŋanha ŋarirrigu bili ŋalapal̲ mit̲t̲ji daguna limalana ŋarirri	At the fish trap, we speak Yan-nhaŋu language: the language of the spirits of the fish trap and its locality. While we were around the fish trap, we must not call out, laugh, or offend the spirits, because the spirits would not give us any fish. Old people would make an incantation at the fish trap to ensure the spirits gave us lots of fish.

Every one of the twenty-four named fish traps of Murruŋga possesses site-specific incantations associated with the *waŋarr* (creator/ancestor/ spirit) that created the site. The proper names of the spirits of the fish trap are withheld to preserve their currency in the ongoing economy of local knowledge. Interestingly, the public hand sign used to signify fish trap spirits at Murruŋga is the same one used for *ragalk* (sorcery). For here today, knowledge, rights to know, and authority over rituals and proper names are decisive elements in exchange and in the reproduction of the institutions of society. What this story illustrates is that not only are rituals for the spirits of the fish trap understood to be essential for providing a good catch, but such ritual is tacitly understood as necessary to the spiritual revivification of the foundations of society as a whole. An unspoken awareness of an ever-present ancestral realm means that in everyday behavior, in ways of speaking and signing, people genuflect to the ever-present spirit world. These rituals and the wider religious system of renewal of ecological and social relations, of which they are part, are replete with notions of ancestral presence, fertility, harmony, and ritual increase at the heart of local knowledge. That is to say, they are essentially focused on the spiritual relationship of people to place, fecundity, and mutually nourishing relations, which are at the heart of the Yan-nhaŋu site-based ontology. The following excerpt from Donald Thomson of an actual site-based ritual contains no secret information.

Donald Thomson's field notes (1937) recorded this brief account of the *Garlayamirriŋguli Betgnu* rite at Murruŋga at Maluwa (place of the father) in 1937. The clan group known as Malarra/Guṇbirritji own the rituals and names for the *Garlayamirriŋguli Betgnu* at Maluwa here transcribed as *Ma'lu'a*. In the following description, a man called Yilkarri (Liyagalawumirri clan), standing in the relation of mother's mother to the fish trap, gives an example of how the *yolngo Mala'rra* (senior men from the Malarra/Guṇbirritji owning clan) of the fish trap incant the rite. Here, at the fish trap, they call out the names of the spirit of the fish trap ancestor [18]

> Dor'narra, Tarri' illi'illi. Koiya ka:n borr kunga:l da:rra'wa kunga:l 'Wa: nga:rr loḻo' Wa:nga:rr yolngo Mala'rra Kaitjpu'yun'ka:n Prr r r r Ta:rrilli'illi koiya'ra':k da:rra'wa kum' lolo'lil nga:rra lukka ma:rna'nirr. Tamirra:ngall yuwalk'ko lolo'wa. Kumur lolo and wanga Ma'lu'a at Mooroonga. (Thomson 1937, 30 August)

This excerpt, part of a larger incantation, entreats the spirit/ancestor of the *loḻo* (fish trap) as a kinsman to "increase the number of fish in the trap," so that "I may eat my fill." The tacit implication of kinship, and thus reciprocity, is here writ large—mutual obligation with ancestral spirits who are kin, and kin quite properly, are expected to provide for their relatives. This ethic of reciprocity is assumed to exist ubiquitously in a kinship-based universe. This notion of spiritual kinship, care, and exchange pervades incantation, songs, paintings, and every day discourse of people on the homelands. What is of overarching significance in reanimating the

Betŋu is the desire to rekindle the deep metaphysical links of ancestral essences, of kinship and connectedness to the spirits of place. It is this profoundly religious urge for spiritual closeness, for renewal in mutual connections through kinship with the living and ancestral elements, that underlies the deep sense of belonging to a place. This is a key understanding of the metaphysics of the fish traps of the Crocodile Islands.

Conclusion

Thomson's evocative depictions of site-based rituals on the Crocodile Islands give visceral recognition to the anchoring force of mythology behind the practices surrounding fish traps and those prevalent in Yolŋu ceremony and society more broadly (Thomson 1938). A mythology and local knowledge shaped by thousands of years of intimate coexistence with the marine environment is revealed in this glimpse of the fish traps of the Crocodile Islands. Here are the coordinates of an imperiled ancestral geography, the exquisite filaments of its metaphysical connections expressed in the idiom of kinship, its preternatural laws shaping the human practices of its survivors. For the Yan-nhaŋu, the sea is not only a physical and temporal space, but also a mental map of ancestral journeys and ritual revivifications celebrated in view of the ever-present spirit world. At the core of this bequest is the responsibility to nurture and pass on this site-based knowledge and its biological, cultural, and linguistic endowment for future generations. This ancestral decree to care whole-heartedly may begin to explain the depth of Yan-nhaŋu attachment to their island home.

Within the alienating circumstances of modernity, the people of the Crocodile Islands struggle, as do we all, to find a quiet place. For them, the legacy of harsh assimilation and settler-state colonialism circumscribe the conditions under which they might thrive. The fish traps have brought together elders, Rangers, and Junior Rangers to revivify site-based ancestral essences through the age-old rituals imbued in these focal ancestral sites. It may be that this is an instance in which indigenous reappropriation of state-sponsored land and sea management priorities can provide opportunities to reinvigorate ancestral responsibilities. Or perhaps it is but a transient window through which to glimpse a passing moment of another world. The question more broadly remains, what light has post-enlightenment modernity thrown on man's relationship with the sea since the Mesolithic? It is certain that state denial of a place for the Yan-nhaŋu will diminish our connectedness with the sea that links us all.

Bentley James has lived in remote indigenous Australia for nearly thirty years. His interest in language, sign, and anthropology began with Warlpiri Media at Yuendumu in the late 1980s. In 1993 in Northeast Arnhem Land, he began the *Yan-nhangu Dictionary* (2003), and since has completed a PhD on Yan-nhangu marine identity, *Time and Tide in the Crocodile Islands* (2009), and the education resource *Atlas and Illustrated Dictionary of the Crocodile Islands* (2014), with Laurie Baymarrwaŋa. His long-term engagement has borne a family of interrelated practical projects, including the Crocodile Islands Rangers and Junior Rangers programs, Language Nests, and bilingual education resources in support of meaningful livelihoods on country. His new book, *Maypal, Mayali' ga Wäŋa: Shellfish, Meaning and Place* (2016), is a bilingual identification guide to shellfish of Arnhem Land for schools in six languages. Currently teaching anthropological linguistics, he continues to visit kin and country from the desert to the islands.

Notes

Many thanks to Professor Nicolas Peterson for access to Donald Thomson's collected field notes.

1. "Yolŋu" is a term increasingly used since the 1970s to describe an Aboriginal person of North East Arnhem Land speaking languages called collectively "Yolŋu-matha" (literally, "people's tongue") and referring to a population of some seven thousand people. Earlier anthropological literature referred to these people as "Murngin" (Warner 1937), "Wulamba" (Berndt 1955, 1957, 348), and "Miwuyt" (Shapiro 1981).

2. The sociolinguistic title "Yan-nhaŋu" represents Yolŋu people inheriting estates and languages endowed by Yan-nhaŋu speaking ancestors in the Crocodile Islands. "Yan-nhaŋu" literally means "the language of this place." The word *yan* denotes "tongue" or "language," and the word *nhaŋu* is the proximal demonstrative meaning "this" or "here." So the language title "Yan-nhaŋu" literally denotes the language of "here," the language of the Crocodile Islands (James 2009, 7, 105).

3. In the Australian indigenous context, homelands are small communities where a number of families from various clans coexist, and where life and work are organized around the management of land/sea country, concern for kinship, ancestral connections, and local languages.

4. As such, marking a difference in orientation from that of coastal dwellers—for example, the Nádja-Nádja, for whom the activities of hunting and fishing were interchangeable (see Petri-Odermann 1963).

5. Recent robust neoliberal ambition in settler-state policy has emphasized assimilation and promotes social indicators that undermine diversity, forcing indigenous citizens into line with narrowly conceived market values (Altman 2009, 54).

6. Starting with the protectionist policy era (*Commonwealth Aboriginal Ordinance Act [1911]*), the process of destroying "aboriginal culture" with compulsory assimilation while "smoothing the dying pillow" by forcibly discouraging nomadism and instituting dependency on missions became a "key instrument" of assimilation policy (Tatz 1964, 18). For a more complete discussion of nomadism, see Stacey and Allison, this volume.

7. I use the expression "local knowledge" to bring attention to the site-based ancestral geography in worldview that underpin Yan-nhaŋu ecological relations, rather than the more generalized terms Indigenous Ecological Knowledge (IEK) or Traditional Knowledge (TK). A growing literature suggests that such labels are problematic, for example, as "traditional" obscures the dynamic nature of such systems and "indigenous knowledge" may exclude other populations perhaps not recognised as indigenous (Berkes, Folke, and Colding 2000). In the Crocodile Islands, the concept "indigenous" is ambiguous in regard to differentiating Yan-nhaŋu speaking Yolŋu from other Yolŋu local groups, whereas the term "local knowledge" recognises the distinctiveness of local forms.

8. Thomson (1938) describes the fish trap *Gurrka-gorl* as a fence or weir; with "stringy-bark" bark-constructed spouts that direct water flow into covered circular bark troughs. These were used to collect fish in the season from about early April to early June in the time known as *Miḏawarr* in the Yolŋu calendar (Thomson 1937, photos 720–50, 862–71; Keen 2004, 86, 101; James 2009).

9. The "Mariŋa" name alludes to the ceremonial alliance of Dhuwa and Yirritja Yan-nhaŋu speaking clans linked to the ownership and matrilineal managerial rights in preexisting ancestral sites, essences, rituals, songs, and names of waters, reefs, and currents in the Arafura Sea surrounding the Crocodile Islands.

10. Seventy kilometres seaward of Milingimbi Island lays the Gamalaŋga Island of Gurriba: Northwest Crocodile Island (see figure 8.2).

11. The names of the cardinal points are loan words in Yolŋu languages derived from the Macassans. For example, "south" is called *selatang* by the Makassarese and a closely homophonous *djalataŋ*, by Yolŋu. "North" in Makassarese is *utara*, and *luŋgurrma* in Yan-nhaŋu; "west" is *barrat* in Makassarese and *bärra* in Yolŋu languages. Lastly, "east," *timor* in Makassarese becomes *dimurru* in Yolŋu-matha. See also, Walker and Zorc 1981; Urry and Walsh 1982.

12. Yolŋu seasons are described in a number of accounts, starting with Thomson 1937. See also, Davis 1982, 7; Rudder 1993.

13. At Murruŋga, the *dililili* (magpie lark, or *Grallina cyanoleuca*) sings in the mornings at the beginning of the season of *dharratharramirr* (the cold season) and tells of the *rika* (wind), the frosty *westerly*, from a place called *Dhamangurra* (James and Baymarrwaŋa 2014, 7).

14. In the Crocodile Islands, the tide is always at its peak when the moon is one hour above the sea in the east, or fifteen degrees past or atop the horizon. This is called *ŋalindi dhawathun* (moon coming out). The tide then *ŋurruthirr* (begins returning) and peaks again twelve and one-half hours later, or when the moon is fifteen degrees below the horizon in the *warnba* (west), at a time called

ŋalindi dhampthana (moon going in). The *raŋithirr* (tide receding) becomes low at one hour past moon zenith, and again when the moon is fifteen degrees past nadir, returning later each day by forty-four minutes (James 2009, 2014).

15. The type of grass fish fence (*yinika lolo*) shown here constructed at the afore-mentioned site, *Djaluwa*, was also commonly made at a number of different but geomorphically similar sites on Milingimbi, including at *Bulmatjirra, Gududutji, Gulaŋbaŋa,* and at *Gurruwa,* and always in the same seasons and at the time of the same moon and associated king tides.

16. Fish traps of the type named *gaṉdamu,* and with the proper names *Naṉḏawarra* and *Betŋu,* were commonly used on the outer islands at sites of geomorphic and geological similarity. More widely, this style of fish trap is named *neny, guluwurrulu, rurrumburru, yambirrpa,* and *yambirrku* (James 2009).

17. The *Betŋu* fish trap at the site named *Garlayamirriŋguli* is named after and designed specifically for catching the species called *garlaya,* (*Gnathanodon speciosus, Cranax sp.*). A number of the ritual songs performed at this site refer specifically to the spirit of the fish *garlaya.* This species' particular ritual is not usual for fish traps in this area; as such, the site-based fish trap ritual is unique to Murruŋga Island. Having said this, the fish trap does not exclusively catch *garlaya,* as many other species are caught: for instance, the ubiquitous mullet *garkuwi* or *wakun* (*Mugil cephalus, Valamugil georgii*) and *meyanga* (*Carangoides gymnostethus, C. chrysophrys*).

18. Totemic increase rites recorded by Thomson at Murrungga in 1937 include this example performed in close proximity to the aforementioned fish trap *Garlayamirriŋguli* at *Maluwa.* The protagonist, a man called Yilkari, (Thomson's Murruŋga informant, a Liyagalawumirr [Kalbanuk] man from Mirramina) guided Thomson to the *lolo* (fish trap) (Thomson 1937, File No. 10).

References

Akerman, K. 1976. "Fishing with Stone Traps on the Dampierland Peninsula. W.A." *Mankind* 10, no. 3: 182.

Altman, J. C. 1987. *Hunter Gatherers Today: An Aboriginal Economy in North Australia.* Canberra: Australian Institute of Aboriginal Studies.

———. 2009. "Contestations Over Development." In *Power, Culture, Economy: Indigenous Australians and Mining.* Edited by J. Altman and D. Martin, 1–15. Canberra: Australian National University Press.

Berkes, F., C. Folke, and J. Colding. 2000. *Linking social and ecological systems: management practices and social systems.* London: Cambridge University Press.

Berndt, Ronald M. 1955. "'Murngin' (Wulamba) Social Organization." *American Anthropologist* 57, no. 1: 84–106.

———. 1957. "In Reply to Radcliffe-Brown on Australian Local Organization." *American Anthropologist* 59, no. 2: 346–51.

———. 1977. *Aborigines and Change: Australia in the '70s.* Canberra: Australian Institute of Aboriginal Studies.

Christie, M. 1994. "Grounded and Ex-centric Knowledges: Exploring Aboriginal Alternatives to Western Thinking." In *International Interdisciplinary Perspectives*. Edited by I. Edwards. London: Hawker Brownlow Educational Press.

Davis, S. 1982. *Report on the Castlereagh Bay and Howard Island Sea Closure Application*. Vol. 1 and 2. Darwin: Aboriginal Sacred Sites Authority.

Ellen, R. 1982. *Environment, Subsistence and System: The Ecology of Small-scale Social Formations*. Cambridge, UK: Cambridge University Press.

Faulkner, P. 2006. "The Ebb and Flow." PhD dissertation. Canberra: Australian National University.

Hale, H. M., and N. B. Tindale. 1933. "Aborigines of Princess Charlotte Bay." Vol. 1. *Records of the South Australian Museum* 5, no. 2: 117–72.

James, Bentley. 1999. "The Implications of Djambarrpuyŋu at Murruŋa Island." Masters dissertation. Darwin: Charles Darwin University.

———. 2009. "Time and Tide in the Crocodile Islands: Change and Continuity in Yan-nhaŋu Marine Identity." PhD dissertation. Canberra: Australian National University.

James, Bentley, and Laurie Baymarrwaŋa. 2014. *Atlas and Illustrated Dictionary of the Crocodile Islands*. Singapore: B. James.

James. B., L. Baymarrwaŋa, R. Gularrbaŋg, M. Darga, R. Nyambal, and M. Nyŋunyuŋu 2. 2003. *Yan-nhaŋu Dictionary*. Milingimbi, CEC Literature Production Centre. Darwin: Northern Territory University Press.

Keen, I. D. 1978. "One Ceremony, One Song: An Economy of Religious Knowledge among the Yolngu of Northeast Arnhem Land." PhD dissertation. Canberra: Australian National University.

———. 1994. *Knowledge and Secrecy in an Aboriginal Religion*. New York: Oxford University Press.

———. 2004. *Aboriginal Economy and Society on the Threshold of Colonisation*. Melbourne: Oxford University Press.

McCarthy, F. D. 1940. "Aboriginal Stone Arrangements." *Australia Australian Museum Magazine* 7, no. 6: 184–89.

McKnight, C. 1976. *The Voyage to Marege: Macassan Trepangers in Northern Australia*. Carlton: Melbourne University Press.

Morphy, H. 1984. *Journey to the Crocodile's Nest: An Accompanying Monograph to the Film Madarrpa Funeral at Gurka'wuy*. Canberra: Australian Institute of Aboriginal Studies.

Petri-Odermann, G. 1963. "The Sea in the Life of a North-West Coastal Population." *Paideuma: Mitteilungen zur Kulturkunde*. Edited by Kim Akerman. Translated by Margaret Pawsey. 9, no. 1: 1–17.

Plumb, K. A. 1965. Wessel Islands/Truant Island: explanatory notes for the 1: 250 000 series maps for the Northern Territory SC315/SC316. Canberra: Bureau of Mineral Resources, Geology and Geophysics. Retrieved 17 May 2018 from https://geoscience.nt.gov.au/gemis/ntgsjspui/handle/1/81792.

Robert, W. C. H. 1973. *The Dutch Explorations, 1605–1756, of the North and Northwest Coast of Australia: Extracts from Journals, Log-books and other Documents Relating to these Voyages*. Amsterdam: Philo Press cv.

Roberts, R. G., R. Jones, and M. A. Smith. 1990. "Thermoluminescence Dating of a 50,000 Year-Old Human Occupation Site in Northern Australia." *Nature* 345: 153–6.

Roth, W. E. 1901. "Food: Its Search, Capture and Preparation." *North Queensland Ethnography*. Bulletin 3. Brisbane: Government Printer.

Rudder, J. 1993. "Yolngu Cosmology: An Unchanging Cosmos Incorporating a Rapidly Changing World?" PhD dissertation. Canberra: Australian National University.

Shapiro, Warren. 1981. *Miwuyt Marriage: The Cultural Anthropology of Affinity in Northeast Arnhem Land*. Philadelphia: Study of Human Issues.

Smith, M. 1983. "Joules from Pools: Social and Techno-economic Aspects of Bardi Stone Fish Traps." In *Archaeology at ANZAAS (Australian and New Zealand Association for the Advancement of Science)*. Edited by M. Smith, 29–45. Perth: Western Australian Museum.

Tatz, C. 1964. "Aboriginal Administration in the Northern Territory of Australia." PhD dissertation. Canberra: Australian National University.

Thomson, D. F. 1937. "Field Notes: Ceremonies and Increase Rites, Elcho Island 7-1-1937 and 115: at Murrungga Island." Nicolas Peterson Collection, Australian National University, Canberra.

———. 1938 "A New Type of Fish Trap from Arnhem Land, Northern Territory of Australia." *Man* 38, no. 216: 193–98.

Trigger, D. S. 1987. "Inland, Coast and Islands: Traditional Aboriginal Society and Material Culture in a Region of the Southern Gulf of Carpentaria." *Records of the South Australian Museum*. 21, no. 2: 69–84.

Urry, J., and M. Walsh. 1982. "The Lost 'Maccassan' Language of Northern Australia." *Aboriginal History* 5, no. 1: 91–108.

Walker, A., and D. Zorc. 1981. "Austronesian Loanwords in Yolŋu Matha of Northeast Arnhem Land." *Aboriginal History* 5, no. 1: 109–34.

Walters, I. 1985a. "The Toorbul Point Aboriginal Fish Trap." *Queensland Archaeological Research* 2: 38–49.

———. 1985b. "Some Observations on the Material Culture of Aboriginal Fishing in the Moreton Bay Area: Implications for Archaeology." *Queensland Archaeological Research* 2: 50–57.

Warner, W. L. 1937. *A Black Civilization: A Social Study of an Australian Tribe*. London: Harper and Brothers Publishers.

Williams, N. 1986. *The Yolngu and Their Land: A System of Land Tenure and the Fight for its Recognition*. Canberra: Australian Institute of Aboriginal Studies.

Woodroffe, C. D., J. M. A. Chappell, and B. G. Thom. 1988. "Shell Middens in the Context of Estuarine Development, South Alligator River, Northern Territory." *Archaeology in Oceania* 23: 95–103.

Woodroffe, C. D., and J. Grindrod. 1991. "Mangrove Biogeography: The Role Quaternary Environmental and Sea-level Change." *Journal of Biography* 18, no. 5: 479–92.

Zorc, R. D. 1986. *Yolŋu Matha Dictionary*. Darwin: School of Australian Linguistics, Darwin Institute of Technology.

CHAPTER 9

A Community-Based Approach to Documenting and Interpreting the Cultural Seascapes of the Recherche Archipelago, Western Australia

David Guilfoyle, Ross Anderson,
Ron "Doc" Reynolds, and Tom Kimber

This chapter discusses a community research program that has adopted an innovative approach to documenting and interpreting the cultural seascapes of the Recherche Archipelago off the southern coast of Western Australia (figure 9.1). Established in 2007, this program provides a holistic, community-based approach to land and heritage management centered on traditional customary practice and protocols (Mitchell et al. 2013). A key feature is the integration of on-ground conservation works with "traditional owners," archaeologists, and environmental scientists as part of a two-way knowledge exchange and collaborative research partnership.

The Recherche Archipelago collectively comprises approximately 105 islands and hundreds more unnamed rocks and shoals. These islands represent the surviving granite peaks of former mountains that once capped a large coastal plain inundated by rising sea levels following the last Ice Age, creating the present-day archipelago, known locally as the "Bay of Isles." The program aims to model this process of coastal change and document the human responses to this change over the last ten thousand years. Although the islands are now part of a protected nature reserve and remain uninhabited, previous research has demonstrated past human occupation on several island groups prior to the formation of the archipelago (Dortch and Morse 1984; Smith 1993).

One of the early aims of the program was to integrate the many perspectives on archaeological places of this region. This required, first, the

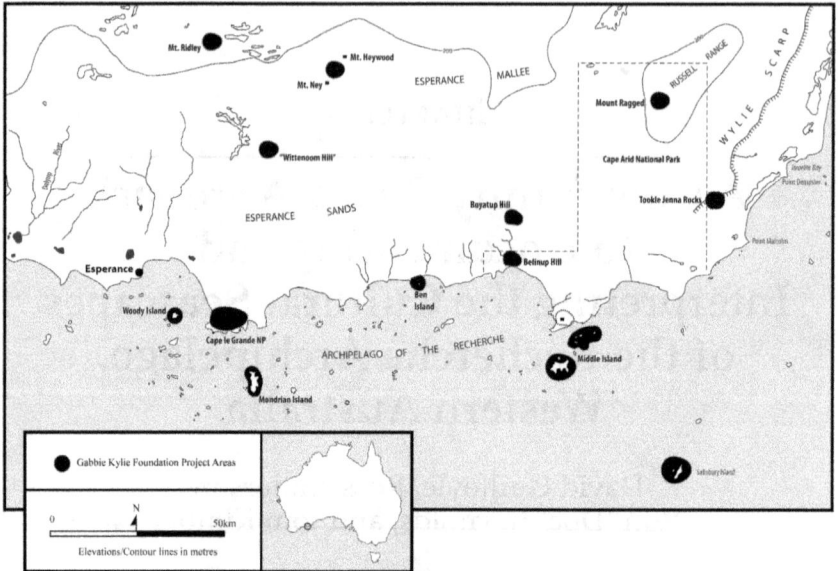

Figure 9.1. Map showing the location of recent Gabbie Kylie projects and the Archipelago of the Recherche. Created by the author.

development of a community research structure and, second, a baseline research framework from which further investigations could unfold. Working with the community-based Gabbie Kylie Foundation (described below), the archaeological research program had two main components: the human–environment relations spanning the late Pleistocene to late Holocene; and the maritime and historical use of the archipelago with a specific focus on relations with the Wudjari (the indigenous, traditional owners) groups of the adjacent mainland.

For the first, the program sought to integrate a diverse dataset in order to document aspects of the human settlement systems and responses to the climate-induced changes associated with this transformation from coastal plain to islands. The region provides a unique insight into documenting spatiotemporal variation in the geographic, environmental, and archaeological record, and its consequences for human habitation of the region. At the same time, the changing social landscape, including traditional creation stories of the islands themselves, together with contemporary cultural values, were integrated into the database of archaeological information and environmental modeling.

Combined ethnographic and ethnohistoric information indicates that these islands were no longer used by people once the islands were formed following sea level rises—until recently. This observation suggests that the islands archaeological record may serve as a time capsule of prehistoric human occupation and activity. However, in order to investigate the archaeology of specific island groups, a model of marine transgression and island formation over the late Pleistocene to the mid Holocene period is needed. This provides the chronological framework for developing testable hypotheses regarding the associated local (island) sequences of human occupation. In addition, such a model facilitates comparative analyses with other archaeological data while, at the same time, providing new data that can refine the marine transgression model itself.

On the subject of writing Australian Aboriginal history, Williamson argues that the "pre- and post-contact worlds are most profitably investigated as a historical continuum and not as being divided by the absence of history or archaeology" (2004, 176). The second component of the program explores the next phase in understanding the cultural seascapes of the Recherche Archipelago, that of the early Dutch, British, French, and American exploration period, pre-colonial and colonial sealing and whaling industries, and the British colonial settlement period. The study examines these historical-era periods in terms of how this unique environment influenced contact between newcomers and Aboriginal people and the development of economic activities in the region, combining evidence from the Archipelago's historical archaeological record, maritime history, environmental studies, and oral histories. An initial "data audit" of the range and type of maritime and historical resources in the Archipelago was undertaken and is presented below. A focus of this study is to identify specific historic events and phases of contact between early newcomers and Wudjari people and any associated archaeological/cultural sites, and then to document the associated cultural values of these places. Archaeological sites include shipwrecks, whaling stations, Aboriginal rock art sites with ship depictions, and pastoral stations.

The findings begin to paint a picture of the dynamic interactions between people and their changing natural and social environments. The innovative community-led structure of the program has been crucial in generating appropriate methodologies for capturing the multiple layers of meaning and understanding of this cultural seascape, to ultimately protect and manage these unique places, landscapes, and values.

The Gabbie Kylie Foundation

The Gabbie Kylie Foundation was established in 2007 under the auspices of the National Trust of Australia (Western Australian branch), and adopts a holistic, community-based approach to land and heritage management based on Wudjari customary practice and protocols (Mitchell et al. 2013). In order to achieve Wudjari objectives, the Foundation integrates education and training programs with on-ground conservation works as part of a bipartisan knowledge exchange and collaborative research partnership. This program provides a mechanism for the implementation of traditional land management, upholding and reinvigorating traditional knowledge systems, while building on existing partnerships with a range of active organizations. It also facilitates the employment of indigenous people in land management and cultural education and delivers projects beneficial to cultural heritage protection, community capacity, bio-diversity, and water quality. For example, the resulting practical conservation projects coordinated by the Gabbie Kylie Foundation and its various partners have removed invasive weeds and feral animals from specific islands, further empowering the community to manage and deliver heritage conservation outcomes. The resultant mechanism for integrated community-based heritage management assists in directing and refining the nature and scope of sustainable management across the region for the future.

The traditional owners present a range of perspectives on the various aspects of the cultural systems of their ancestors' past, as well as detailed knowledge about many different sites and features across the region. Cultural information is derived from oral histories relating to events and sites of the "contact" period associated with early sealing and whaling. Elders work with archaeologists and students to document and interpret archaeological features (created by their ancestors) across the islands. On a spiritual level, the traditional owners walk in the footsteps of their ancestors who once walked across this ancient coastal plain. The traditional owners also walk the islands as part of the important process of sorrowful reflection, as a number of their ancestors were kidnapped from the mainland and kept here by sealers and whalers. Finally, the program is also significant in protecting those cultural values by honoring cultural places (figure 9.1), a mechanism for the cultural practice of "caring for country," or looking after the land (Guilfoyle, Guilfoyle, and Reynolds 2009): "It's a huge responsibility to protect all this for our descendants" (traditional owner Gail Yorkshire-Selby, speaking on Middle Island, Recherche Archipelago, February 2012). This holistic program is documented elsewhere (Mitchell et al. 2013). The focus here is to explore the early stages of establishing a sustainable, long-term, community-based research program, beginning with identifying and addressing gaps in current knowledge and key avenues of future search.

The Archaeology of Esperance and the Ancient Coastal Plain

Archaeological evidence from the Esperance region indicates a regional occupational chronology dating to at least the Terminal Pleistocene, 13,000 years BP (Smith 1993). People adapted to and shaped the natural environment, embedding systems of movement, settlement, and subsistence that exist today in the form of ubiquitous archaeological places and features dotting the terrestrial and oceanic landscape. Such places include stone artifact scatters, *gnamma* (water) holes, lizard traps, quarry sites, scarred trees, burials, rock art sites, hearths, and camps. There is ethnographic information detailing knowledge of people using this area associated with hunting, fishing, settlement, and seasonal movement (Smith 1993) (figure 9.2).

The most distinctive geomorphological characteristics of the Recherche Archipelago and adjacent Esperance mainland are the massive granite domes that protrude from the relatively flat coastal plain. These granite domes, formed through processes of erosion and movement, were largely submerged during the Eocene (forty million years ago), forming tunnels, caves, and overhangs (Ryan et al. 2008, 42). The vegetation is diverse with eucaplypts and paperparks (*Myrtaceae*), banksias and grevilleas (*Proteaceae*), peas (*Papilionaceae*), orchids (*Orchidaceae*), heaths (*Epacridaceae*), sedges (*Cyperaceae*), daisies (*Asteraceae*), and wattles (*Mimosaceae*) all common (Beard 1981). Banksias (*Banksia speciosa, Banksia pulchella*) support an abundance of small native animals (such as the honey possum [*Tarsipes*

Figure 9.2. The team mapping a newly discovered fish trap that was buried by coastal sands as a result of rising sea levels. Photo by the author.

rostratus]) and insects. Some of the area's ecological diversity is attributed to granite outcrops that support microhabitats and provide soil moisture, acting as refuge zones for a number of species, such as prickly honeysuckle (*Lambertia echinata*) and numerous orchids and eucalypts (Hopper, Brown, and Marchant 1997). Hopper et al. (1997) have also indicated that the region has been subject to dramatic climatic changes that may have facilitated genetic divergence and speciation. The Archipelago is the natural habitat for colonies of Australian sea lions (*Neophoca cinerea*) and New Zealand fur seals (*Arctocephalus forsteri*). Seasonal migrating herds of humpback whales (*Megaptera novaeangliae*) and southern right whales (*Eubalaena australis*) follow the southern Australian coastline using sheltered bays as whale nurseries, while sperm whales (*Physeter macroephalus*) are present year-round. Much of the land surfaces between these granite domes are characterized by Holocene sands formed from prevailing winds with rising sea levels following the end of the last Ice Age, approximately seven to ten thousand years ago. These dunes have formed both swales and high ridges, some up to fifteen meters in height.

Site preservation is challenging due to post-glacial shoreline erosion and associated sediment transportation and redeposition. This depositional history suggests that much of the cultural archaeological material is deeply buried. Indeed, blowouts at various locations across the expansive coastline have revealed accumulations of stone artifacts (Smith 1993) that presumably represent several thousand years of deflated cultural deposits. Further, the south coast of Australia, and in particular the Southern Ocean encompassing the Recherche Archipelago, is subject to the most extreme wave energy of the entire Australian coastline (Ryan et al. 2008, 42) and is one of the highest energy coastlines in the world, producing frequent large swells and extreme storms through the winter months. These waves are the dominant marine process across all southern Australia (Short 1988). This pressure would almost certainly mean a significant increase in the rate of shoreline recession and contribute a deleterious effect on site preservation on islands of the Recherche (particularly those outlying the main archipelago), a common issue confronting Australian coastal archaeology (Rowland and Ulm 2012). However, the islands themselves provide a degree of shelter to the mainland from coastal energy. For the island archaeologist working in the Southern Ocean, the challenges faced by the people that have used this area in the past are those same challenges facing the researcher today: unpredictable swells, storms and waves, and limited access opportunities.

Just as the granite domes and hills are known for their ecological diversity, these areas also contain an abundance of archaeological evidence (Smith 1993), their fecundity having made them a target for people searching for camps with desirable water catchment properties together with an abundance of plant and animal resources. Nonetheless, previous researchers have assumed that relatively mobile human settlement systems and resource structures were maintained throughout the late Pleistocene to the late Holocene (e.g. Smith 1993). Smith (1993, 235) has argued that the archaeology of the Recherche represents a system of land use focused on granite domes and pavements. Smith (1993, 235) states that the archaeological pattern so far identified on the islands is assumed to "represent an earlier form of a land use system which still continued on post-transgressive mainland sites" (Smith 1993, 235).

This research is reexamining the notion that the ancient coastal plain archaeological record represents a similar pattern of settlement and subsistence as has been documented for the more recent (late Holocene) mainland. A marine transgression model has been developed (discussed below) that serves as the basis for investigating the likely range of exploitable habitats of the inundated coastal plain in comparison to the present-day mainland (an area of investigations first proposed by Dortch and Morse [1984, 44]). This model is the prerequisite for directing data collection strategies and in developing a range of testable hypotheses related to these broad realms of investigation. Archaeological data, focused on stone artifact assemblages, will serve as the basis for comparing and contrasting certain modes of past economic behavior as determined from different island groups—ultimately, to test notions relating to adoption of alternate land-use strategies across time and space in this ancient coastal plain.

It has been noted that the islands of the Recherche Archipelago are major factors in the evolution and configuration of the present-day mainland (Sanderson et al. 2000; Ryan et al. 2008), which is characterized by a largely high-energy crenulated coastline, granite headlands, and expansive crescent-shaped beaches. The coastal landscape during times when there was no "archipelago" is therefore expected to have been vastly different, presenting a whole set of new challenges, and perhaps opportunities, for hunter-gatherer-fisher societies. In another Southern Ocean context, Bowdler (1979) examined aspects of the archaeological record of the northwest coast of Tasmania, suggesting that the period between 18,000 BP and circa 8000 BP involved a coastal adaptation to a low-energy littoral and open coastal strip—with a productive and diverse settlement-subsistence system. With sea level rise, Bowdler (1979) describes an "ecological squeeze" whereby:

> A new adaptation had to be made to a restricted area of high energy coastline and an "economic" decision was made to drop fish from the diet and concentrate time and energy on higher yielding resources such as seal and abalone. (Bowdler 1979, 425)

This interpretation of the Tasmanian sequence raises the possibility of parallels to the islands of the Recherche. Was the Early and Mid Holocene coastline more productive for hunter-gatherer-fishers than the more recent past? Or, as other researchers have suggested, was there a refocus away from coastal areas during this period of marine transgression that resulted in changing marine productivity and a reduced predictability of coastal resources? (e.g., Ulm 2006, 253). At the very least, some level of *change* should be expected, and not limited to the economic landscape. For instance, the islands are known to be imbued with spiritual significance by the traditional owners for a variety of reasons, but are also an important part of culturally defined "creation stories." Given the distinct periods of island formation expected, with archaeological evidence of people living throughout the area since at least 13,000 BC (Smith 1993), some change and restructuring of the social and cultural world is expected. It can also be surmised that social change and restructuring took place independently from these landscape changes, in the dynamic processes of group formation, territoriality, changing kinship systems, and alterations in trade and alliance patterns.

Terrestrial and maritime archaeological sites provide evidence of the activities of indigenous people, sealers, and whalers in the Archipelago during the historic period (Dortch and Morse 1984; McIlroy 1987; Henderson 1989, 1991; Gibbs 1994, 1995; Bindon 1996; Green, Souter, and Baker 2001; Paterson and Souter 2006; Anderson 2011, 2012, 2016; Anderson, Berry, and Loo 2013). Known sealing-related sites include Middle Island historic site and artifact scatters, Boxer Island sealer's cave complete with rolled up bundles of sealskins from the early twentieth century, mainland camps in the Esperance area, and the shipwrecks of *Belinda* (1824) and *Mountaineer* (1835). Shore whaling sites include Middle Island, Thomas's Fishery and Barrier Anchorage at Cape Arid (McIlroy 1987; Gibbs 1994), and Goose Island. Sites related to ship-based bay whaling include Cape Arid, Middle Island, Point Malcolm, and Rossiter Bay—where Captain John Rossiter of the French whaler *Mississippi* famously rescued explorer Edward John Eyre and his Aboriginal companion, Wylie, following their arduous trek across the Great Australian Bight in 1841.

Modeling Island Formation and Human Responses to Environmental Change

Prior to the work of the Gabbie Kylie Foundation and its predecessor, the Restoring Connections project (Guilfoyle, Guilfoyle, and Reynolds 2009), the archaeological potential of the Recherche Archipelago had been investigated, to a limited degree, in a series of exploratory surveys that took place in the mid 1980s. During an expedition to Middle Island in 1984, archaeologists identified stone artifacts atop the massive granite dome of Flinders Peak on Middle Island (approximately six kilometers offshore from Cape Arid) (Dortch and Morse 1984). The findings indicate that the "chert" (fine grained cryptocrystalline material) and quartz artifacts, some of which were located near shallow *gnamma* (water) holes, were created prior to the island's formation. Dortch and Morse (1984) categorize archaeological deposits on the offshore islands of the Australian continental shelf as invariably relating to one of three modes of occupation: the pre-transgression occupation of the former coastal plain (circa five thousand to thirteen thousand years ago); sporadic Late Holocene (last 1,500 years) visitation by seafaring people; or the remains of post contact settlement predominately associated with the whaling industry. For the latter, several Aboriginal artifacts made of European materials (ceramic) are assumed to be "linked with the presence of European and American sealers, who seem to have had with them Tasmanian women and other Aboriginal people" (Dortch and Morse 1984, 34).

These early surveys indicated that relative to their size, the islands of the Archipelago play host to a rich archaeological record, reflected in ubiquitous evidence of lithic material and other cultural features scattered across the surface of the islands. As is typical in much mainland Australian archaeology, these lithic assemblages lack the chronological controls provided by substantive regional evidence of stratified occupational sequences on the islands and, as such, could be reasonably expected to offer the same broad parameters of data as the mainland assemblages. This can lend itself to interpretations that emphasize homogeneity across time and space, overlooking variation. And yet, despite the lack of stratified sites on the islands to date, current research allows a framework for providing a chronological context to island lithic assemblages through reconstructing the islands' landscape and paleoenvironmental history.

The second mode of potential Holocene occupation identified by Dortch and Morse—that islands were visited and sporadically exploited by seafaring people after the Mid Holocene climatic stabilization—appears to have been confined to northern and eastern Australia. Early investigations by Ronald Lampert and Norman Tindale concluded that there was a substantial "gap" in ocean-going watercraft usage running from the Kangaroo Island in South Australia across to Shark Bay on the Midwest coast of Western Australia (Tindale 1974; Lampert 1981, 174; see figure 9.3). This lack of watercraft usage is corroborated by ethnohistoric accounts from the whaling period, which indicate that the open ocean represented an unfamiliar environment with many traditional songs speaking of the anger

Watercraft usage

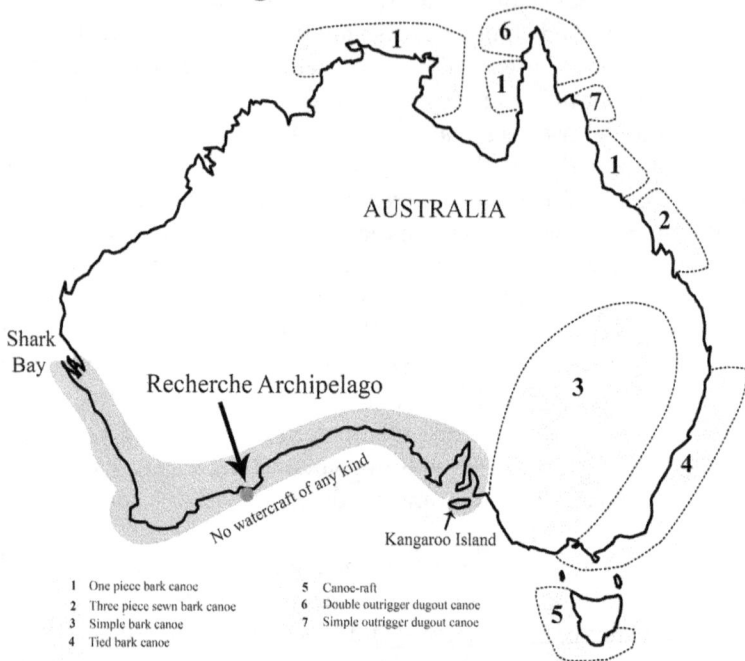

1	One piece bark canoe	5	Canoe-raft
2	Three piece sewn bark canoe	6	Double outrigger dugout canoe
3	Simple bark canoe	7	Simple outrigger dugout canoe
4	Tied bark canoe		

Figure 9.3. Watercraft usage map (after Lampert 1981, 174).

of the seas along the south coast, and to move across them was obviously a courageous act (Gibbs 2003, 9).

A limited amount of evidence has emerged subsequent to the Lampert study hinting that culturally modified trees with scars consistent with cutting bark for canoes may be present at the eastern extent of Lampert's gap on the Fleurieu Peninsula in South Australia (Walshe 2012); however, no such evidence contradicting Lampert's model has been documented in the Esperance Region. Such is the starkness of the contrast observed ethnographically in the eighteenth and early nineteenth centuries of the legacy of watercraft usage between the southwest and other regions of Australia that any notions of watercraft usage in the Esperance region are at present hard to sustain. The granite geology of the majority of the islands in the Recherche would have rendered them largely inaccessible even to well-adapted maritime societies. So with the lack of watercraft usage in the region discounting the probability of continued island exploitation throughout the Holocene, it can be posited that the Recherche Archipelago represents a fleeting glimpse into the occupation of the drowned Australian continental shelf, a relict landscape from the apex of the Pleistocene (with interesting European parallels—see Schulting and Richards 2002; Milner et al. 2004).

The archaeological evidence from the Recherche Archipelago demonstrates great potential, especially if considered in relation to a model of past sea-level change. The first steps toward accomplishing this were undertaken through a Geographic Information System (GIS) by layering broad spectrum eustatic sea level curves over coarse-grained bathymetric data from the seascape surrounding the islands. This facilitated the production of a series of paleocoastline projections for the archipelago at various stages before sea-level stabilization, enabling the delineation of a broad chronology, which would indicate the latest precontact occupational dates to which island assemblages would theoretically relate (figure 9.4).

Eustatic sea-level curves indicate that the Australian coastline underwent a dramatic and consistent recession in the period between the Last Glacial Maximum (at approximately 18,000 BP) and the Mid Holocene, when the global climate stabilized and, after a high sea stand at about 6,000 BP, sea levels receded to more or less their present level (Chappell 1983; Lambeck and Nakada 1990).

With rising sea levels following the end of the last Ice Age, a period of environmental instability and adjustment affected human populations, altering patterns of mobility, technological adaptation, and settlement.

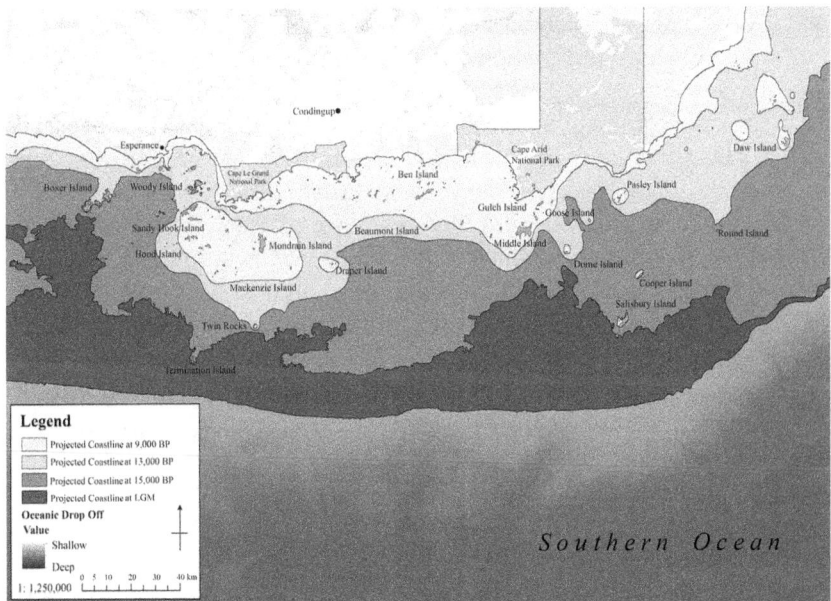

Figure 9.4. A model of marine transgression, Recherche Archipelago. Created by the author.

Numerous archaeological resources can be expected to now lie submerged on the continental shelf and in the deep Holocene sands that are a prominent feature of the Esperance coastline today.

The archaeological implications of changes in eustatic sea level have been recognized for a long time and other Australian coastal landscapes have been examined under the same framework (e.g., Hall 1999). However, for the reasons outlined above, the Recherche Archipelago provides a unique case study for the examination of a variety of archaeological questions, including the varying visibility of marine resources at different periods in the Pleistocene, the differential preservation of coastal archaeological sites, the constraints on human dispersal imposed by the creation and submergence of land bridges, changes in shoreline ecology, and alterations more generally in the palaeo-economic potential of coastlines following the extension or contraction of coastal territory (Hall 1999; Shackleton and Van Andel 1986 cited in Bailey and Fleming 2008, 2153).

The reconstruction of paleo-sea levels and coastlines is therefore significant in the interpretation of Pleistocene and Holocene coastal settlement. At present, however, issues of data access, quality, and availability in relation to bathymetry, sea-level curves, and locally derived paleoclimatic data hinder the potential for exploring these issues to their fullest extent and the ability to create anything more than a broad, necessarily limited model. Bearing these limitations in mind, the present model nevertheless tentatively hints at potential new avenues for research, and reveals important contextual information about the relationships between the geomorphic features of the landscape during the transgression. These allow us to not only comment on the archaeology of the islands themselves, but to also place mainland archaeological sites into a more precise landscape framework. In contrast to other areas of Australia, the mainland Esperance region contains little stratified evidence of Pleistocene occupation. The earliest dated site identified in the region, at Cheetup Cave rock shelter in Cape Le Grand National Park, yielded an initial occupational date of 13,200 BP (Smith 1993). Contrasting this occupation date with the transgression model enables us to hypothesize about this initial occupation.

The model indicates that for the first five thousand years of transgression, the process was comparatively rapid, inundating large swaths of low lying land and creating shallow tidal inlets that as early as 15,000 BP had potentially penetrated as far as sixty-five kilometers inland from the Lowest Glacial Maximum (LGM) coastline (figure 9.4). At this point, the outlying islands of the Recherche formed headlands or peninsulas still attached to the mainland. By 13,200 BP, however, the outlying Salisbury, Termination, and Cooper Islands appear to have been cut off by the fast rising seas. Recent archaeological work by the Gabbie Kylie Foundation at the outer margins of the archipelago on Salisbury Island has identified cultural material that, on the basis of the transgression model, suggests Pleistocene provenance. The model also reveals information about the nature of the relationship between inlying islands. For example, it would appear that a narrow and shallow paleo-channel isolated the Mondrain and Woody Island groupings, indicating that these were the first of the major islands to be isolated from the mainland. The model suggests that these islands were potentially linked to each other as part of a much larger single island some forty kilometers in length, the veracity of which can be further tested with higher resolution bathymetric data. This model also shows that the small islands of Anvil and the Pointer and Spin Islands, at the extreme northeastern end of the archipelago, may have formed a substantial island grouping (figure 9.4).

Archaeological Research

Despite their tightly delineated boundaries, the islands of the Recherche cannot be considered "island laboratories" in the same manner as the Melanesian Islands or, to a certain extent, Tasmania (Spriggs 2008, 216). Instead, the archipelago represents the surviving cultural fragments of a much broader landscape. Whether or not reflective of the wider pattern of landscape used in the area, the granite domes of the archipelago were of great significance to the people of the southwest, both functionally and culturally: "The Australian Aboriginal landscape is one replete with a highly elaborate totemic geography linking together place and people" (Tilley 1994, 38; see also Bradley 2008, 634).

Current evidence is insufficient to conduct meaningful comparative analyses. Accordingly, the approach adopted here is to examine stone artifact assemblages encountered on the islands in relation to technological measures of mobility. Ethnoarchaeological studies suggest that one of the most significant units of behavior causing variation in the archaeological record is mobility. Mobility is seen as a crucial aspect of adaptation in the economic relations of hunter-gatherer societies (Gamble and Boimier 1991, 5). Though settlement patterns may vary, the mobility strategy ensures that settlements are repeated at different times, durations, and places in the regional environments (Gamble and Boimier 1991, 5). In Binford's original thesis, the terms "residential" and "logistical" were used as conceptual frameworks intended to aid researchers in distinguishing the relationships between individual movement and group movement, and its implications for site formation (Binford 1980, as discussed in Kelly 1992, 44–45). There has been widespread application of this conceptual framework to lithic assemblage that builds upon the Binfordian frameworks of residential and logistical mobility. Many researchers have advanced interpretations of lithic assemblages based on assessments of "technological provisioning strategies" (e.g., Kuhn 1995; Boone Law 2005; Mackay 2005; Clarkson 2006; Graf 2010). The theory of mobility and technological provisioning provides a framework for analyzing lithic assemblages within and between different island groups as a means to distinguish between the range of land- and sea-use systems adopted at different times. The marine transgression model provides the necessary chronological context from which such comparisons may be made.

As further work continues to integrate a variety of fragmented datasets, and gather more refined archaeological data from the various island groups, a complex and dynamic picture of human–environmental relations is emerging. The challenge for archaeologists is to generate more effective methods for identifying variation in the archaeological record in the context of dramatic geomorphological change, preservation issues, and the subtlety of the existing datasets, and attempt to identify the social fabric underlying the material cultural record from the distant past. As Veth, O'Connor, and Wallis (2005) note, a dichotomy has arisen in Australian archaeology whereby socially framed approaches to understanding change in the archaeological record (e.g. Lourandos 1997) have been largely confined to the Late Holocene period, whereas discussions of earlier Pleistocene and Early Holocene datasets have remained persistent (for a variety of reasons related largely to poor spatial and chronological control confined to environmentally deterministic frameworks). With these broad chronological frameworks established, the possibility is there to model aspects of human settlement and change, including archaeological site formation processes, and to begin to understand notions of "place" across broad spatial and time scales.

The Historic Sealing and Whaling Period

This aspect of the research combines evidence from historic-era Aboriginal, historical, and maritime archaeological sites with historical sources to allow as comprehensive an interpretation as possible of the diversity and complexity of newcomer–indigenous contacts, early maritime activities and their associated archaeological sites (figure 9.5) in the study area. It adopts a "maritime cultural landscape" approach (Westerdahl 1992) to investigate both submerged and terrestrial archaeological sites within their wider environment. The maritime cultural landscape includes archaeological sites, intangible places, and concepts including cognitive

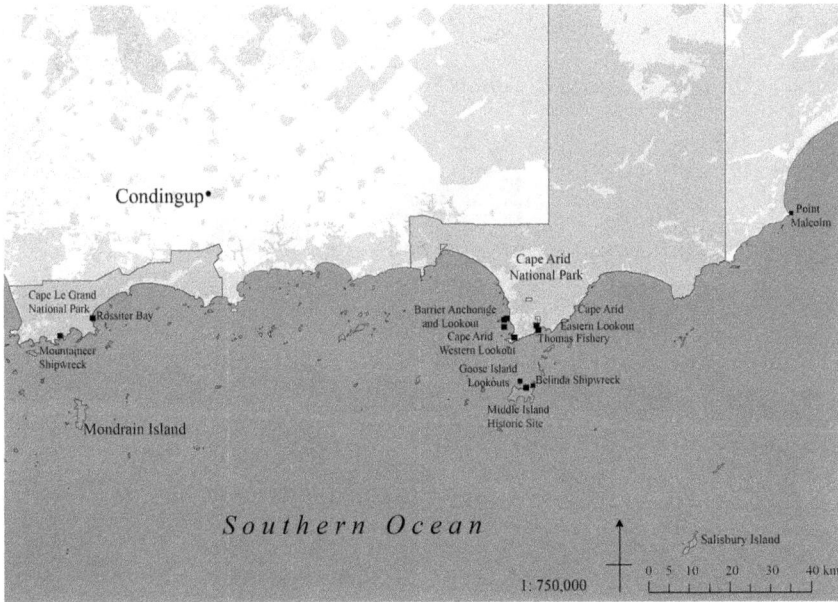

Figure 9.5. Location of key historic sealing and whaling sites in the Recherche Archipelago. Created by the author.

or indicatory aspects such as place names (the "place name landscape"), oral histories, rituals, superstitions, and traditions (Westerdahl 1992, 6; 2005, 2).

The abundance of marine mammal resources along the Southern Ocean coastline saw sealers and whalers visiting the area prior to the British colonization of King George Sound (Albany) in 1826, with the earliest recorded visits by the British whaling ships *Kingston* and *Elligood* in 1800. In 1803, the American sealer Captain Pendleton sailed in the brig *Union* on a speculative sealing voyage and met French explorer Captain Nicolas Baudin in a sheltered bay, which Baudin subsequently named Two Peoples Bay. The shipwreck of the British sealing supply vessel *Belinda* (1824) at Middle Island is the earliest known archaeological site related to sealing activities in the Recherche Archipelago (Bateson and Loney 1972, 66; Henderson 1980, 75; see figure 9.5 and figure 9.6). Sealers were often the first to explore remote, uncharted islands and coastlines in the Southern Ocean, while withholding detailed information from authorities and rival merchants (Ross 1987, vii). Sealers knew many of the safe anchorages, water sources, islands, rivers, and inlets as their small vessels could readily approach the mainland coast. Vessels ranged from brigs and schooners to small open whaleboats or longboats fitted with a lug sail, with built-up canvas sides to keep water and spray out. Subsequent

Figure 9.6. Excavating the hull timbers of the *Belinda* (1824) shipwreck, Middle Island (Patrick Baker/ WA Museum).

explorers obtained invaluable knowledge of the coast and its resources from sealers and whalers.

Pelagic ship-based whaling was conducted by British, French, American, and Australian whalers up until the 1880s when industry and market changes saw the demise of demand for whaling products, and whale populations became depleted through industrial-scale killing. Early maritime visitors made the first contacts between Europeans and Aboriginal people on the south coast, with most contacts apparently friendly. However, some of the early sealers resorted to brutality and violence in their quest for women, which in turn shaped cultural responses. One report stated that the Western Australian coast was visited:

> by parties in search of the fur seal. They frequently made inroads into the territory of the aborigines, and endeavored to carry off the women, which infringement on their natural rights roused the natives to fury, and several collisions between the blacks and whites took place. Even now, talking of these marauders, the natives describe them with symptoms of loathing and innate hatred. (PGWAJ 8 October 1842, 3)

Shellam (2009, 133–37) has described how by the 1830s, "King Ya-nup"/ Minang people at King George Sound chanted and sang to celebrate the arrival of *caibre* (larger ships) that brought goods that could be traded.

The Minang distinguished *caibre* from *potora* (smaller boats) that could be carrying sealers. *Potora* did not bring large amounts of goods but rather presented a potential threat to Aboriginal people, as sealers were known to have killed men and forcibly abducted women and children, and were therefore to be avoided.

Conditions in the sealing and whaling industry were harsh and dangerous, and the men and women involved were usually illiterate and living on the fringes of conventional society. Sealing gangs included escaped convicts or deserters from whaling ship crews, and were multiethnic with European, American, Polynesian, and Aboriginal crew members. When French explorer Captain Durmont D'Urville visited King George Sound in his ship *Astrolabe* in October 1826, he encountered two boats with gangs abandoned by the colonial sealing schooners *Governor Brisbane* and *Hunter*. These crews had been sealing, fishing, and hunting on Breaksea Island for seven months, and included two kidnapped Aboriginal women, a New Zealand Maori named William Hook, and John "Warroba" Pigeon, a New South Wales Aboriginal man from the Killimbagong tribe in the Shoalhaven River area (Smith 2010, 154).

Aboriginal women were highly valued by sealers for their diving, foraging, and hunting skills, as well as for sexual "companionship" (Gibbs 1995, 91; Clarke 1996, 56–59). Aboriginal women from Van Diemen's Land (Tasmania) and Kangaroo Island were bartered in an exchange economy where Aboriginal groups traded women to sealers in exchange for hunting dogs, flour, potatoes, and skinned seals (Plomley 1966, 289, 306, 687, 688). Aboriginal women typically carried out most of the work for sealers, such as cooking, fetching wood, salt scraping and bagging, seal hunting and seal-skin curing, killing, plucking and salting mutton birds, and rowing boats. One Tasmanian woman, "Fanny," told George Augustus Robinson "that she could navigate a schooner and could hand reef and steer" (Plomley 1966, 82). Another unidentified woman traveled to Isle de France (Mauritius) in a French whaler and returned to her country having learnt to speak French (Plomley 1966, 686). It has been argued that the majority of women "were willing participants in this culturally-based barter system, and they became the resource managers and initiators of the small-island mixed economy" of Bass Strait (Cameron 2008, iii). As well as these negotiated exchanges, there are also accounts of sealers violently and forcibly kidnapping Aboriginal women during raids into their country, violent treatment and slavery (Australia Parliament 2011; *Perth Gazette and Western Australian Journal* 3 October 1835, 575; *Cornwall Chronicle* 9 November 1844, 4; Plomley 1966, 82; Merry 2003, 81–82).

D'Urville described the gang from the *Governor Brisbane* having with them on Breaksea Island "two native women they have got either voluntarily or by force" (D'Urville in Rosenman 1987). Five Aboriginal crew in *Hunter*'s gang comprised two young women from the Port Dalrymple region of Tasmania, a male and a female both between eighteen and twenty years old "from the continent opposite Kangaroo Island," and:

> a little girl of about eight or nine, who comes from the mainland opposite Middle Island. All these individuals have been living for several years with the Englishmen except for the little girl whom they have only had for about seven months. (D'Urville in Rosenman 1987, 32, 34)

In reference to this little girl, on 13 January 1827 during the establishment of the first British settlement at King George Sound, Major Edmund Lockyer arrested sealer Samuel Bailey on suspicion of murdering a Minang man found dead on Green Island in Oyster Harbour. Bailey had living with him on Eclipse Island one young Aboriginal woman from Oyster Harbour and a small girl eight or nine years of age, named by him Fanny Bailey, "taken off the mainland opposite Middle Island" (Lockyer 1826–1827, 18), who was no doubt the same girl D'Urville described earlier that year. The Minang people welcomed the return of the woman from Oyster Harbour by Lockyer, though "the little girl, finding she was a stranger to them, one pointed to Pidgen [sic] and then to the child, meaning he must take care of her" (Lockyer 1826–1827, 18). Lockyer obviously recognized the danger Fanny Bailey was in and acted by removing her from the sealer's grasp. However, Lockyer made no attempt to repatriate Fanny to her home country on the mainland opposite Middle Island, instead sending her to Sydney in the care of Thomas Hansen, master of the *Amity*. Hansen took Fanny to the Blacktown Native Institute for Aboriginal children and orphans in western Sydney, where she became the fifteenth student to be enrolled in the school (Brook and Koen 1991, 211–13). The Blacktown Native Institute is today recognized as the earliest institution in Australia associated with the "stolen generations" for its practice of forcibly removing Aboriginal children from families in the Sydney area, as well as taking in legitimate orphans (Lydon 2005).

The following account of the violent methods some sealers employed in South Australia's Spencer Gulf to abduct women is likely to be typical of the tactics used in raids elsewhere along Australia's Southern Ocean coast:

> There was another whale-boat on Long Island, with four men in her, named George Roberts, John Howlett, Harry and William Forbes. In November, on Boston Island, the people in this latter boat caught five native women from the neighbourhood of Port Lincoln; they enticed two of their husbands into the boat, and carried them off to the island, where, in spite of all remonstrance on the part of Manning, they took the native men in Anderson's boat round a point a short distance off, where they shot them, and knocked their

brains out with clubs. Manning believes they still have the women in their possession, with the exception of Forbes, whose woman ran away from him shortly after they were taken to the island. Two of the women had infants at their breasts at the time their husbands were murdered; an old woman was compelled to take them away, and carried them into the bush. (*Perth Gazette and Western Australian Journal* 3 October 1835, 575)

During the 1840s, historical accounts described Middle Island as "the right whale station of the Bight" and "for some time the resort of a set of lawless desperadoes, composed of runaway convicts, sealers etc." (Bécher-vaise 1954, 6; *Perth Inquirer* 5 January 1848). Between the 1860s and 1870s, colonial entrepreneurs established shore whaling stations with between twelve and twenty men, boats, and supplies. Shore whaling stations in the Recherche Archipelago included Middle Island, Thomas Fishery, and Barrier Anchorage. Evidence of these whaling stations remains in the form of stone try-works (furnaces used with iron try-pots to "try out" whale blubber to extract the precious oil), lookout shelters, domestic structures, and their associated artifacts.

Aboriginal Whalers

There is historical, archaeological, and ethnographic evidence for the involvement of Aboriginal people in whaling activities in the Recherche Archipelago. At Marbaleerup (Mount Ridley), 170 km inland north of Esperance, a significant rock art site includes depictions of a ship and a whale. It is considered to be related to whaling activities and is likely to be an example of contact art whereby indigenous people communicated and defined their experiences that had lasting impacts on their traditional culture (Anderson 2016, 246–53).

By 1850, Aboriginal people made up thirty percent of the shore whaling industry on Western Australia's south coast (Gibbs 1995, 91). Many were skilled, long-term workers in the industry who were treated as equals and shared the same "lay" share payments as whalers of other nationalities. Gibbs lists Jack Hardy, Tommy King, Nebinyan, Bobby Noneran, Rattler Nuterwert, and possibly Jack Hansome and Taylor Dickey as Aboriginal crew members working on the East Coast/Cape Arid shore whaling stations during the 1870s (Gibbs 1995, 621–43). Anthropologist Daisy Bates recorded a unique song by Nebinyan, who vividly recreated his whale hunting experiences as part of a shore whaling party (Gibbs 2003). Aboriginal people gathered around shore whaling stations using the opportunity for large amounts of whale meat coming ashore to feast and conduct associated ceremonial activities, although archaeological evidence for contact and possible trade between Aboriginal groups and shore whaling parties has proven difficult to find (Gibbs 1995, 85–89, 307).

Shipwrecks, Survivors, and Aboriginal Contact

The experiences of shipwreck survivors cast ashore on Aboriginal territory are a little-explored area of indigenous and non-indigenous contact. Survivors would often be in distress without trappings of European power (Silvester 1998, 2). Both indigenous and non-indigenous accounts of such events offer potential to researchers and indigenous groups to gain insights into cultural practices and responses, and provide evidence for Aboriginal populations and presence at specific geographic places and points in time.

The sealing and trading cutter *Mountaineer* blew ashore at Thistle Cove, Cape Le Grand, on 20 March 1835. The survivors camped for ten days on the beach, during which time they met with five Aboriginal people, before sailing in a small boat to Middle Island. After living and sealing with John "Black Jack" Anderson and his gang, including three Aboriginal women, on Middle Island for about four months, survivors James Manning and James Newell requested Anderson take them to King George's Sound. Anderson refused but agreed to land them on the mainland at Cape Arid without provisions (PGWAJ 3 October 1835, 575). Manning and Newell's subsequent account of their two-month-long coastal trek from Cape Arid to Cheyne's Beach with the assistance of Aboriginal groups was recorded by Richard Spencer, Resident Magistrate at Albany, who wrote:

> They are reduced almost to skeletons, and have nearly lost their voice. I am delighted to add that the moment the natives (The White Cockatoo, Murray and Will men Tribes) fell in with them, that they nursed, fed and almost carried them to Mr John Cheyne's at Henty, I have requested Mr D. A. C. G. Browne to issue a small portion of flour to each native, and a duck frock each, to two, who were most active, and kind to them on the journey, also to issue one weeks rations to the two men, and a duck frock to each of them. (Resident Magistrate to Colonial Secretary, 10 August 1835, State Records Office of Western Australia, Colonial Secretary's Office, Vol. 42/173)

The *Mountaineer* shipwreck and Manning and Newell's survivor-ordeals culminating in their rescue by Aboriginal people is significant as an early contact event on the south coast, and as the subsequent official correspondence and legal records provide most of the available historical information on the maritime history and sealing activities in the Recherche Archipelago at this time.

In Edward John Eyre's journal of his and Wylie's exploration of the south coast between Fowlers Bay and King George Sound, Eyre noted on 28 March 1841 that for three days, he had passed ship wreckage on a beach in the Great Australian Bight east of the Recherche Archipelago, though the ship did not appear to have been recently wrecked. In 1976, local rabbiter John Carlisle reported to the Western Australian Museum the discovery of ship wreckage and associated indigenous oral history accounts at a beach location pointed out to him by Aboriginal people:

> Two lifetimes before Eyre a ship "with smoke coming from it" was offshore, and a boat with white men came ashore. Some were walking and some lay down. The next morning two men lay dead and others had dug holes in the sand. Later in the day the ship came ashore rolled over and "died." Another boat with five men came ashore, three died and a fourth was speared, but a fifth was spared and lived with the tribe for some time. He eventually left and lived with another tribe west of Eucla. The shipwreck was subsequently inspected and identified as most likely having been a nineteenth century whaler or sealer. (Henderson 1980, 73–74)

Terrestrial Sites

Middle Island is the largest island in the Recherche Archipelago with valuable resources, including a salt lake (with evaporated salt, bagged and collected), fresh water, seals, cape barren geese (*Cereopsis novaehollandiae*), mutton birds (shearwaters, *Ardenna tenuirostris*), and tammar wallabies (*Macropus eugenii*) as food resources (Bindon 1996). Sealers were active on Middle Island up until the 1840s, and sealing probably continued intermittently until the late nineteenth century. In 1862, John Thomas established the first colonial shore whaling station in the Archipelago on Middle Island (Gibbs 1994, 86)—the returns were small and it is unclear how long this station lasted. Middle Island was also used by east coast colonial whaling parties from South Australia in the mid 1840s (Gibbs 1994, 86) and as an anchorage by American and colonial whalers.

The archaeology of Middle Island demonstrates indigenous occupation from prehistory to the twentieth century; evidence suggests activities such as sealing, whaling, fishing, pastoralism, and salt collecting. The main cluster of historic archaeological features consists of five stone ruins, flagstone floors, a forge, stone-lined well, and soak. Nearby features on a granite outcrop include a dam with a garden built over an indigenous *gnamma* hole and artifact scatters (both indigenous and European material), with tramlines and other artifacts near Lake Hillier used for late nineteenth century salt collection. Features in the main historic area were excavated in 2006 (figure 9.7), with analysis of faunal remains indicating that the inhabitants were adapting to their isolation by consuming tammar wallaby, birds, and fish (Marrell 2009).

A sealers cave on another island dates to the early twentieth century based on analysis of the types of tins found. The cave included a bed frame, a canvas sail probably used as a doorway, a block of salt on a wooden tray used in the tanning/curing process, tins and a baking dish stored on wooden shelves built into a crevice, and a wooden pine box with rolled up seal skins (Paterson and Souter 2006) (figure 9.8). Samples of the seal skins were tested for DNA and found to be Australian sea lion (*Neophoca cinearea*) skins (Anderson, Berry, and Loo 2013). That they appear to have been abandoned may be an indication of the overall unsustainability and decline of the industry at this time. Combined zoological, historical, and archaeological studies are important to assist in determining original seal populations, the extent and impact of historic sealing activities, and modern seal population recovery rates.

Between June and September 1840, the American whale ships *Hamilton* and *Julian* (Captain Haws) anchored in Goose Island Bay, Middle

Figure 9.7. Archaeological excavations at Middle Island historic site (Ross Anderson/WA Museum).

Figure 9.8. Archaeologists recording the sealer's cave (Alistair Paterson/University of WA).

Island. Three boat crews from the *Julian* camped on an island in Barrier Anchorage on the west side of Cape Arid between June and September 1840. Lookouts were constructed of stones and canvas sails to protect the crew from the prevailing winds and elements. In 1841, the explorer Eyre recorded lettering on a carved tree at Point Malcolm that said "Haws, 1840/Ship Julian/C. W." Crews from the Middle Island whaling station set up signal flagpoles and lookouts on both Hummock and Goose Island to signal to the anchored whaling ships when whales were sighted. Black rabbits still occupying Goose Island are recorded to have been left by whalers as a food source. The island is also a nesting area for shearwaters, more commonly known as "mutton birds," that the crew of the *Hamilton* collected for food in 1840.

At Cape Arid, Albany, whaler Thomas Sherratt used the sheltered bay of Barrier Anchorage as a shore whaling station between 1871 and 1879 (Gibbs 1994, 90). There are remains of a stone try-works, artifacts, and a lookout on the headland. A sloping granite shelf provided an ideal flensing platform. Artifactual remains include glass, ceramics, clay tobacco pipes, indigenous stone artifacts (that may or may not be associated with the whaling station), and rusting hoop iron. The small bay known as Thomas's Fishery just east of Barrier Anchorage was also used as a shore whaling station, and subsequently as a port for shipment of wool and produce from local farms, including Hill Springs Station, Lynburn Station, and Gabtoobitch Stations. A cast-iron whaling try-pot was removed to Lynburn Station in the early twentieth century. The floor of the bay is said to be covered in whalebone related to the slaughtering and processing of whales (Gibbs 1994, 94).

Conclusions

This developing archaeological research program is necessarily collaborative in nature to ensure those with a connection to the archipelago are involved in the planning and development of the underlying program. Thus, there is a necessary focus of research to ultimately protect and more effectively manage the heritage values associated with the archipelago and the associated ecological platform. At the same time, it requires work to identify the data gaps and the priorities for developing a set of research objectives and a methodology that is inclusive and relevant. Undertaking an "inclusive" research program requires "diverse theoretical and methodological perspectives and integrating multiple lines of evidence" that allow for a rich understanding of archaeological places (Bowser 2004, 2).

The initial documentation and assessment process undertaken thus far is critical to this inclusive, community research program. Investigations into the Pleistocene-Holocene archaeology require the development of the marine transgression model as the platform for directing research. Likewise, for the maritime and historical archaeology component, the first step required to understand the meaning of specific archaeological places is a data audit of the range, types, and context of sites and features currently known within the archipelago.

A strength of this program is that the researchers, traditional owners, students, and volunteers involved all bring different perspectives while sharing the same goal: to learn how best to understand, manage, and protect our shared natural and cultural landscapes. Themes of climate change and human responses, exploration, isolation, industrial activities, contact archaeology, human use of islands, coastal and international trade, colonial administration, and life ways emerge that are essential to understand the early development of Western Australia, and the lives of those Aboriginal people, sealers, and whalers who were "at home on these waves." For this program, the multitude of perspectives mirrors the multiple layers of history of this dynamic and constantly changing landscape.

Acknowledgments

The authors acknowledge the traditional owners who welcomed us to their country, history, and heritage. The research project was developed and delivered via the Gabbie Kylie Foundation, a legal entity first established under the auspices of the National Trust of Australia (WA) and now part of the Esperance Tjaltjraak Native Title Aboriginal Corporation (incorporated in 2015). The Foundation was put on hold with the formation of the Esperance Tjaltjraak Native Title Aboriginal Corporation. The Corporation is supporting the Gabbie Kylie Foundation 2.0 under an informal partnership approach.

The work reported here is also partly funded or supported by the Australian Department of Sustainability, Environment, Water, Population, and Communities; BHP Billiton; South Coast Natural Resource Management Inc.; the Western Australian Department of Indigenous Affairs (now Department of Planning, Lands and Heritage); the Western Australian Museum; and the Western Australian Department of Environment and Conservation (now Department of Biodiversity, Conservation and Attractions).

David Guilfoyle is the managing director of Applied Archaeology Australia/International, operating throughout Australia and the western United States. He works with various community-based organizations, and focuses on strategic planning, landscape mapping and protection, and supporting cultural ranger teams in the integration of natural and cultural heritage management. Aside from managing a variety of community projects with his small team that includes an anthropologist, a GIS specialist, and highly experienced field crews committed to community archaeology, David also works as a Lecturer at the School of Indigenous Studies (UWA) and is a Research Associate with the Centre of Excellence in Natural Resource Management (UWA, Albany). He is an Associate of the Museum of the North, University of Alaska and also the Western Australia Museum. David has also been selected as a key participant of a worldwide program: The Intellectual Property Issues in Cultural Heritage Project, Simon Fraser University, Canada.

Ross Anderson is a maritime archaeologist working as a Curator in the Western Australian Museum's Department of Maritime Archaeology. His PhD from the University of Western Australia researched the history and archaeology of the nineteenth-century sealing and whaling industries and associated cross-cultural contact along Western Australia's south coast (2016). He is also Senior Vice President of the Australasian Institute for Maritime Archaeology (AIMA), and an academic and applied researcher among seafaring families in the Philippines, at sea, and in a number of ports around the world.

Ron "Doc" Reynolds is a recognized Traditional Owner of the Wudjari people, part of the Noongar Nation of Esperance, Western Australia. With a career spanning forty years, Doc has been a leader in the community at the local, regional, State, and national levels. He was the first indigenous person to be elected Shire Councillor in Esperance. He has been President of the Aboriginal Legal Service of WA, Chair of the Aboriginal Lands Trust, and is currently the Chair of the Western Australian Indigenous Tourism Operators Council (WAITOC).

Tom Kimber is Senior Archaeologist with Gavin Jackson Cultural Resource Management in Perth, Western Australia. He holds a BA in History and an MA in Archaeology and Landscape History from the University of Leicester in the UK.

References

Anderson, R. 2011. *Maritime Archaeological Site Surveys Cape Le Grand, Cape Arid, Middle Island and Goose Island 14–24 February 2011*. Department of Maritime Archaeology report 269. Fremantle: Western Australian Museum.

———. 2012. *Report on Maritime Archaeological Fieldwork, Cape Arid and Middle Island, Archipelago of the Recherche, Gabbie Kylie Foundation Field School 20–28 February 2012*. Department of Maritime Archaeology report 295. Fremantle: Western Australian Museum.

———. 2016. "Beneath the Colonial Gaze: Modelling Maritime Society and Cross-cultural Contact on Australia's Southern Ocean Frontier; The Archipelago of the Recherche, Western Australia." PhD dissertation. Perth: Department of Archaeology, School of Social Sciences, University of Western Australia.

Anderson, R., O. Berry, and I. Loo. 2013. "Historical Sealskins from the Archipelago of the Recherche, Western Australia." *Bulletin of the Australasian Institute for Maritime Archaeology* 37: 114–23.

Australia Parliament. 2011. *Historical Records of Australia*. Series 3: Volumes 1–6. Library Committee and Archive Digital Books Australasia. Modbury: Archive CD Books Australia.

Bailey, G. N., and N. C. Fleming. 2008. "Archaeology of the Continental Shelf: Marine Resources, Submerged Landscapes and Underwater Archaeology." *Quaternary Science Reviews* 27, no. 23–24: 2153–65.

Bateson, C., and J. K. Loney. 1972. *Australian Shipwrecks Including Vessels Wrecked en route to or from Australia, and some Strandings: 1622–1850.* Vol. 1. Sydney: AH & AW Reed.

Beard, J. S. 1981. *The Vegetation of the Esperance and Malcolm Area, Western Australia. 1:250 000 Series.* Perth: Vegmap Publications.

Béchervaise, J. M. 1954. "General History: The Archipelago of the Recherche." *Report of the Australian Geographical Society* 1: 3–7.

Bindon, P. 1996. *Report on a Visit to Middle Island, Recherche Archipelago February 1996.* Community Report no. 1996/1. Perth: Anthropology Department, Western Australian Museum.

Boone Law, W. 2005. "Stone Artefact Reduction, Mobility and Arid Zone Settlement Models: A case study from Puritjarra Rockshelter, Central Australia." In *Lithics Down Under: Australian Perspectives on Lithic Reduction, Use and Classification.* Edited by C. Clarkson and L. Lamb, 114–23. Oxford: Archaeopress.

Bowdler, S. 1979. "Hunter Hill, Hunter Island." PhD dissertation. Canberra: Department of Prehistory, Research School of Pacific Studies, The Australian National University.

Bowser, B. J. 2004. "Prologue: Toward an Archaeology of Place." *Journal of Archaeological Method and Theory* 11, no. 1: 1–3.

Bradley, J. 2008. "When a Stone Tool is a Dingo." In *A Handbook of Landscape Archaeology.* Edited by B. David and J. Thomas, 633–37. Walnut Creek: Left Coast Press.

Brook, J., and J. L. Kohen. 1991. *The Parramatta Native Institution and the Black Town: A History.* Vol. 15. Sydney: University of New South Wales Press.

Cameron, P. 2008. "Grease and Ocre: The Blending of Two Cultures at the Tasmanian Colonial Sea Frontier." Masters dissertation. Hobart: University of Tasmania.

Chappell, J. 1983. "Sea Level Changes, Australian Region." In *Sea Level Changes.* Edited by M. J. Tooley and I. Shennan. Special Publications Series no. 20. Oxford: Institute of British Geographers.

Clarke, P. A. 1996. "Early European Interaction with Aboriginal Hunters and Gatherers on Kangaroo Island, South Australia." *Aboriginal History* 20: 51–81.

Clarkson, C. 2006. "Interpreting Surface Assemblage Variation in Wardaman Country, Northern Territory: An Ecological Approach." In *An Archaeological Life: Papers in Honour of Jay Hall.* Edited by S. Ulm and I. Lilley. Research Report Series 7. Brisbane: Aboriginal and Torres Strait Islander Studies Unit, University of Queensland.

Dortch, C. E., and K. Morse. 1984. "Prehistoric Stone Artefacts on some Offshore Islands in Western Australia." *Australian Archaeology* 1, no. 19: 31–47.

Gamble, C., and W. A. Boimier, eds. 1991. *Ethnoarchaeological Approaches to Mobile Campsites: Hunter-gatherer and Pastoralist Case Studies.* Ethnoarchaeological Series 1. Ann Arbor, MI: International Monographs in Prehistory.

Gibbs, M. 1994. *An Archaeological and Conservation Management Study of Nineteenth Century Shore-based Whaling Stations in Western Australia.* Unpublished report to the National Trust of Australia for the Australian Heritage Commission, Perth.

———. 1995. "The Historical Archaeology of Shore-based Whaling in Western Australia 1836–1879". PhD dissertation. Perth: University of Western Australia.

———. 2002. "The Enigma of William Jackman, 'The Australian Captive': A Fictional Account or the True Story of a Nineteenth Century Castaway in Western Australia." *Journal for the Australian Association for Maritime History* 24, no. 2: 3–21.

———. 2003. "Nebinyan's Songs: An Aboriginal Whaler of South-west Western Australia." *Aboriginal History* 27: 1–15.

Graf, K. E. 2010. "Hunter-gatherer Dispersals in the Mammoth-steppe: Technological Provisioning and Land-use in the Enisei River Valley, South-central Siberia." *Journal of Archaeological Science* 37, no. 1: 210–23.

Green, J., C. Souter, and P. Baker. 2001. *Department of Maritime Archaeology Visit to Middle Island, Recherche Archipelago 29 April–4 May 2001.* Report no. 154. Fremantle: Department of Maritime Archaeology, Western Australian Museum.

Guilfoyle, David R., Andrew Guilfoyle, and Ron "Doc" Reynolds. 2009. "Participatory Action Research in Cultural Heritage Management for Indigenous Cultural Heritage: The Gabbie Kylie Foundation, Esperance, Western Australia." *International Journal of Diversity in Organisations, Communities and Nations* 9, no. 6: 95–118.

Hall, H. J. 1999. "The Impact of Sea Level Change on the Archaeological Record of Southeast Queensland." In *Australian Coastal Archaeology.* Edited by H. J. Hall and I. J. McNiven, 169–84. Research Papers in Archaeology and Natural History, no. 31. Canberra: Archaeology and Natural History Publications, Research School of Pacific and Asian Studies, Australian National University.

Henderson, G. 1980. *Unfinished Voyages: Western Australian Shipwrecks 1622–1850.* Perth: University of Western Australia Press.

———. 1989. *Belinda: Unpublished Wreck Inspection Report.* File no. 12/90. Fremantle: Department of Maritime Archaeology, Western Australian Museum.

———. 1991. *Belinda: 1991 Expedition; Preliminary Report.* Fremantle: Western Australian Museum.

Hopper, S. D., A. P. Brown, and N. G. Marchant. 1997. "Plants of the Western Australian Granite Outcrops." *Journal of the Royal Society of Western Australia* 80, no. 3: 141–58.

Kelly, R. L. 1992. "Mobility/Sedentism: Concepts, Archaeological Measures, and Effects." *Annual Review of Anthropology* 21, no. 1: 43–66.

Kuhn, S. 1995. *Mousterian Lithic Technology.* Princeton, NJ: Princeton University Press.

Lambeck, K., and M. Nakada. 1990. "Late Pleistocene and Holocene Sea-level Change along the Australian Coast." *Palaeogeography, Palaeoclimatology, Palaeoecology* 89, no. 1–2: 143–76.

Lampert, Ronald. 1981. *The Great Kartan Mystery.* Terra Australis Volume 5. Department of Prehistory, Research School of Pacific Studies. Canberra: Australian National University. Retrieved 1 June 2018 from http://pacificinstitute .anu.edu.au/sites/default/files/resources-links/TA_05.pdf.

Lockyer, Edmund. 1826–1827. *Papers of Major Edmund Lockyer (1784–1880), 1826–1827 Re Expedition to King Georges Sound.* Australian Joint Copying Project. Microfilm: M 2054. Canberra: West Devon Area Record Office.

Lourandos, H. 1997. *Continent of Hunter-gatherers*. London: Cambridge University Press.

Lydon, Jane. 2005. "'Men in Black': The Blacktown Native Institution and the Origins of the 'Stolen Generations.'" In *Object Lessons: Archaeology and Heritage in Australia*. Edited by Jane Lydon and Tracy Ireland, 201–24. Melbourne: Australian Scholarly Publishing.

Mackay, A. 2005. "Informal Movements: Changing Mobility Patterns at Ngarrabulgan, Cape York, Australia." In *Lithics "Down Under": Recent Australian Approaches to Lithic Reduction, Use and Classification*. Edited by C. Clarkson and L. Lamb, 95–108 British Archaeological Reports International Monograph Series, 1408. Oxford: Archaeopress.

Marrell, J. 2009. "'I do not Believe they are Starving': The effect of Isolation on the Occupation of Middle Island, Recherche Archipelago 1835–1914." BA Honours dissertation. Perth: Centre for Archaeology, University of Western Australia.

McIlroy, J. 1987. *Nineteenth Century Bay Whaling Stations in Western Australia*. Report prepared for the National Trust of Western Australia and Western Australian Museum, Perth.

Merry, K. 2003. "The Cross Cultural Relationships between the Sealers and the Tasmanian Aboriginal Women at Bass Strait and Kangaroo Island in the Early Nineteenth Century." *Counterpoints* 3, no. 1: 80–88.

Milner, N., O. E. Craig, G. N. Bailey, K. Pedersen, and S. H. Andersen. 2004. "Something Fishy in the Neolithic? A Re-evaluation of Stable Isotope Analysis of Mesolithic and Neolithic Coastal Populations." *Antiquity* 78, no. 299: 9–22.

Mitchell, M., D. R. Guilfoyle, R. "D." Reynolds, and C. Morgan. 2013. "Towards Sustainable Community Heritage Management and the Role of Archaeology: A Case Study from Western Australia." *Heritage and Society* 6, no. 1: 24–45.

Paterson, A., and C. Souter. 2006. *Report on Historical Archaeological Expedition to Middle and Boxer Islands, Recherche Archipelago, Western Australia 16–25 April 2006*. Department of Maritime Archaeology. Report no. 222. Fremantle: Western Australian Museum.

PGWAJ. 1835. *The Perth Gazette and Western Australian Journal*, 3 October 1835.

———. 1842. *The Perth Gazette and Western Australian Journal*, 8 October 1842.

Plomley N. J. B. 1966. *Friendly Mission: The Tasmanian Journals and Papers of George Augustus Robinson 1829–1834*. Hobart: Tasmanian Historical Research Association.

Rosenman, H., ed. 1987. *An Account in Two Volumes of Two Voyages to the South Seas by Captain (later Rear-Admiral) Jules S-C Dumont D'Urville of the French Navy to Australia, New Zealand, Oceania 1826–1829 in the Corvette* Astrolabe *and to the Straits of Magellan, Chile, Oceania, South East Asia, Australia, Antarctica, New Zealand and Torres Strait 1837–1840 in the Corvettes* Astrolabe *and* Zélée, *Volume I:* Astrolabe *1826–1829*. Carlton: Melbourne University Press.

Ross, J. O. C. 1987. *William Stewart: Sealing Captain, Trader and Speculator*. Publication no. 37. Canberra: Roebuck Society.

Rowland, M. J., and S. Ulm. 2012. "Key Issues in the Conservation of the Australian Coastal Archaeological Record: Natural and Human Impacts." *Journal of Coastal Conservation* 16, no. 2: 159–71.

Ryan, D. A., B. P. Brooke, L. B. Collins, M. I. Spooner, and P. J. W. Siwabessy. 2008. "Formation, Morphology and Preservation of High-energy Carbonate Lithofacies: Evolution of the Cool-water Recherche Archipelago Inner Shelf, Southwestern Australia." *Sedimentary Geology* 207, no. 1–4: 41–55.

Sanderson, P. G., I. Eliot, B. Hegge, and S. Maxwell. 2000. "Regional Variation of Coastal Morphology in Southwestern Australia: A Synthesis." *Geomorphology* 34, no. 1–2: 73–88.

Schulting, R. J., and M. P. Richards. 2002. "The Wet, the Wild and the Domesticated: The Mesolithic–Neolithic Transition On the West Coast of Scotland." *European Journal of Archaeology* 5, no. 2: 147–89.

Shellam, T. 2009. *Shaking Hands on the Fringe: Negotiating the Aboriginal World at King George's Sound.* Crawley: University of Western Australia Press.

Short, A. D. 1988. "The South Australia Coast and Holocene Sea-level Transgression." *Geographical Review* 78: 119–36.

Shott, M. J. 1986. "Settlement Mobility and Technological Organisation: An Ethnographic Examination." *Journal of Anthropological Research.* 42, no. 1: 15–51.

Silvester, L. 1998. *Strangers on the Shore: Shipwreck Survivors and their Contact with Aboriginal groups in Western Australia 1628–1956.* Report no. 146. Fremantle: Department of Maritime Archaeology, Western Australian Museum.

Smith, K. V. 2010. *Mari Nawi: Aboriginal Odysseys.* Kenthurst: Rosenberg Publishing.

Smith, M. 1993. "Recherche a L'Esperance: A Prehistory of the Esperance Region of Southwestern Australia." PhD dissertation. Perth: University of Western Australia.

Spriggs, Matthew. 2008. "Are Islands Islands? Some Thoughts on the History of Chalk and Cheese." In *Islands of Inquiry: Colonisation, Seafaring and the Archaeology of Maritime Landscapes.* Edited by Geoffrey Clark, Foss Leach, and Sue O'Connor, 211–26. Terra Australis 29. Canberra: Australian National University Press.

Tilley, C. 1994. *A Phenomenology of Landscape.* Oxford: Berg.

Tindale, N. B. 1974. *Aboriginal Tribes of Australia.* Canberra: Australian National University Press.

Ulm, S. 2006. *Coastal Themes: An Archaeology of the Southern Curtis Coast, Queensland.* Vol. 24. Canberra: Australian National University Press.

Veth, P., S. O'Connor, and L. A. Wallis. 2005. "Perspectives on Ecological Approaches in Australian Archaeology." *Australian Archaeology* 50, no. 1: 50–66.

Walshe, K. 2012. "Canoe Scars in the 'Gap': Fleurieu Peninsula, South Australia." The Nawi Conference, Sydney, 30 May 2012.

Westerdahl, C. 1992. "The Maritime Cultural Landscape." *The International Journal of Nautical Archaeology* 21, no. 1: 5–14.

———. 2005. "Seal on Land, Elk at Sea: Notes on and Applications of the Ritual Landscape at the Seaboard." *The International Journal of Nautical Archaeology* 34, no. 1: 2–23.

Williamson, C. 2004. "Contact Archaeology and the Writing of Aboriginal History." In *The Archaeology of Contact in Settler Societies.* Edited by T. Murray, 176–99. Cambridge, UK: Cambridge University Press.

CHAPTER 10

Recognized Seaworthy

Resistance and Transformation among Icelandic Seawomen

Margaret Willson and Helga Tryggvadóttir

> The struggle for recognition is the nexus of human identity
> and national identity, where much of the most important
> work of politics occurs.   —Melissa Harris-Perry, 2011

In Iceland (Skaptadóttir and Proppé 1996, 1998; Proppé 2004) and else-where (Danowski 1980; Ellis 1984; Thompson 1985; Dowling 2011), the gendered division of fisheries work has generally been described as a system where women work on land (making and mending nets, working in fish processing plants, etc.) while the men fish at sea. The activity of fishing is also universally described as "male" (Danowski 1980; Ellis 1984; Thompson 1985; Dowling 2011). Yet, despite this pervasive perception, women in Iceland have been a discernible part of the fishing fleet from medieval times to the present (Magnúsdóttir 1984; Willson 2014, 2016). Additionally, in contrast to most other industrialized countries where most women fishing at sea work on small inshore family boats with their husbands (Munk-Madsen 2000), consistent numbers of Icelandic women have, since the early to mid 1900s, worked independently in various positions on trawlers and other larger deep-sea fishing vessels. Although women in Iceland have also worked in small family-run inshore fisheries for centuries, the social situation on these boats is distinctly different from that of the larger vessels. In the smaller boats, women tend to start in their teens, fish with other family members, and encounter little resistance or the need for "proving" themselves. The focus of this chapter, however, is solely on women working on the larger deep-sea fishing vessels that stay at sea for weeks or more at a time.

In this chapter, we argue that the decision by modern Icelandic women to fish is an active political choice, one in which they understand they are resisting restrictive gendered social norms. These women do this through transforming themselves from a generic, unacceptable "woman at sea," to a specific individual who rises above gender classifications through becoming recognized as a capable, strong, knowledgeable—and known— female "seaman" (*sjómaður*). Through this process of "proving," these women deliberately overcome suspicion and even hostility to their female presence. In doing this, they do not become "male," but instead undergo a calculated transformation from sexualized stereotype of the disruptive outsider to the specific, known, and trusted crewmate. Through doing this, they negotiate a space of recognition and equality among fellow crew within the prescribed hierarchy of a ship's social system.

In presenting this argument, we first establish the presence of large-vessel, Icelandic crews with seawomen, and then, using their own accounts, explore their process of transformation from generic "woman" to a recognized seaworthy seafarer. These women's experiences show that this process of transformation occurs through four critical periods: their decision to fish; getting their first job at sea; overcoming resistance at sea; and eventual acceptance or balance among crewmates.

In looking for explanations as to why this significant large-vessel contribution from Icelandic seawomen exists, we examine the agency of the women themselves as they align themselves with the Icelandic notion of the strong and independent female individual (Brynjólfsson 2010). In this context, the actual experiences of these Icelandic seawomen present insights into the complexities of sex-segregated work, negotiations of gendered social norms (both at sea and on shore), and the interrelationships of hierarchy, power, and identity.

The ethnographic research for this chapter is based on formal and informal interviews Willson conducted in all regions of Iceland between 2009 and 2014 with almost 200 Icelandic seawomen, whose fishing experiences span the 1950s to the present. This research also included discussions with numerous men who are involved in fishing, either as regular seamen or as skippers, and included extensive archival, governmental, and library research. This ethnographic research is supported through statistical data and analysis done by Tryggvadóttir, which establishes the level of these women's large-vessel presence.

The Modern Large-Vessel Engagement of Icelandic Seawomen

With the arrival of trawlers in the early 1900s, Iceland underwent social, economic, and cultural change on such a large scale that the effects of these boat technologies are often called Iceland's Industrial Revolution. Although few women worked on the earliest trawlers, beginning in the 1930s, they began to find their way aboard, first as cooks, and then as deckhands and other positions. More women began working on these boats in the 1940s, increasing gradually with a surge in the 1970s (Magnúsdóttir 1984; Willson 2016). In the early 1980s, an estimated 71 percent of Icelandic seawomen worked as cooks, while 29 percent worked as deckhands (*háseti*) (Magnúsdóttir 1984, 80); but by 2003, a majority of these large-vessel seawomen were working as deckhands (Tryggvadóttir 2008).

Starting from 1991, figures on the number of people working as fishers are available according to gender from an employment survey conducted by the Statistics Bureau (table 10.1).[1] Because these data were collected and rounded to the nearest hundred, they should be taken as approximations. In addition, we base the findings on our own statistical analysis of data from the Seafaring and Vessel Registry, which was available from 2007–2011. The data we are using for this chapter from the Seafaring and Vessel Registry is based on only vessels over twenty tons, reflecting only women working on these larger vessels, not the many inshore family vessels where women have traditionally fished in Iceland for centuries.[2]

Looking at the overall numbers from 1991 (table 10.1) a peak in women fishing from the larger vessels can be seen in 1999–2000, a surge that echoes that of the 1970s. Although many other factors influenced these surges, women who went to sea during the 1970s stated that they were influenced by the women's rights movements in Iceland, saying it was a time that encouraged freedom for women, allowing them to try new things; as a part of this, seawomen said they "wanted to prove that they could do anything as well as any man could do" (Willson 2014, 532).

Table 10.1. Comparison of the number and ratio of Icelandic women fishing, 1991–2011 (Hagstofa Íslands 2012).

Year	Number of women fishers
1991	400 (ratio: 6.5 percent)
1992	500 (ratio: 7.5 percent)
1993	200 (ratio: 3.0 percent)
1994	400 (ratio: 6.3 percent)
1995	600 (ratio: 8.6 percent)
1996	600 (ratio: 8.5 percent)
1997	400 (ratio: 6.4 percent)
1998	600 (ratio: 9.7 percent)
1999	900 (ratio: 12.5 percent)
2000	800 (ratio: 13.1 percent)
2001	500 (ratio: 8.3 percent)
2002	500 (ratio: 9.4 percent)
2003	400 (ratio: 7.8 percent)
2004	400 (ratio: 8.7 percent)
2005	400 (ratio: 7.8 percent)
2006	300 (ratio: 6.5 percent)
2007	200 (ratio: 4.4 percent)
2008	400 (ratio: 9.5 percent)
2009	300 (ratio: 6.8 percent)
2010	300 (ratio: 6.0 percent)
2011	300 (ratio: 6.5 percent)

Both the 1970s and 1990s were also periods when the economics of fishing meant fewer Icelandic men wanted fishing jobs. This shortage created an opening for women and, in the 1990s, also for immigrant men (Willson 2016). Since the early 2000s, the numbers of people fishing overall in Iceland has decreased dramatically to less than 5 percent of the total population (Einarsson 2011, 274), but women more so than men. The causes for this are complex, including the interrelationships of increased mobility, economics, increased educational and professional opportunities for rural women, as well as the gendered influences of technology and Iceland's Individual Transferable Quota system, all of which have strongly affected women's desire for, and access to, sea work (Willson 2016).

From 2007 to 2011, we have numbers for the average size of vessel upon which these women were working, showing that they were working on the very large deep-water vessels (table 10.2). We also have figures on the positions they held (table 10.3).

Table 10.2. Average weight of fishing vessels where women worked, 2007–2011 (Siglingastofnun 2012).

Year	2007	2008	2009	2010	2011
Average weight (tons)	1152	1191	1030	1115	1092

Table 10.3. Percentage of registered positions for women (ships over 20 tons) (Siglingastofnun 2012).

Position	2007	2008	2009	2010	2011
Deckhands	45.5	46.3	41.9	54.5	49.5
Research positions	10.1	8.9	12.2	17.5	13.8
Command positions	1.7	1.1	1.2	2.1	1.0
Administration	4.5	3.2	4.1	4.2	2.0
Engineering	0.0	1.1	2.3	2.8	0.5
Service (incl. cooks)	38.2	39.5	38.4	36.4	33.2

In addition to showing the high percentage of women working in deckhand positions, these figures reflect the small number of women working in command positions on larger deep-sea vessels. The job category of "administration" (*umsjónarstörf*) includes fish assessors (*matsmaður*), processing supervisors (*vinnslustjóri*), and inspectors (*eftirlitsmaður*). Cook jobs account for around half of the service positions (*þjónustustörf*), while the other half include cook's assistant and beginner deckhand.

Comparisons with Seawomen
in Other Industrialized Countries

If we compare these figures to the available research on seawomen in other industrialized nations, we see distinct differences. In the United States in the 1970s, the numbers were about 9–10 percent, with more women fishing on the West Coast than the East, in part because the women were more accepted working at sea in the West (Allison 1988, 243–49). In fisheries-dependent countries in Europe in the 1990s, the average was 3 percent (MacAlister Elliot and Partners 2002). Dowling (2011, 140) reports that no statistics are available for Australia, although Stella (1996, 176) put the number in the 1990s at about 1 percent. Atlantic Canada has seen a surge in the numbers of women fishing, increasing dramatically in small-scale fishing from 8 percent in 1981 to about 20 percent in 1990 (Grzetic 2004). But of these, in Newfoundland at least, women feel they have little choice but to fish in a subordinate and underpaid role (Grzetic 2004; Binkley 2005). In these circumstances, not entirely surprisingly, a majority of the women say they would not be fishing if they had a choice, and are doing it because of family economic stress, fisheries restructuring, and male expectations (Gerrard 1995; Yodanis 2000; Binkley 2002; Grzetic 2004; Power 2005). By contrast, the decision by Icelandic women to fish is a political one of gendered independence in which they knowingly confront assumptions about their character and identity. An important factor here is that in Iceland, unlike other areas such as Atlantic Canada and Australia (Stella 1996; Grzetic 2004; Binkley 2005; Dowling 2011), the women expect that, if they are able to get a job at fishing, they will make equal pay to men. This share equality stems in part from a 1720 law that accorded women equal pay to men for the "men's" work of cutting hay, cutting sod, and "rowing," which at the time meant fishing. Although this law is little remembered or considered in Iceland today, the precedent of equal pay for equal work aboard fishing vessels has almost always been followed throughout the centuries to today (Willson 2016).

Although Icelandic seawomen tend to be consistently marginalized in Icelandic popular imagination (Karlsdóttir 2009, 74), superstition regarding the bad luck of women on boats was clearly imported from other countries in the late 1800s and early 1900s (Magúsdóttir 1984, 84; Pálsson 1991, 93; Willson 2016). In modern times, although a majority of male skippers are resistant to the idea of taking on unknown female crew, actual superstition against a female presence at sea appears to be less than in many other industrialized countries (Willson 2016; see also King 2011). The women's path to acceptance is a process we shall now explore.

Phase One: Misrecognition, Political Knowledge of Difference, and the Decision to Fish

The majority of women, and men, who fish in Iceland have come from rural coastal communities where, until very recently, poor—or nonexistent—roads, combined with arctic weather conditions, made access to the outside world limited, at best. In this situation, the women who chose to fish saw it as their only option for escaping local low-paying female-specific jobs, mostly at fish processing plants. Icelandic women in rural and coastal communities in the 1990s earned 55 percent less than Icelandic men and had a lower educational level (Karlsdóttir 2008, 68). Young women recognized this and saw fishing as *the* local activity where they had a chance of earning decent money equal to what they saw among local males their own age. The women also saw fishing as their way out of the constraints village life placed on women, and as an avenue for adventure and freedom, as the following comments attest:

> I was fourteen when I started. For me, there were only two choices: work at the fish factory or go fishing.

> I was in school and I saw my fellow classmates going to sea and making money, so I wanted to do it too.

> I was tired of the female jobs where you earn nothing, you never have a definition of a job, you are just expected to do everything.

> We went because it was easy money—or maybe not so easy, but quick money—to prove we could do it, for the freedom and the adventure.

These Icelandic women's accounts reflect an ever-present consciousness of resistance, of knowledge that they are "swimming against the current" and that they are confronting social norms for women. Many encountered direct opposition to their going to sea from their parents and other community members. The women knew that this disapproval from their community was unlikely to change because regardless of their success at sea, their difference and nonconformity among shore people would remain a constant. In the face of this, the women still persisted in their desire to enter a profession that was central to not only the identity of their coastal communities, but their country as a whole.

> I had always said I wanted to go to sea since I was seventeen. I worked at the processing plant from five [a.m.] until nine [p.m.], so I knew I could do it. I was always calling the ship [asking for a job]. I thought it wasn't fair that the boys could make more money. I was faster [at cutting and processing the fish], so why couldn't I go?

> In 1979, I finished school and I didn't want to go to college, all I wanted to do is go fishing. My mother didn't want me to go and the women in the village stared at me, talking to my mother about my going.

In all of these accounts, the women are reflecting a political knowledge of their misrecognition by the society as incapable of doing this "man's" job, and are understanding that they are expressing resistance to the conformity and constraints of their society by doing it. Their assertion is that they are thinking and acting independently, regardless of attitude or repercussions. However, actions take more than desire, and their next struggle was to actually get a job aboard a fishing vessel in the face of this fairly consistent disapproval.

Phase Two: Resistance to Marginalization and Getting Their First Job at Sea

In any sex-segregated occupation, a prominent hurdle is access, and this is true with fishing. Nearly all the skippers are male, the fishing firms are controlled almost entirely by males, and the society at large does not provide avenues for women to enter commercial fishing. The seawomen recognize that their first chance to work at sea in commercial fishing was exactly that—a chance: a specific incident, action of their own doing, or opportunity that allowed them to break through their gendered exclusion from the large-vessel fishing profession. For most women, these moments are cause for remembered stories, pivotal moments. Some women foregrounded their own agency, stressing that when an opportunity came, they grabbed it. Or, despite a general impression in coastal communities that wives of seamen are resistant to other women being at sea, some seawomen also credited help they received from seamen's wives:

> I signed on at [a bar]. They needed a second cook, and I was just out of high school. My brother-in-law was there [at the bar], and we ran into the skipper and his wife. The skipper said, "No girls, they don't last at sea; some people have tried to take a girl but it has never lasted." But then his wife said, "No, give the girl a chance." This went on and on, back and forth, until the skipper said, "Okay, okay." He couldn't stand up against us both.

Women growing up in fishing families also often had to convince their parents. If they were not able to convince them, some women just went fishing anyway:

> When I was seventeen, I decided I wanted to go to sea and my father hit the roof. His brother, who was more conservative, was even worse. The house has a huge fight about that, but then I thought, "Well, I can really just do what I want to do. They can't tell me what I should be doing." So, I went to the harbor and spoke to the captain of the boat that my father owned. I said to the captain, "I hear you need extra people to work on the boat." He replied that he did. I said, "Well, I'm offering myself." He looked at me, a minute of silence, and then he said, "You get seasick?"

"No," I said.

"Have you had any experience?" he asked.

"No," I said.

"Well," he said, "then you can start tomorrow. Report first thing in the morning."

So, I went home quietly, packed my bags, and left the next morning.

For those without connections, their persistence had to be with resistant skippers and fishing companies.

I was on another job and decided, "I can't do this anymore; I am going to be a fisherman." Everyone laughed at me, but some guys I knew at the bar gave me the information to call the skipper. I called every day for a month. Finally, he said, "Okay, you can try it."

Basically, women told stories of doing whatever they had to do to get on a boat. This included finagling their way on:

It was always a dream for me to fish. My father owned a ship and was dead set against me going. So I knew this skipper. One night, he was dead drunk and wanted to go to a dance. I said I would take him if he would take me on his ship. So he said yes.

Some women, even when they had special qualifications, took jobs on boats no one else wanted.

In the beginning, I had learned to be a paramedic. The money was bad, so I thought, "What can I do to make money so I can be independent?" It was a dream; it was in my blood. My brother, my father, my grandfather—everyone—was fishing, and I thought, "How can I do this?" You can't just ask for it, you have to go through the back door. So I went to fish school . . . first and I had to do some research, so I decided that my research would be on the freezing process on a trawler. I went to one of the big quota firms, the fishing industry, and asked if I could do this research. But no skipper would take a woman in 1993, except an old man whose boat went overseas, so he was gone a month at a time. That's how I first got on.

In all of these accounts, the women are confronting community and parental resistance, usually alone and each in her separate way. This achievement, on its own, is one in which each seawoman claims respect and recognition, if not in the eyes of others, then certainly in her estimation of herself.

Phase Three: Transformation, Proving Oneself, and the Acquisition of Knowledge

Women who enter male occupations such as fishing are often considered controversial, a challenge to the status quo, and held accountable for engaging in "gender inappropriate" behavior (West and Zimmerman 1987, 136–39). According to common perception, even in nondangerous occupations, women are relegated to less physically demanding jobs while men are accorded the more demanding ones (Anker 1998). Despite the overt contradiction of women, for example, having consistently performed the acceptable and under-paid physically demanding shore work in fishing communities (see Karlsdóttir 2007, 2009), such perceptions tend to make it challenging for women to enter physically demanding, male-dominated occupations. This is particularly true in professions that are considered dangerous and where a team or crew is reliant upon each other for actual survival. As with fire fighting and mining (Tallichet 1997; Baigent 2005), the male-dominated, sex-segregated occupation of fishing is considered dangerous (Jónsson 1981; Van Den Hoonaard 1992; Binkley 1994). Danger is both construed as an exclusively male space (Dowling 2011, 143) and the "burden of danger" means that one's survival can depend upon the abilities, including the strength, of one's workmates (Stefánsson and Roughton 2010). Thus, for a woman to be accepted in fishing, her crewmates have to be completely assured that in a dangerous situation, they can rely upon her.

From what is reported in other industrialized countries, women are generally not expected or allowed to become equal crewmates. In Australia, women at sea are accorded the jobs men do not wish to do, such as "cleaning and cooking" (Stella 1996, 177), reflecting a pervasive pattern that women in fishing are always subordinate to men and are seen as "helpers" rather than "genuine" (Power 2005). In Maine fishing communities in the United States, women who "helped their husbands fish" expressed their resistance to being economically forced to fish by positioning themselves as "women" through complaining about seasickness and refusing to lift heavy boxes (Yodanis 2000). By contrast, the possibility of shipboard equality in work and pay is part of why Icelandic women see themselves as having, in practice, to be equal to the men and do equal (or better) work. In doing this, the Icelandic women talk of going through a process where they prove themselves to be *not* incapable women, but respected female seamen.

An aspect of what is considered lacking in women is the "natural" physical strength and endurance to work the long hours demanded by fishing. Another determinate of "natural" ability is whether or not a person gets seasick. In Iceland, seasickness is a metaphor for the lack of practical knowledge, while getting over seasickness, or "getting one's sealegs," acts as a metaphor for an ability to learn at sea (Pálsson 2000, 27). For this reason, women who do not get seasick on their first trips saw this as a quality that counted toward being a "natural" seaman (Willson 2016).

> I went on my brother's boat, fishing in winter. The winter was cold and high seas. It was natural to have me aboard because I wasn't seasick.

> I was never seasick. I liked to be at sea, working with nets, especially when the weather was really bad, to see it and feel it, when the boat was moving a lot.

If the women do get seasick, they told stories about how they either overcame or dealt with it. Thus, through presenting themselves as having an ability to *overcome* seasickness, the women are placing themselves as sea-worthy.

> It was a *bræla* [extremely bad weather], but we would steam for twenty-four hours to get to the fishing grounds. I was really seasick, but I always stuck to my watch. I would stir the porridge, throw up, and go back, stir the porridge again, throw up again. But after four days, it was okay.

A specific and more human aspect of learning to be at sea, which is a fairly constant theme among the large-vessel seawomen, is the initial hazing or overt hostility they encountered on their first boats. The hazing emerges in several categories. One is what the women consider "normal" or expected hazing that is common for every "greenhorn" or new crew member, but which is often delivered with a special strength when the novice is a woman. In all cases, the women reiterated the importance of reacting with humor, tolerance, cleverness, and defined personal boundaries. Here are a couple of examples women gave of overcoming what they considered normal hazing:

> They were always trying to fool me, telling me to cut off tails to count the fish, but I never bought it. They did this kind of teasing with all the new young boys too.

> It was a certain kind of guy who would be doing this. They would tease me; they put a crab in my bed once. I didn't do anything—just put it in a plastic bag and threw it away. They wanted a reaction; but since they didn't get it, they stopped.

For the women who went out on local boats, where the crew were fathers of friends or young men with whom they had grown up, this hazing was generally minimal or nonexistent; the most problematic occurred on boats where the seawoman was unknown and the crew were from disparate areas of the country. Most of the seawomen had grown up in fishing communities hearing stories of hazing between males, so they knew what was possible if the men felt they had an upper hand. A constant theme of these women is their understanding that in order to work as equals with the men on board, they not only have to be better but they also have to be clever in reacting to the teasing, harassment, or hazing, to not let the men know they are irritated. If they appeared intimidated, they said, the men would know they have gained power over them, the harassment would get worse, they would lose respect, and their chance to become an accepted crewmate would collapse.

There is also a constant theme from the women, that after working so hard to get on the boat and encountering a consistent and often hostile attitude from both the crew and shore community—both insistent that the women will not be capable of doing the work—that they have to prove this to be wrong and to establish a reputation as being tough and able to stand up for themselves:

> [There was] one old man who didn't want women at sea. So he was sometimes out of line. But he also encouraged me, when he said these things; I wasn't going to prove him right. I worked really hard. He was about sixty-five and the engineer. Then later, the best thing he said to me was, "If you stayed here [working] for seventy years, that would be good."

Another aspect of stabilizing equality is contending with men who wish to "protect" female crew. Each woman also handled this in her individual way, depending upon the situation and her own personality, with the ultimate aim of establishing relationships of respect and friendly companionship.

> At first [the men] wanted to protect me, they treated me differently, but I didn't want this. At the beginning they tried looking after me, but they soon found they couldn't do that and it became evident that I could do it, and then it was the same for me as the men. When the new men came after that, they heard that I worked well so they treated me with respect.

> I wasn't very popular at the beginning. I woke up one night and there was a huge cod in my bed. The two worst guys at the beginning, two brothers, didn't want me on the ship, but later they changed. They would later fix my hands, the bandages or cream when they would hurt from the work, sharpen my knives, and they protected me. I didn't want this either. I just answered them back, worked very hard, and was tough, which is why they changed. Another one of the guys, in trying to attract me, put on aftershave. It didn't go very well with the fish smell.

An attitude expressed often on shore is that women cannot work on boats because, the ship being a closed environment often for weeks at a time, the sexual tension from the men will cause problems to the effective working of the ship. The women recognize, however, that sexual harassment is an expression of attempted dominance and, on a case-by-case basis, worked to establish themselves not as sexualized inferiors, but as equal and dependable crewmates.

> They were showing really hard porn, all looking at me to see if I would react. Finally, the old man leaned over and said, "Come on boys, give the girl a break. Take this off." I said, "It's okay. This is nothing. If they can show me good sex, great, but this won't affect me. It's nothing." After that, they turned it off. They never did it again.

The guy [who had been cook] before me was very bad, I grew to understand. He used drugs. I noticed in one corner a cupboard full of [porn] video-tapes. Then one night, I hear sounds of a pornographic video being played loud. I thought this was not going to work, so I just put the food away so it wouldn't fall off the table and went to my room. I waited for the sounds to stop. Then I waited a bit longer. Then I came back up and put the food on the table. Nothing was said, but it never happened again.

Another aspect of power and positions at sea relates to the nature and stewardship of knowledge. Pálsson (2000, 27) describes fishing "en-skilment" or "embodied knowledge" (Pálsson and Helgason 1995) as "not just a cognitive process taking place in the mind; rather it involves the whole person actively engaged with a social and natural environment." This knowledge, in other countries, is always presented as male, and can include a special relationship with God (Dowling 2011, 143). Aragon (2011), in considering the knowledge of textile artists, places knowledge as either "circulating," as a common good that is shared, or as "sequestered," exclusive to a specific group, which in the case of fishing is usually men. A "guardianship" of this knowledge and the power associated with it is thus unevenly accessible. In Newfoundland and Australia, women are appar-ently excluded from this knowledge because they do not have a lifelong experience of fishing, nor "saltwater in their blood" (Dowling 2011, 158). This is also one reason for saying women working at sea in Newfound-land are not "genuine" (Power 2005, 98).

Likewise, most Icelandic women who choose to fish encounter the atti-tude that the sea is a "male" space and that they will never be able to—or in numerous cases should not be allowed to—acquire the boat and sea knowledge required of all seamen. This is where the women know they need to transform themselves in the eyes of their fellow crewmates from "not genuine" and lacking in knowledge to capable, knowledgeable, and trustworthy. Many of the hurdles they encounter toward reaching this goal they say they encounter on their first trip.

In keeping with this attitude, some women, who had less experience with fishing and the sea when they first went aboard, told stories of their process of learning. This is always set in contrast to their knowledgeable present self; this is what they did then, certainly not what they would do now. In this, they are acknowledging their own transformation, showing themselves now as capable female seamen in contrast to what they were at the beginning.

One time, I was taking this night shift and I had to pee, and I didn't pee out-side like the boys so I went back to the toilet. When I came back, I couldn't see the [buoy] light. The current had taken the boat away. I steered, looking for it, but I couldn't find it. Finally, I saw a light but then I saw that it was at the lighthouse on land. So then I woke the captain and he found the light. I thought the captain would tell everybody, but he didn't. He showed me how to use the compass. That was good.

Occasionally, women find a crew member who acts as their mentor:

As a teenager, I had worked a lot at the fish factory—it is similar to being at sea, but at sea we have the movement of the sea and fewer people doing the job. At sea, I had to go and to learn how to do all the things. There was one guy doing the grading control, he found it very interesting that there was a girl on board who was interested in everything, so he taught me everything. He taught me how to behave: you have to be a little bit better than the rest, he said. Always be the first to go on deck after dinner, the last to leave the work. So I followed his advice. And at the end of that first trip, the captain asked me if I wanted to stay.

Despite their equality at sea however, Icelandic, and other, seawomen are in many ways "invisible" (Karlsdóttir 2009) to the general land population. However, Icelandic seawomen note that, although in many contexts this is true, they are also highly visible, not as participants in the fishing industry but as curiosities. Seawomen find it intrusive when people gather to watch them as they work on boats at dock. They express irritation at their misrepresentation in journalistic articles, which focus entirely on their difference and their sex, depicting them as mascots or anomalies rather than as an integral component of a ship's functioning. Such articles, they say, do not work to inform, but instead increase systematic misrecognition through fuelling negative stereotypes among those who do not fish. Recognizing this combination of shore invisibility with continued shore misrepresentation, these seawomen say they are frustrated because their presence is not accurately recognized as a valuable contributor to the industry:

That is what is holding us back; we never get credit for what we do. You never see women getting credit in the fishing world. I know that if I am doing something right, someone else is taking the credit for it.

Through their stories of knowledge acquisition and transformation, these women demonstrate their agency, taking actions that transcend negative stereotypes and transforming them from sexualized "other," or "woman outsider" at sea, to a respected, known individual. In this way, they mobilize the stereotype of the "strong Icelandic woman" to include themselves, superseding other roles in which they are cast. They are moving themselves away from images of weakness, sexual prey, and incapable generic woman, instead claiming respect as tough, capable, and clever seawomen.

Phase Four: Recognition, Negotiation, and Balance of Being a Seawoman

Once the woman becomes an individual who is known, her recognized ability and acceptance among crew and skippers shifts dramatically and, unless the economics makes it very hard for men to get work, she does not find it hard to secure jobs:

> I was at sea for seventeen years and seldom found people to say, "Oh, she's a woman, and she can't do this," even when I was working as a deckhand on a new boat.

> There are many men who are opposed to having a woman aboard boats. But, there is a captain who says he is against women onboard, but he is always asking me to work for him. And when I am onboard, they always treat me just like everyone else onboard.

> They asked an old guy to cook for them, and he said he had never been so humiliated to have to work with two girls. But later, we became best friends. When he got drunk, he said if he got money and bought a boat, he would give it our name, or if he had a girl, he would give her our name. Seven years ago, he called. I hadn't talked with him for years, and he said, "Now I will do my promise."
> I said, "Oh, maybe you have won the lottery and bought a boat?"
> "No," he said. "I have a little girl and I have given her [a combination of your two names]."

The ultimate recognition comes with women taking officer positions on large-vessels. The 1970s saw the first Icelandic women enter the College of Navigation, with four graduating with qualifications as large-vessel skippers, all in the early 1980s. Two more women qualified in the early 2000s, and another seven women qualified between 2008 and 2013. Women who work in command positions are confident in their abilities, while the strict boundaries of a ship's hierarchy makes a command role clearly defined regardless of the officer's gender. One such woman noted that women are particularly suited for such roles because they know how to be calm when surrounded by chaos and they are used to doing multiple, complex tasks. Another expressed her opinion that women in Iceland are on the ascendancy:

> The captain's job, that was symbolic for men. But as the time went by, and women earned more rights . . . women realized that they should of course have the same abilities and opportunities as men. I think we all know that women can be just as physically strong and hard working as men, even though some generations of men don't believe it. It is my opinion that the male generation is growing rapidly weaker, physically, due to poor life-

style choices. At the same time, the female generation is growing stronger because of greater opportunities. And the time has told them that, why shouldn't they be able to work at sea? Even though being a deckhand may be too much hard work for some women, the captain's job requires no physical demands, unless we mention the great responsibility that comes with it. But I have personally done the job of manually steering an about 14,000-ton ferry, and it does not require a penis.

Conclusions

In this chapter, we have argued that these women are initially misrecognized by seamen and generally among non-fishing people, as generic females who are not competent, strong, or tough enough to be trustworthy sea crew. However, the women who choose to go to sea actively counter this misrepresentation through becoming known individuals who draw upon the accepted Icelandic image of the "strong Icelandic woman." In this, they do not become "men" or even gender-neutral in this predominately male profession, but instead, through a process of transformation, make themselves acceptable as known individuals. In doing this, the women act with agency at the onset, in first expressing their desire to work at sea, countering accepted gendered social norms. They then show their resistance through devising ways in which they can get hired on boats, going sometimes against their families as well as sceptical and often negative attitudes of skippers to get their first job. Then, once they obtain this job, they exhibit no illusions about the tough conditions in which they are expected to work, including the hazing and often outright hostility they will encounter initially from some male crew members. In confronting these attitudes and shipboard actions, they do not give up their femaleness, but, through their actions of strength, hard work, and cleverness, prove themselves as seaworthy. In this, they are exhibiting their ability to not only do the work the profession demands, but also their ability to get along with fellow crew. Their accounts reflect how they do not allow themselves to become victims, be intimidated, or give up their identity as women, but instead prove themselves as, in the eyes of fellow crew, seawomen who can hold their own at sea.

As this study has shown, the Icelandic seawomen present a different perspective on women who enter the fishing profession, not as subservient helpers to men, but as active participants in their own right, with sea experience and who have valuable contributions to make to fisheries knowledge in general.

Margaret Willson is a cultural anthropologist with interests in gender and fisheries, sustainable coastal communities, international development, issues relating to the polar regions, and Brazil. She is Affiliate Associate Professor with the Department of Anthropology, and Canadian Studies Jackson School for International Studies, Arctic Program at the University of Washington. Her latest book is *Seawomen of Iceland: Survival on the Edge* (2016).

Helga Tryggvadóttir† was a PhD student in Anthropology at the University of Iceland, where she was doing research on the experience of asylum seekers in Iceland. She completed an analysis on the discourse of development and the experience of seawomen in Iceland. She also worked as a research assistant in History at the University of Iceland, Faculty of Education, where she conducted demographic data processing and statistical analysis on Icelandic censuses from 1703–1920.

Notes

This chapter is dedicated to my coauthor Helga Katrín, who passed away, far too young, while this book was in press.

We firstly thank all the Icelandic seawomen and others in Iceland for their insights, support, and participation in this research. Funding from the Wenner-Gren Foundation for Anthropological Research and the National Geographic Society made Willson's fieldwork for this research possible. Many of the interviews for this article were done with research assistant Birna Gunnlaugsdóttir. Willson would also like to thank Águsta Flosadóttir, Álfrún Sigurgeirsdóttir, and Thóra Lilja Sigurðardóttir for translation and library assistance. She also thanks Joan Sharp for pointing out Melisa Harris-Perry's work, Bobbi Ballas for her generous hospitality during Willson's initial writing of this chapter, and Gísli Pálsson for introducing her to the editors of this volume. We would also like to thank the Seafaring and Vessel Registry for the access to their data.

 1. These numbers are based on an employment survey made regularly by the Icelandic Statistical Bureau since 1991. Since 2003, the sample has been around 3,800 people and the response rate is between 80–85 percent. The sampling frame is all residents between the ages of sixteen and seventy-four.
 2. Before 2011, registration was only obligatory for vessels over twenty tons, but since 2011, registration is necessary for everyone working in commercial fishing in Iceland.

References

Allison, C. 1988. "Women Fisherman in the Pacific Northwest." In *To Work and to Weep. Women in Fishing Economies*. Edited by D. L. Davis and J. Nadel-Klein, 230–60. St. John's, Newfoundland: Institute of Social and Economic Research, Memorial University of Newfoundland.

Anker, R. 1998. *Gender and Jobs: Sex Segregation of Occupations in the World*. Geneva: International Labour Office.

Aragon, L. 2011. "When Commons Meets Commerce." *Anthropology of Work Review* 32, no. 2: 63–76.

Baigent, D. 2005. "Fitting In: The Conflation of Firefighting, Male Domination, and Harassment." In *In the Company of Men: Male Dominance and Sexual Harassment*. Edited by J. Gruber and P. Morgan, 45–64. Boston: Northeastern University Press.

Binkley, M. 1994. *Voices from Off Shore Narratives of Risk and Danger in the Nova Scotia Deep-Sea Fishery*. St. John's, Newfoundland: Canada: Institute of Social and Economic Research.

———. 2002. *Set Adrift: Fishing Families*. Toronto: University of Toronto Press, Scholarly Publishing Division.

———. 2005. "The Bitter End: Women's Crucial Role in the Nova Scotia Fishery." In *Changing Tides: Gender, Fisheries and Globalization*. Edited by C. McGrath, B. Neis, and M. Porter, 64–75. Black Point and Winnipeg: Fernwood Publishers.

Brynjólfsson, B. 2010. "Strong Women in Small Towns." *Iceland Review* 48, no. 4: 16–22.

Cohen, A. 1977. "For a Political Ethnography of Everyday Life: Sketches From Whalsay." *Ethnos* 13, no. 3–4: 180–205.

Danowski, F. 1980. *Fishermen's Wives: Coping with an Extraordinary Occupation*. Narragansett, RI: University of Rhode Island, Marine Advisory Service, Publications Unit.

Dowling, J. 2011. *"Just" a Fisherman's Wife: A Post Structuralist Expose of Australian Commercial Fishing, Women's Constitutions and Knowledge, Sustainability, and Crisis*. Cambridge, UK: Cambridge Scholars Publishing.

Einarsdóttir, S. S. 2002. "'Meykóngur' og Þjóðsagnahetja: Sagnir og Samtímaheimildir um Þuríði Einarsdóttur." ("'Maiden King' and Folk Hero: Myth and Contemporary Sources on Þuríður Einarsdóttir.") PhD dissertation. Reykjavík: University of Iceland.

Einarsson, N. 2011. *Culture, Conflict and Crises in the Icelandic Fisheries. An Anthropological Study of People, Policy and Marine Resources in the North Atlantic Arctic*. Uppsala: University of Uppsala Press.

Ellis, C. 1984. "Community Organization and Family Structure in Two Fishing Communities." *Journal of Marriage and the Family* 46, no. 3: 515–26.

Gerrard, S. 1995. "When Women Take the Lead: Changing Conditions for Women's Activities, Roles, and Knowledge in North Norwegian Fishing Communities." *Social Science Information* 34, no. 4: 593–631.

Grzetic, B. 2004. *Women Fishes These Days*. Hallifax: Fernwood Publishing.

Harris-Perry, M. 2011. *Sister Citizen: Shame, Stereotypes, and Black Women in America.* New Haven: Yale University Press.

Hagstofa Íslands. 2012. *Vinnumarkaður (Labor Market).* Retrieved 21 May 2018 from http://hagstofa.is/Hagtolur/Laun,-tekjur-og-vinnumarkadur/Vinnu markadur.

Jónsson, S. 1981. *The Development of the Icelandic Fishing Industry 1900–1940.* Reykjavík: Ministry of Fishing.

Karlsdóttir, A. 2007. "Kvinders Deltagelse I Beslutningsprocessor I Fiskeopdraet ok Fiskeri: Kon Sekvenser for Regional Udvikling." In *Arbete och Valfard: Arbete och Demokrati.* Edited by G. L. Rafnsdottir, 182–95. Reykjavík: Nordisk Ministerrad/Vestnorden/Haskolautgafan.

———. 2008. "Not Sure about the Shore! Transformation Effects of Individual Transferable Quotas on Iceland's Fishing Economy and Communities." In *Enclosing the Fisheries: People, Places and Power.* Edited by M. E. Lowe and C. Carothers. Reykjavík: American Fisheries Society.

———. 2009. "Are Living Fish Better Than Dead Fillets? The Invisibility and Power of Icelandic Women in Aquaculture and the Fishery Economy." In *Gender, Culture, and Northern Fisheries.* Edited by J. Kafarowski, 67–84. Edmonton, Alberta: CCI Press.

King, T. 2011. "The 'Skipper Effect': Riddles of Luck and Rhetorics of Individualism." *Human Organization* 70, no. 4: 387–96.

MacAlister Elliott and Partners. 2002. *The Role of Women in the Fisheries Sector.* A Final Report to the European Commision Directorate for Fisheries. Lymington: MacAlister Elliott and Partners Ltd. Retrieved 21 May 2018 from http://ec.europa.eu/fisheries/documentation/studies/role_of_women/mainreport_en.pdf.

Magnúsdóttir, Þ. 1984. *Sjósókn Sunnlenskra Kvenna, frá Verstöðvum í Árnessýslu 1697–1980 (Sea-fishing of Southern Icelandic Women from the Fishing Stations of Árnessýsla County, 1697–1980).* Reykjavík: Sagnfræðistofnun Háskóla Íslands.

Munk-Madsen, E. 2000. "Wife the Deckhand, Husband the Skipper: Authority and Dignity among Fishing Couples." *Women's Studies International Forum* 23, no. 3: 333–42.

Pálsson, G. 1991. *Coastal Economies, Cultural Accounts. Human Ecology and Icelandic Discourse.* Manchester University Press, Manchester.

———. 2000. "Finding One's Sea Legs: Learning, the Process of Enskilment, and Integrating Fishers and Their Knowledge into Fisheries Science and Management." In *Finding Our Sea Legs.* Edited by B. Neis and L. Felt, 26–40. St. John's, Newfoundland: Institute of Social and Economic Research.

Pálsson, G., and A. Helgason. 1995. "Figuring Fish and Measuring Men: The Individual Transferable Quota System in the Icelandic Cod Fishery." *Ocean and Coastal Management* 28, no. 1: 117–46.

Power, N. 2005. *What Do They Call a Fisherman?: Man, Gender and Restructuring in the Newfoundland Fishery.* St. John's, Newfoundland: Institute of Social and Economic Research.

Proppé, R. 2004. "Hér Er Ég, Bara Kyngdu Því: Rými, Vald og Andóf í Íslenskum Sjávarbyggðum" ("Here I Am, Just Accept It: Space, Power and Protest at the

Icelandic Seaside"). In *Fléttur II: Kynjafræði: Kortlagningar.* Edited by I. Erlings-dóttir, 293–311. Reykjavík: Rannsóknarstofa í kvenna- og kynjafræðum.

Siglingastofnun. 2012. *Lögskráningagrunnur Sjómanna.* Reykjavík: Siglingastofnun.

Skaptadóttir, U., and H. Proppé. 1996. "Housework and Wage Work: Gender in Icelandic Fishing Communities." In *Images of Contemporary Iceland: Everyday Lives and Global Contexts.* Edited by G. Pálsson and P. Durrenberger, 87–106. Iowa City: University of Iowa Press.

———. 1998. "Verkaskipting Kvenna og Vinnulag í Fiskiðnaði" ("Job Roles of Women and Work Methods in Fish Processing"). In *Rannsóknir í Félagsvísinum II.* Edited by F. H. Jónsson, 253–62. Reykjavík: Háskólaútgáfan.

Stefánsson, J., and P. Roughton. 2010. *Heaven and Hell.* London: MacLehose Press, Quercus.

Stella, L. 1996. "No Place for Wimps: Working on Western Australian Trawlers." *Anthropologica* 38, no. 2: 173–95.

Tallichet, S. 1997. "The Underground Proving Ground: Women and Men in an Appalachian Coal Mine." In *Women Working in the Environment.* Edited by C. Sachs, 31–48. Washington, DC: Taylor and Francis.

Thompson, P. 1985. "Women in the Fishing: The Roots of Power between the Sexes." *Comparative Studies in Society and History* 27, no. 1: 3–32.

Tryggvadóttir, H. 2008. "Vinna Kvenna á Sjó: Skýrsla um Hlutverk og Stöðu Sjókvenna á Íslandi" ("Women's Work at Sea: A Report on the Role and Status of Seawomen in Iceland"). An internal report prepared for the Ministry of Communications/Transport. Retrieved 21 May 2018 from http://fishernet.is/images/stories/sjokonur_skyrsla_2.pdf.

Van Den Hoonaard, W. 1992. *Reluctant Pioneers: Constraints and Opportunities in an Icelandic Fishing Community.* Berlin: Peter Lang Publishing.

West, C., and D. Zimmerman. 1987. "Doing Gender." *Gender and Society* 1, no. 2: 125–51.

Willson, Margaret. 2014. "Icelandic Fisher Women's Experience: Implications, So-cial Change, and Fisheries Policy." *Ethnos: Journal of Anthropology* 79, no. 4: 525–50.

———. 2016. *Seawomen of Iceland: Survival on the Edge.* Seattle: University of Washington Press.

Yodanis, C. 2000. "Constructing Gender and Occupational Segregation: A Study of Women and Work in Fishing Communities." *Qualitative Sociology* 23, no. 3: 267–90.

CHAPTER 11

"It Is Windier Nowadays"
Coastal Livelihoods and Seascape-Making in Qeqertarsuaq, West Greenland

Pelle Tejsner

Coastal fishermen and whalers on the island of Qeqertarsuaq (English: Disko Island) in Disko Bay, West Greenland, have relied on the harvest of marine resources for the continuation of livelihoods across the generations. More recently, however, Qeqertarsuarmiut (residents of Qeqertarsuaq) and residents in other parts of the Circumpolar North have increasingly been portrayed as somehow more "exposed" or "vulnerable" victims located on the frontline of a geographically determined global crisis narrative about climate change, which inadvertently ignores the reality of coastal livelihoods in the Arctic today. Qeqertarsuarmiut often narrate a different story about their experiences with environmental changes, which is instead rooted in their continued familiarity and engagement with nonhuman agents (such as winds, sea ice, and marine mammals), as these are encountered during seasonal harvesting efforts along the coast. So while environmental fluctuations are certainly observed, interactions with a familiar coastal environment, nevertheless, continue to foster a relationship predicated on an enduring patience and concomitant flexibility toward shifting ice conditions, local weather vagaries, and the moods of nonhuman agents rather than risks or vulnerable exposures.

In this chapter, I will discuss how what we might call "coastal"—as opposed to "crisis"—narratives about Qeqertarsuarmiut livelihoods reflect the complexities of Arctic livelihoods in ways that immediately contradict a, more or less, dominant global vocabulary of risk in popular portrayals of the human (in this case Inuit) condition in the face of an ever-looming mainstream sensationalist narrative about particular population exposures to climate change in the Arctic. Most settlements and towns in the Disko Bay area are located either on or immediately adjacent to the coast, and since there are no road networks connecting towns and settlements in Greenland, people rely on boats or planes when commuting in Greenland (figure 11.1). The town's geographical position as an island situated between the west coast of Greenland and the wider Davis Strait has always provided rich access to a multispecies habitat, and since there are

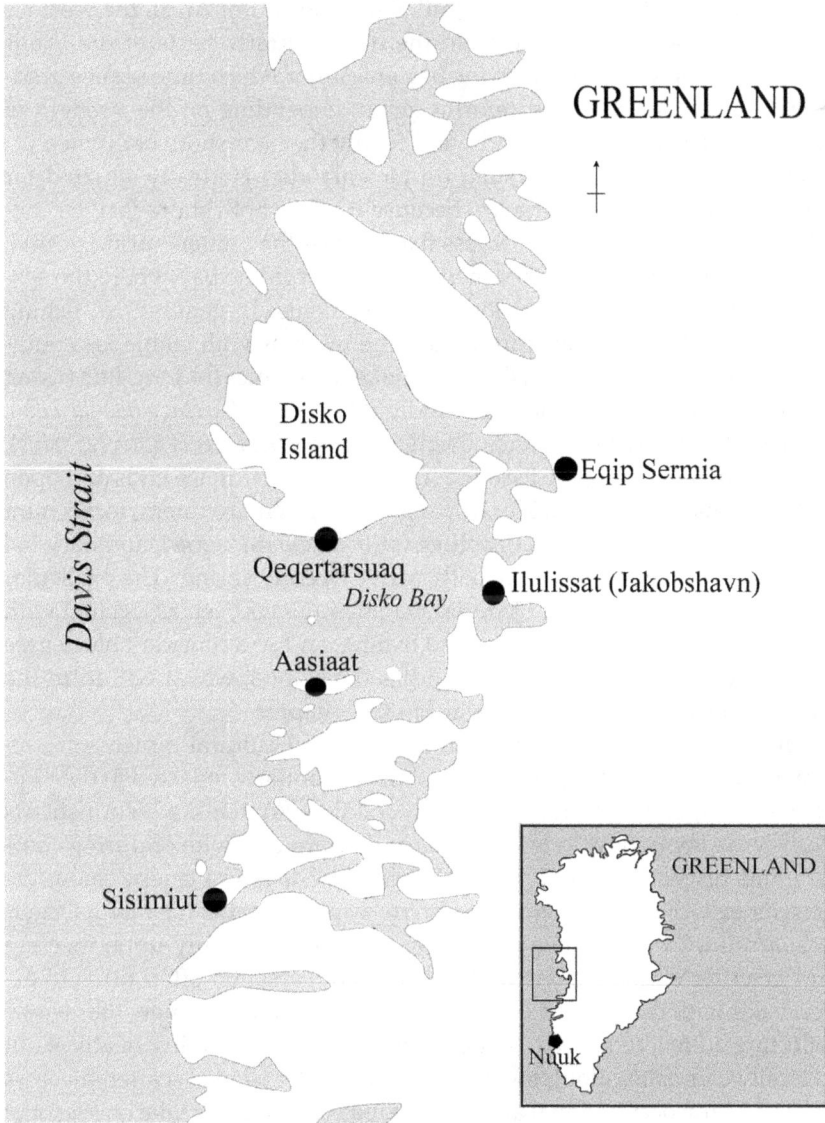

Figure 11.1. Map showing the location of Qeqertarsuaq and other towns and settlements in Disko Bay. Created by Tanya J. King.

no muskoxen or caribou on the island, Qeqertarsuarmiut are primarily dependent upon the sea around them.

In addition, the bathymetry of the bay indicates a sharp drop of the seabed, to a depth of 250–300 meters, less than a kilometer offshore. The sudden drop in the seabed often triggers strong currents, which then influences the condition, movement, and annual formation of winter sea ice. From around early January until about the end of April, the west ice (named so due to its arrival from the northwesterly parts of the Davis Strait) effectively encapsulates the bay area, after which time sea-ice gradually forms, dissolves, and reforms again, depending on the strength of currents, tides, prevailing winds, and finally the near-shore bathymetry.

Disko Island or Qeqertarsuaq (in Greenlandic) is ideally situated for studying people's use of the ice, because it offers both shore-fast ice conditions, which remain more or less fixed across the winter–spring period, and a wider floe-edge environment further out in the bay where the sea-ice is consequently more prone to the elements. In general, ice fishing is common along the coast in wintertime in areas with stable ice conditions; in these places, local fishermen make catch holes for long-line (using around thirty to forty hooks) for landing Arctic cod (*Arctogadus glacialis*), wolfish (*Anarhichas lupus*), and Greenland shark (*Somniosus microcephalus*). Further offshore along the ice edge (the area where firm ice ends and open water begins) and in the wider drifting floe edge environment, locals hunt for ringed seal (*Phoca hispida*), beluga (*Delphinapterus leucas*), and narwhal (*Monodon monoceros*), which usually arrive in early spring. The particular richness of the sea around Qeqertarsuaq has always been associated with certain risks attached to hunting and fishing, and so a considerable degree of knowledge, experience, and skill has developed, which will form the basis for the arguments put forward in this chapter.

The sea, and its manifold environmental and cultural dimensions, remains central to Inuit experiences and this is similarly reflected in the popular Inuit legend and stories of the *Sedna* (Sea-Woman), which instructs the listener about how to treat the sea and its animals with enduring courtesy and respect (Holtved 1967). After a few days in Qeqertarsuaq, the newcomer will notice that the sea holds a special status for many Qeqertarsuarmiut. During coffee breaks, over dinner, or simply upon meeting and greeting with someone on the street, conversation often turns to experiences with the sea and its animals. Some locals are human "libraries," reflecting a life lived at sea, while others simply enjoy taking relatives out to family campsites along the coast or the smaller islands scattered across the bay. Many occupational and nonoccupational hunters take on seasonal work on the shrimp trawlers or join the halibut fisheries in summer while others continue to hunt as a way of life. In most houses, there is either a balcony or a window facing the bay and binoculars are often found on people's windowsills, while short-range radios, used by local hunters, are left on in the kitchen most of the day.

Local fishermen often hang around the pier, meeting and greeting with people upon their return from the day's work at sea, while learning news and picking up relevant stories and insights concerning ice and wind conditions around potential harvesting grounds. In a culture where oral traditions are still valued, such informal exchanges draw on socioenvironmental experiences, accumulated over a lifetime as a body of knowledge about the coastal environment, which is often shared and affirmed in conjunction with other members of the community (Bird-David 1992, 39; Wenzel 1995). Qeqertarsuarmiut attentiveness to environmental fluctuations and consequent ecological variations not only used to be, but continues to remain, key to subsistence livelihoods on the island. These fluctuations inform day-to-day decision-making, such as where and what species to harvest among local Inuit hunters and their families. During fieldwork in 2008, the mixed cash-subsistence economy, which defines local household economies, was based on a multispecies approach to the harvest of renewable resources in the coastal environment (see also Caulfield 1997, 25); during more recent research stays (2014–2015), it was found that this approach is still practiced. Inuit reliance on marine resources has influenced historical, social, and economic developments in Qeqertarsuaq and simultaneously continues to shape present-day discourses about issues, such as national fisheries regulations, whaling quota allocations, and climate change among Greenlandic politicians, government resource managers, and foreign stakeholders.

The Vocabulary of Risk in Climate-Crisis Narratives

This chapter focuses on the discrepancies in receptions of the global climate-change discourses as we move from the global stages to the local shores—more specifically, on how an externally derived discourse is conversely interpreted and negotiated among Qeqertarsuarmiut on a daily basis. Recently, in debates about representations of the Arctic, scholars have started to comment on what is often referred to as a crisis-driven narrative of global climate-change science, which frames an Arctic commons as a unified, at-risk community (Duerden 2004; Martello 2004, 108; Bravo 2009). In the scientific climate-crisis narratives, Inuit are typically represented as having to cope with environmental uncertainties by being more profoundly exposed to climatic fluctuations than people elsewhere in the world (see, for example, ACIA 2005, IPCC 2007). Indeed, as I want to show here, Arctic residents (or Pacific Islanders for that matter) are frequently depicted as located on an imaginary environmental frontline in the struggle against global warming. The iconography, and accompanying captions, in the climate-crisis narrative includes photographs of indigenous Inuit (mostly men) in their supposed "natural" habitat (typically on melting sea ice) practicing traditional activities, such as hunting or herding (ACIA 2005; Martello 2008). The natural science discourse on climate change can be read as a vocabulary of risk employing headlines such as "impact" and "vulnerability" (IPCC 2001), which consequently omits key aspects of socioenvironmental interactions that are central to local subsistence practices. The climate-crisis narrative and its particular iconography inadvertently obscure vital Inuit concepts of human agency, such as patience or flexibility, when negotiating responses to changeable weather or melting sea-ice (Tejsner 2012, 2013).

This kind of representation of Arctic residency is not new to the region, and in cultural representation debates, popular accounts of Inuit livelihoods have often shared a long and, at times, uneasy relationship with their subject matter. Fienup-Riordan (1990, xiv) finds that the Western imagination, or, better, how life in the Arctic is commonly envisioned and depicted beyond Arctic shorelines, has had serious cultural repercussions, including an attempt by contemporary Inuit to depict themselves in accordance with a stereotypical Western portrait. Fienup-Riordan finds that even early-twentieth-century, deliberately staged films such as *Nanook of the North* (Flaherty 1922) still continue to feed the Western imagination and contemporary representations in ways that inevitably distort public perceptions of arctic livelihoods (Fienup-Riordan 1990, 14). Although such "encounter narratives" tend to originate in the past, they can, nevertheless, be read as long-contested views of nature and conservation because they "continue to resonate with contemporary debates about history, science, and colonial practices as well as with current struggles surrounding environmentalism" (Cruikshank 2005, 9; see also Bankoff 2001, 20). In Greenland, these encounter narratives are rooted in a very long line of complex stories and social recollections of oppression, paternalistic protectionism, military-scientific colonialism, and socioeconomic injustices (KVUG 1925; Brøsted and Fægteborg 1985). From the images of colonialism to contemporary displays of select (especially indigenous) peoples, dependency upon a climate variable, such as in the case of the ice, climate-crisis narration is simply the newest edition of dependency. These very similar resonations will endure as long as we continue to portray the entire Arctic region and its diverse populace as being "at risk."

In an analysis of popular representations of Inuit as increasingly exposed or vulnerable due to impending climate change, Martello finds that their implications for the global community inevitably dictates "who is made visible as a global citizen and who speaks for global citizenries" (2008, 354; see also Jasanoff and Martello 2004). The prevalent image of Inuit livelihoods as somehow more exposed to climatic variations is not exclusive to the Arctic but is similarly found in narratives of climate change in other, typically "peripheral" parts of the world. Farbotko's analysis of representations of Tuvaluans in Australia's *Sydney Morning Herald* suggests that their identities, to the outside world, are framed in terms of environmental displacement consequently fusing perceptions of climate change and coastal livelihoods in ways that then portray these islanders as "tragic victims" (Farbotko 2005, 280; Farbotko and Lazrus 2012). The images commonly associated with climate change tend to originate in places far away from Tuvalu, or Qeqertarsuaq for that matter, circulating via complex networks that subsequently reemerge at international fora for debating global warming (Hulme 2009, 219). Farbotko and Lazrus suggest that "cultural values and practices of particular groups of people in particular places are important for understanding the meanings and consequences of climate change" (2012, 382), and this is a point to keep in mind as we examine Qeqertarsuarmiut responses to climate change. The particular tone, inherited, as Cameron (2012) similarly suggests, from a common experience of colonialism, weaving an uneasy thread of commonality between what continues to feature as an inhospitable Arctic or a remote Pacific island in the global climate-crisis narrative. Qeqertarsuarmiut are optimistic about the prospect that increasingly warming ocean currents should bring cod and, more recently, mackerel to the Arctic. This particular kind of optimism is anchored in historical experiences of warmer northerly currents back in the 1950s, which led to a boom in cod fishing that secured the foundations for what was to become the modern Greenlandic fishing industry (Smidt 1983; Hamilton, Lyster, and Otterstad 2000, 199).

In "Voices from the Sea Ice," Michael Bravo (2009) suggests that Inuit responses to melting ice and glaciers are better understood by eliciting aspects of social inclusion of Inuit populations in debates about receptions of change rather than simply subscribing to a climate change "crisis narrative" where Inuit feature as more exposed, and increasingly vulnerable, victims of global warming. So in representing Inuit communities as endangered, crisis narratives continue to depict global climate systems as threatening to the pan-Arctic region (Bravo 2009, 256), despite the fact that the impacts of changing weather and climate are experienced differently in Greenland when compared to other parts of the Arctic.

The crisis narrative relies upon a vocabulary of scientific expertise that is poorly equipped to address the workings of socioecological relations and human–environmental interactions, and this has become increasingly apparent in cross-cultural translation attempts of Inuit concepts such as *Sila* (Leduc 2007, see below). The quality of cross-cultural translation also echoes the historical precedent for reducing or narrowing the scope of indigenous environmental knowledge in attempts at integrating it into national wildlife management frameworks (Nadasdy 2004; Huntington 2005). This particular kind of knowledge ambiguity is frequently observed in relation to previous decades' debates about hunting regulations where the local context of Arctic environmental knowledge has largely been ignored (Usher 2000). In contrast, recent local knowledge or observations of climate change are accepted for inclusion in scientific reports on Arctic climate change. But whether ignored or accepted, local voices are still obscured because the storyline in climate-crisis narration focuses solely on the challenges associated with climate while other, often more pressing social challenges or economic forecasts, which locals repeatedly express severe concerns about, do not fit well into a natural science agenda and are consequently ignored.

The crisis narrative—which drives the discussion of environmental risks facing Inuit populations—relies on making melting sea-ice synonymous with global warming; more precisely, politicians and activists attribute local observations of change to global warming. However, such associative linkages continue to remain a frequent bone of contention in the scientific community (Kerr 2007, 1413; Sorteberg et al. 2008). Nuttall states that he has:

> never felt entirely comfortable with the mere chronicling of indigenous observations . . . particularly when such observations are removed from their lived, everyday social and cultural context and offered as supporting evidence for scientific research on climate change. (2009, 292)

Since the pan-Arctic crisis narrative as a discursive monopoly maintains dominant global currency, Bravo asks whether better counter-narratives can be found. He finds that only by placing greater emphasis on "contextual complexities" can we hope to make climate-policy analysis more specific to place than has been the case so far (Bravo 2009, 258). I take a similar view, querying any argument that suggests that any changes reported by Inuit observers can simply be reduced to climate change.

After a few months of fieldwork in Qeqertarsuaq, I became increasingly puzzled by the fact that Qeqertarsuarmiut never sought to address environmental changes and ecological fluctuations in the same way as audiences beyond their shores envision Arctic livelihoods today. So in light of this observation, and with a view to the dominance of a climate-crisis narrative, I want to explore what is at once represented as a population at risk due to climate change, while simultaneously on the ground, Qeqer-tarsuarmiut do not perceive such a risk but instead view the environment as benevolent by continuing, in their words, to provide them with the means to get by.

Qeqertarsuarmiut Relations with the Coastal Environment

Examining Qeqertarsuarmiut relations with the surrounding coastal environment and wider sea, its significance as subsistence base and how it is conversely perceived among local everyday users, as opposed to the way it features in the crisis-narrative, may provide a useful platform from which to explore and discuss coastal dwellers' relations with their immediate marine environment. In what follows, I argue that the social role often attributed to marine mammals also reflects local perceptions of the surrounding coastal and sea environment. I explore coastal dwellers' relationship with the sea by showing how the sea, often conceived as *mare nullius* or "ocean void of humans" (Mulrennan and Scott 2000) by outsiders, nevertheless, continues to be thought of and spoken about as "home" among the Qeqertarsuarmiut. The point I wish to make in relation to the climate-crisis narrative is that this way of representing Arctic environments often appears meaningless to hunters and fishers because their stories tend to focus on individual experiences with the sea and their cherished family camp sites and harvest locations along the coast. This is confirmed by Qeqertarsuarmiut enduring interactions with coastlines, sea-ice, tides, and currents, which reflects a socioenvironmental relationship that crucially signifies how they choose to receive and negotiate a natural world that has always been perceived as changeable, willful, and therefore sentient as a nonhuman actor and force to be reckoned with in the course of their labors.

Navigation along the coast is always informed by the movement of natural forces, a constant awareness for fluxes of stronger or weaker currents, tides, and wind patterns. In the course of the whaling season, hunters rely on prior experience and intuition while patiently waiting for the timing to be right when they suspect that schools of beluga might be feeding underneath the shore-fast ice. They know that beluga are sensitive to ebbs and flows and how their prey travel back and forth with them, and so knowing where, and especially when, beluga make their way back toward open waters is often key to initiating a successful hunt. Morseth makes a similar observation about the role of high tides in relation to the movement of beluga in Eschscholtz Bay, noting that the whales "are highly sensitive to tidal fluctuations . . . and when the tide ebbs, leaving the eastern end of the bay too shallow, the northern channel serves as their escape route" (1997, 244). But unlike Eschscholtz Bay, however, the waters around Qeqertarsuaq are immediately exposed to the wider bay waters, so hunters, therefore, have to observe the right ice conditions and tidal fluctuations carefully since beluga escape routes (although also dependent upon the degree of ice cover) remain fairly open.

Hunters display an ongoing awareness for prevailing tidal conditions, which is crucial for success in everyday hunting and fishing. Since winds have been known to deviate unexpectedly from the observable norm, fishers often focus on tidal states, which can be far more reliable. An almost-guaranteed indicator of tidal conditions and the onset of either ebbs or flows are the icebergs situated in and around the shore fast ice. During tidal ebbs, a narrow strip consisting of bluish ice and a distinct protruding edge can easily be identified between the icy surface and the foot of the berg itself, and this distinctive marker is always a useful tidal indicator. By assessing the particular current and tidal conditions at the catch site, a hunter may be able to assess whether possible changes to weather or ice conditions are imminent.

One day, while out tending to our long-lines, my companion assessed the current by suspending his glider (a shovel-shaped anchor used to disperse the long-line across the seabed) in the water beneath the catch site, thus revealing the strength and direction of the current. This method not only provides a useful clue about which way to cast the glider (ideally against the current for optimal dispersal of the line), but also provides an indication of immediate tidal conditions. Qeqertarsuarmiut fishermen maintain that the reason for attaining familiarity with tidal cycles is based on the observation that tidal conditions always influence the volume of a potential catch. Similarly, fishermen exhibit a constant awareness of relevant currents along the coast, around rocky outcroppings, and when seal hunting on drifting ice floes further out in the bay.

If one fishing spot produces less fish, fishermen are quick to seek their fortunes in nearby locations where previous experience has taught them to try their luck. While journeying on sea-ice along the coast in winter, whether by dogsled or snow-scooter, familiarity with *sarfaqtoq* (places with strong currents) and their location is always vital to travel safety. Stronger currents during tidal intervals may result in areas with undercurrents, which "chew away" at the ice, causing it to thin out from underneath. Along the western shoreline, places where stronger currents chew away at the ice can be difficult to detect and people must often probe the thickness of the ice by jabbing once or twice using a self-made ice pole (called a *tooq*).

Because currents often influence the presence of Arctic cod along the coast, fishers are often seen using four or five catch sites at a time around a common area, so when one catch site is depleted, users quickly swap to the next and so on, thereby following the catch as it moves in accordance with prevailing currents. Naming cliffs and rock formations, outcroppings, and other prominent features along the coast is based on visual and other sensory experiences that reflect the Qeqertarsuarmiut relationship with the coastal environment. A place called *Issittunnguit* (the cold place) refers to a stretch of the coast that is exposed to winds coming down from the valley. Similarly, place names that describe topographic features such as outcroppings, inlets, or the particular shape of a protruding rock serve to guide wayfarers and reveal their importance as points of reference in immediate orientation and wider coastal navigation.

Another sensory association often made with features of the coast involves taste sensations and how these influence people's opinions about where they prefer their trout or salmon to be caught. One day, while I was attending a *kaffemiq* (the Greenlandic word for a social gathering in the form of a celebration) in a local home, and before being invited to enjoy the smorgasbord of locally procured delicacies, I was carefully instructed on when, and where, the different foodstuffs had been obtained. Familiarity with various places along the coast conveys the sense of an environment that is alive and endowed with intent, in which local wildlife is always consumed with a sense of regret, appreciation, and respect for the animal that has given itself to the hunter.

Across the seasons, as they are being hunted and fished, animals remain important coauthors in community narratives about the coast. They are perceived as willful agents who leave their imprint, just as people would, upon local seascapes. (One example of this is the story of *Eqaluit*, the trout place.) When people sit down to enjoy a meal consisting of *kalaalimerngit* (the Greenlandic word for locally procured wildlife, as opposed store-bought food, which is called *qaluunaamerngit*, namely Danish food), the story about the hunt itself, where the animal was caught and the weather and ice conditions of that place, is often retold.

Family members recall trips made along the coast, exchanging experiences of weather and stories of events that unfolded around these places. And in this way, a connection is established, not only between the family and the animal, but also between family members and the place where the animal was caught. The sharing and subsequent consumption of local foods reveals an intimate connection between Qeqertarsuarmiut and local animals, but also reinforces a sense of belonging, which people share with familiar places along the coast. In this sense, whales and other maritime species emerge on a common horizon alongside other nonhuman actors such as winds, tides, and other turbulent forces.

Among the Western Apache Indians, Keith Basso (1996) has found that the importance of place naming is tied to the fact that they may often act as moral tokens when stories about events that unfolded there are narrated. In much the same way, Qeqertarsuarmiut stories about places along the coast act as moral anchors that remind the listener about certain events or specific encounters with animals or other nonhuman (environmental) forces that exist there (Hunn 1996). These narratives range from recollections of bountiful harvests to less fortunate experiences with shallow reefs or unreliable ice conditions, which a traveler might face from time to time. They serve to remind the attentive listener about what to expect and what to look out for upon encountering these places along the coast or further out at sea. The narrations reveal how to comport oneself during times of uncertainty and suggest an enduring sense of familiarity with the coastline. In accounting for the workings of tides, currents, or winds as turbulent force and nonhuman environmental forces, the coastal narrative draws upon aspects of *Sila* as part of everyday Inuit ontology.

How do Qeqertarsuarmiut then receive weather fluctuations in relation to the crisis narrative and essentially deal with a primarily Western discourse about environmental fluctuations and change? Nuttall has argued that among hunting communities across Greenland, Inuit often talk about the environment as being in "a constant process of *becoming*" (2009, 299—original emphasis). People perceive every feature of the environment as endowed with its own *inua* (essence), so that, for example, *sermersuap inua* becomes the "essence of the great ice." He also notes that concepts related to weather or climate are known and addressed with reference to *Sila*, and thus expressed as *silap inua*, or the "the essence of *Sila*" (Nuttall 2009, 299). The concept of *Sila* is often used as an external reference to both ice and weather conditions, but it also pervades the individual and shapes his or her conscience. *Sila* contains a sense of openness toward the world, where what we perceive is already with us and not somehow external or removed from our engagement. In many coastal communities, hunting and fishing activities are always about more than skill or a sole reliance upon experience, and aspects of luck are often invoked when fishermen talk about their interactions in the course of fishing (Paolisso 2003, 78).

Many of the questions brought up while getting underway in the early morning hours deal with issues of prevailing winds and presumed ice conditions around prospective hunting or fishing grounds. In the practical everyday language of Qeqertarsuaq, *Sila* refers to the weather in general and may be expressed as *sillagippoq* (nice weather) or *sila allanngoqattartoq* (changing weather). And whether one is speaking about local weather or global climate in general (an impressive geographical shift), *Sila* is used interchangeably to describe and address both, although *klima* (i.e., the Danish word for "climate") is often deliberately employed when Qeqertarsuarmiut reflect on climate change as communicated via national media outlets or in scientific reporting. This trend is further observed in Leduc's cross-cultural evaluation and discussion of the shortcomings in contemporary translations of the Inuit concept of *Sila* into the vernacular of science and climate policy formulations.

Sila conveys the notion that environments (forces and actors such as winds, ice, and animals) are not part of imaginary realms that exist beyond our sensory experiences or individual conscience, and, in this sense, *Sila* is perhaps not so different from the way in which Western forms of expression refer interchangeably to the "moods" of people and the weather. If we consider words in English derived from the root "temper," such as "temperature" and "temperament," we can see how they carry double connotations as they refer interchangeably to both the moods of people and given weather conditions (Ingold 2010, 133). Through the continual unfolding of relations between people, weather, ice, and animals, any distinction between beings and environments evaporates. In this way, *Sila* is consistent with what Ingold describes as a kind of openness toward the world, which remains fundamental to an animistic way of being (2006, 18).

Sila points to the way in which, as people grow into their local environment, the environment grows in them, saturating individual and group perceptions as it oscillates between beings—human and nonhuman forces (such as ice, weather, and animals)—and their surroundings. Inuit ontology, as conveyed through *Sila,* sheds light on aspects of conscience, in this case patience, when used as a personal attribute. A person described as *silarqisitsiivuq* is "someone who waits for good weather," and in so doing, exhibits both the use of reason and sensible conduct. In relation to the moods of the weather, or *Sila*, this point became clearer to me while waiting for the right conditions for going hunting or fishing. The rhythm that hunters must observe entails following the rising sun and the returning tide while patiently waiting for the right moment to get underway. Through its everyday practical usage, *Sila* refers to both the outward means of orientation among people in the living environment, while simultaneously conveying an introspective reflection on how one feels and should act. As Qeqertarsuarmiut address environmental fluctuations, they also invoke emotional aspects of being. Specifically, they emphasize that one should aim to approach the uncertainties, which characterize harvesting methods, by changing the pace of work routines to match the rhythms of the environment. So when we ask about local climatic changes, in other words "the weather," we are tapping into an issue that is not only very personal, but also charged with a range of emotional responses based upon a lifetime of interactions with ever-changeable environmental conditions.

Wayfaring along the coast entails a figurative embracement of a life-world composed of varying environmental conditions, such as the vagaries of weather, or ecological fluctuations, as these unfold over the course of a day's journey. The coastal ranges of Disko Bay are a mix of drifting floe ice, shifting tides, and strong currents, to which hunters are deeply attuned, relying on years of individual experience and timely recollection of narratives about what to expect at certain moments in given places. There are also stories about places around smaller islands or near reefs that yield an abundance of food or where, while sailing under certain conditions, sea and sky are so at peace with one another that an absence of any bilge allows them to emerge as one.

Living in tandem with weatherly fluctuations, as continually reflected through the appreciation for *Sila* (i.e., the environment), where success in hunting rests on the continued affirmation of relations between people, animals, and the immediate environment entails an opening of our anticipations toward the natural world. Seasonal fishing activities follow harvesting cycles, and success is often based on previous encounters where the behavior of different species, their presence or absence, is familiar to the hunter. Local fishermen remain open to species fluctuations as yields inform what sorts of harvests can be made at which locations and, more importantly, for how long. A drop in harvested numbers triggers the relocation of harvesting activities to other known locations along the coast. These everyday observations of tides and related environmental forces along the coast are anchored in a long history of interaction between Qeqertarsuarmiut and the sea. One night, while enjoying a meal at the house of an old hunter and his son, a teacher at the local school, our conversation turned to the old days:

> Back in those days, some of the older people would go down to the shore at Kangidlersuit (Black Sands) and observe the seaweed. They would study the flow pattern of the seaweed which the current produced and predict whether or not the weather would be good for fishing and then people would respect their observations and adhere to their remarks. (Field notes, Qeqertarsuaq, 4 January 2008)

People's experiences with coastal waters, offshore islands, strong currents, or windy areas comprise a rich repository for both collective memories and contemporary ways of understanding and thus relating to the immediate environment. Nelson suggests that the Koyukon "must move *with* the forces of their surroundings, not attempting to control, master, or fundamentally alter them" (1983, 240—original emphasis), and I would argue that Qeqertarsuarmiut relate to their environs in the same way by continuing to employ attributes of *Sila* as a guiding principle. In the eyes of many local hunters and fishers, territorial hunting and fishing grounds are important because they shape the fishers' self-perception. Harvey Feit's observation that people's histories are "part of both hunting and landscape making" (2004, 94) cogently applies to Qeqertarsuarmiut narratives about the coast as they form a vital part of both fishing and seascape making.

The coastal waters around Qeqertarsuaq are perceived as abundant, nourishing environments of seasonal opportunity; but at the same time, I have often heard the expression that "life is hard here," uttered with a sense of reverence for the sea, as people talk about relatives and friends they have lost along the way. Some places along the coast are talked about and remembered for yielding abundant harvests, while others are best avoided or tabooed since they are places from where loved ones or close relatives never returned. But there is always a sense of keeping things going in what can best be described as a "give-and-take" relationship, and it is this assurance that allows locals to trust in their relations with familiar places and those animal partners they encounter along the coast and further out at sea. Just as the sea sometimes places heavy burdens on individuals through the hardships or sorrows one must endure, it is also talked about as a source of nourishment, strength, and renewal.

As suggested previously, patience, as borrowed from *Sila*, lies at the heart of a hunter's ability to anticipate those moments where immediate weather and ice conditions and the presence of animals come together. According to Inuksuk, an Inuit elder from Igloolik:

> It is never safe when people are impatient to use the ice when it is newly formed. . . . As far as anyone can remember, people have had accidents on ice due to their impatience and I have known cases of accidents that happened regarding the water and the ice. (Inuksuk 1988, cited in Aporta 2002, 347)

Personal interactions are informed by the task at hand and a sense of patient anticipation and timely flexibility, for instance, when poorer ice conditions might prompt an adjustment of strategy to match the intentions of nonhuman forces. Conditions that leave travelers stranded are not unheard of, but instead of immediately citing changes to climatic conditions or loss of predictability, local hunters point to impatience or inexperience as more likely causes.

Conclusions

By isolating local Inuit observations of climate change from their lived social context, we risk burying them in an externally imposed crisis narrative of exposure and vulnerability, which consequently silences the more enduring and versatile aspects of socioenvironmental relations as expressed by Qeqertarsuarmiut. Locals consider changing ice conditions (irrespective of any associations with climate change) alongside a range of related interactions with the coast, which makes it difficult to speak about responses to melting ice in relation to one, single force (i.e., climate change). When I critique the vocabulary of risk as it currently features in Arctic crisis narration, it is not to say that people are not vulnerable to environmental change. On the contrary, it is rather to point out that such portrayals inevitably reduce Arctic residents to helpless victims of externally imposed narratives, which reinforces an already existing historical (or colonial for that matter) representation of northern livelihoods.

Through a long history of entwined interactions with familiar places, recollections of encounters with nonhuman environmental forces, and *Sila*'s manifold expressions, Qeqertarsuarmiut share a connection with coastal waters that rests on a personal, emotionally charged sensitivity toward its fluctuations. So when they address a topic like climate change, the reply will almost certainly be charged with a profound personal insight. Coastal dwellers' narratives convey a sense of enduring patience that reveals how they live with—and accept—an environment perceived as living, intentional, and ever changeable. From this point of view, counter narratives are important for redressing the current trend so that Inuit are not solely portrayed as people having to cope with an unforgiving environment but rather as those who respond and constantly act upon the changes they experience.

By repositioning the commonly construed climate-crisis narrative as coastal narratives about coexistence with a myriad of environmental forces, I have sought to avoid the otherwise dominant vocabulary of risk as it fails to capture culture-specific relations—such as the concept of *Sila*—as these continue to inform coastal livelihoods. In considering, and accounting for, Qeqertarsuarmiut socioenvironmental interactions with their coastline, deeply engaging narratives emerge in which Greenlandic Inuit are not just passive victims of climate change, but rather mediators on how to relate and incorporate ongoing changes. From this perspective, counter-narratives reflect the kind of flexibility, patience, and enduring openness that coastal dwellers bring to any engagement with their local habitats.

Pelle Tejsner is an Assistant Professor with the Arctic Research Centre (ARC) and with the Department of Anthropology at Aarhus University in Denmark. His PhD thesis and related publications are based on long-term, ongoing fieldwork in the Disco Bay region in Northwest Greenland, and he focuses on local receptions of climate change as part of his interests in subsistence strategies and coastal resource harvesting among Inuit hunters and fishermen. His recent postdoctoral research (2015–2017) examines local expectations and receptions of plans for offshore oil exploration, mining, and wider Arctic industrialization. The research assesses the status concerning indigenous people's (Inuit) rights in Greenland through a focus on traditional notions of tenure and custodianship of local marine resources vis-à-vis the interest of the state and multinational resource exploration companies.

References

Aporta, C. 2002. "Life on the Ice: Understanding the Codes of a Changing Environment." *Polar Record* 38, no. 207: 341–54.

ACIA (Arctic Climate Impact Assessment). 2005. Cambridge, UK: Cambridge University Press Scientific Report.

Bankoff, G. 2001. "Rendering the World Unsafe: 'Vulnerability' as Western Discourse." *Disasters* 25, no. 1: 19–35.

Basso, K. H. 1996. *Wisdom Sits in Places: Landscape and Language among the Western Apache.* Albuquerque: University of New Mexico Press.

Bird-David, N. 1992. "Beyond 'the Hunting and Gathering Mode of Subsistence': Culture-sensitive Observations on the Nayaka and Other Modern Hunter-gatherers." *Man* 27, no. 1: 19–44.

Bravo, M. 2009. "Voices from the Sea Ice: The Reception of Climate Impact Narratives." *Journal of Historical Geography* 35, no. 2: 256–78.

Brøsted, J. and M. Fægteborg. 1985. *Thule: Fangerfolk og Militæranlæg.* København: Jurist- og Økonomiforbundet.

Cameron, E. 2012. "Securing Indigenous Politics: A Critique of the Vulnerability and Adaptation Approach to the Human Dimensions of Climate Change in the Canadian Artic." *Global Environmental Change* 22, no. 1: 103–14.

Caulfield, R. K. 1997. *Greenlanders, Whales and Whaling: Sustainability and Self-determination in the Arctic.* Lebanon, NH: University Press of New England.

Cruikshank, J. 2005. *Do Glaciers Listen? Local Knowledge, Colonial Encounters and Social Imagination.* Vancouver: University of British Columbia Press.

Duerden, F. 2004. "Translating Climate Change Impacts at the Community Level." *Arctic* 57, no. 2: 204–13.

Farbotko, C. 2005. "Tuvalu and Climate Change: Constructions of Environmental Displacement in the Sydney Morning Herald." *Geographical Annals* 87, no. 4: 279–93.

Farbotko, C., and Lazrus, H. 2012. "The First Climate Refuges? Contesting Global Narratives of Climate Change in Tuvalu." *Global Environmental Change* 22, no. 2: 382–90.

Flaherty, Robert J. 1922. *Nanook of the North*. Pathé Pictures.

Feit, H. A. 2004. "James Bay Crees' Life Projects and Politics: Histories of Place, Animal Partners and Enduring Relationships." In *In The Way of Development: Indigenous Peoples, Life Projects and Globalisation*. Edited by M. Blaser, H. A. Feit, and G. McRae, 92–110. London: Zed Books.

Fienup-Riordan, A. 1990. *Eskimo Essays: Yup'ik Lives and How We See Them*. London: Rutgers University Press.

Hamilton, L., P. Lyster, and O. Otterstad. 2000. "Social Change, Ecology and Climate in Twentieth Century Greenland." *Climatic Change* 47, no. 1–2: 193–211.

Holtved, E. 1967. "The Eskimo Myth about the Sea-Woman: A Folkloristic Sketch." *Folk* 8/9: 145–53.

Hulme, M. 2009. *Why We Disagree about Climate Change: Understanding Controversy, Inaction and Opportunity*. Cambridge, UK: Cambridge University Press.

Hunn, E. 1996. "Columbia Plateau Indian Place Names: What Can They Teach Us?" *Journal of Linguistic Anthropology* 6, no. 1: 3–26.

Huntington, H. P. 2005. "We Dance around in a Ring and Suppose": Academic Engagement with Traditional Knowledge." *Arctic Anthropology* 42, no. 1: 29–32.

Ingold, T. 2006. "Rethinking the Animate, Re-animating Thought." *Ethnos* 71, no. 1: 9–20.

———. 2010. "Footprints through the Weather-world: Walking, Breathing, Knowing." *Journal of the Royal Anthropological Institute* 16, no. 1: 121–39.

IPCC (Intergovernmental Panel on Climate Change). 2001. *Climate Change 2001: Impacts, Adaptation, and Vulnerability: The Contribution of Working Group II to the Third Scientific Assessment of the Intergovernmental Panel on Climate Change*. Edited by J. J. McCarthy, O. F Canziani, N. A. Leary, D. J. Dokken, and K. S. White. Cambridge, UK: Cambridge University Press. Retrieved 21 May 2018 from http://hcl.harvard.edu/collections/ipcc/docs/27_WGIITAR_FINAL.pdf.

———. 2007. *Fourth Assessment Report: Climate Change 2007: Synthesis Report*. Contribution of Working Group I, II and III to the Fourth Assessment Report of the Intergovernmental Panel on Climate Change. Edited by R. K. Pachauri and A. Reisinger. Geneva, Switzerland. Retrieved 21 May 2018 from https://www.ipcc.ch/pdf/assessment-report/ar4/syr/ar4_syr_full_report.pdf.

Jasanoff, S., and L. M. Martello. 2004. *Earthly Politics: Local and Global in Environmental Governance*. Cambridge, MA: MIT Press.

Kerr, R. 2007. "Pushing the Scary Side of Global Warming." *Nature* 316, no. 5830: 1412–15.

KVUG (Kommissionen for Videnskabelige Undersøgelser Grønland). 1925. *Stiftende Møde 1925 for Indenrigsministeriets Udvalg*. Fond No. A 022. København: Arktisk Institut.

Leduc, T. B. 2007. "Sila Dialogues on Climate Change: Inuit Wisdom for a Cross-cultural Interdisciplinarity." *Climatic Change* 85, no. 3–4: 237–50.

Martello, M. L. 2004. "Global Change Science and the Arctic Citizen." *Science and Public Policy* 31, no. 2: 107–15.

———. 2008. "Arctic Indigenous Peoples as Representations and Representatives of Climate Change." *Social Studies of Science* 38, no. 3: 351–76.

Morseth, C. M. 1997. "Twentieth-Century Changes in Beluga Whale Hunting and Butchering by the Kaṇiġmiut of Buckland, Alaska." *Arctic* 50, no. 3: 241–55.

Mulrennan, M., and C. Scott. 2000. "*Mare Nullius*: Indigenous Rights in Saltwater Environments." *Development and Change* 31, no. 3: 681–708.

Nadasdy, P. 2004. "The Politics of TEK: Power and the Integration of Knowledge." In *Hunters and Bureaucrats: Power, Knowledge, and Aboriginal-State Relations in the Southwest Yukon*, 114–47. Vancouver: University of British Columbia Press.

Nelson, R. K. 1983. "Nature and the Koyukon Tradition." In *Make Prayers to the Raven: A Koyukon View of the Northern Forest*, 239–47. Chicago: University of Chicago Press.

Nuttall, M. 2009. "Living in a World of Movement: Human Resilience to Environmental Instability in Greenland." In *Anthropology and Climate Change: From Encounter to Action*. Edited by S. Crate and M. Nuttall, 292–310. Walnut Creek: Left Coast Press.

Paolisso, M. 2003. "Chesapeake Bay Watermen, Weather and Blue Crabs: Cultural Models and Fishery Policies." In *Weather, Climate, Culture*. Edited by S. Strauss and B. Orlove, 61–82. Oxford: Berg.

Smidt, E. L. B. 1983. "Om Overgangen fra Fangst til Fiskeri i Vestgrønland." *Grønland* 5, no. 5: 125–45.

Sorteberg, A., X. Zhang, J. Zhang, R. Gerdes, and J. C. Comiso. 2008. "Recent Radical Shifts of Atmospheric Circulations and Rapid Changes in Arctic Climate System." *Geophysical Research Letters* 35, no. 22: L22701.

Tejsner, P. 2012. "It Is Windier Nowadays": Coastal Livelihoods and Changeable Weather in Qeqertarsuaq." PhD dissertation. Aberdeen: University of Aberdeen.

———. 2013. "Living with Uncertainties: Qeqertarsuarmiut Perceptions of Changing Sea Ice." *Polar Geography* 36, no. 1–2: 47–64.

Usher, P. J. 2000. "Traditional Ecological Knowledge in Environmental Assessment and Management." *Arctic* 53, no. 2: 183–93.

Wenzel, George W. 1995. "Ningiqtuq: Resource Sharing and Generalized Reciprocity in Clyde River, Nunavut." *Arctic Anthropology* 32, no. 2: 43–60.

CHAPTER 12

Home-Making on Land and Sea in the Archipelagic Philippines

Olivia Swift

While industrial and post-industrial workplaces are commonly thought to oppose the space of the home, they vary in the extent to which they facilitate workers feeling at home within them.[1] Few workplaces seem as alienated from home as ships: ships are mobile, isolated, institutionalized, industrial spaces on water, typically with an all-male crew accustomed to dangerous and grueling work and a specific occupational culture that is stereotypically masculine. Workplaces of various types have been recognized as sites in which class-related masculinities are produced (e.g., Willis 1977; Kimmel 1996; Ashcraft and Flores 2003). Few workplaces, however, equal ships in terms of masculine spaces. For Raewyn Connell, seafarers are "'exemplars of masculinity': heterosexual, competitive, homo-social and able to dominate women as well as other men" (cited in McKay 2007, 619). Home, in comparison, is usually perceived as land-based, static, domestic, and typically associated with family, caring relationships, and women. It is this tendency to contrast spaces of industrial and postindustrial work with domesticity—and production with reproduction—that has spawned a tradition of scholarship that emphasizes the interrelationships between these dichotomous entities, particularly highlighting the way in which women's home-based labor underpins the reproduction of the labor force and processes of accumulation (e.g., Redclift 1985; Fortunati 1995). This chapter follows in this tradition, but examines the gendered and other symbolic inversions that take place when the workplace—in this case, the ocean—is also considered "home."

In what follows, I reflect upon what it means to feel at home aboard a ship and in a union-run village of seafaring families from the Philippines. People's sense of home can be defined and studied in different ways: through the physical and conceptual media and resources people use to make a home (Rapport and Dawson 1998, 11) and the routine practices, social interaction, and ritual use of personal names (Rapport and Dawson 1998, 27) that take place within them. My own focus is on the gendering of home on land and sea. I emphasize how the ship is less "masculine" than stereotypes suggest and, equally, how the village and its women are more integrated with the global shipping industry than their seafaring husbands. The extent to which seafarers feel at home at sea is somewhat rooted in the widespread image in the industry of Filipinos as "natural seafarers" on account of the country's archipelagic ecology. However, more significant in determining whether Filipinos feel at home in this environment are their own, active practices of making contractual, isolated employment meaningful, as well as employer policies that shape the extent to which crew interact with one another and value their work as part of a long-term, professional career.

Scholars of contemporary labor migration from the Philippines—a phenomenon unrivalled by other labor-supply nations—have tended to laud the ease with which Filipinos are innately "at home in the world" on account of their sacrificial flexibility and the contribution of this to the global economy. In contrast, my discussion of the experience of feeling at home across land and sea offers an alternative model of Filipino subjectivity in the world, in which Filipino seafarers feel "at home in the world" not on account of their submissive adaptability as a hangover of colonial domination, but rather their professional confidence and competence and active search for meaning in the neoliberal context of flexible labor and impermanence.

This discourse turns on a particular conception of Philippine history, one which I have explored in more detail elsewhere (Swift 2011, 284–88). Specifically, it concerns the way in which transforming the Philippine archipelago into a modern nation-state has meant forging a land-based nationhood and territorializing precolonial seafaring people in order for the sea to become a liberal, vacuous space of trade. The people of the premodern Philippines are thought to have been sea-going since at least the fourth century (Abinales and Amoroso 2005, 34). Their islands comprised a series of chiefdoms (Junker 1999) rather than a centralized or autocratic political system based on abstract principles or institutions. Each chiefdom was headed by a *datu*—the native term for chiefs, sovereign princes, and monarchs—whose power was based on personal relationships, not territorial boundaries, and whose position relied on his ability to protect his people through war and accumulation, helped by having control of waterways, which enabled him to collect harbor fees and tributes, backed by armed force when necessary (Abinales and Amoroso 2005, 23).

A more notorious form of chiefdom violence was the raiding and enslaving of neighboring villages by the Illanun (or Iranun) tribe and Sama sea nomads in the Sulu sea to the south of the now Philippines. It was not until the US took over control of the Philippines from Spain, insti- gating antipiracy patrols and bloody "pacification" campaigns between 1903 and 1913, that the southern Philippines was mostly brought under government command and relative law and order was established in the southern seas (Eklof 2009, 12). As precolonial chiefdoms gave way to the centralized modern state (initiated by Spain), and as the US freed the sea of piracy making it a liberalized space of trade, the archipelago became a territorialized nation-state in the European sense. While political power in both the premodern archipelago and European style of nation-state relied ultimately on coercion, only with these developments did political power in the Philippines become aligned with a fixed territory on land, rather than personal relationships spanning both land and sea (Eklof 2009, 13).

In these ways, the conceptual separation between land and sea in the Philippines emerges as contingent and political. In a similar vein, the oft-cited stereotype of the contemporary global Filipino seafarer being "naturally inclined" to go to sea is a political construction based on little empirical evidence of continuity between indigenous and contemporary forms of seafaring (Swift 2007, 12–16). The image of Filipinos as "nat- urally" inclined to go to sea on account of their country's archipelagic ecology is promoted by the Philippine state and actors across the mar- itime industry (Swift 2007, 6; McKay 2014). This image naturalizes and disguises the exploitative global division of labor in which Filipinos have come to dominate the labor market on account, first and foremost, of their labor being cheap (cf. Elson and Pearson 1981).

Home-Making at Sea

I sailed aboard the ship described in this chapter as a researcher for one month in 2007, following a year of doctoral fieldwork in Manila, and in a union-run village for seafarers and their families in Cavite, further south. Housing some 450 families, the AMOSUP[2] Seamen's Village is the only union-run settlement for seafarers in the country. Seafarers in the village and aboard the ship comprise just a fraction of the Filipinos who have come to dominate the global seafaring labor market since the industry deregulated in the latter decades of the twentieth century, massively ex- panding the number of cheaper seafarers from the Global South. In 2013, 367,000 Filipino seafarers were deployed, according to Philippine govern- ment statistics. Instead of ships being crewed by nationals of their own flags and ports of registry as they were thirty years ago, typical twenty- first century ships have mixed nationality crews working under foreign flags. Seafaring has always been contractual work and, typically, contemporary Filipino seafarers are employed for single voyages lasting six to twelve months.

The ship on which I researched is a car-carrying vessel crewed by just twenty-three Filipino men. It has twelve decks, a total area equivalent to nine football fields, and the capacity to carry some six thousand cars, or fewer larger vehicles. The ship's hot and noisy engine rooms are blind to the world in its bowels. The ramp providing access on and off the ship is on deck five; accommodation quarters are on deck twelve with the bridge above it, toward the bow. Most of my time aboard was spent on the bridge and deck twelve, on which the cabins, gym, and laundry rooms of officers are divided from those of ratings (nonofficers) by the officer and main recreation rooms; slop chest; two lobbies; sanatorium; offices of the captain, chief engineer, and chief officer; a meeting room; public toilets; galley; kitchen; and officer snack room. The ship is registered in the Bahamas and operated and managed by two subsidiaries of a company incorporated in Bermuda with head offices in Norway. The operator has transportation contracts with the world's key car manufacturers and operates approximately fifty vessels at any one time.[3]

Before my joining the ship, friends and colleagues quipped about the lair of masculinity I was preparing to enter. I had read up on safety aboard ship and sought advice from the few female researchers who had spent time aboard ships before me. I had also hired a satellite telephone so I could call for assistance without needing to rely on the permission of the captain to access the ship's communication equipment. In short, I was excited and apprehensive in equal measure, unsure of what to expect but in practical terms, prepared. Once aboard, the environment felt surprisingly familiar to me. The sound of spoken Tagalog and Tagalog pop songs floating down corridors, the taste of Filipino food, the videoke machine, and the collection of Tagalog DVDs and reading materials were all a continuation of the Philippines where I had been conducting fieldwork on land. The clean, pleasant, brightly lit corridors and rooms of deck twelve were more comfortable than the humid shell of a vacant house in which I had lived in the Seamen's Village.

The increased use of technology, larger ships, and smaller crew sizes have resulted in seafarers often working alone or in small groups. Social isolation is one of the largest challenges aboard modern-day car carriers, as it is in other sectors of industry (Kahveci 2006, 111). Motivated by a desire to reduce the social isolation among crew that threatens the cooperation and harmony necessary for safe and efficient ship operations, the crew's employer has a long history of trying to create onboard environments that are "humane" and "responsive" (Roger 1983). High-quality food and leisure activities are consistent across its fleet and informality is encouraged by having self-service food in one room for both officers and ratings, whereas traditionally, ratings eat separately to officers, to whom food is served by members of the galley. This serves to bridge the divide between ranks and departments that is likely to arise given the distance between the engine and bridge that separates the departments for most of the working day.

Having an all-Filipino crew helps foster cohesion among members. While many companies employ Filipino ratings and often also junior officers, this company is relatively unusual in having Filipino ratings, junior officers, and senior officers. In my conversations with the crew, I would often be told that the positive atmosphere aboard the ship was down to the captain and chief engineer, who worked hard to maintain crew morale. They would compare the captain to others under whom they had sailed on previous voyages: "Sometimes they can be real assholes. We are lucky because this captain, he's a good man. And he's a Filipino: that helps." The captain encouraged parties for all crew at the smallest of excuses. Crew in jeans and t-shirts came together for beer and snacks in the recreation room benches—chatting, singing videoke, or playing guitar and drums. The captain was also known for blasting rock music from his office and calling for games of basketball on deck.

Although these parties and other initiatives may sound in keeping with the machismo typically associated with sailors, the levels of alcohol were limited and the atmosphere was more one of tired bodies relaxing than fervent masculinity. Parties were light-hearted and ended early; even as the sole female, I never felt in any way uncomfortable at these gatherings. Interactions between the crew and myself were good-natured, and while I did receive disproportionate amounts of attention from some crew members, this never felt aggressive. The masculinity I observed aboard struck me as something apart from the type of masculinity historically associated with tough working conditions and with hierarchical relations among crew aboard ships. While I do not mean to imply that the crew was entirely lacking in tensions, the company largely succeeded in meeting its need for safe and efficient transportation through its use of onboard space, food, leisure, and by employing a single-nationality crew.[4] In so doing, it also created an onboard environment that, in spite of the dangers and challenges of seafaring work, was more comfortable, informal, and friendly than is reported by these and other seafarers aboard the majority of ships.

Versed in the stereotype of sailors' machismo, I was surprised to find men engaging not just in sport, music, and traditionally relaxing pursuits during their limited time off, but an array of other activities. The oiler made necklaces from melted-down loose change, the messman baked nut brittle, the chief officer wrote poetry, the third engineer made films and computer programs, the second officer sketched; everyone did this without attracting undue interest from their peers. Almost all crew members spoke of taking time to pray and meditate daily and in private, something they said helped them feel close to their wives and families on land, and several spent some of their free time studying for additional qualifications necessary for promotion on subsequent voyages. While the gender associations of different creative activities vary, with none being as stereotypically feminine as crafts such as embroidery (Parker 1984), the fact that crew used their leisure time at sea to learn and practice new skills, develop their careers, and attend to their physical and spiritual wellbeing is significant.

While seafarers often describe time at sea as a liminal "hermitage" in which time "stands still" or "doesn't count" (Swift 2010a), how they relate to this experience reflects the wider professionalizing of Filipino seafaring. On occasion, crew used the idea of the ship as a "time out" space as justification for engaging in high-risk activities that were not part of their lives among family in the Philippines, such as smoking, drinking, and occasionally paying for sex when opportunities arose in port. More commonly, however, men drew upon the notion of a hermitage in relation to the self-improving behaviors described above (cf. Aguilar 2002, 33). When men use time at sea to improve their skills, health, and general wellbeing, they are engaging in an upwardly mobile lifestyle while improving their career prospects. Given that more than half of Filipino seafarers originate from fishing and farming families with only two percent being the children of professionals (Amante 2003), seafaring offers many the opportunity for significant social mobility (McKay and Lucero-Prisno 2011).

The difference between the two types of "hermitage" behaviors might represent a divergent point in Filipino global seafaring. Seafarers from cheap-labor supply countries are stereotypically assumed to go to sea for a limited number of years in order to secure sufficient capital to set up a petty enterprise on land, without developing the experience and qualifications needed to progress to senior ranks. Given the trend toward larger ships with smaller crews and increasing use of technology, seafaring labor and education have become increasingly professionalized (McKay and Lucero-Prisno 2011). At the same time, a global shortage of officers has led the industry to nurture an ethos of seafaring as a professional career for life among Filipinos (Swift 2010a). At present, Filipinos are over represented among ratings but under represented among senior ranks at sea (Wu and Sampson 2005; McKay 2007, 622–23). Such efforts complement those of the Philippine state, which is keen to retain its dominance over the global labor market and the remitted income this provides: the Philippine government requires its seafarers to remit at least 80 percent of their basic wage to a Philippine bank account, a practice that in 2014 earned the national economy US$5.5 billion according to the Philippines' central bank.

The view that Filipinos go to sea as a short-term strategy purely for financial gain is also being challenged increasingly by Filipino seafarers themselves, who McKay and Lucero-Prisno (2011) describe as projecting "a more professional and self-disciplined" image by "distancing themselves from what they described as the 'older' negative image of Filipino seamen from the 1970s and 1980s." The authors quote a seafarer to illustrate their point:

> Before, the Filipinos were known for . . . drinking and fighting but not anymore. Before, maybe they are just hiring anyone around Luneta [a city park in Manila, where seafarers congregate] asking, "Hey, do you want to become a seaman? Ok, come on." Like a market. Some of these guys were not so good. Now, almost all Filipino seamen are graduates [of maritime colleges], more professional. Most of us are also married, have families. (Quoted in McKay and Lucero-Prisno 2011, 25—parentheses in original)

For McKay and Lucero-Prisno, this professionalizing of Filipino seafarers manifests itself as a particular form of cautious, middle-class masculinity, based on competence and self-control, which they depict as one form of multiple and often conflicting masculinities performed by Filipino seafarers on ship and on land. On account of their historically subordinate position in the global labor market and aboard mixed-nationality crews characterized by ethnic and racial division of labor (Reid 1993; Frost 1995), Filipino seafarers use leisure time among compatriots aboard and in port, as well as their roles as breadwinner and patriarch at home, to forge an "exemplary" style of masculinity. This "hyper" masculinity, they argue, helps Filipino seafarers invert exploitation on the job and compensate for the harshness of the workplace. At the same time, it counters the cautious, self-controlled form of masculinity Filipino seafarers may be forced to perform in their subordinate position among mixed-nationality crews and the labor market at large (McKay 2007).

While I support McKay and Lucero-Prisno in their depiction of Filipinos as marginalized within shipping (based on a long history of American imperialism and Philippine state policies [see McKay 2014]), the particular crew with whom I sailed were not subordinate to senior ranks of other nationalities in the actual workplace, since the entire crew was Filipino. As a result of being an all-Filipino crew, these men were able to engage in activities such as basketball and karaoke, which McKay and Lucero-Prisno understandably associate with exemplary, hyper-masculinity, without this having to be read as an inversion of their subordinate positions during the working day, and without this behavior having to be at odds with the softer, more professional masculinity the crew of all ranks shared as part of their social mobility. I would argue that among this crew, this more cautious masculinity was actively and willingly adopted rather than imposed on account of the seafarers' marginalization within the global division of labor. While I am not suggesting that crew members performed only one masculinity, or that their inevitably multiple masculine identities lacked conflict, the predominant shared masculinity I observed was one based on professional, middle-class values and aspirations, and that the contrast between the class-based masculinities McKay and Lucero-Prisno describe is considerably less apparent aboard this single-nationality ship, as it is increasingly across the labor market with more and more Filipinos occupying senior ranks at sea.

This professionalization among the crew and the shift away from the image of working-class, exemplary, or hyper-masculinity that accompanied it, coupled with the company's efforts to make a softer, more humane work environment, made for a "feminizing" of the ship space. This was furthered by encouraging the spouses of senior officers to sail with their husbands for a period of weeks or months. According to employers, having wives aboard is good for crew morale in general, helps individual seafarers sustain marriages, and assists the wives of seafarers in understanding their husbands' lives as sea, thereby giving them the knowledge and empathy they need to support their husbands. Some of my neighbors in the Seamen's Village who had joined their husbands described being assigned a status and role aboard ship that was not sexual but maternal: these women spoke of winning affection through baking and offering a sympathetic, outsider's ear to crew members who came to them with concerns they felt they were unable to share with peers aboard ship. A similarly caring dynamic was also present between the actual crew. Indeed, company policies fundamentally shaped the nature of onboard interactions such that relations between crew were considerably more supportive than is to be expected from other accounts of life at sea (e.g., King 2007).

Specifically, the company achieves high levels of retention, in spite of employing crew for single contracts, by offering a range of incentives other than wage increases. These include vacation and standby pay; bonuses for returning to work for the same company once a contract has expired; medical insurance; subsidized, land-based training; basic pay while training; extended work-related insurance cover during vacation and training; performance-based bonuses; conferences; seminars; family courses; and an annual party in the Philippines. As a result, several crew members described staying with the company for repeated contracts over a number of years because of these incentives, the onboard conditions, and particularly the camaraderie between crew, even though the wages were not as high as could be earned with other companies. All those aboard, bar the cadet, had worked for the company for a number of years, which is not the norm in the industry. As a result, many knew one another from previous voyages or company events.

The camaraderie to which the crew referred was helped by the company offering cadetships in which the company funds promising high school students through maritime university on the condition that they then work aboard the company's fleet for a minimum duration (typically two years). In my conversations during fieldwork in the Philippines, seafarers would often comment that friendships formed at sea end at the gangway when they disembark. Rarely do they work with the same people more than once, nor do they maintain regular contact once on land, either because they live far apart from one another or because their acquaintances were based on shared experience aboard ship, rather than the common ground needed for longer-term friendships. In contrast, the sociality I observed among this crew sometimes struck me as that of institutionalized peers (such as at boarding schools or military training camps). For me, it was reminiscent of my own experience of single-sex schooling, which, given that several younger crew members first met in their mid-teens while studying together, is not so far-fetched a comparison. When there was a partial changeover of crew in Amsterdam, the farewells to some crew and the welcoming of others felt like the start and end of school terms combined. Similarly, when I went ashore in Gdansk with some of the younger crew members to walk around the snowy old town, visit a shopping mall, check emails, and to play pool over a beer, it felt like a precious excursion of a few hours away from teachers' supervision. Two young members of the crew—an officer and an engineer—were among those who met at university. Their cabin doors were often open, and they had configured their laptops so that they could challenge one another at computer games. When they sang or played together in the recreation room, they reveled like old friends. The two men who were in the deck and engine departments respectively said that one day they would be captain and chief engineer together.

Through this kind of friendship between peers, crew members were able to find light relief from the boredom and isolation of seafaring, help one another with work tasks when time allowed, relate to one another's lives in the Philippines, and share in a sense of meaningful career progression. Crew described these kinds of bonds as like those of a *barkada*. In Tagalog, the word *barkada* means a peer group of (usually same-sex) friends and derives from the Spanish for "boat-load" or "passage in a boat," *barcado*—itself stemming from the Spanish for boat, *barco*—referring to the islands' first Malay settlers (Kelly 2000, 104). Consequently, the use of the word *barkada* by crew referring to relations aboard etymologically enriches the idea of "being in the same boat." A key form in Philippine society (Dumont 1993), *barkada* offers an egalitarian space apart from traditional society and in this sense exists in the present. Crucially, however, members of a *barkada* also continue to relate to one another as such while progressing through life together.

In addition, hierarchical relations between crew members of different ages who knew one another from previous contracts and sometimes also from other connections in the Philippines were described in kin terms. Several of the junior officers and the cadet described the wiper in particular as their *kuya*, meaning older brother, on account of his cheery nature and readiness to listen to others' problems. The wiper himself had been promoted from messman when I joined the ship, which he attributed to the kindness of the chief engineer who lived in the same village as the wiper's sister and recommended him to the company for promotion.

What I hope to have portrayed in these mere glimpses into life aboard this particular ship is the way in which caring relationships between crew, a professional and feminized form of masculinity among them, and the comfortable and informal living quarters of the ship all combined to create an onboard environment that was less liminal and grueling and more feminized than the stereotypical ship crewed entirely by men would suggest. I argue that in these ways, the ship emerges as more "homely" a space than might be expected of such a workplace and not so dissimilar to the nature of the Seamen's Village to which I now turn. While it is tempting to assume that the village is a fixed, closed site of stability and domesticity (cf. Cohen 1996; Rapport and Dawson 1998, 6) in opposition to that of the ship, I am keen to disrupt this view and to demonstrate instead the ways in which the meaning of "feeling at home" in both spaces is neither clearly distinct nor mutually exclusive from the other space (cf. Rapport and Dawson 1998, 7).

Home-Making on Land

The AMOSUP Seamen's Village, where I lived and researched for eight months in 2006, is a housing project intended to enable members to own their own homes.[5] The village is an enclosed subdivision in Cavite, some thirty-five kilometers south of Manila, covering an area of nineteen hectares. Housing approximately 450 seafaring families, the first of whom arrived in 1993, the village is equipped with a clubhouse, basketball court, swimming pool, canteen, playground, chapel, primary school, library, and small lagoon. Outside the village gate, there is a small barangay (smallest unit of governance, akin to a village) of houses, stalls, and fields connected by a short tarmac road that links to the highway to Manila through the province's mix of towns, malls, industrial sites, and agricultural land. The village is run by the daughter of the union's president with the assistance of his nephew and an unrelated engineer—who all live off-site—as well as by a local team of staff, some of whom live in the village. Members of the union can apply to live in the village and, if accepted, make a payment toward the construction cost of their property to the union every month, without a down payment or interest for up to fifteen years, until they take over ownership upon completion of payments.

Village families have migrated from different parts of the Philippines and usually live apart from extended kin as a nuclear family of seafarer, his wife, and any children. Since the seafaring men of the village spend most of the calendar year aboard ship, the number of women far outweighs that of men in the village at any one time. Seafarers' wives remarked routinely on the multiple roles and responsibilities they take on as a result of their husbands' absence: they are both mother and father to their children, they manage household finances, engage in various economic activities, mediate relationships between children and their distant fathers, interact with neighbors and extended kin on both sides of the family and with their husbands' company and union, and take on all household tasks. If, as I have emphasized, home is associated with women, the Seamen's Village represents two possibilities: on the one hand, it is an exaggerated home space; on the other, it is hard to recognize as a "home" in the common sense of the word, due to the abnormal lack of men in the domestic setting.

Moreover, the recent development of the village and the active shaping of community among inhabitants with diverse backgrounds means it lacks a sense of security and continuity from the past into a certain future one usually attributes with home (cf. Bourdieu 2005, 20). Villagers are of varying shades of class, faith, and place of origin, with lifestyles that embody different traditions and practices. They differ in the degree to which they are embedded within networks of extended kin in provinces of origin, in their plans for the future, and whether these include remaining in the Seamen's Village. As a result, the future of the village project is always uncertain and a sense of shared community and civic-mindedness have to be actively encouraged through the built environment (cf. Kotkin 1995; Holston 1989; Alexander 2002) and union-led policies and activities (Swift 2010b). While one might understandably assume the village to be a site of stability and permanence in opposition to the impermanence of seafaring and the moving ship, the reality is one in which this comparison is somewhat inverted.

Just as the village lacks stability in the ways I have described, so too do individual village households. Instead of having settled, clear-cut rhythms, routines, and ways in which family members relate to one another, family dynamics are disrupted with the departure and return of seafarers to and from the sea. Young children may not remember their returning fathers and have to adjust repeatedly to their strange presence. Older children sometimes struggle to acclimatize to suddenly having two parents who might vary in their parenting style and degree of emotional connection to their children. Village wives describe their lives as a series of cycles in which they await their husbands' return while getting on with life in their absence, or adjust to a very different way of life while their husbands are home between contracts, during which time a family is typically together visiting relatives and enjoying meals and days out. These adjustments involve mixed emotions for seafarers' wives. On the one hand, women cope with their husbands' suspected or actual infidelity while at sea, dieting and visiting the beauty parlor in excited anticipation of the man's return and glowing with contentment during his stay. On the other hand, these same women complain about their husbands' desire for them to stay home in their company, in lieu of socializing with neighbors outside the house. Similarly, when husbands are at sea, their wives alternate between talk of keeping busy so as not to miss them and being glad of their absence.

Neither seafarers nor their wives could provide a clear sense of what constitutes "normality." Some said the norm was having men at sea while others associated normality with men being back with their families in the Philippines. The net effect of these comments is that a sense of normality is not associated solely with the familiar, or with a sense of belonging to family and nation, but rather involves aspects of the two. Similarly, a sense of being at home in the village involves an uncertain setting in which the rhythm of family life is routinely disrupted and reconfigured, accompanied by tensions and emotional upheaval for seafarers, wives, and children. A sense of the village as home does not equate, as is commonly assumed, to continuity in the village or its households' dynamics. Nor does the village equate to a domestic space opposed to the ship as the "shop floor" of the global shipping industry, in spite of the union's efforts to maintain the village as a site of nonproductivity.

While villagers are not officially allowed to keep livestock or run commercial businesses within the subdivision, the union tolerates small-scale enterprising activities, such as households selling phone cards. Despite being a residential area to which seafarers return when on vacation, the Seamen's Village is a space conceptually linked to seafaring work by its maritime references. Its grocery stores are called "slop chests" and at the village gate there is a large anchor dedicated to the AMOSUP member-ship. Several houses have anchor motifs in their ironwork or on plant pots in front gardens, and many have ship-wheel or life-buoy clocks on the walls inside. Moreover, although seafarers refer to their time in the village as "vacation," company training, bureaucratic tasks, household repairs, and visiting kin make for a vigorous schedule that is far from leisurely.

Unlike in similar subdivisions in other parts of the Philippines, many of which are home to families of Overseas Filipino Workers (OFWs), build-ings are not overtly inspired by, or marketed as, part of an Italian, Amer-ican, or British aesthetic, but as something more generic designed by the union's famous, octogenarian president, Captain Oca.[6] Both staff and res-idents in the village mentioned the captain's role in the creation of houses with a nod of appreciation for his thoughtful and creative input; thus they also sanctioned his symbolic presence in their homes. These buildings form a unique village and represent a unique figurehead's wish for the betterment of Filipino seafarers. Each style of house is named—as are the streets—after shipping companies, unions, and individuals whom Cap-tain Oca deemed supportive of the Filipino seafarer. Many of these names are Norwegian. This Scandinavian presence extends further. For example, on the side door of the house in which I lived, "Maersk" was graffitied in a penciled, childish scrawl. Maersk is the name of the Danish employer of my neighbor's husband. It is also the name of the artist himself: my neigh-bor conceived while honeymooning with her husband aboard the ship on which he was working. Maersk's twin brother is Odense, a name taken from a Danish shipbuilding town. Another neighbor said her son, Mark, was named after the same company "without the extra letters."

In some ways, the village women are woven into the world of global shipping, at least as much, if not more, than the union's actual seafaring members (their husbands). This is especially the case given the lack of union stewards aboard ships. As already noted, while men earn the ma-jority of a household's income, it is typically their wives who manage at least 80 percent of this income once remitted.[7] Secondly, it is women who head households and are "both father and mother" to their children for much of each calendar year, and it is also women who are most active in maintaining varying degrees of contact with kin on both their own and their husbands' sides of the family. Thirdly, women glean from conversa-tions with other wives an extensive knowledge of different companies and contracts, such that they advise their husbands about which companies to switch to and when (assuming such scope is available, which often it is not). And fourthly, it is women who have most regular contact with AMOSUP officers; some only do so when making a house payment at the village office, while others have more regular, social involvement with the union's village officers. For the latter set of women, friendship and play contribute to their pseudo membership of AMOSUP, in a way not dissimilar to that described by Turner within Japanese trade unions (1995, 59, 64).

Wives are also often involved in their husbands' companies, possibly spending time aboard, attending seminars, or visiting the office while a husband is at sea to deliver mail or to address a remittance problem. Most of all, however, women create relative surplus value for shipping employers through their domestic labor (cf. Redclift 1985; Fortunati 1995) and other income-generating activities that sometimes prove crucial to a household staying financially afloat. These factors also make sense of why an International Transport Workers' Federation (ITF)[8] unionist once told me of trying to convince her colleagues that organizing seafarers' wives was just as, if not more, important as organizing seafarers themselves.

Conclusions

In all the ways explored above, the Seamen's Village is not a stable site with a shared past or certain future. Although a domestic site occupied primarily by women, neither the village's built environment nor its women are detached from global shipping. Equally, the ship of this case study is not as liminal, harsh, and hyper masculine an environment as the stereotypical conception of "the ship" suggests. If home is traditionally associated with certainty, domesticity, and often contrasted to sites of work, then it is difficult to see how the Seamen's Village unequivocally fulfills this image and how the ship does not. Instead, I have stressed how the boundaries between these sites are unclear (cf. Swift 2010b), a notion that should be examined with an awareness of the distinction between Philippine land and sea as one shaped by a particular history.

While any connection between historical forms of Filipino seafaring and Filipinos' contemporary role in merchant shipping is at best unclear, what I have shown in this chapter is how this one, particular crew does indeed feel—to quote the title of this collection—"at home on the waves." This is not because of any "natural" affinity to the sea; it is through forging a sense of meaning and belonging in their profession—a long-term, career-minded project of building a better future for their families. Extensive literature explores the Philippines' colonial experience as justification for the image of Filipinos as typically submissive, sacrificing, and adaptable workers (McKay 2007, 624) who are unusually "at home" in—and open to—the world. Rafael (1995, xiv) describes the borders between the Philippines and the rest of the world as "fluid and indeterminate," while David (2004, 40) remarks that Filipinos are predisposed to work beyond their national boundaries because the nation's 350 years of Spanish rule, as well as another fifty under American control, stripped Filipinos of a sense of a land-based nation they could call their own. The implication of these remarks is that Filipino nationhood is subsequently dispersed, some of which buys into the state's rhetoric of seafarers and other overseas Filipino workers as *bagong bayani*—modern heroes—on account of the remittances they bring to their families and nation (Lamvik 2002, 123; McKay 2007; Swift 2010a). I would argue that in this case study, Filipino seafarers feel "at home on the waves" not because they cope with marginalization in the global division of labor, nor because of a colonial legacy that has characterized them as flexible workers *par excellence*. Rather, it is because of a professionalizing process that has seen Filipinos actively find meaning and a sense of the future in seafaring. Rather than feeling "at home in the world" as a euphemism for reactive adaptation to, instead of selective mastery of, one's environment, the men of this crew are not viewing seafaring as a short-term strategy to be endured purely to earn sufficient amounts to fund an alternative livelihood on land. Like an increasing number of other Filipino seafarers, these men—as able professionals—are engaging in a long-term project of home-making aboard ship and in the industry at large.

Olivia Swift is an academic impact manager at Royal Holloway, University of London. She has been a Lectuer in Anthropology. Research interests include maritime trade unionism, piracy, and various aspects of seafarers' welfare including health, communication technologies, and welfare structures and financing.

Notes

1. Exceptions include scholars who use anthropological models of village social organization in order to present workplaces as "homes" or "communities" (e.g., Aguilera 1996, 737).
2. Associated Marine Officers' and Seamen's Union of the Philippines.
3. In this chapter, my use of the term "company" actually refers to the two companies—operator and manager—since employees make little distinction between the two. I also use the words "employer," "company," and "ship owner" interchangeably.
4. See Swift (2010b, 159–63) for a discussion of active efforts to maintain onboard harmony.
5. In spite of this utopian vision for the village, unexpected tensions and disputes over property have arisen (Swift 2010b, 67–75). For a fuller discussion of motives for establishing the village, see Swift (2010b, 55–56).

6. Described by some as the "godfather of Filipino seafaring," Captain Oca passed away in 2010. Since AMOSUP is the largest maritime union in the country providing the largest number of seafarers, Oca was a key player in the international maritime industry and synonymous with the union that he founded and presided over until his death. See Swift (2010b) for further discussion of Captain Oca as union leader and patron to his members.
7. I use "manage," aware that there are differences between management, control, and budgeting within household finances. See Pahl (1983).
8. The ITF is an international umbrella organization to which AMOSUP is affiliated.

References

Abinales, P., and D. Amoroso. 2005. *State and Society in the Philippines*. Pasig City, Metro Manila: Anvil.

Aguilera, F. 1996. "Is Anthropology Good for the Company?" *American Anthropologist* 98, no. 4: 735–42.

———, ed. 2002. *Filipinos in Global Migrations: At Home in the World?* Manila: Philippine Migration Research Network and Philippine Social Science Council.

Alexander, C. 2002. *Personal States: Making Connections between People and Bureaucracy in Turkey*. Oxford: Oxford University Press.

Amante, M. S. V. 2003. "Philippine Global Seafarers: A Profile." Cardiff: Seafarers' International Research Centre. Retrieved 21 May 2018 from http://www.marinerssystem.net/L4SS/images/2014/june/Amantepercent202003percent20Philippinepercent20Globalpercent20Seafarerspercent20SIRCpercent20Cardiffpercent2097percent20pp.pdf.

Ashcraft, K., and L. Flores. 2003. "'Slaves with White Collars': Persistent Performances of Masculinity in Crisis." *Text and Performance Quarterly* 23, no. 1: 1–29.

Bourdieu, P. 2005. *The Social Structure of the Economy*. Cambridge, MA: Polity Press.

Cohen, P. 1996. "Homing Devices." In *Re-Situating Identities: The Politics of Race, Ethnicity, and Culture*. Edited by V. Amit-Talai and C. Knowles, 68–82. Ontario: Broadview.

David, R. 2004. *Nation, Self and Citizenship: An Invitation to Philippine Sociology*. Pasig City, Metro Manila: Anvil.

Dumont, J-P. 1993. "The Visayan Male *Barkada*: Manly Behavior and Male Identity on a Philippine Island." *Philippine Studies* 41, no. 4: 401–36.

Eklof, S. 2009. *Pirates in Paradise: A Modern History of Southeast Asia's Maritime Marauders*. Copenhagen: Nordic Institute of Asian Studies.

Elson, D., and R. Pearson. 1981. "'Nimble Fingers Make Cheap Workers': An Analysis of Women's Employment in Third World Export Manufacturing." *Feminist Review* 7, no. 1: 87–107.

Fortunati, L. 1995. *The Arcane of Reproduction*. Milan: Autonomedia.

Frost, D., ed. 1995. *Ethnic Labour and British Imperial Trade: History of Ethnic Seafarers in the United Kingdom*. London: Frank Cass.

Holston, J. 1989. *The Modernist City: An Anthropological Critique of Brasilia.* Chicago: University of Chicago Press.

Junker, L. 1999. *Raiding, Trading and Feasting: The Political Economy of Philippine Chiefdoms.* Honolulu: University of Hawaii Press.

Kahveci, E. 2006. *The Other Car Workers: Work, Organisation and Technology in the Maritime Car Carrier Industry.* London: Palgrave.

Kelly, P. 2000. *Landscapes of Globalisation: Human Geographies of Economic Change in the Philippines.* London: Routledge.

Kimmel, M. 1996. *Manhood in America: A Cultural History.* New York: Free Press.

King, Tanya J. 2007. "Bad Habits and Prosthetic Performances: Negotiation of Individuality and Embodiment of Social Status in Australian Shark Fishing." *Journal of Anthropological Research* 63, no. 4: 537–60.

Kotkin, S. 1995. *Magnetic Mountain: Stalinism as a Civilization.* Berkeley: University of California Press.

Lamvik, G. 2002. "The Filipino Seafarer: A Life Between Sacrifice and Shopping." PhD dissertation. Trondheim: Department of Social Anthropology, Norwegian University of Science and Technology.

McKay, S. 2007. "Filipino Sea Men: Constructing Masculinities in an Ethnic Labour Niche." *Journal of Ethnic and Migration Studies* 33, no. 4: 617–33.

———. 2014. "Racializing the High Seas: Filipino Migrants and Global Shipping." In *The Nation and Its Peoples: Citizens, Denizens, Migrants.* Edited by J. Park and S. Gleeson, 155–66. New York: Routledge.

McKay, S., and D. E. Lucero-Prisno III. 2011. "Masculinities Afloat: Filipino Seafarers and the Situational Performance of Manhood." In *Masculinities in Southeast Asia.* Edited by M. Ford and L. Lyons, 34–51. London: Routledge.

Pahl, J. 1983. "The Allocation of Money and the Structuring of Inequality within Marriage." *Sociological Review* 31, no. 2: 237–62.

Parker, R. 1984. *The Subversive Stitch: Embroidery and the Making of the Feminine.* London: The Women's Press.

Rafael, V., ed. 1995. *Discrepant Histories: Translocal Essays on Filipino Cultures.* Philadelphia: Temple University Press.

Rapport, N., and A. Dawson. 1998. *Migrants of Identity: Perceptions of Home in a World of Movement.* Oxford: Berg Publishers.

Redclift, N. 1985. "The Contested Domain: Gender, Accumulation and the Labour Process." In *Beyond Employment: Household, Gender and Subsistence.* Edited by N. Redclift and E. Mingione, 92–125. Oxford: Blackwell.

Reid, A. 1993. *Southeast Asia in the Age of Commerce 1450-1680: Volume Two: Expansion and Crisis.* New Haven, CT: Yale University Press.

Roger, S. 1983. "American Seamen on the *Hoegh Mallard.*" In *Industrial Democracy at Sea: Authority and Democracy on a Norwegian Freighter.* Edited by R. Schrank, 33–104. Cambridge, MA: MIT Press.

Swift, O. 2007. "'Natural Born' Sailors? Reconsidering Stereotypes of Filipino Global Seafarers." *Ugnayang Pang-Agham Tao* (Journal of the Anthropological Association of the Philippines) 16: 1–28.

———. 2010a. "'Looking For a Horizon That's Real in This Sea That's Fantasy': Temporalities of Land and Sea in a Changing Global Shipping Industry."

Economic and Social Research Council (ESRC) Research Network: Grant no. RES-451-26-0456. *Conflicts in Time: Rethinking "Contemporary" Globalisation.* Rethinking Global Workplaces: Polychrony and Uncertainty (A workshop to examine the time-spaces of global labor), London, 3–4 May 2010. London School of Economics.

———. 2010b. "Making a Model Union Village in the Philippines: Labour, Gender and Global Shipping." PhD dissertation. London: Department of Anthropology, Goldsmiths, University of London.

———. 2011. "Seafaring Citizenship: What Being Filipino Means at Sea and What Seafaring Means for the Philippines." *South East Asia Research* 19, no. 2: 273–91.

Turner, C. 1995. *Japanese Workers in Protest: An Ethnography of Consciousness and Experience.* Berkeley: University of California Press.

Willis, P. 1977. *Learning to Labor: How Working Class Kids Get Working Class Jobs.* New York: Columbia University Press.

Wu, B., and H. Sampson. 2005. "Reconsidering the Seafarer Labor Market: A 21st Century Profile of Global Seafarers." *Ocean Yearbook* 19: 357–80.

CHAPTER 13

Fishing for Food and Fun

How Fishing Practices Mediate Physical and Discursive Relationships with the Sea in Carteret County, North Carolina, US

Noëlle Boucquey and Lisa Campbell

Carteret County is situated along the central coast of North Carolina (figures 13.1 and 13.2). When Edward Earll visited in the 1880s, he observed:

> Carteret County . . . is long and narrow. . . . Its shores are so frequently interrupted by bays, rivers, and creeks, and the whole country is so cut up by water-channels, that wagons are almost wholly dispensed with, and the communication between different sections is carried on by means of boats. (Earll 1884, 485)

Despite the addition of cars and bridges in the intervening years, Earll's physical description of the county remains apt. It is the many distinct water bodies that continue to give the county its character and to delineate the different areas, islands, and communities within the region. Today, there are dozens of commercial, recreational, and mixed-use harbors throughout the county, ranging from tiny hideaways with a handful of boats to large marina developments with electricity, covered storage spaces, and haul-out services. A diversity of fishing, ranging from creek-side subsistence to medium-scale commercial to multi-million-dollar sport fishing tournaments, means that many different people and boats, with a variety of purposes and gears, use Carteret County's seascapes at any given time.

Carteret County represents a microcosm of socioeconomic trends in commercial and recreational fishing activities that have played out in North Carolina and the United States over the past century. Despite a long history as the region's dominant industry, commercial fishing in Carteret County has been in decline since the mid 1980s (Bianchi 2003). Although "as recently as thirty years ago, the poundage of commercial catch in

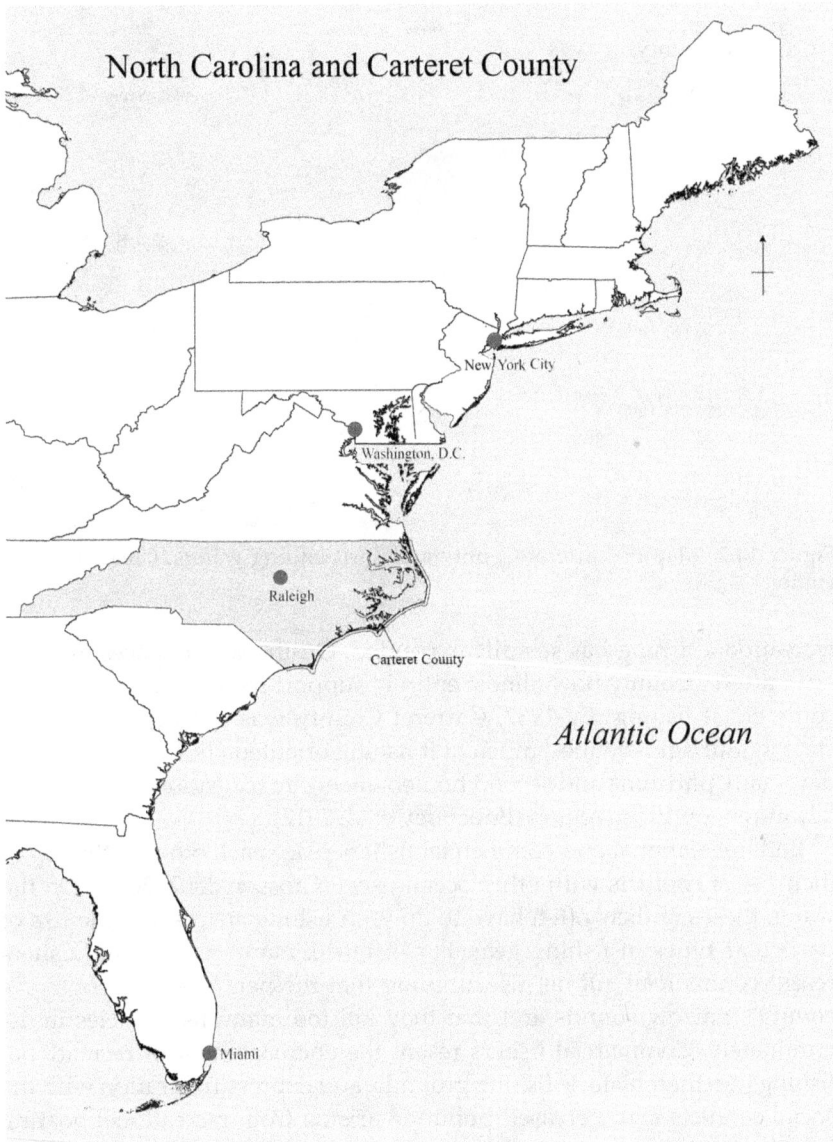

Figure 13.1. Map of North Carolina and Carteret County. Created by the author.

this small area exceeded that of any other region of the North Carolina coast," commercial fishers today struggle to make a living (Crosson 2007, 4). Changes over the past decade are largely attributed to falling seafood prices, rising fuel prices, and increases in waterfront land values (and thus property taxes) (Crosson 2007). In contrast to commercial fishing,

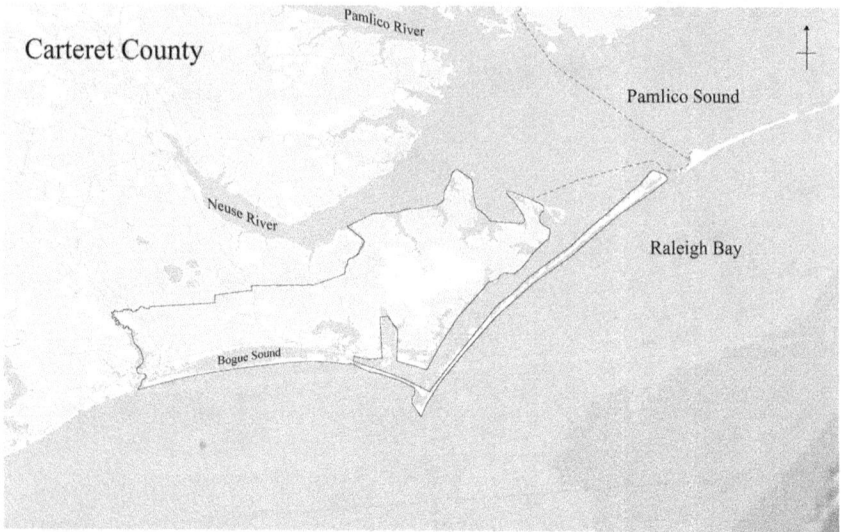

Figure 13.2. Map of Carteret County and surrounding waters. Created by the author.

recreational fishing has steadily expanded. On-the-water spaces in western Carteret County now almost entirely support recreational rather than commercial fishing. By 1987, Carteret County was already leading the state in tourism revenues, much of it fishing oriented (Tschetter 1989). Today, many part-time and second homeowners cite recreational fishing as a key attraction to the region (Boucquey et al. 2012).

Both recreational and commercial fishers place each other at the top of their list of conflicts with other ocean users (Crosson 2007, 2010). On the water, these conflicts often have to do with fishing spaces and the use of particular types of fishing gear. For instance, many recreational fishers resent commercial gill net use, arguing that the nets block access to the county's narrow sounds and that they kill too many fish species indiscriminately. Commercial fishers resent the encroachment of recreational fishing into their historic fishing grounds, and express frustration with the social conflicts and increased pollution arising from recreational boating infrastructure (often attached to new housing developments). Off the water, political and managerial conflicts are even more pronounced. In addition to disagreements over sector allocation (i.e., who gets how many of what fish), in recent years, prominent recreational fishing groups have repeatedly petitioned the state legislature to have several species[1] declared "game fish," which would reserve them for recreational catch only (Designation of Coastal Game Fish 2009; Designation of Coastal Game Fish 2011; *Fisheries Economic Development Act [2013]*). Related campaigns by these groups have pushed for a gill net ban on the grounds that too many turtles and recreational fish are being killed (SaveNorthCarolinaShores.org 2018). While these propositions have not yet passed, they are a constant source of tension between commercial and recreational fishers.[2] In this chapter, we examine how commercial and recreational fishers' experiences of fishing contribute to the feelings of cultural difference that underlie these political tensions.

Theoretical Context

In analyzing the underlying causes of social and political conflict between commercial and recreational fishers, it is necessary to consider how their fishing experiences differ, despite sharing on-the-water spaces. The idea that economic and material activities are always embedded in social relations (Polanyi 1944; Granovetter 1985) is useful for thinking about the particular nexus of socioeconomic experiences from which individual fishers approach the activity of fishing. However, because these social relations are at the same time discursively ordered, embodied, and "spaced" (Macnaghten and Urry 1998), there are many (physical and discursive) points at which fishers' experiences cross and overlap. This web of interactions— the everyday relations fishers have with each other and with the tangible "stuff" of fishing: seawater, boats, fish, bait, gear—helps to produce a divergent cultural politics of fishing.

Harvey's (2002) notion of "geographical lore" adds yet another component to social conceptualizations of embeddedness. For Harvey, all social groups possess this "lore," which consists of "a working knowledge of their territory, of the spatial configuration of use values relevant to them, and of how they may intervene to shape the use values to their own purposes" (Harvey 2002, 108). Thus, the working knowledge of commercial and recreational fishers might diverge over time as fishers pursue different goals. Since such knowledge is "acquired through experience, is codified and socially transmitted as part of a conceptual apparatus with which individuals and groups cope with the world," fishers' own experiences are also influenced by other fishers and stories they encounter in their daily lives (Harvey 2002, 108). The "geographical lore" of both recreational and commercial fishers is extensive and, combined with the concept of embeddedness, is especially useful in thinking about how the social geographies of fishing influence fishers' material experiences, and how those material experiences likewise work to reproduce social differences.

Considering more explicitly fishers' interactions with the landscapes (and seascapes) around them is also useful for understanding their conceptualizations of particular places and the role these play in fishing conflicts. Indeed, a landscape itself can be considered "a cultural image, a pictorial way of representing, structuring, and symbolizing surroundings" (Cosgrove and Daniels 1988, 1). Transformations in the common uses of particular places are far from culturally neutral and instead "result from continuous, dialectical struggles of power and resistance" among the users (in this case fishers) and mediators (i.e., regulators, law enforcement) of a landscape (Aitchison, MacLeod, and Shaw 2000, 19). Though in seascapes there may be few permanent structures, the spaces of fishing are well known by users and are full of symbols and meaning. Further, because "place meanings encompass . . . utilitarian values as well as intangible values such as belonging, attachment, beauty, and spirituality," conflicts over the use of a place are inevitably also over these less tangible qualities (Cheng, Kruger, and Daniels 2003, 89, 91). While embedded in a social structure, meanings and values also constitute part of the identities of individuals; "how one understands, evaluates, and acts in a geographic setting directly reflects one's self-identity" (Cheng, Kruger, and Daniels 2003, 93). Understanding how places—whether at sea or on land—are integrated into people's identities (and expectations of others' behavior) can help illuminate why conflicts over fishing areas and practices are often so intense.

The meaning of place is also intertwined with varied understandings about the value and purpose of a place's resources. Differing ideas about the role of resources in socioeconomic life (as manifested in attitudes toward landscape, work, and ideas about environmental practice) can be a further source of conflict (Davenport and Anderson 2005), and are instrumental in explaining the ideological positions and actions taken by opposing groups (Smith and Krannich 2000; McCarthy 2002; Walker and Fortmann 2003). Particularly where common-pool resources such as fisheries are concerned, ideas about the nature of the resource itself can influence normative arguments about how it should be governed and who should benefit from it (Schlager and Ostrom 1993; McCay 1998; Acheson and Brewer 2003; Campbell et al. 2009). These arguments have real consequences in terms of the distribution of resources among different groups, and frequently such divides occur along the lines of social class (McCarthy 2002; Wolford 2004). Given the diversity in types of both recreational and commercial fishing, it is not possible to categorically assign these groups to particular social classes. In North Carolina, however, recreational fishers on average have higher incomes than commercial fishers (Crosson 2007, 2010); sport fishers in particular often belong to more powerful social classes than commercial fishers (Kitner and Maiolo 1988; Smith and Jepson 1993; Garrity-Blake 1994). Regardless of class, fishers understand the role of fishing in their lives in unique ways.

The remainder of this chapter draws on semistructured interviews conducted with thirty commercial and thirty recreational fishers in Carteret County (in 2010–2011), and more generally on five years of research (between 2007 and 2012) analyzing fishing histories, fisheries and development politics, and coastal land use change in the county, to explore how meaning and materiality come together in influencing fishers' personal experiences and collective ideas about the value of fishing. In the course of the interviews, about a third of the subjects took photos of meaningful places and practices, and we include some of these to further illustrate recreational and commercial fishers' relationships with the sea and each other.

Fishing Histories

Both recreational and commercial fishers emphasize their long-time linkages with fishing activities. When asked how they began fishing, most recreational fishers described learning to fish as a child, often with their fathers. As one man recalled, "My father . . . started me fishing in freshwater, and then when I was about nine or ten years old, he brought me on one of his trips over to Drum Inlet" (R4).[3] Others began saltwater fishing at an early age. One fisher explained that he grew up "outside of Houston, with a father who loved fishing . . . so we fished throughout all my growing up time down there" (R22). Recreational fishers' memories are generally intertwined with the male family members who introduced them to the activity, and are recalled fondly as time well spent.

Recreational fishing memories are also associated with particular adventures or regular vacations. As one fisher explained, "My family has had a summer cottage in Nags Head since 1950 so . . . summers at the coast, holidays at the coast, so I was always somewhere close to the coast even though we lived three hours away" (R14). Another recalled, "I was born in New Jersey. . . . When I was eleven years old, I went on a trip with my grandfather and a couple of his buddies, and we caught so many striped bass" (R20). These recollections emphasize the discrete experiences and specific places that first engaged people in fishing. Charter captains in particular described "falling in love" with fishing and wanting to do it for a living or for retirement income. One fisher related, "As a young teenager, I just went to the beach and fell in love with saltwater fishing. And I lived 250 miles from the coast and it became a goal to live on the coast at some point in my life" (R7). Another related that he had "been coming down here since 1958. . . . And I had an opportunity to come back [and] buy this place . . . [and I] have been running trips out on my charter boat ever since" (R8). In this way, whether now fishing for personal or for-hire recreation, many recreational fishers had experienced the coast as young adults and purposely returned for the fishing.

Commercial fishers, rather than remembering individual fishing trips or vacations, often described their family lineage in fishing. As one fisher recalled, "My family was a commercial fishing family. My grandfather was the number one pogy captain on the east coast. . . . I was born into it. I started helping him on the boat at three . . . by my sixth birthday he bought my first clamming license" (C9). Another related, "I started with my dad . . . I guess I was maybe five where I would go with him and pull nets. I started getting paid when I was eight. . . . So, I guess it's more or less in my blood" (C1). Sometimes, these recollections were accompanied by laments about how fishing used to be and how times have changed. As one fisher remembered, "I just grew up as a small boy; grandfathers, great-grandfathers, uncles, cousins, everyone was fishermen. . . . It's the greatest job on the face of the Earth [but] it's going away. We're losing it every day with laws and regulations and habitat pollution" (C30). Thus, while fishers often spoke fondly about their memories of growing up fishing commercially, few mentioned passing on the occupation to their own children. Instead, commercial fishers were pessimistic about the future of commercial fishing in Carteret County.

Closely tied to discussions about the heritage of commercial fishing were bittersweet recollections and commentary about specific places within the county. As one fisher explained, "Look, back in the beginning . . . all this—all Down East, Beaufort was nothing but a commercial fishing town. It was born on commercial fishing . . . every one of these little towns was founded on commercial fishing. Now they're turning more to charter boats and sports fishing . . ." (C15). Another remembered the bustle of activity that used to occur in the many rural communities: "Every community had a fish house. . . . Williston had a clam house. . . . You could ride into any of the harbors . . . out of Marshallberg it was shrimp boats, Davis Shore, even Williston had shrimp boats. But that's a thing of the past" (C13). Eating fish on a daily basis was often described with pride by commercial fishers. One fisher described coming home each day to his grandmother's cooking on Cedar Island, one of the most remote communities:

> We'd be down in the bay [when] she'd holler down the path, "Come and get it!" We'd run up the path . . . pour a bucket of water over us . . . [and] sit down to fried fish, stew potatoes, squash, cucumbers, tomatoes out of the garden—six days [a week]. Just as good the sixth day as it was the first. (C4)

As these stories illustrate, the daily practices of catching, selling, and eating fish that commercial fishers associate with home and community—

and which used to sustain the region economically—have shifted in ways that fishers find unsettling.

Valuing Fishing

Recreational Values: Excitement, Beauty, and Social Space

When discussing reasons why they fish, about half of recreational fishers described the aesthetics of fishing and a sense of closeness to "nature": "I like being outside and seeing all the different life you see and the different geographic areas—I mean it's beautiful around here" (R15). The beauty of the Carteret County area specifically was emphasized; one fisher related: "Now I've fished all over the world, but particularly here it's beautiful" (R19). Another explained: "My boat is named *Sunrise*, and as my wife asked me the first night we met, 'Why would you go out there?' [I responded], 'If you don't see anything but that sunrise over the cape, then that makes the trip worthwhile'" (R7). In addition to sunrises and sunsets, recreational fishers express the value of the marine life they were able to enjoy through fishing:

> It's the whole kind of bonding with nature thing. . . . Some mornings . . . you'll be out there and you'll come across basking whales or mola,[4] or schools of fish just leaping and jumping . . . you get to see weather phenomenon, you get to experience great views of the sky at night, it's like being in a cathedral and a museum all the time. (R6)

In expressing their enjoyment at being on the water, most recreational fishers explained that they felt lucky to "see and do things that most people won't ever experience" (R3). For those working day jobs, getting on the water was also described as an outlet for stress and escape from computers and cell phones—a place where they could "choose to be in contact with the world or not" (R18). The beauty of Carteret County's seascape and people's interactions with different species were valued as contributing to quality leisure time or (for recreational captains) as creating an attractive workplace.

While being on the water was highly valued, recreational fishers discussed even more frequently the excitement and challenge of fishing itself. Many described the pleasure they felt in thinking through the steps necessary to catch a fish. As a fly-fishing enthusiast said, "I think it's the hunt; you've got to find them. You've got to get very close with a fly rod. So you've got to sneak up, essentially, and you sight cast to them rather than just throw and hope there's a fish coming by" (R16). Another fisher described how rod-and-reel fishing could be equally challenging, particularly when going after speckled trout:

> In order to get speckled trout to bite, I believe that's a measure of a true
> angler. They won't just come by and snatch something. You've got to . . . it's
> got to be bait presentation, you've got to know where they are in the water
> column, you have to know how to present the bait. (R21)

Charter captains venturing into deeper waters conveyed similar challenges on a larger scale. One described the excitement of catching dolphin
fish,[5] explaining that "my most favorite thing is . . . working the weed line,
catching dolphin. Watching them come up and take the bait, and tail walk
. . . you know, they're just an incredible game fish" (R4). For recreational
fishers of all types, anticipating fish behavior, learning new techniques,
and enjoying the "bite" are essential elements of fishing.

Recreational fishers also emphasized the social aspects of fishing as
important components of the experience. For guides or charter captains,
interacting with people is part of their jobs and they expressed fulfillment
at teaching others (especially children) how to fish:

> There's a lot of teaching involved in what I do. . . . I'm not just putting them
> on a boat and putting out lines. . . . I'm teaching them how to cast, how to
> hook flounder on the bottom, how to cast a fly rod. . . . I just get a pleasure
> out of all those things. (R1)

Another part-time guide explained that he loves:

> Taking kids fishing and watching youngsters catch fish. Because there's
> nothing in the world like a nine or ten year old fisher that's catching 'em . . .
> you know, one or two of them every time they drop to the bottom. I mean
> they'll just get so excited" (R4).

Rather than emphasizing teaching, non-guide recreational fishers were
more likely to associate fishing with time to bond with friends or family.
Fishing is often "a social thing, because I'll take a friend or two with me
and we can spend a day just bonding and having fun and experiencing the
same thing" (R18). For one casual fisher, "the camaraderie with my friends
and my family, more than anything" is what he enjoys about fishing (R26).
Sharing the fishing experience with others, whether in a formal teaching
role or simply by spending time together, was strongly valued by those
recreational fishers being interviewed.

Commercial Values: Livelihood, Independence, and Connection to Place

In discussing why they continue to fish despite concerns for the future
of fishing in Carteret County, commercial fishers point to the independence that fishing affords them in managing their time. As one explained,

"You're self-employed, I mean you can come and go as you please. That's a big advantage of it" (C13). One fisher described the challenges and rewards of self-employment: "The hardest boss you can have is being your own boss, because, you know, there's nobody else to blame," but at the same time there is "the satisfaction of knowing that I got by this week on my own, you know? I did it, I didn't have to depend on anybody; I didn't have to worry about being fired" (C5). When relating how they valued the independence of fishing, several fishers also explained that they felt regulations were diminishing their choices:

> I'm my own boss . . . and [I like] knowing that I don't have nobody telling me, pick this up or do that. . . . But it's getting to the point where they're telling me when I can fish, where I can fish, and so we really do have someone over us, so to speak. (C15)

Though fishers felt frustrated by some of the constraints of fisheries regulations, they very much valued making their own decisions. For commercial fishers, independence was primarily about flexibility, in organizing their time and choosing when and how to fish.

In addition to independence, commercial fishing also offers a livelihood for many fishers in Carteret County. Often, fishing was linked to supporting a family. As one fisher explained, the primary reason he fished was "to provide for my family. . . . I got four kids and . . . if it wasn't for being able to fall back on this, I really don't know what I would do in this time of hardship" (C28). Another fisher explained that he thought of fishing as "something that is natural, put there by nature, and I believe to feed yourself and your family" (C6). Sometimes after acknowledging their reliance on commercial fishing income, fishers alluded to its decline. As one commercial fisher explained, "I really just enjoy going [fishing] . . . that's about the only reason I go 'cause there ain't no money in it these days" (C3). Another fisher expressed frustration that he was losing control over his income: "My dad always taught me: 'Son, the harder you work, the more nets you fish, the more money you make. The harder you work, the more money you make.' That's not the way it is anymore . . ." (C15). For many commercial fishers, income was a highly valued but precarious aspect of fishing.

A final value expressed by commercial fishers was an attachment to being on the water. Sometimes this attachment was expressed as experiencing and enjoying nature, and other times it was described as a less tangible feeling. One fisher explained that his "favorite thing is just being able to go out and enjoy Mother Nature. Catch fish, just our way of life" (C17). Another related, "When I go down to the Outer Banks in the mornings and the sun's rising over that ocean . . . there's a peace that passes all understanding" (C15). Another fisher simply stated, "I love it all. I mean from A to Z. I can't put my finger on one thing that I don't love more or less . . . I can't describe it in words what fishing is like and what it means" (C30). One fisher who had moved in and out of fishing several times described that he always goes "back to the water" (C8). Another long-time fisher explained:

> I sleep on the land but I live on the water. You can't take this away from me no more than you can take a cowboy's horse from him. It's the same thing, I got saltwater—I can't go inland . . . when I get in there, I can't stand to go in the woods. I want to be down here, and the further out in the ocean I go the better I like it. (C4)

For these commercial fishers, the experience of being on the water is not always easy to describe. Nevertheless, it is a central reason why they continue to fish, and—as in the previous quote—often becomes a part of their identity as fishers.

Emphasizing Values: Fishing Photos

The photos that fishers took are revealing in the ways that they depict people and places in the region, emphasizing how each group fishes and how their activities both produce and reflect particular values. Though each group calls the same waters home, the character of this home is often portrayed quite differently by commercial and recreational fishers. Table 13.1 gives an overview of the themes in photo content.

Table 13.1. Themes in commercial and recreational fishing photographs (author's data).

Content theme	Commercial		Recreational	
	# participants N=9	# photos (percent) N=202	# participants N=10	# photos (percent) N=225
People in the process of fishing	8	74 (37 percent)	8	47 (21 percent)
Scenery/seascape	7	70 (35 percent)	8	53 (24 percent)
Social "message" photos[6]	2	38 (19 percent)	2	21 (9 percent)
Fish/catch alone	6	12 (6 percent)	6	22 (10 percent)
People holding fish, facing camera	2	5 (2 percent)	9	63 (28 percent)
Children fishing	2	3 (1 percent)	8	19 (8 percent)

Mutual Appreciation of the Seascape

The experience of "being on the water," as reflected in scenery or seascape photos, was a popular theme. This category of photos showed the most similarity across fishers, illustrating the importance of the physical beauty of the region to both groups. Sunrises, sunsets, and panoramas of Carteret County's characteristic marshy inshore waters were common. Figures 13.3 and 13.4 show such typical photos.

Figure 13.3. A commercial fisher's photo of sunset on the water (C9). Used with permission of interviewee.

Figure 13.4. A recreational fisher's photo of inshore marshes in Carteret County (R25). Used with permission of interviewee.

People and Fish: A Complex Mix

In depicting people, fish, and their interactions with each other, commercial and recreational fishing photos contained some basic similarities in content, but substantial differences in how such content was displayed. For both commercial and recreational fishers, photos of people in the act of fishing were popular (see figures 13.5 and 13.6). The contrast in fishing methods become evident here, however, as recreational fishers are universally shown with fishing rods while commercial fishers are shown with various types of net. Another difference was the frequency with which children were portrayed—only two commercial fishers included photos of children fishing, while eight recreational fishers did so. While not a large percentage of total recreational photos (8 percent), the common inclusion of one or two photos of children among a collection of recreational photos is further evidence of the "family bonding time" that many recreational fishers described as part of the social aspect of fishing. Furthermore, fishing is a leisure activity for many, done when children are out of school. The relatively few children in commercial fishing photos may simply reflect that the photos were taken during schooldays rather than weekends, but may also indicate a broader trend: fewer commercial fish-

Figure 13.5. In the process of commercial fishing (C21). Used with permission of interviewee.

Figure 13.6. In the process of recreational fishing (R7). Used with permission of interviewee.

ers introducing their children to an occupation increasingly characterized by pessimism about its future. It reinforces interview comments by fishers expressing concern about whether their children could continue to call Carteret County home in a future without commercial fishing.

Once fish were caught, both recreational and commercial fishers took photos of the fish without people in the shot. In photos taken by commercial fishers, the fish are generally shown on the deck of the fishing boat. In recreational photos, they are either displayed on a dock or are held for a close-up. The careful display of recreational fish reflects the fisher's pride at successfully overcoming the challenge of hunting and capturing them. A boat full of fish casually displayed, on the other hand, illustrates the importance of a quantity of fish in maintaining livelihoods. Individual fish are of little significance, except as contributing incrementally to a daily catch.

One stark contrast between the recreational and commercial photos was the frequency of photos featuring people holding fish and facing the camera. Only two commercial participants returned such photos, while nine out of the ten recreational participants did. Like the act of displaying the fish, this indicates different attitudes toward the goal of fishing and the level of interest in individual fish. As figure 13.7 shows, for recreational fishers, each fish is cause for excitement and worthy of a photo. In addi-

Figure 13.7. A recreational fisher displays a red drum (R14). Used with permission of interviewee.

tion, if fishers are actually paying for a recreational fishing experience (or advertising their guide service), each fish may become more valuable and worthy of documentation.

Fishing "Messages"

Most commercial and recreational fishing photos centered on the activity itself, but some photos contained a pictorial message. Only four people included these "message" photos, but we highlight them here because they deal with issues that are continually controversial in Carteret County and in state fisheries policymaking. For one commercial and one recreational participant, the message was about pollution, and photos showed closed-area signs and trash along the waterways. The other commercial participant dedicated his entire collection of photos to showing out-of-work commercial fishing boats and memorials to fishers, emphasizing both a fishing heritage and the difficult state of commercial fishing today (figure 13.8). The remaining recreational participant dedicated his entire collection of photos to showing various marine life—fish, turtles, dolphins—entangled in commercial fishing gear (figure 13.9). These photos begin

Figure 13.8. A commercial fisher displays pocket change next to an out-of-work vessel (C22). Used with permission of interviewee.

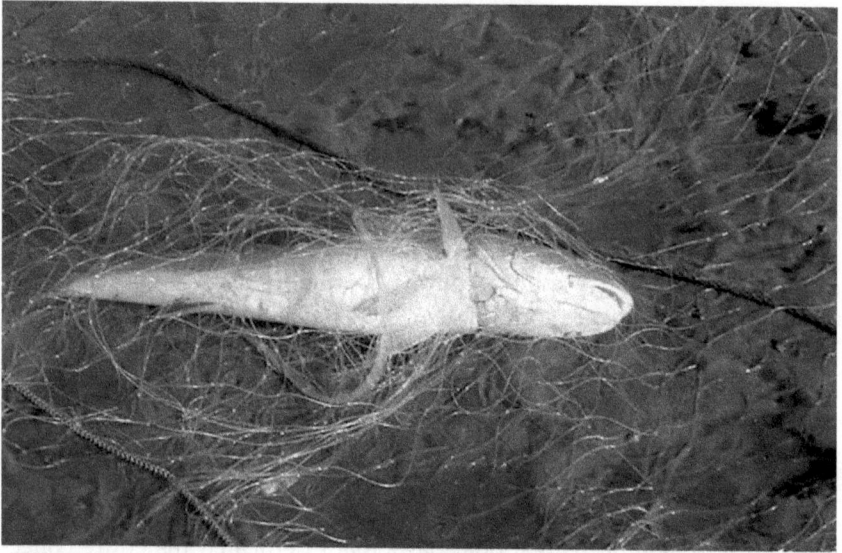

Figure 13.9. A recreational fisher's photo of a red drum entangled in a gill net after the tide has gone out (R3). Used with permission of interviewee.

to hint at some of the concrete topics where commercial and recreational fishers have difficulty finding common ground.

Discussion

Fishers' verbal and pictorial accounts of fishing highlight both commonalities and differences in the material and social experiences of recreational and commercial fishing. In terms of their "geographical lore" (Harvey 2002), recreational and commercial fishers overlap the most in their knowledge of and appreciation for Carteret County's waters. Whether they've lived there since birth or are retiree transplants, the material aspects of the region's waterways shape fishers' sense of home and purpose. Both types of fishers value "nature"—the islands, channels, and sea life, as well as a more intangible feeling of peace on the water. However, for recreational fishers, this feeling of peace is associated with an *escape* from the world of work, while for commercial fishers (and some for-hire recreational captains), the feeling is associated with *connecting* to work and a traditional livelihood. For most recreational fishers, a fishing trip is a discrete event— something slightly outside the everyday, an interaction between people and fish worth documenting with photos of both facing the camera. That commercial fishers rarely pose with their catches, however, illustrates that for them fishing is a part of daily working life. Thus, while both celebrate beauty and peace on the water, the "use values" these provide for recreational and commercial fishers are experienced in different ways. While seemingly subtle, these distinctions in the ways fishers interpret their experiences on the water have important implications for shaping social differences between the two groups.

Beyond this appreciation of the seascape, there were some superficial similarities in commercial and recreational fishing histories: both groups generally grew up fishing with their fathers, and they linked this experience to particular places in Carteret County and along the coast. However, recreational fishers associated these early experiences with vacations or memorable adventures, whereas commercial fishers associated these experiences with daily home life and viewed them as preparation for a commercial fishing vocation. Herein are signs of class tension; for recreational fishers, fishing is associated with leisure time and a growing industry, while for commercial fishers, it is associated with a fading livelihood. Early fishing histories are instructive in that they reveal the beginnings of a "shared moral universe" (Scott 1976, 167) within commercial and recreational groups based on how fishers have interacted with fish over time, and the types of experiences they learned to value. Indeed, in fishers' descriptions of their histories, we begin to see the formation of "place-identities," or "cognitions about the physical world [that] represent memories, ideas, feelings, attitudes, values . . . and conceptions of behavior" which then influence their sense of self (and in turn "other") (Proshansky, Fabian, and Kaminoff 1983). The stories fishers tell about the people and places in their fishing histories serve to reinforce their sense of identity as belonging to either a commercial or a recreational community.

In terms of portraying their interactions with fishery resources, all fishers are fascinated and excited by the very process of fishing. The challenge of finding and catching fish is a central component of the fishing experience for recreational fishers, who often relate techniques for pursuing specific species of fish. In further ascribing meaning to the act of fishing, recreational fishers value the pleasure of fishing as a social act, sharing it with friends and family, or customers. Commercial fishers describe an intangible combination of lifestyle and feeling on the water that keeps them attached to fishing in spite of its financial and physical hardships. Instead of emphasizing its social qualities, commercial fishers value the flexibility, independence, and the opportunity to be "in nature" that fishing affords them on a daily basis. These discursive "cultural images" of the fishing landscape (Cosgrove and Daniels 1988) are reflected in fisher photos as well. As discussed above, though people and fish both feature prominently in photos by all fishers, the relationships between them are depicted differently; individual fish and fishers take a more prominent role in recreational photos. The "message" photos further reflect some of the more extreme views among fishers about which activities do or do not constitute appropriate use of fishery resources. The recreational fisher's depiction of dead fish in commercial nets demonstrates an especially strong "environmental imaginary," reflecting a desire for fishing spaces without particular types of fishing equipment (Peet and Watts 1996 in Walker and Fortmann 2003). These examples underscore again that while recreational and commercial fishers share some fundamental feelings toward fishing (such as its being a rewarding activity), how these feelings are translated into social meanings differ in ways that are important for understanding on- and off-the-water conflict in Carteret County.

Conclusions

To return to some of the tensions and political clashes mentioned in the introduction to this chapter (such as proposals for recreational "game fish" designations), we argue that the intertwined cultural and material experiences of fishing are relevant to the persistence of social and political conflicts between fisher groups. Recreational fishers' accounts of interactions with the sea and its fishery resources are highly ordered—in stories of discrete adventures, species-specific fishing techniques, and photos of fish neatly arranged on the dock, these accounts reflect a vision of fishery resources as valuable in very specific ways. Commercial interpretations of being "at home on the sea" are more diffuse—with generally longer memories of change in the region, commercial accounts of fishing blend on- and off-the-water experiences and are fraught with anxiety about their identity and future as fishers. As a result of these social filters, commercial and recreational fishers can share ocean space and experience similar emotions related to fishing, yet support very different management proposals for divisions of ocean space and fishery resources. Our research suggests that management interventions focused on allocating space and resources are unlikely to solve conflicts, as conflicts are about much more than "who gets more fish" or "who gets which fish"; rather, they demonstrate how such decisions reinforce or deny particular understandings of the world and the role of fishers in it. Further, if a place is partly a product of the social struggles of its users, Carteret County's seascapes are continually being molded by these diverse resource visions (Aitchison, MacLeod, and Shaw 2000). At the same time, the commonalities between fisher groups suggest there are some grounds for beginning more productive political conversations about new environmental imaginaries for Carteret County.

Recognizing that "natural resource management . . . always brings diverse individuals and groups in relationship to one another," and that while conflicts are almost inevitable, "such conflicts do not wholly preclude the possibility of discovering common place-based group identities" (Cheng, Kruger, and Daniels 2003, 95). In this vein, a more explicit attention to the socionatural experiences of fishing in the region, and to the overlapping ways fishers feel at home on the water, could potentially serve to promote understanding between fishing groups.

Noëlle Boucquey is Assistant Professor of Environmental Studies at Eckerd College. Her research examines human–environment relationships and the role of coastal and marine spaces in mediating those relationships. Her work has analyzed the social and political-economic consequences of fisheries conflicts as well as ongoing negotiations over marine spatial planning in the United States. Her publications include "From Vegetable Box to Seafood Cooler: Applying the Community Supported Agriculture Model to Fisheries" (2014) and "Interpreting Amenities, Envisioning the Future: Common Ground and Conflict in North Carolina's Rural Coastal Communities" (2012).

Lisa Campbell is the Rachel Carson Professor of Marine Affairs and Policy, in the Nicholas School of Environment, Duke University. For a variety of marine topics, she studies the interactions of policy-making and practice across local, regional, national, and international governance levels. In North Carolina, her research focuses on coastal community responses to social and environmental impacts associated with the economic change. She has published widely in geography and interdisciplinary journals, including *Annals of the American Association of Geographers, Geoforum, Conservation Biology, Ecology and Society, Journal of Rural Studies,* and *Conservation and Society.*

Notes

1. Red drum (*Sciaenops ocellatus*), speckled trout (*Cynoscion nebulosus*), and striped bass (*Morone saxatilis*).
2. Not all recreational fishers support efforts to declare "game fish," including many of those interviewed in this research. Nonetheless, these efforts exacerbate tensions between commercial and recreational fishers generally.
3. To preserve the privacy of those interviewed for this research, numbered codes have been substituted for fishers' names. Codes beginning with "R" re-

fer to recreational fishers while those beginning with "C" refer to commercial fishers.

4. Ocean Sunfish (*Mola mola*).
5. Mahi-Mahi, dorado, dolphinfish (*Coryphaena hippurus*).
6. These included photos of pollution (both groups), boats out of work (commercial), and animals entangled in fishing nets (recreational).

References

Acheson, J. M., and J. Brewer. 2003. "Changes in the Territorial System of the Maine Lobster Industry." In *The Commons in the New Millenium: Challenges and Adaptation*. Edited by Nives Dolšak and Elinor Ostrom. Boston: Massachusetts Institute of Technology.

Aitchison, C., N. E. MacLeod, and Stephen J. Shaw. 2000. *Leisure and Tourism Landscapes: Social and Cultural Geographies*. London: Psychology Press.

Bianchi, A. 2003. "An Economic Profile Analysis of the Commercial Fishing Industry in North Carolina Including Profiles for the Coastal Fishing Counties." Morehead City, NC: North Carolina Department of Environment and Natural Resources, Division of Marine Fisheries. Retrieved 21 May 2018 from http://portal.ncdenr.org/c/document_library/get_file?p_l_id=1169848&folderId=31440743&name=DLFE-137050.pdf.

Boucquey, N., L. M. Campbell, G. Cumming, Z. A. Meletis, C. Norwood, and J. Stoll. 2012. "Interpreting Amenities, Envisioning the Future: Common Ground and Conflict in North Carolina's Rural Coastal Communities." *GeoJournal* 77, no. 1: 1–19.

Campbell, L. M., N. J. Gray, E. L. Hazen, and J. M. Shackeroff. 2009. "Beyond Baselines: Rethinking Priorities for Ocean Conservation." *Ecology and Society* 14, no. 1. Retrieved 21 May 2018 from https://www.ecologyandsociety.org/vol14/iss1/art14/main.html.

Cheng, A. S., L. E. Kruger, and S. Daniels. 2003. "'Place' as an Integrating Concept in Natural Resource Politics: Propositions for a Social Science Research Agenda." *Society & Natural Resources* 16, no. 2: 87–104.

Cosgrove, D., and S. Daniels, eds. 1988. *The Iconography of Landscape: Essays on the Symbolic Representation, Design and Use of Past Environment*. Vol. 9. Cambridge, UK: Cambridge University Press.

Crosson, S. 2007. "A Social and Economic Analysis of Fisheries in North Carolina: Core Sound." Morehead City, NC: North Carolina Department of Environment and Natural Resources. Retrieved 21 May 2018 from http://digital.ncdcr.gov/cdm/compoundobject/collection/p249901coll22/id/46281/rec/6.

———. 2010. "A Social and Economic Survey of Recreational Saltwater Anglers in North Carolina." Morehead City, NC: North Carolina Department of Environment and Natural Resources. Retrieved 21 May 2018 from http://digital.ncdcr.gov/cdm/compoundobject/collection/p249901coll22/id/444843/rec/7.

Davenport, M. A., and D. H. Anderson. 2005. "Getting from Sense of Place to Place-based Management: An Interpretive Investigation of Place Meanings and Perceptions of Landscape Change." *Society and Natural Resources* 18, no. 7: 625–41.

Designation of Coastal Game Fish (Bill). 2009. North Carolina General Assembly. House Bill 918. Sponsor, Justice Luebke. 113 (Chapter); 113–75.1, 113–92 (Sections). Retrieved 21 May 2018 from https://www.ncleg.net/gascripts/Bill LookUp/BillLookUp.pl?Session=2009&BillID=h918.

Designation of Coastal Game Fish (Bill). 2011. North Carolina General Assembly. House Bill 353. Sponsor, Glazier McCormick and Ingle Samuelson. 113 (Chapter); 113–75.1, 113–92 (Sections). Retrieved 21 May 2018 from https://www.ncleg.net/gascripts/BillLookUp/BillLookUp.pl?Session=2011 percent20 percent20&BillID=h353.

Earll, R. E. 1884. "North Carolina and Its Fisheries." In *The Fisheries and Fishery Industries of the United States*. Edited by George Brown Goode. Government Printing Office.

Fisheries Economic Development Act (2013). North Carolina General Assembly. Sponsor, Tom Murry, Michael Wray, Tim Moffitt and John Bell. 105, 113, 143 (Chapters); 105–449.126, 113–74.2, 113–75.1, 113–92, 143–215.73F (Sections). Retrieved 21 May 2018 from https://www.ncleg.net/gascripts/BillLookUp/BillLookUp .pl?Session=2013&BillID=H983.

Garrity-Blake, B. 1994. *The Fish Factory: Work and Meaning for Black and White Fishermen of the American Menhaden Industry*. Knoxville: The University of Tennessee Press.

Granovetter, M. 1985. "Economic Action and Social Structure: The Problem of Embeddedness." *American Journal of Sociology* 91, no. 3: 481–510.

Harvey, D. 2002. *Spaces of Capital: Towards a Critical Geography*. London: Routledge.

Kitner, K. R., and J. R. Maiolo. 1988. "On Becoming a Billfisherman: Study of Enculturation." *Human Organization* 47, no. 3: 213–23.

Macnaghten, P., and J. Urry. 1998. *Contested Natures*. Thousand Oaks, CA: SAGE Publications.

McCarthy, J. 2002. "First World Political Ecology: Lessons from the Wise Use Movement." *Environment and Planning A* 34, no. 7: 1281–1302.

McCay, B. J. 1998. *Oyster Wars and the Public Trust: Property, Law, and Ecology in New Jersey History*. Tucson: The University of Arizona Press.

Polanyi, K. 1944. *The Great Transformation: Economic and Political Origins of Our Time*. New York: Rinehart.

Proshansky, H. M., A. K. Fabian, and R. Kaminoff. 1983. "Place-identity: Physical World Socialization of the Self." *Journal of Environmental Psychology* 3, no. 1: 57–83.

SaveNorthCarolinaShores.org. 2018. "The Hidden Cost of Destructive Fishing Gear in North Carolina." Retrieved 21 May 2018 from http://savencsounds .org/gillnets/.

Schlager, E., and E. Ostrom. 1993. "Property Rights Regimes and Coastal Fisheries: An Empirical Analysis." In *The Political Economy of Customs and Culture: Informal*

Solutions to the Commons Problem. Edited by T. L. Anderson and R. T. Simmons, 13–41. Lanham, MD: Rowan and Littlefield.

Scott, J. C. 1976. *The Moral Economy of the Peasant.* New Haven, CT: Yale University Press.

Smith, M., and R. Krannich. 2000. "'Culture Clash' Revisited: Newcomer and Longer-term Residents' Attitudes Toward Land Use, Development, and Environmental Issues in Rural Communities in the Rocky Mountain West." *Rural Sociology* 65, no. 3: 396–421.

Smith, S., and M. Jepson. 1993. "Big Fish, Little Fish: Politics and Power in the Regulation of Florida's Marine Resources." *Social Problems* 40, no. 1: 39–49.

Tschetter, P. D. 1989. *Characterization of Baseline Demographic Trends in the Year-round and Recreational Populations in the Albemarle-Pamlico Estuarine Study Area.* Raleigh, NC: North Carolina Department of Natural Resources and Community Development.

Walker, P., and L. Fortmann. 2003. "Whose Landscape? A Political Ecology of the 'Exurban' Sierra." *Cultural Geographies* 10, no. 4: 469–91.

Wolford, W. 2004. "This Land Is Ours Now: Spatial Imaginaries and the Struggle for Land in Brazil." *Annals of the Association of American Geographers* 94, no. 2: 409–24.

CHAPTER 14

Sea Nomads

Sama-Bajau Mobility, Livelihoods, and Marine Conservation in Southeast Asia

Natasha Stacey and Edward H. Allison

Sama-Bajau Mobility and Livelihood

Scattered throughout island Southeast Asia are three groupings or clusters of specialist maritime populations commonly referred to in academic and popular literature as "sea nomads" and "sea gypsies." These ethnolinguistic groups are the Moken, Orang-Laut, and the Sama-Bajau. Each of these groups are geographically, linguistically, and culturally distinct and have developed various modes of adaptation in the ecosystems of Southeast Asia to support their livelihoods (Sather 1997).

The Moken (or Moklen, Selung) are found in the Mergui Archipelago and coastal waters of Myanmar (Burma) and around the coasts and islands along the southwest part of Thailand. The Orang Suku Laut (Sea Tribe People) or Orang Laut (Sea People) consider themselves to be Malays and are found in the Riau archipelago region of Indonesia, the east coast of Sumatra, the islands of Banka and Belitung, and the southern coasts of the Malay Peninsula in Malaysia (Chou 2003; Lenhart 2002) (figure 14.1).

The final group in question, the Sama-Bajau, comprise the most widely dispersed ethnolinguistic group indigenous to insular Southeast Asia (Sather 1997). Sama-Bajau speakers live scattered over a vast maritime zone 3.25 million square kilometers in extent. This range stretches from eastern Palawan, Samar, and coastal Mindanao in the Philippines in the north, through the Sulu Archipelago to the northern and eastern coasts of Borneo, southward through the Straits of Makassar to Sulawesi, and through large areas of eastern Indonesia (Sather 1997). It is estimated there are between 750,000 and 1.1 million Sama-Bajau speakers in Southeast Asia (Sather 1997; Clifton and Majors 2012).

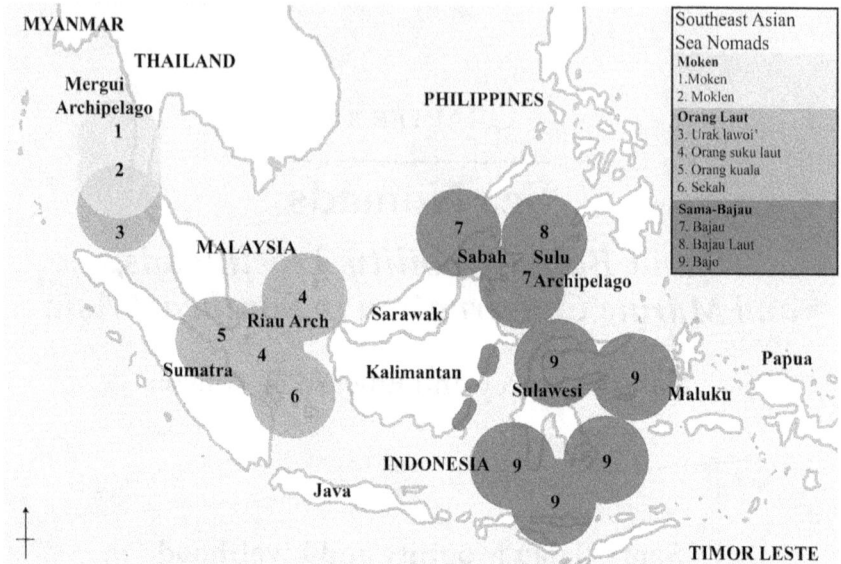

Figure 14.1. Distribution of the three main sea-nomad groups in Southeast Asia (after Lenhart 1995).

The term "Sama-Bajau" is used as a composite label to cover all languages spoken by members of this group in Southeast Asia, which not only incorporates most exonyms commonly used by outsiders, but also includes terms of self-designation used by Sama-Bajau speakers themselves. Most Sama-Bajau speakers refer to themselves as Sama or A'a Sama or Orang Sama (Sama People). Outsiders describe groups in the Philippines, Malaysia, and Indonesia by a host of names, including Bajo, Bajau (and its many cognates), and Bajau Laut (Sea Bajau).[1] Families of boat-dwelling Sama-Bajau or former "boat nomads" comprise only a small proportion of Sama-Bajau, estimated to be less than five thousand across the three countries of Malaysia, Philippines, and Indonesia (Sather 1997), with the majority of speakers being strand and land based (Sather 1997).

In this chapter, we explore the history, dispersal, and settlement of one group of Sama-Bajau in eastern Indonesia and examine their nomadic livelihood strategies from the eleventh century to the present. We examine the concept of maritime nomadism and the terms used to describe livelihood strategies involving mobility. We draw on historical literature and ethnographic data concerning Sama-Bajau from settlements of Mola and Mantigola in the Wakatobi district of Southeast Sulawesi and the related Sama-Bajau settlement of Tanjung Pasir in the village of Pepela on the island of Rote in East Nusa Tenggara Province. We examine the global policy frameworks around indigenous and nomadic peoples in the conservation arena and how a significant marine conservation initiative in the Indonesian region has considered the rights and needs of such groups. We show that rather than affording special and supportive attention to nomadic groups such as the Bajo, some conservationists have made misleading and inappropriate representations. This has resulted in negative associations of Sama-Bajau nomadic behavior and its impact on the environment. Such responses tend to ignore social complexities of migratory maritime-orientated livelihoods. We highlight the need for better understanding of livelihood mobility and how it can be accommodated in conservation and fisheries management, as well as the need to afford special attention to groups who engage in mobile livelihood strategies within marine conservation areas.

Nomadism

The term "nomadic" comes from the French word *nomade*—via Latin from the Greek word *nomad,* meaning "roaming in search of pasture" (OED 2018)—and has been used to describe people who have no permanent home but who move from one place to another with their herds. Over time, it has been used in reference to tribes of hunters and gatherers whose livelihoods specialize in foraging for (undomesticated) plants and animals in both terrestrial and marine environments over a large geographical area.

To historical observers, the Sama-Bajau—with their extensive dispersion and mobile economic pursuits on the sea and along coastal areas—did not appear to have a homeland or home base (Gaynor 2005). This contributed to European observers labeling them as "sea nomads" and "sea gypsies," "a designation at once romantic and derogatory" (Gaynor 2005, 90).

The term "sea nomad" was introduced into American scholarly literature by geographer David Sopher in his 1965 book *The Sea Nomads.* Sopher described the life of sea nomads as characterized by "families living in boats, and moving about the sea coasts in nomad fashion" throughout Southeast Asia (1977, 47). Sopher specifically stated that activity which involves male crew on boats, leaving families at home—namely shore-dwelling communities—is not considered nomadic in its truest sense. (See Swift, this volume, for other types of circumstances where the ocean is considered home by seafarers in the Philippines.)

But in the anthropological literature from the 1980s and 1990s (when research on sea nomad groups by anthropologists increased considerably), the term "nomadism" was used more generally to refer to the "phenomenon of mobility and in principle, refers to all populations which migrate in a reasonably regular fashion, primarily for economic reasons" (Lenhart 1995, 245). According to Lenhart, if spatial behavior and economic activities are the two key variables important in the characterization of nomadism, "it seems reasonable to characterize the mobile sea hunter-gatherers of Southeast Asia as the 'nomads of the sea'" (Lenhart 1995, 245).

Some scholars have disagreed with using the term "nomad" or "sea nomad" for mobile maritime peoples due to its etymological roots, and argue that the term should be used exclusively for pastoralists (Lenhart 1995). In a 1984 dictionary of anthropology, the term "nomad" refers to not only pastoral nomads, but "other social types characterized by the lack of a permanent residence or settlement" (Seymour-Smith 1986, 209). Groups who alternate periods of nomadism and extended residence in a particular location are called "seminomadic" (Seymour-Smith 1986). Further, this categorization is grounded in ecological and seasonal factors, but also in symbolic and sociopolitical ones (Seymour-Smith 1986, 209).[2]

The term "migration" is also used in the literature to refer to the nomad-like characteristics of fishing populations around the world who follow opportunities based on spatial and temporal movements of fish populations (Jorion 1988; Aburto, Thiel, and Stotz 2009; Cripps 2009; Njock and Westlund 2010; Crona and Rosendo 2011), but also for other reasons as discussed later in this chapter. Crona and Rosendo (2011) define migration in the context of small-scale fisheries as "various forms of voluntary, permanent or temporary/return migration." Here, the focus is on voluntary migration, rather than displacement or forced migration due to the impacts of natural disasters and wars.[3]

Drawing on an example from West Africa, seasonal movements and migration strategies from home (or ancestral villages) can be classified into three main categories: movement to "satellite bases" (short stays in other locations or villages); movement to seasonal encampments (for example up to a month in a hut on a beach near fishing grounds); or, migration to another place for years as a permanent move. (However, after a period of time—years or decades—in another location, one may be back to one's ancestral village [Jorion 1988]).

"Nomadism" is thus used in this chapter to describe livelihood strategies characterized by a lack of permanent residence or settlement in one place, where families or crews dwell on boats for extended periods of time—months or years—and where "seminomadic" refers to strategies that alternate between periods of nomadism and periods of residence in a single location. Cultures with a tradition of migrating for fisheries and other livelihood strategies, such as the Sama-Bajau in Southeast Asia, can therefore be characterized both as nomadic and seminomadic, depending on the type of activity and residence arrangements.[4] In the next section, we show that nomadism and mobility remain important Sama-Bajau livelihood strategies.

Sama-Bajau Dispersal, Settlement, and Nomadism into Eastern Indonesia

Sama-Bajau dispersal into eastern Indonesia via Borneo and Sulawesi from homelands in the Sulu region of the Southern Philippines is believed to have commenced at the beginning of the ninth century (Pallesen 1985). Over the following centuries, movement of Sama-Bajau in small boats throughout the eastern regions was dictated by the search for marine commodities (Fox 1977, 2000). By the time of European arrival in the Southeast Asia region, Sama-Bajau speakers were already "widely dispersed, internally diverse and heavily engaged in sea-going commerce and already fissiparous" (Sather 1997, 36).

The fourteenth century La Galigo epic provides the earliest recorded evidence of Bajo in Sulawesi (Pelras 1972).[5] A Portuguese apothecary, Tomé Pires, documented the presence of Sama-Bajau in the Makassar region in 1511 (Reid 1983) and described Sama-Bajau, residing on islands offshore from Makassar, who were compelled to "always be ready to go with their vessels in any direction they are sent" by the Raja or King of Makassar to collect, for example, a turtle shell as a tribute (Speelmen 1967, 43 quoted in Reid 1983, 126). The specialized maritime skills of the Sama-Bajau played an important role in the rise of power of Makassar (State of Gowa) in the sixteenth and seventeenth centuries and later the Bugis Kingdom of Bone. The Sama-Bajau were their explorers, messengers, and exploiters of sea products, trading commodities on international markets (Reid 1983). They were also the kingdom's naval power.

Further dispersal and later settlement of Sama-Bajau in eastern Indonesia (during the eighteenth and nineteenth centuries) were closely linked to the Bugis and Makassarese political and commercial expansion and migration in the region and the development of a region-wide trading network in marine products, particularly turtle shell and sea cucumber species; this network ranged as far as the northern coast of Australia (Fox 1977). Dutch records from the 1720s indicate the presence of Sama-Bajau in the Timor-Alor region of eastern Indonesia shortly after; they were noted to have been engaged in fishing ventures from Rote Island south to the Ashmore Reef region in the Timor Sea (Fox 1977, 2000), voyages which continue in the twenty-first century and are discussed further below (Stacey 2007).

Englishman G. W. Earl noted the presence of Sama-Bajau *perahu* (boats) from the region of Makassar collecting turtle shell at the colonial settlement of Port Essington on the Northern Territory coast of Australia; in 1840, Earl described them as "that singular people the Badju, a tribe without fixed home, living constantly on board their *perahus*, numbers of which congregate among the small islands near the southern coast of Celebes" (Fox 2005, 50, citing Earl 1846, 65). Earl also mentioned that the Sama-Bajau frequented the northwest region of the Australian coast (Macknight 1976). Matthew Flinders encountered Sama-Bajau participating in the Makassan-led sea cucumber industry; this was Australia's first fisheries industry, operating from the late 1700s and continuing into the early 1900s (Macknight 1976).

Various historical sources show differentiation in the living arrangements and extent of nomadic behavior among Sama-Bajau groups in the Sulawesi region of Indonesia. Sources distinguish between Sama-Bajau who lived on shore (*aan den wal wonende Orang Badjos*) and roaming Sama-Bajau (*rondzwervende Orang Badjos*) (Vosmaer 1839 cited in Mead and Lee 2007, 115).[6] These groups were attached to particular islands and localities. Adriani noted during his visit to Tomini Bay in Central Sulawesi at the turn of the nineteenth century: "They move sometimes to one place, and sometimes another, but they have never entirely abandoned the Togian Islands" (Adriani 1900, 460).

Permanent boat dwelling, it appears, was declining in this period (Sopher 1977). In the Wakatobi (Tukang Besi) region of Southeast Sulawesi, based on oral accounts, the first Sama-Bajau settlement or congregation area for boat dwelling Sama-Bajau was in the nineteenth century, near Lembonga, near the present-day settlement of La Hoa on the northern side of the island of Mantigola, Kaledupa Island. These Sama-Bajau had come from the region of Pasar Wajo on the south coast of Buton Island in their boats. Later, many Sama-Bajau moved to the south side of the island to what is now Mantigola Village to fish during the east monsoon, returning to the north side of the island at the onset of the west monsoon. Mantigola Village was established around 1850 when the Sama-Bajau sought permission from the government (Sultan of Buton) to build pile house dwellings over the reef and littoral zone at Mantigola to be closer to offshore reefs (Stacey 1999).

Sama-Bajau Population and Settlements in Indonesia

The Sama-Bajau of eastern Indonesia reside in settlements in areas of high biodiversity, mostly in the eastern region of the Indonesian archipelago (figure 14.1). Although a comprehensive survey has never been conducted in Indonesia, it is estimated that Sama-Bajau speakers number between 150,000 and 230,000 (Sather 1997). However, the figures for Indonesia vary. It has been estimated (based mostly on 1980s data) the total Indonesian Sama-Bajau population is likely to number around 150,000 people, with approximately 90,000 (living in 150 known settlements) in Sulawesi; however, this does not necessarily reflect the number of speakers and does not include areas outside of the eastern Indonesian region such as Kalimantan (Mead and Lee 2007). By far, the largest number of speakers live on the island of Sulawesi (table 14.1).

Nagatsu (2007) estimated there to be around 193,000 Sama-Bajau in Indonesia, including Sama-Bajau settlements in Kalimantan and Java/Bali that are unlikely to have been accommodated in the assessment by Mead and Lee and more recent figures (table 14.2).

The majority of Sama-Bajau speakers in eastern Indonesia now live in pile or stilt house settlements built over the water in coastal areas and on the land. Some Sama-Bajau still spend short or extended periods of time at sea and living on boats pursuing fishing activities. This will be discussed further below. Small numbers of boat dwellers remain along the coasts of eastern Sulawesi, particularly to the north of Kendari at La Solo and around island groups in Central Sulawesi. The number of remaining boat dwelling people in Indonesia is unknown, but two decades ago, in the mid 1990s, it was estimated that a few hundred families remained living on boats (Alimaturahim, Yayasan Sama, pers. comm., 1994).

Sama-Bajau groups in Indonesia are often considered to be of very low status in the social and political hierarchies, locally and nationally (Gaynor 2005). A

Table 14.1. Areas of Sama-Bajau settlement in Indonesia. (Source: Mead and Lee 2007. The estimates for Lesser Sunda Islands by Mead and Lee could be overestimates, as twenty-four of the settlements identified by Verheijen [1986] are former settlements.)

Province	Population estimate
Southeast Sulawesi	40,000
Central Sulawesi	36,000
South Sulawesi	9,000
North Sulawesi and Gorontalo	7,000
North Moluccas	5,000
Lesser Sunda Islands	40–45,000

Table 14.2. Estimated Sama-Bajau population in Indonesia by region. (After Clifton and Majors 2012 from Nagatsu 2007 based on 2000 census data and field research during 1995–2007.)

Province	Population estimate
Kalimantan	21,921
Maluku and Papua	13,978
Nusa Tenggara	18,006
Sulawesi	90,522
Sumatra	31,815
Java and Bali	16,905

lifestyle that involves moving from place to place with apparently no fixed address, homeland, or base camp has led to a perception that Sama-Bajau are "uncivilised, backward, alien mobile citizens" (Lowe 2006). In an attempt to "civilize," government programs have settled some communities into land-based housing so they could be included in administrative systems of governance (Gaynor 2005).

Sama-Bajau Livelihood Strategies

The degree of engagement in maritime-orientated lifestyles and economic pursuits, in inshore and distant shore marine environments, varies across Sama-Bajau communities. Anthropologically informed studies of Sama-Bajau livelihoods (e.g., Gaynor 2005; Lowe 2006; Stacey 2007) describe the existence of patterns of fishing activity defined by the particular environment fished and the distances traveled. The Wakatobi Islands form a Kabupaten (regency) in the region of Southeast Sulawesi, which supports five Sama-Bajau villages with an approximate population of 7,000 (Stacey 2007; Clifton 2010). Generally landless, the marine environment constitutes "culturally defined living spaces" (Chou 1997) and Sama-Bajau spend their entire life in the vicinity of the sea. It is often said by Sama, and by other indigenous groups with which they reside, that Sama feel sick if they spend too much time on the land or away from the sea (see also Nolde 2009). They maintain a rich indigenous marine cosmology and ritual practice, with belief in supernatural beings—ancestors of the sea—that control the universe of the sea and all the creatures in it for Sama-Bajau people (Stacey 2007).

The Sama-Bajau classify their fishing activities into four main types: *nubba* (gleaning/collecting), *pali libu* (inshore coastal fishing), *pongka* (sea or reef fishing for days or weeks), and *lama* (long-distance, or nomadic fishing). The practice of *nubba* is generally undertaken by women and children to support household subsistence needs. Excess products are sometimes exchanged, shared, or sold. Gleaning can take place along the beach, in mangroves, shallow waters, and fringing reefs at low tide. A diverse range of products, such as crustaceans, sea cucumber, edible seaweed, shellfish, small fish, hard corals, sponges, and sea urchins—a particular delicacy fancied by the Sama—may be gleaned. Gathering may be done by hand or using various tools.

Pali libu means to go and seek a living in coastal waters, nearby to the village, or in offshore open waters and coral reefs, and to return home the same day. These activities include hand lining, trolling, and spearing from canoes to catch reef fish and pelagics such as tuna, skipjack, mackerel, squid, and octopus. They are conducted by men, women, and children.

Pongka means to go and seek a living in the sea or on the reefs of nearby islands for periods of a few days to several weeks at a time. The type of boat used could be a *soppe* (a *perahu lambo*), sail or motorized. It commonly involves families or male-only crews who may live in a pile hut above a reef, which is used as a sleeping area and as a place to dry and process products (such as reef fish, sea cucumber, and clams). *Pongka* is not confined to a particular fishing method, but describes the type of activity, including the length of time it takes to complete, and can involve travel to and from markets to sell the catch and purchase provisions (Gaynor 2005).[7] It is likely that many historical observations of Sama-Bajau were made while they were engaged in *pongka* activities.

The historical context of Sama-Bajau in eastern Indonesia, and their acquisition of sea-going watercraft, has enabled Sama-Bajau to engage in long-distance voyaging to fish for a range of marine products, including shark fin, trepang (sea cucumber), trochus (sea snail) shell, tuna, and turtle.[8] This kind of economic activity is called *lamaq*, meaning "to sail," but can also refer to long distance voyages on motorboats (Stacey 2007).[9] A large proportion of the male population of Mola and Mantigola spend weeks, months, or years living on boats, making voyages around Indonesia and beyond to search for a living. This form of livelihood behavior is considered an important rite of passage for young men (Stacey 2007; Nolde 2009).

At times, such activities have extended into neighboring countries of Australia, Papua New Guinea, Palau, Singapore, and Malaysia (Stacey 2007). Long distance voyaging by Mola and Mantigola Sama-Bajau to north and northwest Australian waters in timber sailing boats is believed to have commenced some time between 1908 and 1924 (Stacey 2007). For decades, Pepela Village on Rote Island operated as a stopping-off point (satellite base) for these voyages further south. In 1992, changing circumstances around shark fisheries markets in Indonesia and Southeast Asia resulted in some Sama-Bajau settling in Pepela permanently and establishing a new enclave of Sama-Bajau called Tanjung Panjang. (In the mid 1990s, there were more than seventy *perahu* engaged in shark fishing in Australian waters, with fishers hailing from home villages of Mola and Mantigola in Sulawesi and from the Sama-Bajau settlement at Tanjung Panjung.[10] The majority of these boats and crews returned to their home islands and settlements at the end of the season [Stacey 2007]. However some households remained and have thus migrated to Pepela permanently.)

Sama-Bajau livelihoods are supported by social and economic networks spread over a vast area within the Indonesian archipelago. People move regularly, and may spend short or extended periods of time in settlements. Communities of Sama speakers move around the archipelago to visit relatives, find marriage partners, fish, secure financial assets to support fishing ventures, and purchase boats. Villages with Sama-Bajau speakers also provide places for families and boat crews to stop, take shelter from bad weather, and stock up on supplies of food and water. This is demonstrated by Sama-Bajau of Wakatobi, who engage in seminomadic livelihood pursuits following seasonal and market opportunities, but periodically return to their home villages.

Mobile Peoples and Conservation

There is a growing global policy framework that exists to support equity and indigenous rights and access to natural resources, participation in management of conservation areas, and compensation resulting from loss of access to resources (Krueger 2009). The rights of indigenous and tribal peoples were recognized in 1989 under the International Labor Organization (ILO) Convention, ratified in 1991 (*Indigenous and Tribal Peoples Convention, 1989* [No. 169], a forerunner to the *United Nations Declaration on the Rights of Indigenous People,* adopted by the UN in 2007). The Convention establishes a framework for the rights of indigenous peoples under international law. Part 2, Articles 13 to 19 of the Convention "protects the rights and values and livelihoods of indigenous people and recognizes the rights of indigenous people to their lands and traditional activities, and to participate in use, management and conservation of those lands." Article 14 notes that particular attention should be given to nomadic peoples (and shifting cultivators) (International Labor Organization 1989, Article 14).

In April 2002, prior to the fifth World Parks Congress (WPC)—held in Durban, South Africa, in September 2003—a group of scientists met to discuss mobile peoples and conservation and commit to five overarching principles for conservation practice application. The outcome was the Dana Declaration.[11] Mobile peoples were defined as a:

> subset of indigenous and traditional peoples whose livelihoods depend on extensive common property use of natural resources over an area, who use mobility as a management strategy for dealing with sustainable use and conservation, and who possess a distinctive cultural identity and natural resource management system. (Dana Declaration 2002)

One of ten outcomes of the Durban Action Plan at the World Parks Congress was that "the rights of indigenous peoples, including mobile indigenous peoples, and local communities should be secured in relation to natural resources and biodiversity conservation" (outcome 5 cited in

Adams and Hutton 2007). This was documented in WPC Recommendation 5.27 on Mobile Indigenous Peoples and Conservation, which endorsed the Dana Declaration and draft *UN Declaration on the Rights of Indigenous Peoples* and urged governments to ratify and implement the ILO Convention no. 1969. Since then, the Dana Declaration has been endorsed at subsequent World Conservation Congresses and side events around the *United Nations Forum on the Rights of Indigenous People.* Nonetheless, as will be shown in the next section, there are large gaps between policy and practice, particularly within the marine or coastal domain.[12] Practice continues to be hindered at the national level by numerous problems, including the absence of an enabling environment of good governance. This hampers application of culturally appropriate policies, undermining conservation practitioners' awareness of local context, and subsequent application of best practice in the field (Springer 2009).

Coral Triangle Initiative on Coral Reefs, Fisheries, and Food Security

The global epicenter of marine biodiversity is the Asia-Pacific region, with Indonesia at the center. In 2009, as a response to global and national concerns over degraded coral reefs, threats to the marine environment, and declining ecosystem services from climate change in Southeast Asia and the Pacific, the leaders of Indonesia, Malaysia, Papua New Guinea, Philippines, Solomon Islands, and Timor Leste launched the Coral Triangle Initiative on Coral Reefs, Fisheries and Food Security (CTI-CFF). The Coral Triangle region spans 5.7 million square kilometers in the Asia-Pacific region, linking six countries. The CTI Regional Plan of Action (RPoA) (National Secretariat of CTI-CFF Indonesia 2009)[13] seeks to address priority risks or threats to biodiversity from impacts of climate change, unsustainable fishing methods, and land-based sources of pollution through five overarching goals, including establishing a regional system of Marine Protected Areas (MPAs). The goals are supplemented by nine guiding principles, including the need for active engagement of stakeholder groups, including indigenous peoples and coastal communities (National Secretariat of CTI-CFF Indonesia 2009, 9). However, there is no mention of regional commitment to addressing the needs of indigenous and nomadic and seminomadic populations in the Coral Triangle Asian countries of Malaysia, the Philippines, and in particular Indonesia.

The Indonesia *National Plan of Actions* under the CTI-CCF Program sets out a mandate to increase its area of MPAs to complement existing MPA networks (National Secretariat of CTI-CFF Indonesia 2009; Wilson et al.

2011). A significant proportion of the existing and proposed areas in eastern regions of Indonesia are either home to—or seasonally accessed by—highly mobile Sama-Bajau communities. Given the nature of Sama-Bajau livelihood strategies and the connections between settlements, these proposed MPAs could have significant social and economic impacts.

Migratory Behavior and Conservation

Long gone are the romanticized portrayals of nomadic populations of the eighteenth and nineteenth centuries living in harmony with the environment (Sopher 1977). In an era of increasing alarm and concern over marine biodiversity loss, the migratory fishing behavior of mobile Sama-Bajau groups (and other maritime populations such as the Bugis, Madurese, and Butonese) is often considered a threat to biodiversity conservation and marine resource sustainability (Lowe 2006; Majors 2008; Clifton and Majors 2012; Stacey et al. 2012).

Despite being increasingly recognized for their rich marine wisdom and dependence on the marine environment (Stacey et al. 2012), Sama-Bajau, as nonresident fishers and characterized by migratory behavior, are often blamed for overfishing and destructive fishing practices (DFP) such as blast fishing, cyanide fishing, trap, trawl, or fish drive methods (Lowe 2003, 2006; Majors 2008; Clifton 2010; Peterson et al. 2010). This view is exemplified by the statement by conservation practitioners that:

> extreme mobility results in two important characteristics of DFP in Indonesia: 1) Paradoxically, the most remote reefs in Indonesia are often the most destroyed; and 2) As these fishers are not bound to a home reef system, they are never forced to deal with the destruction they bring to bear. Rather, as one reef system becomes unproductive, they simply move on. (Pet-Soede and Erdmann 1998, 33)[14]

This view was also echoed in the "Coral Triangle and Climate Change: Ecosystems, People and Societies at Risk Report" (Hoegh-Guldberg et al. 2009), launched at the CTI-CFF RPoA signing in 2009. The report claims, via its subtitle, to be a "comprehensive study involving over twenty experts and based on three hundred peer-reviewed scientific articles" (Hoegh-Guldberg et al. 2009, 1) and professes to consider the strong links between people and coastal ecosystems within the Coral Triangle. In effect, it presents the commonly held conservationist view of nomadism and in particular Sama-Bajau and associated maritime populations in Indonesia:

> Coral reefs have a very important meaning for the coastal community from an economic and cultural point of view. One third of the Indonesian population living in coastal areas depend on shallow water fisheries which originate

from coral reefs, mangroves and seagrasses. The largest proportion of them consists of traditional fishermen using simple fishing gear to capture small benthic and pelagic fish. The dependency of their livelihoods needs [sic] to the attachment of strong cultural values to sea life. Some tribal groups such as the Sama-Bajau, Bugis and Maduranese [sic] dramatically follow fishing opportunities in groups of 5–10 boats, catching what they will and selling it to the nearest market. The take all practices of these wandering fishermen leave the locations that they exploit highly degraded with very few fish stock left. This behavior contrasts other traditional stationary communities that live in relative harmony with local coastal resources. (Hoegh-Guldberg et al. 2009, 45)

This negative view of migratory behavior is often in contrast to conservationist views of "fixed" sedentary coastal communities whose strategies are viewed as having a positive impact on the marine environment (Lowe 2006; Clifton 2010). In writing about the Sama-Bajau in the Togean Islands of Central Sulawesi, Lowe states, "Imagining the Sama as 'nomadic,' conservationists, bureaucrats, and others expect landscapes to be of little relevance to Sama people's lives" (Lowe 2003,116).

Such views are underpinned by a narrow understanding of the social, cultural, spiritual, economic, and historical complexities and livelihood strategies of mobile fishing communities. This is itself a symptom of absent and/or poor quality social science research and analysis, a history of limited local engagement in marine conservation planning (Gaynor 2005; Afiff and Lowe 2008; Majors 2008; Clifton 2009), and insufficient attention paid to local and indigenous technical knowledge about the marine environment (e.g., Berkes 1993). Overall, the social sciences and resource-users' knowledge have been insignificant in the design and implementation of conservation policy when compared to the input from the biological and ecological sciences (Christie et al. 2003; Mascia et al. 2003; West, Igoe, and Brockington 2006; Springer 2009; Peterson et al. 2010).

Mobility is employed by Sama-Bajau communities as a practice to avoid local over-exploitation of resources. A key livelihood strategy among the Sama-Bajau of the Togean Islands region of Central Sulawesi involves groups moving between places in search of species they know are abundant (Lowe 2006). Lowe (2009, 85–86) further explains, "To *pongkat* means to have access to remote fishing grounds, both on distant off-lying reefs and on coastal shores, spreading one's use thinly across the resource." And as pointed out by Lowe, "Living aboard a boat is never a sign that one lacks connections to a village or to the land . . . or that one is drifting aimlessly or endlessly in some Robinson Crusoe adventure" (2006, 81). Indeed, nomadic or seminomadic livelihood strategies do not render Sama-Bajau disinterested in protection of the environment or unconcerned for overharvesting of particular species.

As noted by Allison and Ellis, "Geographical mobility is necessary to sustain catches of mobile or fluctuating fish stocks. Mobility can also be beneficial to stock conservation in that it enables fisheries to move away from locally depleted resources" (2001, 387). However, this proves extra challenging in regions like Indonesia, where locally depleted resources are common. Nonetheless, the presence of migratory fishermen and their families in towns and regions can also have a positive economic impact on that area; this is often overlooked (Allison and Ellis 2001). The families of fishers in home villages often rely on fishers returning home at the end of fishing in distant regions to provide a cash injection to households and the community (Jorion 1988).

The impact of conservation initiatives and MPAs can result in a loss of territory (Chou and Wee 2002), resulting in changing livelihood strategies and further mobile and shifting fishing activities (Lowe 2006; Majors 2008; Clifton 2010). There is also evidence to suggest flow-on effects from changing livelihood circumstances can lead to fishers taking on illegal activity, such as people-smuggling across permeable sea boundaries (namely between Australia and Indonesia) (Dwyer 2001). Changes in fishing practices by people experiencing vulnerable conditions and events (be they economic hardship, illness, or theft), have also been shown to lead to the use of illegal methods (Barratt 2012).

Conclusions: The Future of the Sama-Bajau

In this chapter, we have examined what it is like for the Sama-Bajau to be "at home on the waves," while being excluded by others from a role in managing and conserving what is "beneath the waves" (Gaynor 2010, 74): the resources that their livelihoods depend upon. Outside of the discipline of anthropology, various interpretations of the term "nomadic" have been used and misused by historians, colonial observers, scholars, and popular media for centuries, with consequences for those thus labeled. There is no accepted definition of nomadism and the type of lifestyle or economic production it represents. Following this analysis, the *pongka* and *lama* (long distance) strategies of Sama-Bajau populations in eastern Indonesia can be characterized as nomadic and seminomadic.

However, continued application of the term "sea nomads" to the majority of Sama-Bajau who now reside in strand/coastal and land areas rather than as permanent boat dwellers can be misleading, and tends to promote negative views of Sama-Bajau and lack of recognition of their associations to place. As demonstrated through historical and contemporary perspectives, mobility and adaptability underlie the social and economic life of this maritime population. Sama-Bajau have strong connections to home villages from which they originate, as well as to the temporary bases or seasonal camps associated with migratory fishing, a part of cultural practice. Sama-Bajau wellbeing is very much predicated on mobile diversified livelihoods across a large geographical region, extending at times into neighboring countries. Moreover, Sama-Bajau communities in eastern Indonesia play an important role in small-scale fisheries, providing for local consumption as well as export trade.

However, many of the fishing grounds on which Sama-Bajau have so long depended for subsistence, cash income, and other forms of social wellbeing are in areas of high biodiversity either earmarked for, or already designated as, conservation areas. Seasonal mobility and periodic migration to fishing grounds—on nearby outer reefs or in more distant island locations—are important components of livelihood strategies of small-scale fisheries in Indonesia. Specifically, this is the case for men catching fish, and women in post-harvest production.

However, such mobility is not well regarded among fisheries managers, nor consistent with conservation approaches to fisheries management that deal with stationary resident populations (Allison and Ellis 2001; Binet, Failler, and Thorpe 2012). The conservation agenda has often sought to blame mobile fishers for much of the overfishing or overexploitation in Indonesia (Stacey et al. 2012; Foale et al. 2013) and exclude them from management discussions (Majors 2008; Clifton 2010; Clifton and Majors 2012; Fitriana and Stacey 2012).

To date, the CTI-CFF Program and associated plans and reports appear to give little consideration to indigenous mobile peoples and application of the global conservation policy regarding indigenous and nomadic peoples. In Indonesia, there is no apparent evidence that consideration has been given to the social impacts of proposed marine management initiatives (West, Igoe, and Brockington 2006; Springer 2009) and in particular the needs of marginalized indigenous mobile fishing communities (Clifton and Majors 2012; Foale et al. 2013). Conservation efforts must be better informed, with greater levels of social impact analysis and linked conservation and development agendas, to accommodate the diversity, mobility, and livelihood needs and strategies of mobile maritime populations. Culturally informed approaches are also important for avoiding the potential negative impacts of conservation initiatives, such as displacement of local people and increased pressure on local human populations and fisheries resources.

There is no doubt that special, flexible strategies are required to ensure food security and access to fisheries for these vulnerable peoples, particularly when areas that are restricted or closed to fishing within MPAs are established in locations where they have demonstrated fishing activity (Foale et al. 2013). Moreover, with little power or unity as a group, mobile groups such as the Sama-Bajau are often marginalized within land-based governance systems, and overlooked as key stakeholder groups in marine conservation and management programs (Gaynor 2005; Jones, Qiu, and De Santo 2011).

There are growing calls for inclusion of indigenous mobile peoples in environmental management and conservation initiatives along with recognition of their value as biodiversity stewards (e.g., Bloomfield 2013). Sama-Bajau knowledge systems, cultural beliefs, and world-views could be valuable in biodiversity monitoring, management, and conservation of migratory species such as whale sharks (where culturally driven prohibitions on whale shark captures can support conservation measures [Stacey et al. 2012]). Such activities can provide employment or supplementary income opportunities, as has been successfully developed in parts of Northern Australia through establishment of indigenous land and sea ranger groups (e.g., Altman and Kerins 2012).

Recently, the innovative involvement of Rotinese fishermen from east Nusa Tenggara in sea cucumber catch surveys has been shown to not only deliver accurate results on population and exploitation rates but also play an important educational role in supporting the development of fisheries management in heavily depleted areas (Prescott et al. 2013). Other opportunities could involve employment of Sama-Bajau as roving ambassadors for conservation and sustainable fisheries, which consider not just the threats posed by harvesting but also the opportunities posed by knowledge of predictable patterns of migratory behaviors (e.g., Chou and Wee 2002; Stacey et al. 2012).

Instead of demonizing Sama-Bajau migratory lifestyles, and overlooking their potential roles in conservation, new approaches are required. Local knowledge, ethics, and respect for people's connections with nature should be promoted. This could allow nomadic fishers to maintain livelihoods consistent with their wishes and strong identity with the sea.

Natasha Stacey is an applied anthropologist with an interest in maritime anthropology and sea nomadic populations in Southeast Asia. She is currently Associate Professor at the Research Institute for the Environment and Livelihoods, Charles Darwin University, leading a multidisciplinary group of scientists and postgraduate scholars working on natural resource management and livelihood research projects in Northern Australia and Southeast and mainland Asia. Her recent research projects have included improving coastal livelihoods and fisheries management in the cross-border regions of the Arafura-Timor Seas; small-scale fisheries: the roles of women, and opportunities for improving livelihoods in Indonesia; building indigenous science capacity for aquaculture enterprise development; social impacts of artisanal mining in eastern Indonesia; and rehabilitating blue carbon mangrove habitats in Indonesia. She lectures in "Natural Resources and Indigenous Livelihoods," and her publications include *Social Wellbeing and the Values of Small-scale Fisheries* (2017), and *Boats to Burn: Bajo Fishing in the Australian Fishing Zone* (2007).

Edward H. Allison is currently a Professor of Marine and Environmental Affairs at the University of Washington, Seattle. His work spans research, policy, and practice in both fisheries science and international development. He has worked on the coasts and inland waters of sub-Saharan Africa, Asia, Oceania, Latin America, and Europe, principally on the contribution of fisheries and aquaculture to food and nutrition security and to coastal livelihoods, the governance of small-scale fisheries and aquaculture production, and people's vulnerability and adaptation to climate change. Since working in Malawi for the UK Department for International Development in the early 1990s, he has held a faculty appointment in the School of International Development, University of East Anglia, has advised the UN Food and Agriculture Organization, and was Director of Policy, Economics and Social Science at the WorldFish Center, Malaysia.

Notes

1. For consistency, we use the term "Sama-Bajau" throughout the chapter rather than local designations.
2. In another *Dictionary of Anthropology*, "nomadism" is defined as "regular seasonal or cyclical movements of a group to obtain sustenance. . . . There are nomads who hunt and nomads who collect food, as well as pastoral and even agricultural nomads" (Winick 1970, 384).
3. See also Chatty (2012), who discusses mobility in relation to indigenous people in the context of on-going restrictions, evictions, and dispossession from natural resources and their traditional production areas.
4. Cripps (2009) examines the seminomadic fishing activity of Vevo from Madagascar, which is contrasted against what he identifies as the truly nomadic boat dwelling tribes of Southeast Asia, such as the Moken.
5. The La Galigo is an epic myth from the Bugis people of South Sulawesi.
6. Sopher (1977), in his postscript to the 1965 edition, starts to appreciate the

house-dwelling and boat-dwelling groups from the Sulu region of the Philippines based on research by Nimmo. Nimmo's (1968) work identifies among the Tawi Tawi islands group in southern Philippines a southern group who are less nomadic than northern Bajau groups, who focus on fishing nearby reefs rather than more seasonal, distant shore activity.

7. Some scholars, such as Gaynor (2005), working on the Tiworo region of Southeast Sulawesi have identified some variation in styles of fishing and collecting practices. In Tiworo, Gaynor states the term *pongkeq* means "to make a living by going out in a boat, by oneself or with one's family, for a few days, weeks, or months, usually travelling from market to market in order to sell ones catch and to buy necessities" (Gaynor 2005). In the Tomini Islands region of Central Sulawesi, Lowe (2006) describes *ponkat* activities by Bajo as "periodic extended collecting trips around the Togean Islands living aboard their canoes . . . or living in shelters . . . over coral reefs for several days or weeks at a time."

8. See also Nolde (2009) for a brief coverage of turtle fishing by Bajo from Sampela village, Kaledupa Island, Wakatobi Islands.

9. Gaynor (2005) notes that among the people she worked with, the term *sakei* was used instead of *lamaq*, meaning "to go off to another region for a long period of time, usually a year or more with a relatively larger boat that is fully equipped for the trip." This may include trips for shark fin, trochus (sea snails), and trepang (sea cucumber), and male only crews—but also families, including women and children who may reside in a base camp while men take part in actual fishing activity offshore. Gaynor notes that in contrast to *ponkeq, sakei* and *lamaq* involve a significant capital investment. Sather (1997) also notes for the Bajau Laut of Semporna region in the 1960s, it was not uncommon for families and fleets of boats to sail 20–80 km to fish and return to their settlements.

10. For detailed coverage of the arrangements allowing traditional Indonesian fishing in waters inside Australia's Exclusive Economic Zone, refer to Stacey 1999 and 2007.

11. The *Dana Declaration on Mobile Peoples and Conservation* was agreed in Wadi Dana Jordan in 2002 (Dana Declaration 2002). The Declaration was the outcome of an international meeting of social and natural scientists and NGOs that took place in Wadi Dana Nature Reserve in Jordan in early April 2002.

12. Much of the policy dialogue and assessments are driven and relate to rights of indigenous people in terrestrial protected areas.

13. Over US$350 million was pledged by bilateral and multilateral donors to implement the CTI regional Plan of Action (National Secretariat of CTI-CFF Indonesia 2009) signed by leaders of the six countries in May 2009. Following this, the CT6 drew up National Plans of Action to mirror regional objectives (Foale et al. 2013).

14. Clifton (2010) states that there is very little data to support such statements on the environmental impacts of the fishing and gathering practices used by Bajo.

References

Aburto J., M. Thiel, and W. Stotz. 2009. "Allocation of Effort in Artisanal Fisheries: The Importance of Migration and Temporary Fishing Camps." *Ocean and Coastal Management* 52, no. 12: 646–54.

Adams, W. M., and J. Hutton. 2007. "People, Parks and Poverty: Political Ecology and Biodiversity Conservation." *Conservation and Society* 5, no. 2: 147–83.

Adriani, N. 1900. "De Talen der Togian-Eilanden." *Tijdschrift voor Indische Taal-, Landen Volkenkunde* 42: 428–90, 539–66.

Afiff, S., and C. Lowe. 2008. "Collaboration, Conservation and Community: A Conversation between Suraya Afiff and Celia Lowe." In *Biodiversity and human livelihoods in protected areas: case studies from the Malay Archipelago*. Edited by N. S. Sodhi, G. Acciaioli, M. Erb, and A. Khee-Jin Tan, 153–64. Cambridge, UK: Cambridge University Press.

Allison, E. H., and F. Ellis. 2001. "The Livelihoods Approach and Management of Small-scale Fisheries." *Marine Policy* 25, no. 5: 377–88.

Altman, J., and S. Kerins, eds. 2012. *People on Country: Vital Landscapes, Indigenous Futures*. Sydney: The Federation Press.

Barratt, C. 2012. "Netting the Benefits Now or Later? Exploring the Relationship between Risk and Sustainability in Lake Victoria Fisheries, Uganda." In *Risk and Africa Multi-Disciplinary Empirical Approaches*. Edited by Lena Bloemertz, Martin Doevenspeck, Elísio Macamo, and Detlef Müller-Mahn, vol. 51, 243–64. Berlin: LIT Verlag Münster.

Berkes, Fikret. 1993. "Traditional Ecological Knowledge in Perspective." In *Traditional Ecological Knowledge: Concepts and Cases*. Edited by J. T. Inglis, 1–10. Ottawa: Canadian Museum of Nature and the International Development Research Centre.

Binet, T., P. Failler, and A. Thorpe. 2012. "Migration of Senegalese Fishers: A Case for Regional Approach to Management." *Maritime Studies* 11, no. 1: 1–14.

Bloomfield, B. 2013. "Anthropology: A Monochrome Eden." *Nature* 496, no. 7443: 28–29.

Chatty, Dawn. 2012. Dana Declaration + 10. Refugee Studies Centre Report, 05/2012, University of Oxford.

Chou, C. 1997. "Contesting the Tenure of Territoriality: The Orang Suku Laut." *Bijdragen Tot de Taal-, Land- en Volkenkunde* 153, no. 4: 605–29.

———. 2003. *Indonesian Sea Nomads: Money, Magic and Fear*. London: Routledge Curzon.

Chou, C., and V. Wee. 2002. "Tribality and Globalisation: The Orang Suku Laut and the 'Growth Triangle'; A Contested Environment." In *Tribal Communities in the Malay World*. Edited by G. Benjamin and C. Chou, 318–63. Singapore: IIAS (International Institute for Asian Studies) and ISEAS (Institute of Southeast Asian Studies).

Christie, P., B. J. McCay, M. L. Miller, C. Lowe, A. T. White, R. Stoffle, D. L. Fluharty, L. Talaue McManus, R. Chuenpagdee, C. Pomeroy, D. O. Suman, B. G. Blount, D. Huppert, R. L. Villahermosa Eisma, E. Oracion, K. Lowry, and R. B. Pollnac.

2003. "Towards Developing a Complete Understanding: A Social Science Research Agenda for Marine Protected Areas." *Fisheries* 28, no. 12: 22–26.

Clifton, J. 2009. "Science, Funding and Participation: Key Issues for Marine Protected Area Networks and the Coral Triangle Initiative." *Environmental Conservation* 36, no. 2: 91–96.

———. 2010. "Achieving Congruence between Conservation and Community: The Bajau Ethnic Group and Marine Management within the Wakatobi and South-east Asia." In *Marine Research and Conservation in the Coral Triangle: The Wakatobi National Park.* Edited by J. Clifton, R. Unsworth, and D. J. Smith, 171–92. New York: Nova Science Publishers.

Clifton, J., and C. Majors. 2012. "Culture, Conservation and Conflict: Perspectives on Marine Protection Among the Bajau of Southeast Asia." *Society and Natural Resources* 25, no. 7: 716–25.

Cripps, G. 2009. *Understanding Migration among the Traditional Fishers of West Madagascar.* London: Blue Ventures Conservation Report for ReCoMaP Indian Ocean. Retrieved 21 May 2013 from https://blueventures.org/wp-content/uploads/2015/10/Cripps_2009.pdf.

Crona, B., and S. Rosendo. 2011. "Outside the Law? Analyzing Policy Gaps in Addressing Fishers' Migration in East Africa." *Marine Policy* 35, no. 3: 379–88.

Dana Declaration on Mobile Peoples and Conservation. 2002. Retrieved 21 May 2013 from http://www.danadeclaration.org/main_declarationenglish.shtml.

Dwyer, D. 2001. "Borders and Bounders." Understanding the Cultural and Natural Heritage Values and Management Challenges of the Ashmore region Symposium, Darwin, 4–6 April 2001. Darwin: Museum and Art Gallery of the Northern Territory.

Fitriana, R., and N. Stacey. 2012. "The Role of Women in the Fishery Sector of Pantar Island, Indonesia." *Asian Fisheries Science* (Special Issue) 25: 159–75.

Foale, S., D. Adhuri, P. Aliño, E. Allison, N. Andrew, P. Cohen, L. Evans, M. Fabinyi, P. Fidelman, C. Gregory, N. Stacey, J. Tanzer, and N. Weeratunge. 2013. "Food Security and the Coral Triangle Initiative." *Marine Policy* 38: 174–83.

Fox, J. J. 1977. "Notes on the Southern Voyages and Settlements of the Sama-Bajau." *Bijdragen Tot de Taal-, Land-en Volkenkunde* 133, no. 4: 459–65.

———. 2000. "Maritime Communities in the Timor and Arafura Region: Some Historical and Anthropological Perspectives." In *East of Wallace's Line: Studies of Past and Present Maritime Cultures of the Indo-pacific Region.* Edited by S. O'Conner and P. Veth, Modern Quaternary Research in Southeast Asia, vol. 16, 337–56. Rotterdam: A. A. Balkema.

———. 2005. "In a Single Generation: A Lament for the Forests and Seas of Indonesia." In *Muddied Waters: Historical and Comteporary Perspectives on Management of Forests and Fisheries in Island Southeast Asia.* Edited by P. Boomgaard, D. Henly, and M. Ossewijer, 43–60. Leiden: KITLV Press.

Gaynor, J. L. 2005. "The Decline of Small-scale Fishing and the Reorganization of Livelihood Practices among Sama People in Eastern Indonesia." *Michigan Discussions in Anthropology* 15, no. 1: 90–149.

———. 2010. "Flexible Fishing: Gender and the New Spatial Division of Labour in Eastern Indonesia's Rural Littoral." *Radical History Review* 107: 74–100.

Hoegh-Guldberg, O., H. Hoegh-Guldberg, J. E. N. Veron, A. Green, E. D. Gomez, J. Lough, M. King, Ambariyanto, L. Hansen, J. Cinner, G. Dews, G. Russ, H. Z. Schuttenberg, E. L. Peñaflor, C. M. Eakin, T. R. L. Christensen, M. Abbey, F. Areki, R. A. Kosaka, A. Tewfik, and J. Oliver. 2009. *The Coral Triangle and Climate Change: Ecosystems, People and Societies at Risk.* Brisbane: WWF Australia.

International Labor Organization. 1989. *Indigenous and Tribal Peoples Convention.* No. 169. Geneva: International Labour Organization. Retreived 22 May 2018 from http://www.ilo.org/dyn/normlex/en/f?p=NORMLEXPUB:12100:0::NO::P12100_ILO_CODE:C169.

Johnson, D. S., T. G. Acott, N. Stacey, and J. Urquhart, eds. 2017. *Social Wellbeing and the Values of Small-scale Fisheries.* New York City: Springer.

Jones, P. J. S., W. Qiu, and E. M. De Santo, eds. 2011. *Governing Marine Protected Areas: Getting the Balance Right.* Vol. 2. Nairobi: Technical Report to Marine and Coastal Ecosystems Branch, UNEP.

Jorion, P. 1988. "Going Out or Staying Home: Seasonal Movements and Migration Strategies among Xwla and Anlo-Ewe Fishermen." *Maritime Anthropological Studies* 1, no. 2: 129–55.

Krueger, L. 2009. "Protected Areas and Human Displacement: Improving the Interface between Policy and Practice." *Conservation Society* 7, no. 1: 21–5. Retrieved 2 May 2009 from http://www.conservationandsociety.org/text.asp?2009/7/1/21/54793.

Lenhart, L. 1995. "Recent Research on Southeast Asian Sea Nomads." *Nomadic Peoples* 36/37: 245–60.

———. 2002. "Orang Suku Laut Identity: The Construction of Ethnic Realities." In *Tribal Communities in the Malay World.* Edited by G. Benjamin and C. Chou, 293–317. Singapore: IIAS (International Institute for Asian Studies) and ISEAS (Institute of Southeast Asian Studies).

Lowe, C. 2003. "The Magic of Place Sama at Sea and on Land in Sulawesi, Indonesia." *Bijdragen tot de Taal-Land-en Volkenkundre* 159, no. 1: 109–33.

———. 2006. *Wild Profusion: Biodiversity Conservation in an Indonesian Archipelago.* Princeton: Princeton University Press.

Macknight, C. 1976. *The Voyage to Marege': Macassan Trepangers in Northern Australia.* Melbourne: Melbourne University Press.

Majors, C. 2008. "Seas of Discontent: Conflicting Knowledge Paradigms within Indonesia's Marine Environmental Area in Sohhi." In *Biodiversity and Human Livelihoods in Protected Areas: Case Studies for the Malay Archipelago.* Edited by Navjot S. Sodhi, Greg Acciaioli, Maribeth Erb, and Alan Khee-Jin Tan, 241–65. Cambridge, UK: Cambridge University Press.

Mascia, M. B., J. P. Brosius, T. A. Dobson, B. C. Forbes, L. Horowitz, M. A. McKean, and N. J. Turner. 2003. "Conservation and the Social Sciences." *Conservation Biology* 17, no. 3: 649–50.

Mead, D., and M.-Y. Lee. 2007. *Mapping Indonesian Bajau Communities in Sulawesi.* Summer Institute of Linguistics Electronic Survey Report, vol. 2007-019. Dallas: SIL International.

Nagatsu, K. 2007. "The Sama-Bajau in and around Sulawesi: Basic Data on their Population and Distribution of the Villages." Department of Sociology, Toyo

University. Retrieved 8 December 2012 from http://www-archive.cseas.kyo
to-u.ac.jp/sulawesi/final_reports2007/article/46-nagatsu.pdf.

National Secretariat of CTI-CFF Indonesia. 2009. *CTI Indonesia National Plans of Actions*. Jarkarta: Ministry of Marine Affairs and Fisheries. Retrieved 22 May 2018 from http://www.coraltriangleinitiative.org/sites/default/files/resources/Indonesiapercent20NPOA_Final.pdf.

Nimmo, H. A. 1968. "Reflections on Bajau History." *Philippines Studies* 16, no. 1: 32–59.

Njock, J.-C., and L. Westlund. 2010. "Migration, Resource Management and Global Change: Experiences from Fishing Communities in West and Central Africa." *Marine Policy* 34, no. 4: 752–60.

Nolde, L. 2009. "Great is Our Relationship with the Sea: Charting the Maritime Realm of the Sama of Southeast Sulawesi, Indonesia." In *Explorations: A Graduate Student Journal of Southeast Asian Studies* 9(1): 15–33. Retrieved 22 May 2018 from http://religiondocbox.com/Buddhism/70337679-Explorations-a-graduate-student-journal-of-southeast-asian-studies.html.

OED (Oxford English Dictionary). 2018. "Nomad." Oxford University Press. Retrieved 21 May 2018 from https://en.oxforddictionaries.com/definition/nomad.

Pallesen, A. K. 1985. *Culture, Contact and Language Convergence*. Monograph no. 24. Manila: Linguistic Society of the Philippines.

Pelras, C. 1972. "Notes sur Quelques Populations Aquatiques de l'Archipel Nusantarien." *Archipel* 3, no. 1: 133–68.

Peterson, R. B., D. Russell, P. West, and J. P. Brosius. 2010. "Seeing (And Doing) Conservation Through Cultural Lenses." *Environmental Management* 45, no. 1: 5–18.

Pet-Soede, L., and M. Erdmann. 1998. "An Overview and Comparison of Destructive Fishing Practices in Indonesia." *SPC Live Reef Fish Information Bulletin* 4: 28–36. Retrieved 22 May 2018 from https://spccfpstore1.blob.core.windows.net/digitallibrary-docs/files/cf/cf45b29997fe13e57923f7880d175b69.pdf?sv=2015-12-11&sr=b&sig=Ipercent2FQHdH9percent2B2W4KoKGOmPTvT8ETu4SkwcAiFwuxWY7percent2FSg8percent3D&se=2018-11-18T01percent3A49percent3A20Z&sp=r&rscc=publicpercent2C percent20max-agepercent3D864000percent2Cpercent20max-stalepercent3D86400&rsct=applicationpercent2Fpdf&rscd=inlinepercent3Bpercent20filenamepercent3Dpercent22LRF4_28_Pet-Soede.pdfpercent22.

Prescott, J., C. Vogel, K. Pollock, S. Hyson, D. Oktaviani, and A. Panggabean. 2013. "Estimating Sea Cucumber Abundance and Exploitation Rates using Removal Methods." *Marine and Freshwater Research* 64, no. 7: 599–608.

Reid, A. 1983. "The Rise of Makassar." *Review of Indonesian and Malaysian Affairs* 17: 117–60.

Sather, C. 1997. *The Bajau Laut: Adaptation, History and Fate in a Maritime Fishing Society of South-eastern Sabah*. New York: Oxford University Press.

Seymour-Smith, C. 1986. *Macmillam Dictionary of Anthropology*. London: Macmillam Press.

Sopher, D. (1965). 1977. *The Sea Nomads: A Study of the Maritime Boat People of Southeast Asia.* No. 5. Singapore: National Museum Singapore.

Springer, J. 2009. "Addressing the Social Impacts of Conservation: Lessons from Experience and Future Directions." *Opinion, Conservation and Society* 7, no. 1: 26–29.

Stacey, N. 1999. "Boats to Burn: Bajo Fishing Activity in the Australian Fishing Zone." PhD dissertation. Darwin: Northern Territory University.

———. 2007. *Boats to Burn: Bajo Fishing Activity in the Australian Fishing Zone.* Asia-Pacific Environment Monograph Series. Canberra: ANU E Press.

Stacey, N., J. Karam, M. Meekan, S. Pickering, and J. Ninef. 2012. "Prospects for Whale Shark Conservation in Eastern Indonesia through Bajo Traditional Ecological Knowledge and Community-based Monitoring." *Conservation and Society* 10, no. 1: 63–75.

Verheijen, J. A. A. 1986. *The Sama/Bajau Language in the Lesser Sunda Islands.* Canberra: Pacific Linguistics.

West, P., J. Igoe, and D. Brockington. 2006. "Parks and Peoples: The Social Impact of Protected Areas." *Annual Review of Anthropology* 35: 251–77.

Wilson, J., A. Darmawan, J. Subijanto, A. Green, and S. Sheppard. 2011. Scientific design of a resilient network of marine protected areas. Lesser Sunda Eco region, Coral Triangle. TNC, *Asia Pacific Marine Program. Report* 2/11.

Winick, C. 1970. *Dictionary of Anthropology.* New Jersey: Littlefield, Adams & Co.

CHAPTER 15

Formal and Informal Territoriality in Ocean Management

Tanya J. King

Fishing for gummy shark (*Mustelus antarcticus*) from the Australian port of Lakes Entrance, the fishermen heard over the radio that the *Sally Anne* had been seen working close by. Owen, one of the listening deckies, responded with indignation to the news of a vessel from another port: "*Sally Anne*! That's a San Remo boat!"

"Port Albert," corrected the skipper, calmly.

"Ahh, Port Albert," continued Owen, studying the gently rolling deck and shaking his head. "They're bad men. They should stay in their own backyard. And those San Remo blokes, too. They shouldn't come out of their back yard. They're poaching!"

Later, I asked Owen what he had meant. He qualified his comments carefully, explaining that everyone was allowed to fish wherever they liked. "But," he continued, "it's a territoriality thing." He explained, "West of the Prom is San Remo, Port Albert have the islands, and Lakes is more the east side of Flinders, the rigs, and the edge of the shelf."

At the time I had this conversation, I had been conducting participant observation with the shark fishing industry of southeast Australia for around twenty months. Steeped in the maritime anthropology literature that described the informal territoriality of commercial fishermen (e.g., Acheson 1988; White 1988; Palmer 1990), I had diligently tried to establish who was able to fish where within the formally open-access domain of the Southern Shark Fishery (the SSF, as it was then known). In two years of intensive fieldwork, however, Owen's brief, frank explanation, prompted as it was by a perceived infraction, was the closest I ever came to an explicit explanation of "the rules."

Australian commercial shark fishermen say that they are "allowed" to fish anywhere they like. Some declare that the sea belongs to everyone and to no one. Certainly, within the official parameters of the SSF, which incorporates Commonwealth waters adjacent to the States of South Australia, Tasmania, and Victoria (figure 15.1), a shark license permits the holder to fish in any location.

In practice, the majority of fishing occurs in Bass Strait, a plateau that once connected the mainland State of Victoria to the island of Tasmania, roughly 240 km wide and 50–70 m deep (figure 15.2). These shallow waters are the only place where the bottom-set gillnets used to catch shark can be set and retrieved safely. Shark fishing within Bass Strait is further restricted by the human relationships among those who, individually, take to sea with a license to fish "anywhere they like." Particular fishermen regularly work particular regions, informed by the productive possibilities afforded by those places, as well as the social possibilities afforded through their home port, working history, and personal associations. To gain access to a particular location is not as simple as taking to sea and plotting a course. Rather, the "open" space of Bass Strait is heavily signposted by the history of the people who dwell there, and the messages encountered range from "stop" to "go" to "enter at own risk," depending on who you are and who you know. The integrity of the "traditional fishing area" boundaries generated by these signs are enforced through the subtle—and sometimes not-so-subtle—exclusion of "outsiders." "Outsiders" are not necessarily

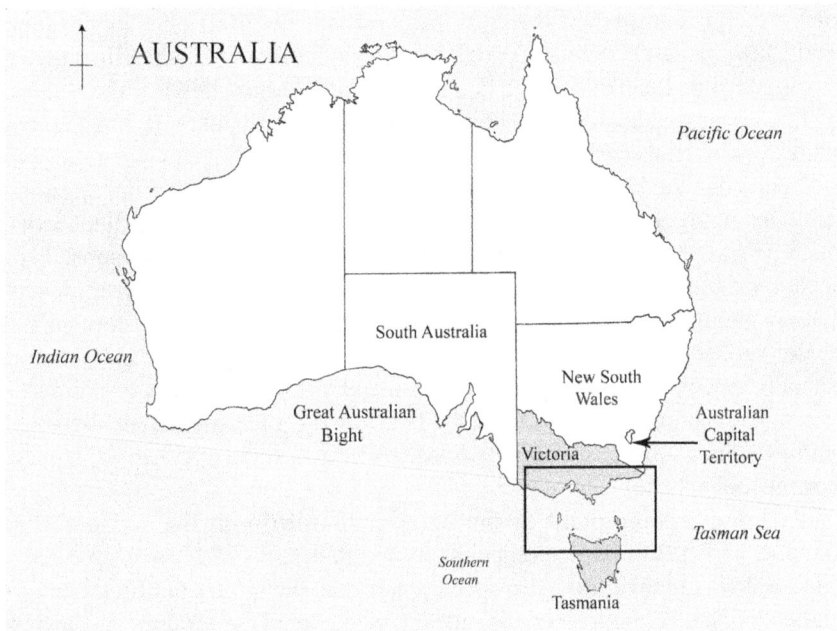

Figure 15.1. Map of Australia, showing research focus region. Created by the author.

Figure 15.2. Map of Bass Strait, showing various salient features. Created by the author.

strangers, and the boundaries are not fixed. Rather, these divisions on the water of Bass Strait reflect the dynamic social connections and fissions at play among members of the community at sea (White 1988; Dwyer, Just, and Minnegal 2003; Kitner 2006; King 2011). I consider this territoriality a component of the Traditional Ecological Knowledge (TEK) of the region, as it is generated by the local community over many years of intimate engagement with the ocean and with each other (Inglis 1993, vi).

In places like Australia, the United States, and Europe, formal territoriality arrangements always exist in tandem with formal management tools, such as gear restrictions, quotas, marine parks, and closed seasons. Typically, the boundaries drawn by formal managers are precise, rigid, and clearly defined using a map or specific coordinates. These "lines on the water" contrast in form with the more subtle, malleable, ambiguous, and socially embedded constraints that informally limit particular fishermen's access to certain regions. Indeed, the two "types" of management—formal and informal—are often depicted as standing in stark opposition, at least conceptually, if not in practice.

Forming a component of the broader literature on the conservation benefits of Traditional Ecological Knowledge (Berkes 1987), a sizable body of literature in maritime anthropology laments the failure of official governance tools to acknowledge the efficacy of informal constraints on the harvesting capacity of fishing fleets (Risien and Tilt 2008; Carter and Nielsen 2011). In some cases the local-user representations of spaces are depicted as being somehow "better" than formal understandings, both environmentally and morally (Berkes 1993, 6; Nadasdy 1999; Wenzel 1999). This link between how we imagine spaces and the value of that mode of appreciation is captured by Van Houtum, who is describing the increasingly poststructuralist tendency of twentieth-century studies in geopolitics:

> The overall view was that "good" were generally those borders that were seen as natural, that is, made by nature in terms of its physiographic variation (seas, mountains, deserts) and borders were generally seen as "bad" when they were human-made, "artificial." (2005, 675)

While anthropological depictions of ocean territoriality recognize the constructed nature of informal territories, there is a tendency to favor, promote, and idealize those depictions of space and ownership generated by local users as "good" rather than the "bad" political boundaries imposed by the state.

Typically, discussions about formal and informal management systems focus on how the informal practices operate in the background of the broader management story (Cinner and Aswani 2007), or how the imposition of formal arrangements undermines the established informal management system (Meinzen-Dick and Knox 2001). It is well recognized that fishermen must negotiate both systems (Acheson and Gardner 2004), but less acknowledged that managers, too, encounter both the formal and informal rules of ocean management. Rather, managers tend to be depicted as myopic, only recognizing—or caring to see—the formal constraints at play. But of course, both managers and fishers negotiate both systems. While the relative salience of formal and informal territoriality will necessarily vary from person to place to context, to describe them as competing systems fails to take into account the degree to which they overlap in a modern fisheries management context. This chapter illustrates that overlap by describing several cases in which formal and informal territoriality in Bass Strait are practically intertwined.

The first half of this chapter provides a description of the "traditional fishing areas" of Bass Strait shark fishermen, as described during fieldwork between 2000 and 2003. The second half of the chapter describes a meeting that occurred in Victoria in 2002, during which knowledge of informal territoriality was explicitly used to inform the development of formal restrictions.

Fishermen's Territoriality

One of the better-known descriptions of informal territoriality in a fishing community comes from Acheson's work in the Maine lobster fishery (Acheson 1988). Acheson draws on Hockett's account of primate behavior

(Hockett 1973, 69) in his distinction between "perimeter" and "nucleated" territoriality (Acheson 1988, 79; 2003, 29). Nucleated territoriality, according to Hockett:

> is not defined, except by increasing distance from home base [or port] and by the increasing chance of encountering another member of the same species if the latter happens to be wandering equally far, in just the right direction, from his own headquarters. (Hockett 1973, 69—brackets added)

Basically, the closer to one's home port, the stronger the sense of rightful access by "insiders" or incursion by "outsiders." The exclusion of "outsiders" tends to be achieved by using (sometimes) veiled coercive tactics employed cooperatively by a group of fishermen who variously cooperate and compete on the basis of a set of shared community rules (King 2007). While these may be fishermen from the same port, as this chapter shows, this is not necessarily the case.

Perimeter-defended territories, in Acheson's account, are associated with particular groups, or "gangs" of men, who fish from a particular harbor. Entry to these gangs is strictly limited. Precise boundaries are determined in relation to salient features of the environment, such as river mouths, islands, big trees, or underwater channels. The boundaries themselves are not official, but are determined by locals, and may shift subtly over time. Only those with an intimate knowledge of the region are even aware of these markers, and those from only ten miles away may have no familiarity with the relevant boundaries of a particular harbor (Acheson 1988, 71–73).

Acheson's research, conducted in the 1970s, found that perimeter defended territoriality was more effective than nucleated territoriality in terms of maintaining the biological and economic health of the fishery (Acheson 1988, 153); lobsters were larger, more fecund, and more plentiful than in the regions organized by nucleated territoriality. This was partly due to the restrictions on entry to gangs, the ferocity with which informal boundaries were enforced, and the self-imposed restrictions on effort imposed by individual gangs (Acheson 1988, 153–54). Other particularities of Acheson's example lend themselves to the success of perimeter-defended territoriality in this case, including the relatively small size of the fishing grounds, the productivity of the region, and the close social (including familial) ties among gang members and on-shore producers. Acheson's account, and several since, have emphasized the benefits of locally conceived and enforced effort restriction, including in cases when the system of territoriality could best be described as nucleated (e.g., Aswani 2002). This is not least because restrictions on access and effort designed by local fishermen are more likely to be respected—and therefore enforced—by fishermen themselves. The key lesson from Acheson's account is not that perimeter or nucleated territoriality is necessarily better, but that local management systems should be carefully accounted for and incorporated into successful management systems.

Notwithstanding the example provided by Acheson, it is important not to assume that perimeter-defended territoriality is the business of formal managers while nucleated territoriality tends to be the style favored in informal systems. Certainly, perimeter-defended territoriality reflects an unambiguous, "lines on the water" style of restriction typically favored by formal management institutions. Boundaries can be policed more precisely by the use of enforcement personnel, Vessel Monitoring Systems (VMS), or the threat of penalties, than can more subjectively articulated restrictions such as defined within nucleated territoriality; one person's definition of "too far from home" may reasonably be different to another's. However, in keeping with the theme of this chapter, despite our capacity to distinguish between perimeter and nucleated territoriality, as between formal and informal systems, we should not imagine that each develops in isolation from the other. Acheson's lobster gangs negotiate a range of management restrictions, and their territoriality—whether nucleated or perimeter defended—arises in the context of these other systems.

Perhaps counter-intuitively, I will now describe two sets of examples, the first of which could be described as informal territoriality and the second as formal territoriality. In both instances, it will become apparent how blurry these boundaries are, and the extent to which formality, in the first instance, and informality, in the second, bleed into the realization of each set of strictures.

Informal Territoriality

Shark fishermen tend to fish in small groups of two or three boats. The reason relates to the physiology of the shark, which cannot be detected using modern fish-finding technology. In order to catch fish, gillnets are deployed for six to eight hours and rest on the bottom of the seabed waiting to ensnare passing sharks. Gillnets therefore act to both catch shark and also to indicate the presence—or absence—of a shoal of shark in the region (up to six to eight hours swim in any direction). A skilled fisherman can also take the information gleaned from a hauled gillnet and determine which direction the sharks were swimming, what they had been eating, and their possible speed. Necessarily, two lengths of net can monitor at least twice as much space as one, and three nets even more again. Collaboration with one or more other boat 'better' enables fishermen to both catch and to "stay on" the shoal as it swims across Bass Strait.

Shark fishermen from the same port will generally fish in a common area, relatively close to their home port. These areas are somewhat "nucleated," in that divisions on the water correlate somewhat to terrestrial locales, and shark fishermen have the strongest territorial "rights" closest to their "home" port. However, in the middle of Bass Strait, or among men from the same port, the "rules" of territoriality are more open to strategic manipulation. While every fisherman with a valid permit can, legally, fish wherever he pleases, it is more accurate to suggest that a fisherman gains access to particular marine regions through his *social* relationships. There are examples of fishermen being "able" to fish in "non-traditional" regions due to a social connection with other men who fish those areas. This connection is not necessarily one of friendship, but may be financial, familial, or broadly political. Lines on the water emerge, shift, and dissolve in ways that reflect the dynamic social relationships among men, both on land and at sea. The engagement of men in the marine environment informs their interpersonal relationships, and this community is simultaneously mapped onto the water.

Though I asked several men if the "traditional fishing areas" could be drawn on a map, they all felt that to do so was somehow inappropriate. To do so would rigidify something that was necessarily vague, and might be seen as tantamount to "claiming" a space to which one had no explicit right (see figure 15.3 for an exception to the rule). Nonetheless, a general picture of the regional zones should be sketched, to give a sense of the basic patterns from which fishermen variously deviate.

From Port Albert and neighboring Port Welshpool, fishermen tend to fish south, past "The Prom" and places known as "Hogans," "Erith," "Deal," or "Kent," around "The Sisters," further down to "Prime Seal" and even to "Banks."[1] Lakes Entrance fishermen may also steam across to the Furneaux Group (of which Flinders Island is a part), but tend to stay further east, around the oil rigs (which all have names, such as "Kingfisher"), and closer to the continental shelf. San Remo fishermen may steam east, but tend toward King Island. Those from Tasmania tend to focus on the islands closest to them (either King or Flinders), while the South Australian fishermen do not often steam east in search of shark, but remain on the west side of the fishery.

The salience of the port distinctions is evident in the way that shark fishermen group together, and classify each other, at sea. While small groups of individual fishermen explicitly cooperate, a lot of chatter occurs between men who are at least known to each other. Indeed, part of the fun of fishing, I was told, was playing the ongoing game of trying to elicit information from others without giving away too much of one's own vital knowledge. One of the topics of radio discussion is the movement, and success, of other boats. While the individuals may be known, a fisherman

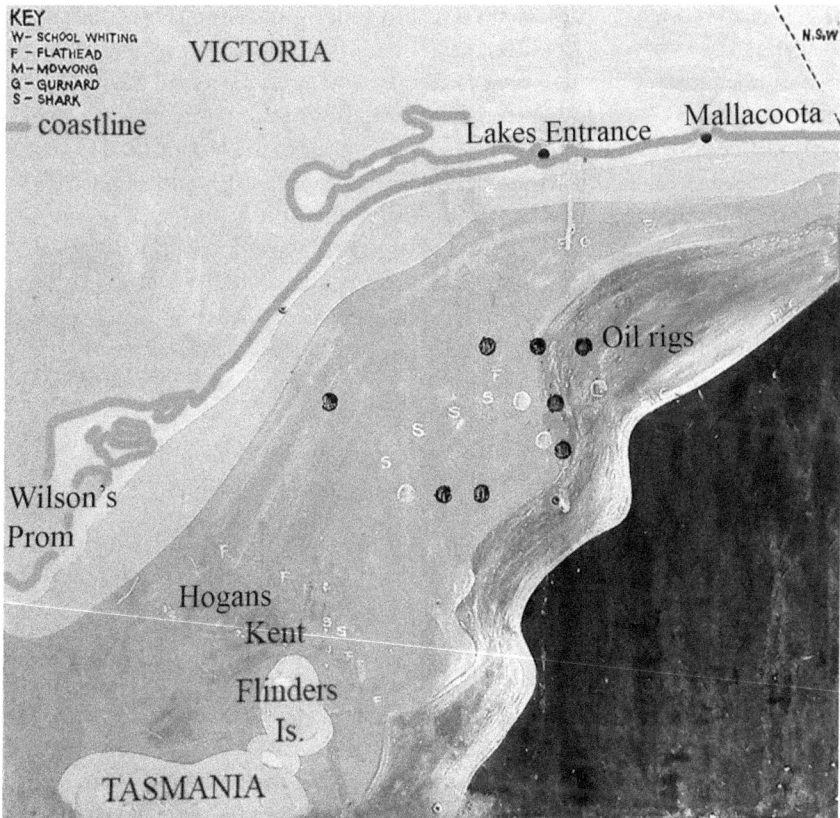

Figure 15.3. Section from display located at the Lakes Entrance Fisherman's Co-operative. The map shows parts of Victorian and Tasmanian coastline, with letters representing ocean locations where particular species are often found. Note that the "shark grounds" depicted reflect the perspective of Lakes Entrance fishermen, with the majority of Ss located to the east of Bass Strait. Indeed, Port Albert and Port Welshpool are not marked on the map (Corner Inlet is represented just east of Wilson's Promontory), nor are the shark fishing grounds that are most salient to the fishermen of this region, around the islands south of these ports. Photo by the author. (Note that this image has been slightly enhanced to improve legibility.)

from Corner Inlet may refer to a group of boats as "Lakes Boys" or "San Remo Boys" or "Tassie Boys" (the degree of specification increasing with the proximity).[2] The following stories are examples of how fishermen subtly enforce these divisions.

One afternoon while his boat was being unloaded, I asked Ollie, an owner and skipper from Lakes Entrance, where he fished and with whom. He explained that he usually fished to the east, and mainly communicated via radio with other boats from Lakes Entrance, several men in particular. If he happened to encounter boats from Port Albert (the closest shark fishing port to the west), he saw no harm in talking to them; it was better, he asserted, for everyone to talk to each other. Occasionally, particularly earlier in his career, Ollie had steamed west and fished around King Island. He did not, however, talk to the San Remo Boys who fished the same area but, rather, worked with his brother: "You only need a couple of boats to find the fish." I asked if the San Remo Boys resented his presence at King Island. "Not that they said . . ." Ollie laughed, adding, "I don't know what they said to each other when they got back in," implying that he suspected these exchanges were less than complimentary. While the San Remo Boys did not actively prevent Ollie from fishing the region, they had nonetheless withdrawn their voices from the interloper, essentially denying him the chance to exchange local knowledge with them and, in that way, reduced his chances of success.

Paul, a skipper from Port Welshpool, had also tried to fish King Island, but had found it difficult to elicit productive radio exchanges with the San Remo Boys. He had come back, unsuccessful, and without the intention to return. Bass Strait is "a big paddock," he explained, and there was little reason to steam all the way to King Island to take a "blind shot" when he had a "guaranteed wage" in an area "close" to home. Of course, had Paul been able to tap into the network of information possessed by the San Remo Boys, he may have placed his shots with greater effect.

Paul, in turn, actively excluded "outsiders" from "his" area, a tactic he explained one day on the wharf. Note that Paul did not claim "rights" to Banks Strait, he merely noted that this was where he fished regularly. He and two other young skippers regularly, and collaboratively, fished a notoriously treacherous area called Banks Strait. It is a considerable challenge to set gillnets effectively across the uneven strata of the region, and to negotiate the strong tides that often "scream through" the narrow pass between the southern tip of the Furneaux Group and northeast Tasmania. Those without experience risk losing their gear over ledges, their nets rolling up in the tide, or worse. Occasionally, other fishermen, respecting his authority on, and perhaps his first rights to, the region asked him, "Where should I put the gear?" Paul, sitting on the wharf with a mischievous grin, imitated his mock indifference with a shrug and recounted his response: "Put them anywhere you like!" Still grinning, he explained that "they" ripped up their nets, or lost them and had to come back with a grapple to retrieve the gear. They rarely bothered to try fishing that area again. Perhaps catching my horrified look at the thought of someone losing AU$25,000 worth of fishing gear, he noted, somberly, "You've got to do it to protect your patch." It is important to note that Paul did not actively contribute to anyone's misfortune. He merely withdrew his voice from the interlopers, essentially denying them the chance to exchange knowledge with him, thus minimizing their chances of success. (See also, Howard, this volume.)

Sometimes this "territoriality" is overtly demonstrated through the sabotage of fishing gear, or worse (McGoodwin 1990, 128; Acheson 2003, 27). Illustrative is the following excerpt from a legal case during which the plaintiff had described some of the factors that had prevented him from fishing during a particular period.³ The record shows:

> Because his hand was still not healed, Mr. Walton could not yet take his boat out on his own and his brother had other commitments. He was still at home on 30th May 1986. That day he received advice from a friend, who had passed through Port Welshpool, that the engine room of his vessel was full of water. It seemed that his boat had been interfered with. Somebody had damaged the switch in his ice room. He suggested that it may have happened because there was animosity between ports, and he was a San Remo fisherman who had fished out of Port Welshpool and left his boat tied up at Port Welshpool.

Through the strategic negotiation of social bonds and alliances, some fishermen are able to more successfully encroach on someone else's "traditional area" and perhaps receive assistance in the form of information. Part of the histories that fishermen draw upon relate to their classification within the formal management structures of the shark and other fisheries, as this next example shows.

Quinn, a Victorian fisherman who now employs a skipper to run his shark boat, laughs when he tells the story of sending his skipper, Ron, to fish in South Australian waters. Ron found himself in a volatile standoff with another skipper who wanted to shoot his gear in the same place. The South Australian was reportedly livid with indignation at the audacity of the Victorian who had come to steal his fish! The situation was on the verge of becoming quite nasty, and both skippers called their bosses. Quinn and the other owner had both worked in the scallop fishery years earlier, and both had served on a scallop comanagement board, during which time they had endured several political threats to the scallop industry, shared many discussions, and more than a little beer. They both told their skippers, "It's okay! Let it go fo' Christ's sake!" The skippers grudgingly conceded to maneuver around each other without further incident. This example illustrates the way that social connections can be stretched and transferred across water, time, and apparent allegiances in order to manipulate social boundaries and facilitate access to otherwise restricted regions. It also suggests how formal management structures may impose themselves on the informal operation of fishing boats at sea.

The following example describes how fishermen are sometimes compelled to acknowledge relationships they would rather ignore, and how the strategic manipulation of certain social connections can elicit important information. In 2002, asleep in the fo'c'sle of the San Remo boat, *Golanding*, we were awoken to action on the deck. The deck lights were on and there was a boat beside us that I did not recognize. Deckies, Simon, Travis, and I stood quietly to one side, smoking, watching. Though our skipper, Victor, and the skipper of the other boat were exchanging "pleasantries," there seemed to be something not quite right. Victor was tense. The exchange ended and we all went back to our bunks. The next day, I queried Victor about the stranger. His name was Walter, Victor told me, and he was the hired skipper of the *Cape Blair*, from Port Albert. Victor squinted and stared ahead as he noted quietly that they did not personally know each other. He had not known who it was when the *Cape Blair* skipper had hailed him over the radio: "You there, *Vic*?" Victor's tone suggested that he felt the man had been somewhat presumptuous in hailing him by his given name, and not the vessel name. Why had he answered, I wanted to know. Victor explained that Walter's boat was owned by a man named Bernard. Bernard leased shark quota to Victor's regular fishing companion, Allen. Though this connection had not been an explicit point of discussion between the two men, Walter had worked this tenuous bond to force Victor to recognize a connection between them and, through that connection, to behave cooperatively. Walter's knowledge of the formal social terrain had granted him access to a physical space that may have been more difficult to negotiate without Victor's cooperation. Victor could only shrug his shoulders: "What can you do, Tanya?"

The "bundle of rights" associated with one's "traditional area" is often difficult to explain, particularly because the style of "ownership" is unsuited to explication. As shown above, one's connection to place can change with shifting social relationships and contexts, and these relationships are necessarily informed by the experiences of fishermen with formal management structures.

Though the salience of "territoriality" among fishermen can manifest tangibly, informal boundaries are typically irrelevant to those concerned with the official management of the region. The uneasy function of territoriality within an official context is illustrated in the following example, as is the difficulty of formalizing knowledge that is only efficacious as long as it remains ambiguous, or open to reformulation.

Formal Territoriality

At a formal fisheries meeting in Melbourne in late 2002, an Australian Fisheries Management Authority (AFMA) manager was seeking information that blurred the distinction between formal and informal territoriality. He was encouraging a small group of fishermen to pass comment upon various regions of Bass Strait that were not necessarily within their "traditional fishing areas." The aim of the exercise was to designate a number of regions that would become closed to all shark fishermen in a trial "Fixed Station Survey." A series of large maps and fishing charts were spread across a long table. For a number of minutes, Adam, the manager coordinating the process, and Brett, the recorder for AFMA, sat alone beside the maps on one side of the table. Several scientists, two AFMA managers, and a data modeler filled the other side of the table and, for the majority of the time, stayed seated. The four fishing industry representatives—all with affiliations to different ports—moved nervously around the table, talking, drinking coffee, occasionally standing beside Adam and Brett, crossing and uncrossing their arms, mostly keeping their eyes on the map in front of them, but occasionally darting glances at each other. I had been permitted to film the meeting.

Cam, a fisherman, was directly asked by Adam to suggest a specific point within a region close to his hometown of Devonport (Tasmania). Obviously nervous and reluctant, he eventually stabbed his finger at the map and said, "There!" and went to walk away. However, Cam had—it was well known—also fished around King Island, and he was asked to suggest another site. Skillfully diverting attention from himself, Cam suggested they ask Daniel, who was more familiar with the region than he. Daniel was a white-haired man of roughly seventy years of age. Though shrewd as a fox, Daniel sometimes liked to don what he called his "blonde wig" to affect an appearance of ignorance. Daniel was called back from the tearoom where he had been murmuring quietly with another fisherman. Appearing startled, looking dazed, Daniel eventually—comically—bumbled out, peered around for somewhere to rest his coffee cup, fumbled with his glasses for a while, asked a litany of questions about the King Island site, and eventually suggested, thoughtfully, that they had best ask Eamon—or perhaps Cam—who both had superior knowledge of that region. Cam rapidly declined: "Eamon'd kill me!" However, the attention was diverted from Daniel long enough for him to slip back to the safety of the tearoom. As he quietly sidled past me, he grinned and winked: "I'd rather be out of *this* shit!"

A little later, another shark fisherman, Gerard, was being pressed for information about where to locate the Fixed Station Survey. Gerard was pointing out large areas on a map of Bass Strait, but Adam, the fisheries manager discussing the project, needed a specific location, one that Gerard was obviously hesitant to supply. The process of extracting this information from Gerard had been going on for some time. It was a verbal dance in which questions were asked, answers half implied, more subtle questions posed, the inquiry thoughtfully "misinterpreted," and so on. Gerard had recently suspended a fishing trip and flown to Melbourne from a South Australian port with the intention of resuming the trip once the meeting was over. He was somewhat frustrated, somewhat resigned, and visibly exhausted, rubbing his red eyes and massaging his pale, stubbled face in his hands. Brett, the AFMA member recording the discussion, was also keen for a prompt resolution to this particular agenda item, and sat with pen poised. Eventually, with some resignation, Gerard conceded the information.

> *Gerard*—So when I say northeast of King Island, I'm generalizing on a fairly large area.
>
> *Adam*—*[quietly]*—Now we, for the sake of exercise, just basically just want the specific GPS coordinates.
>
> *Gerard*—*[staring ahead, with minimum inflection]*—45°16′150″07.

Evident on the video recording of this exchange is the sudden cessation of background chatter: the room is momentarily completely silent.

> *Adam*—*[somewhat taken aback]*—You realize what you're doing? You realize that that's then going to be. . . . So don't make it a point that's particularly special to you . . .
>
> *Brett*—*[interjecting as he writes]*—45°16′150″07: thank you very much!

Commonwealth employed fisheries "experts" who talk with shark fishermen about their resource use—managers and scientists in particular—tend to be well aware of the informal zoning that takes place, as Adam's comments indicate. Nonetheless, they are required to adhere to the administrative regulations of their employers. This exchange illustrates how informal lines on the water can be blurred with the official lines, and the personalities involved, in the creation of new lines. In this way, "official" categories are infused with some of the ambiguity characteristic of unofficial categories. When the social or environmental or productive contexts in which these official categories are embedded shift—say, Gerard leaves the fishery, or Fixed Station Survey locations are subsequently employed to determine the sites of marine parks—the residual administrative boundaries can appear to exist independently of any human input. Rather, as the creative roles of particular people recede from memory or are obliterated in reams of paperwork, marks on a map that were established in a particular context take on a legitimacy afforded through their incorporation in official fisheries administration. However, unlike the ambiguous boundaries of fishermen, these formal markers cannot be easily renegotiated to accommodate shifting circumstances.

Both "official" lines and those boundaries relevant within the community of fishermen must be simultaneously negotiated. However, these lines are not necessarily easy to distinguish and often inform one another. Official restrictions that distinguish among men who can fish in a particular region, or target a particular species, or use a particular type of equipment, can be reflected in the way those men subsequently define social boundaries for themselves and others, as the following, final example illustrates.

Formal Informalities

Following a meeting in Canberra in which "exclusion zones" were discussed, I found myself at a restaurant with a group of shark fishermen. Though there used to be—and sometimes still is—intense rivalry among shark fishermen of different states (particularly Victoria and Tasmania), our group consisted of shark fishermen from all three states regulated under the Commonwealth's shark management plan: Victoria, Tasmania, and South Australia. This grouping was in the context of the scope of the meeting, in which a variety of fishermen were present, including trawl fishermen and "non-trawl" fishermen (distinct in fishing method, target species, or both, from shark fishermen). The meeting had been arranged to discuss details of an amalgamation of these sectors, and representatives of each were vying for the best outcome for their particular fishery. Though the "Non-Trawl Boys" had courteously asked us to accompany them to the city, our group, the "Sharkers," had decided to go to a steak house in the nearby suburb of Manuka. As we walked in the door, I felt Michael stiffen beside me, and looked up to see two "Trawl Boys" talking at the bar. The scene reminded me of an old Western film, as we all paused, just inside the swinging doors, waiting for the whistle in the air to die away. Instead of a greeting, Michael gave a small grin and acknowledged our embarrassing mistake: "Is this the exclusion zone?" he asked. The men at the bar grinned back and one drawled: "No, it's just the Non-Trawl exclusion zone."[4] There was a smattering of laughter, and we walked past the bar to the restaurant area. Already seated was a large group associated with the Trawl Fishery. A number of vague, even surprised, greetings were exchanged. Observant waitresses hurriedly began pulling tables together. Several people from both groups leapt in to stress that such rearrangement would not be necessary. In the crowded restaurant, the tables were nonetheless close together, and when several latecomers arrived, and our table was extended to accommodate them, the two groups were effectively joined anyway. With droll resolution, the Sharkers and Trawl

Boys managed to ignore each other, and we left separately. Evident in this encounter is that years of institutionalized differentiation between these fishermen, some of whom live in the same port and several of whom have fished in the same fishery in the past, informs their relationships, at least in contexts where these groupings are relevant.

The argument of this chapter is that the distinction between the formal boundaries that restrict commercial fishers, and those informal limitations that are sometimes denied by fishermen (i.e., shark fishermen can work "anywhere they like"), while tending to be emphasized by scholars interested in drawing attention to the power of informal territoriality (e.g., Acheson 1988), unfold simultaneously in the strategic negotiations of those who live the boundaries and open spaces at sea. Just as the relationships and social dynamics among shark fishermen and managers were shown to influence the way in which a Fixed Station Survey was designed, formal categories and rules impact the way that fishermen behave with each other both at sea (in the case of Vic and Walter, as with Quinn and his skipper) and on land (as in the case of the restaurant meeting in Manuka). While, as Van Houtum (2005, 675) suggests, some styles of delineation may be imbued with more or less "morality" than others, overemphasizing the distinction between formal and informal styles of management—drawing clear and unambiguous lines around places or people, versus a more subtle, socially-informed process that allows for agency and strategy—does not adequately convey the concert in which such styles often emerge. Rather than suggesting that either system is more or less valuable or effective, this chapter merely presents the reality in which many fishers—and fisheries managers—work, one in which both formal and informal territoriality are encountered simultaneously.

Tanya J. King is a maritime anthropologist who focuses on the social and ecological implications of environmental policy implementation in Australia. She lectures in environmental anthropology at Deakin University, and is a director of the national women's commercial fishing organization, Women in Seafood Australasia, or WISA. Her publications include "'A Different Kettle of Fish': Mental Health Strategies for Australian Fishers, and Farmers" (2015).

Notes

1. These regions refer to, consecutively, Wilson's Promontory, the Hogan Group, Erith Island, Deal Island, the Kent Group (of which Erith and Deal make up a part), Inner Sister Island and Outer Sister Island, Prime Seal Island, and Banks Strait.
2. While not necessarily an expression used by all in the industry, the description of other groups of fishermen as "such-and-such boys" was common.
3. *Walton v Australian Fisheries Management Authority* (2002) 68 ALD 193, 201.
4. Various tensions between Trawlers and Non-Trawlers sometimes surfaced, particularly in relation to the public perception of their relative environmental credentials.

References

Acheson, J. M. 1988. *The Lobster Gangs of Maine*. Hanover: University Press of New England.

———. 2003. *Capturing the Commons: Devising Institutions to Manage the Maine Lobster Industry*. Hanover: University Press of New England.

Acheson, J. M., and Roy J. Gardner. 2004. "Strategies, Conflict, and the Emergence of Territoriality: The Case of the Maine Lobster Industry." *American Anthropologist* 106, no. 2: 296–307.

Aswani, S. 2002. "Assessing the Effects of Changing Demographic and Consumption Patterns on Sea Tenure Regimes in the Roviana Lagoon, Solomon Islands." *AMBIO: A Journal of the Human Environment* 31, no. 4: 272–84.

Berkes, F. 1987. "Common-Property Resource Management and Cree Indian Fisheries in Subarctic Canada." In *The Question of the Commons: The Culture and Ecology of Communal Resources*. Edited by B. J. McCay and J. M. Acheson, 66–91. Tucson: The University of Arizona Press.

———. 1993. "Traditional Ecological Knowledge in Perspective." In *Traditional Ecological Knowledge: Concepts and Cases*. Edited by J. T. Inglis, 1–10. Ottawa: Canadian Museum of Nature and the International Development Research Centre.

Carter, B. T. G., and E. A. Nielsen. 2011. "Exploring Ecological Changes in Cook Inlet Beluga Whale Habitat though Traditional and Local Ecological Knowledge of Contributing Factors for Population Decline." *Marine Policy* 35, no. 3: 299–308.

Cinner, J. E., and S. Aswani. 2007. "Integrating Customary Management into Marine Conservation." *Biological Conservation* 140, no. 3: 201–16.

Dwyer, P. D., R. Just, and M. Minnegal. 2003. "A Sea of Small Names: Fishers and their Boats in Victoria, Australia." *Anthropological Forum* 13, no. 1: 5–26.

Hockett, C. F. 1973. *Man's Place in Nature*. New York: McGraw-Hill Companies.

Inglis, Julian, ed. 1993. *Traditional Ecological Knowledge: Concepts and Cases*. Canadian Museum of Nature and the International Development Research Centre.

King, T. J. 2007. "Bad Habits and Prosthetic Performances: Negotiation of Individuality and Embodiment of Social Status in Australian Fishing." *The Journal of Anthropological Research* 63, no. 4: 537–60.

———. 2011. "The 'Skipper Effect': Riddles of Luck and Rhetorics of Individualism." *Human Organization* 70, no. 4: 387–96.

Kitner, K. R. 2006. "Beeliners, Pinkies, and Kitties: Mobility and Marginalization in the South Atlantic Snapper Grouper Fishery." *Human Organization* 65, no. 3: 294–306.

McGoodwin, J. R. 1990. *Crisis in the World's Fisheries: People, Problems, and Policies.* Stanford: Stanford University Press.

Meinzen-Dick, R., and A. Knox. 2001. "Collective Action, Property Rights, and Devolution of Natural Resource Management: A Conceptual Framework." In *Collective Action, Property Rights, and Devolution of Natural Resource Management: Exchange of Knowledge and Implications for Policy.* Edited by R. Meinzen-Dick, A. Knox, and M. D. Gregorio, 41–74. Proceedings of the International Conference, Puerto Azul, Philippines, 21–25 June 1999. Feldanfing, Germany: DSE/ZEL.

Nadasdy, P. 1999. "The Politics of TEK: Power and the 'Integration' of Knowledge." *Arctic Anthropology* 36, no. 1/2: 1–18.

Palmer, C. T. 1990. "Balancing Competition and Cooperation: Verbal Etiquette among Maine Lobstermen." *Maritime Anthropological Studies* 3, no. 1: 87–105.

Risien, J. M., and B. Tilt. 2008. "A Comparative Study of Community-based Sea Turtle Management in Palau: Key Factors for Successful Implementation." *Conservation and Society* 6, no. 3: 225–37.

Van Houtum, H. 2005. "The Geopolitics of Borders and Boundaries." *Geopolitics* 10, no. 4: 672–79.

Wenzel, G. W. 1999. "Traditional Ecological Knowledge and Inuit: Reflections on TEK Research and Ethics." *Arctic* 52, no. 2: 113–24.

White, D. R. M. 1988. "Knocking 'em Dead: Alabama Shrimp Boats and the 'Fleet Effect.'" Marine Resource Utilization: A Conference on Social Science Issues. Mobile, AL: University of South Alabama.

At Home on the Waves?

A Concluding Comment

Tim Ingold

Human beings did not arise from the sea. Notwithstanding some rather fanciful theories[1] that, among other things, have attributed the orientation of masculine chest hair to the prowess of ancestral swimmers, or the origins of language to the breath control required of them, there can be little doubt that humans evolved on land, probably far from any ocean, with bodies well adapted to the conditions of life in relatively open, terrestrial environments. Among mammals of the land, we are certainly not alone in our capacity to swim, and even to dive, but even the most athletic of humans can swim unaided over only a relatively short distance, and hold their breath underwater for no more than a few minutes. To go further, or to spend a longer time at sea, our ancestors needed some kind of watercraft. It is hard to know when they first took to the waves, for things that float tend not to last, being necessarily fashioned from lightweight and perishable materials. Most likely, the first voyages were accidental, when storm or tide took craft designed for inshore waters far out to sea. But the subsequent development of ocean-going vessels, along with the ways of life that have surrounded them, has been among the most remarkable chapters of human technical evolution. In many ways and for several millennia, it turned the world inside out, as the great expanses of the sea offered the best opportunities for long-distance travel and trade. The land, by contrast, became a barrier, with its fast-flowing rivers, treacherous marshes, deserts, and mountain ranges presenting formidable obstacles to movement. Islands, once remote and cut off, became centers of human commerce—a situation that persisted until the transport revolutions of modern times brought road, rail, and, latterly, air travel to the fore, relegating many islands once again to the periphery. I will return to this.

First, however, it is important to stress that no comparison of life on sea and on land could be complete without introducing the element of air. Whether on land or at sea, we humans must have air to breathe. In earth, without air we would be buried; in water, without air we would drown. We live, necessarily, beneath the sky, on or at the surfaces formed where earth, air, and water meet and mingle. There are surfaces where water meets air: such are the waves. But there are also surfaces where air meets earth, and surfaces where earth meets water. Which, then, is above, and which below? Air is above water; water is above earth. Are people living on the earth, then, living underwater? Perhaps it's all a matter of perspective. In a tale from medieval Ireland, told by Bishop Patrick of Dublin in the eleventh century and retold by the poet Seamus Heaney in the twentieth, worshippers at prayer espied a ship floating in the sky, whence descended an anchor rope (Carey 1992; Heaney 2014). The anchor itself, having snagged in a rail of the altar, had brought the ship to a juddering halt. A crewman shinnied down the rope to try to free it, but could not. Realizing that the man was close to drowning, the abbot ordered his congregation to help. The anchor was eventually released and—in the nick of time—the crewman made it back up the rope to rejoin his ship, which sailed on out of sight. The swirling medium of air that we mortals breathe to stay alive was for the celestial seafarer a realm of "surge, swell and brine . . . inimical to human life" (Cohen 2015, 121).[2] It would have killed him, were it not for the abbot's timely intervention. Would the salty sea not kill us too, were we to spend too long beneath the waves?

Our ships, too, would appear celestial to the denizens of the deep, and many must have wondered at the strange things that have fallen from this heavenly realm: chests of gold and precious goods, cannon shot, anchor chains, and, of course, human beings, drowning if not already dead. Few are those who, with the assistance of marvelous underwater creatures (or *mer*-people), have made it back up alive. But some perhaps, long presumed dead by relatives left at home, are living still, having metamorphosed into sea creatures and joined their own, underwater congregations. Maritime lore is full of such perspectival inversions, long familiar to anthropologists from their studies of Amerindian and northern circumpolar cosmologies, but by no means limited to the peoples of these regions (de Castro 2012). What they tell us is that the surface of the sea is far more than a division, within the known physical world, between the sky above and the waters below. It is also a threshold between parallel worlds of existence, of life and death. To venture out upon the waves is to inhabit this threshold, at every moment to place one's very existence on the line. Whereas on land, we experience the ground—in the words of philosopher Alphonso Lingis (1998, 14)—as "a reservoir of support extending indefinitely in depth," the sea offers only conditional support, its depth ever threatening to swallow us up. Depth at sea is not a cushion but an abyss. That's why there is more to landing and to setting sail than exchanging one surface of support for another. The harbor quay or jetty, jutting out into the water, only goes so far, until the earth gives out or sinks too deep for any pillar of support, mounted on the bed, to reach the surface. The jetty is a one-ended bridge that casts off into the midst. Beyond it, our umbilical connection to the land is lost.[3]

On land, we can count on the ground to hold us. Indeed, it is precisely to this holding capacity that we refer when we speak of place. But once at sea, we must necessarily hold on to one another and to our craft if we are to stay afloat. Does this mean the sea is placeless? Do we, on setting sail, leave behind the safety and security of our places of abode, our homes, for a life of peril? Is it possible even in principle, let alone in practice, to be at home on the waves? Some might argue that such a thing is simply impossible. What is a home, after all, if not a place of shelter to which we, and those with whom we live, return—again and again—to eat and sleep? Nor is it confined to the shelter alone, since home is also the familiar world that unfolds along the many paths or tracks that take us to the places where we spend our days, with their accustomed horizons. Everywhere we go, when we are at home, is inscribed with the memories of earlier perambulations, which we redouble in our present movements. How, then, can we be at home in a watery environment that offers no secure bed on which to found a shelter, and which erases every trace of movement on the instant it is formed? How can the sea—that great dissolver of human ambition, where nothing lasts—be a place of memory? People may, of course, live by the coast or even on the shore, making daily or longer forays out to sea in their pursuit of livelihood, by fishing or hunting, while their homes yet remain on land. But the opposite—a people of the sea, launching forays onto land for food and water—would better describe a naval or piratical expedition, intruding on alien shores, than a way to dwell.

The chapters of this book, however, have encouraged us to think otherwise. They suggest possibilities not just of going to sea from home, but of making a home at sea. One way is to cast one's lot beneath the waves, as do trawler-men and underwater archaeologists,[4] so as to think of the sea, in the first place, not so much as a body of water than as ground that happens to be submerged. This ground can be worked, surveyed, dredged, even cultivated just as surely as farmers or field-based archaeologists work the land above. Fishers who trawl the bed know it and its features like the backs of their hands, even though it remains invisible to the naked eye. They have their places, their grounds, often named after them or after the experience of working them. Even as they ride the swell and communicate with their fellows over the airwaves, they are vicariously at home on the bed, which they work and cultivate as assiduously as the farmer would work a field. Underwater archaeologists likewise make places for themselves on the seabed through the gestural reenactment, on deck, of their underwater movements, drawing in the air what they have observed below. Home at sea, for those whose fortunes rest upon its bed, is like inhabiting a house with a cellar. You live upstairs, but your riches lie in the airless caverns below. The problem, in such a split-level existence, is to connect the cellar with the living room, the level of technical operations on the seabed with the level of social interaction at the surface. Whether for trawler-men operating from on deck, or for subsea divers, this calls for the deployment of copious amounts of gear. Both, however, have to live with the ever-present danger that the gear may be cut, disconnecting the two levels with potentially fatal consequences.

There is another way to conceive of home at sea, however, rather than by anchoring one's fortunes to the bed. It is, perhaps paradoxically, to think again about the land, and to question whether land and sea are really as fundamentally distinct in nature as we are inclined to suppose. Consider, for example, the indigenous peoples of the Sahara, traders and nomadic pastoralists, whose camels have been compared by travelers to ships of the desert, roaming waves not of water but of sand. Or think of the herdsmen roaming the grassland steppes of Central Asia, far from any substantial body of water. Or again, let us call to mind the Inuit inhabitants of the Greenlandic arctic, in whose winter landscape, blanketed in snow, any transition from land to frozen sea is imperceptible: the salient division is not there but at the floe's edge, where ice gives way to open water.[5] Sands, steppe, and ice are all examples of what the philosopher Gilles Deleuze, and his collaborator Félix Guattari, call "smooth space." This is a space that cannot be apportioned, that resists measurement or survey of any kind. It is a space of continuous variation, stirred up by wind and weather, and suffused with light, sound, and feeling. In smooth space, as Deleuze and Guattari say, "There is no line separating earth and sky" (Deleuze and Guattari 2004, 421; see also Ingold 2011, 132–33). Such is the space, they say, of pastoral nomadic peoples whose homes, principally tents or tent-like, are not fixed in place but move as people and their animals do. Or rather, since all move together, they offer havens of stillness in a world of perpetual flux. And yet the archetypal exemplar of smooth space, according to Deleuze and Guattari (2004, 528–29), is the sea. Might there be a parallel, then, between the ways that pastoralists and mariners make themselves at home? Might we compare tents and igloos to boats and ships?

The term "nomadic" has frequently been applied, often pejoratively, to both land and sea dwellers, to connote a state of enduring homelessness comparable to that of wild beasts.[6] Yet even the animals make homes for themselves! They do so, however, not by pegging themselves down to an appointed place, but by drawing their own movements into a kind of knot, or holding formation. Tents and boats, likewise, are holdings rather than held. In both, one can be fully at home without an anchor, without the kind of place-attachment that only *terra firma* can provide. The tent, as the design theorist Vilém Flusser has remarked, answers, like the sail of a ship, to the wind rather than gravity. It is "a place where people assemble and disperse, a calming of the wind" (Flusser 1999, 57). Might not the same be said of a ship? After all, the very word *ship*, used alternately as noun and suffix, connotes both the vessel and a gathering (as in "fellow-ship"). However, the modern ocean-going vessel—oil tanker, container ship, or cruise liner—answers neither to the wind nor the waves. Rather than riding the swell, its propellers drill a tunnel through the sea, much as the propeller of a plane drills through the air. The sea has been homogenized. And those who make their home on it, on gargantuan vessels the size of skyscrapers, are nomads of a new sort. Besides their luxury apartments, the well-heeled residents of the largest cruise-ship ever built, *The World*, have access to shops, swimming pools, tennis courts and putting greens, a jogging track and fitness center, cinema, cocktail lounges, and restaurants—everything, indeed, that they could expect of a luxury onshore hotel. They might witness the sea as a blue expanse and enjoy the uninterrupted skies. But the last thing of which they would have any direct experience would be the waves.

At the other extreme are professional surfers, for whom the wave is everything. At least while riding, their entire existence is borne along in this one, overwhelming movement. So which of them is more at home on the waves, the resident of *The World* or the surfer on their board? The one, we might say, cannot tell the waves from the sea; the other cannot tell the sea from the waves. One hankers for an eternity; the other lives only for the moment. They represent, if you will, the opposite poles of a world that has been refashioned as a globe. Where once the mariner had been at the center of a world, with the sea below and the sky above, the sea is now imagined as an all-around, outer covering for planet Earth. The oceans, divorced from their intercourse with sky and wind, have no waves. And conversely, waves have no ocean: they could just as well be made by a machine. As the residents of *The World* glide serenely over the planetary surface, much like the celestial ships of medieval lore, blithely indifferent to the suffering of those condemned to live below, the surfer inhabits a bubble that will burst at the instant it breaks upon the shore. Both *The World* and the surfboard afford means not to inhabit a world but to escape from it, though one more lasting than the other. For the real world to reassert itself, from either end, spells disaster. Residents of the cruise liner, like the passengers on board the *Titanic*, will only experience the waves as the ship goes down; surfers experience the sea when the wave becomes a tsunami and engulfs them. We discover, in these catastrophic events, that the waves and the ocean can be held apart only by artifice, by feats of engineering on an ever-greater scale, and that all such attempts are bound, ultimately, to fail.

For waves are the ocean's way of making itself felt. We are told that at present, thanks to the effects of an overall rise in global temperatures and the consequent rapid melting of ice-sheets in the Arctic and Antarctica, sea levels are rising fast. They have risen before, of course, most notably at the end of the last glacial period, and many once-inhabited lands—from Doggerland in the North Sea to much of the Recherche Archipelago of Western Australia[7]—now lie underwater, silent and mysterious. But the level did not inch up, imperceptibly, inundating the land so gradually that no one in their lifetimes would have noticed it. Rather, sea-level rise was witnessed then, as it is now, in increasing susceptibility to catastrophic events. The massive Storegga tsunami, attributed to a landslide in the North Sea and dated to around 6200 BC, is thought to have finally overwhelmed Doggerland. In living memory, too, tidal floods, storm surges, and typhoons, along with earthquake-induced tsunamis, have eaten away at coastlines and brought massive destruction and loss of life to people in many parts of the world. Each time they strike, they remind us that the surface of the sea *is not level*. It sloshes about: one huge, continuous mass that is stretched, crumpled, and swirled by forces of earthly and lunar gravity, by the rotation of the planet, by the differential heating of the sun, by the friction of the irregular sea bed below and the convulsions of the atmosphere above. Along the coasts, this sloshing is visible in the cycle of the tides, and the formation of beaches, alternately over- and underwater. But for mariners at sea, it is experienced as currents and gradients. If you are operating a fishing boat from the shore, you can save fuel by leaving at high tide, "free-wheeling" down the slope of the sea, and then returning once the gradient is reversed.

"Sea level," in short, is a cartographic abstraction, and a strange one at that. For on the map, the sea appears to have solidified into a homogeneous and featureless surface. Though this surface shares its curvature with that of planet Earth, it is otherwise a perfect plane. It has no waves, and there is nothing underneath. And the land, rather than rising up at the coasts from beneath the sea, is depicted as if it were built up, contour by contour, upon the marine base level. Thus, the lowest contour, closest to sea level, covers the greatest area. This describes the shoreline. The mass of the land, then, appears contained within its shores. We see land masses as continents, bounded by their shores, rather than oceans bordered by coasts. Oceans are more often perceived to fill the spaces between continents than continents to fill the spaces between oceans. We say that the Atlantic is between Africa and America, and the Pacific between America and Asia, not that America is between the Atlantic and the Pacific. Yet across these oceans, between continents, we send gigantic ships, that are either containers in themselves (such as oil tankers) or laden with containers, destined on arrival for ground transportation by road or rail. In reality, of course, no continent is fully contained, nor any ship. Both continents and ships discharge into the sea, which is gradually filling with such quantities of waste as to form floating islands, which people may end up living on. In the meantime, land and sea will continue their dialogue as they have always done. What's new is only this: more humans are on the planet than ever before, a greater proportion are living in cities than ever before, and most of these cities are low-lying. Finding ways to be at home on the waves may, in time, become a strategy for survival, not just for a few but for millions.

Tim Ingold is Professor of Social Anthropology at the University of Aberdeen and a fellow of the British Academy and the Royal Society of Edinburgh. Following twenty-five years at the University of Manchester, Ingold moved to Aberdeen in 1999, where he established the UK's newest Department of Anthropology. Ingold has carried out ethnographic fieldwork among Saami and Finnish people in Lapland, and has written on environment, technology, and social organization in the Circumpolar North; the role of animals in human society; issues in human ecology; and evolutionary theory in anthropology, biology, and history. In his more recent work, he has explored the links between environmental perception and skilled practice. Ingold is currently writing and teaching on issues of the interface between anthropology, archaeology, art, and architecture. He is the author of *The Perception of the Environment* (2000), *Lines* (2007), *Being Alive* (2011), *Making* (2013) *The Life of Lines* (2015), and *Anthropology and/as Education* (2017).

Notes

1. Most famously, the so-called "Aquatic Ape" hypothesis, originating with Alister Hardy and popularized by Elaine Morgan (1982) in *The Aquatic Ape: A Theory of Human Evolution.*
2. The words are taken from an extended commentary on the tale by literary historian Jeffrey Jerome Cohen in "The Sea Above" (2015).
3. On landing places as "the interface between sea and land," see Robinson (this volume, chapter 7).
4. See Howard, and Simonetti (this volume, chapters 2 and 6).
5. See Elixhauser, and Tejsner (this volume, chapters 5 and 11).
6. See Stacey and Allison (this volume, chapter 14).
7. See Wickham-Jones, and Guilfoyle, Anderson, Reynolds, and Kimber (this volume, chapters 4 and 9).

References

Carey, J. 1992. "Aerial Ships and Underwater Monasteries: The Evolution of a Monastic Marvel." In *Proceedings of the Harvard Celtic Colloquium*, vol. 12, 16–28. Department of Celtic Languages and Literatures, Faculty of Arts and Sciences, Harvard University. Retrieved 15 June 2018 from https://www.jstor.org/stable/pdf/20557234.pdf?seq=1#page_scan_tab_contents.

Cohen, J. J. 2015. "The Sea Above." In *Elementary Ecocriticism: Thinking with Earth, Air, Water and Fire.* Edited by J. J. Cohen and L. Duckert, 105–33. Minneapolis, MN: University of Minnesota Press.

de Castro, E. B. T. 2012. "Cosmological Perspectivism in Amazonia and Elsewhere." Four lectures given in the Department of Social Anthropology, Cambridge University, February–March 1998, introduced by Roy Wagner. *HAU Journal of Ethnographic Theory*, vol. 1. https://haubooks.org/cosmological-perspectivism-in-amazonia/.

Deleuze, G., and F. Guattari. 2004. *A Thousand Plateaus: Capitalism and Schizophrenia.* Translated by Brian Massumi. London: Continuum International Publishing Group.

Flusser, V. 1999. *The Shape of Things: A Philosophy of Design.* London: Reaktion Books.

Heaney, S. 2014. "Lightenings." In *New Selected Poems: 1988–2013.* Edited by Seamus Heaney, 32. London: Faber & Faber.

Ingold, T. 2011. *Being Alive: Essays in Movement, Knowledge and Description.* Abingdon: Routledge.

Lingis, A. 1998. *The Imperative.* Bloomington, IN: Indiana University Press.

Morgan, E.. 1982. *The Aquatic Ape: A Theory of Human Evolution.* London: Souvenir Press.

Glossary

Compiled by Caroline Wickham-Jones

Artifact: An object made by human hand. Artifacts may be ancient or modern, and they may be of any size.

Birlinn: Traditional wooden sailing ship used in western Scotland from the thirteenth century.

Bronze Age: Period of prehistory when metal first came into household use. The adoption of metal took place at different times around the world. In Britain, it occurred around 2000 BC.

Doggerland: Dryland area of continental shelf in the southern North Sea between Britain and Western Europe that was revealed by lower global sea levels during the last Ice Age. Doggerland was flooded as sea levels rose after deglaciation, and by 6200 BC, it had disappeared.

Early Holocene: First two millennia of the Holocene, the period that began with deglaciation around 10,000 BC.

Fieldwalking: A technique of archaeological survey in which an area of ground is walked in order to locate upstanding remains or scatters of ancient artifacts.

Fishing Hands: Areas of sea used by local fishermen, where a good catch might be expected.

Ground-truth: An archaeological technique in which a previously surveyed area is examined in order to evaluate the existence, or not, of remains identified by the survey.

Holocene: The geological period that began with deglaciation around 10,000 BC.

Homo Erectus: An extinct species of hominin that lived from about 2 million years ago to about 70,000 years ago. Experts are divided as to whether it was a direct ancestor of modern humans.

Martello Tower: Defensive towers built around the coasts of the UK in the early nineteenth century to warn of invasion and assist in defence.

Mesolithic: Period of Prehistory in the Early and Mid Holocene, immediately after deglaciation. Mesolithic communities were stone-age hunter–gatherers who practiced a mobile way of life.

Midden: Household rubbish incorporating mainly organic material that was left to rot before reuse as fertiliser and in other ways.

Moai: Human figures of stone carved, from the thirteenth century, on Rapa Nui.

Neolithic: Period of Prehistory after the Mesolithic. The Neolithic is distinguished by a switch to farming as the economic mainstay of life, and it often incorporates settled communities and the introduction of monumental architecture. In Britain, it occurred around 4000 BC.

Norse: Medieval inhabitants of the Scandinavian countries, including parts of Britain and Ireland.

Palaeolithic: Period of Prehistory during and preceding the last Ice Age. The Palaeolithic starts with the development of stone-tool-using societies around 2.5 million years ago and ends with deglaciation about 10,000 years ago.

Palaeo-shoreline: Fossilized shoreline now occurring away from the modern shore. Palaeo-shorelines may lie above the present shore or below sea level depending on the relative sea-level change that has led to their existence.

Scapa Flow: Land-locked, natural harbour in Orkney, circa 125 square miles in area.

Shieling: Settlement remains relating to the practice of taking cattle up to high pastures during the summer in Scotland.

Storegga tsunami: Tsunami triggered by an undersea landslide in the North Sea. The Storegga tsunami occurred circa 6200 BC.

Index

www.ingramcontent.com/pod-product-compliance
Lightning Source LLC
Chambersburg PA
CBHW070900030426
42336CB00014BA/2273